REMAINS

Historical and Literary

CONNECTED WITH
THE PALATINE COUNTIES OF

Lancaster and Chester

Volume XLI – Third Series

MANCHESTER
Printed for the Chetham Society
1996

The Lordship of Man
Under the Stanleys

Government and Economy
in the Isle of Man, 1580–1704

J. R. Dickinson B.A., Ph.D.

General Editor: P. H. W. Booth

MANCHESTER

1996

Manx
National
Heritage
Eiraght Ashoonagh Vannin

The publication of this book has been assisted by a generous grant from Manx National Heritage, for which the Society is most grateful.

The Lordship of Man Under the Stanleys
Government and Economy in the Isle of Man, 1580–1704
by J. R. Dickinson

ISSN 0080–0880

Published for the Society by Carnegie Publishing Ltd,
18 Maynard Street, Preston
Typeset in Linotype Stempel Garamond by Carnegie Publishing
Printed and bound in the UK by Cambridge University Press
Also published concurrently by the Centre for Manx Studies

British Library Cataloguing-in-Publication Data
A catalogue record for this book is available from the British Library
ISBN 1-85936-037-8

Contents

Acknowledgements

This book is a revised version of a University of Liverpool Ph.D. thesis submitted in the spring of 1991. In the course of my research and revising the text, I have incurred a great many debts and it is a pleasure to have the opportunity to thank those individuals and institutions who have provided assistance in one way or another. In particular, I wish to acknowledge a generous grant from the Veitch Fund which helped to sustain me during one of my regular visits to the Isle of Man in the early stages of the project. I also owe a debt to the librarians and archivists at the following insitutions for their courtesy and unflagging assistance: the Manx Museum Library (now the Manx National Heritage Library), Douglas; the Public Record Office, Chancery Lane; the British Library; Lancashire Record Office, Preston; Liverpool City Record Office; Chester City Record Office; Clwyd Record Office, Hawarden; and the Sydney Jones Library, University of Liverpool. I would also like to express my especial thanks to Miss A. M. Harrison, the former librarian/ archivist in the Manx Museum Library, who provided much valuable advice and encouragement.

I am extremely grateful to the late earl of Derby for permitting me to consult the manuscripts relating to the Isle of Man in the library at Knowsley Hall. I would also like to thanks Mrs B. Burgess, the librarian at the Hall, who offered every assistance during my visits to Knowsley.

No historian can work successfully in isolation and I have benefited greatly from the advice of friends and colleagues. For sometimes lengthy discussions on a wide range of specialist subjects I am particularly indebted to Mr N. G. Crowe, the late Mr R. A. Curphey, Dr R. Gillespie, Mr C. S. Miller, Dr B. W. Quintrell, Mrs C. K. Radcliffe and Mr A. N. Ryan. I must also thank Dr J. I. Kermode, who supervised the thesis, for her advice, encouragement and criticism over more years than either of us might care to remember. Finally, I must thank Penelope Wilson, not least for her assistance in the preparation of the maps. My greatest debt, however, is to my parents, who have been a constant source of support.

List of Maps

List of Illustrations

These illustrations are taken from J. Chaloner, *A Treatise of the Isle of Man*, appendix to *The Vale-Royall of England. Or, the County Palatine of Chester Illustrated* (Daniel King, 1656)

List of Tables

Abbreviations

A.P.C.E.	*Acts of the Privy Council of England*
Ag.H.R.	*Agricultural History Review*
Blundell, *History*	W. Blundell, *A History of the Isle of Man*, ed. W. Harrison, Manx Society, vols xxv and xxvii (1876, 1877)
B.L.	British Library
B.L. Add. MS	British Library, Additional Manuscript
C.C.R.O.	Chester City Record Office
Chaloner, *Treatise*	J. Chaloner, *A Short Treatise of the Isle of Man*, ed. J. G. Cumming, Manx Society, vol. x (1864)
Chet. Soc.	Chetham Society
Cl.R.O.	Clwyd Record Office, Hawarden
C.C.R.	*Calendar of Close Rolls*
C.J.	*Journal of the House of Commons*
C.P.R.	*Calendar of Patent Rolls*
C.S.P.D.	*Calendar of State Papers, Domestic*
C.S.P.Ire.	*Calendar of State Papers, Ireland*
C.T.B.	*Calendar of Treasury Books*
Craine, *Manannan's Isle*	D. Craine, *Manannan's Isle. A Collection of Manx Historical Essays* (Douglas, 1955)
Denton, 'Description'	T. Denton, 'A Description of the Isle of Man with its Customs (*c.* 1681)', ed. G. W. Wood, *Y.L.M.*, vol. iii (1902)
D.N.B.	*Dictionary of National Biography*
Ec.H.R.	*Economic History Review*
E.H.R.	*English Historical Review*
E.R.S.	*Exchequer Rolls of Scotland*
G.R.	General Registry, Douglas
H.M.C.	Historical Manuscripts Commission
H.M.C. Egmont	*Historical Manuscripts Commission, Report on the Manuscripts of the Earl of Egmont* (2 vols in 3 parts, 1905–9)
H.M.C. Kenyon	*Historical Manuscripts Commission,*

	Fourteenth Report, Appendix part iv, The Manuscripts of Lord Kenyon (1894)
H.M.C. Ormonde	*Historical Manuscripts Commission, Calendar of the Manuscripts of the Marquess of Ormonde, preserved at Kilkenny Castle*, new series (8 vols, 1902–20)
H.M.C. Salisbury	*Historical Manuscripts Commission, Calendar of the Manuscripts of the Marquess of Salisbury, preserved at Hatfield House* (24 vols, 1883–1976)
History and Antiquities of the Isle of Man	'J. Stanley, Earl of Derby, History and Antiquities of the Isle of Man', in F. R. Raines (ed.), *The Stanley Papers*, pt iii, vol. iii, Chet. Soc., O.S., vol. lxx (1867)
I.O.	Manx Museum Library, Ingates and Outgates
I.E.S.H.	*Irish Economic and Social History*
I.H.S.	*Irish Historical Studies*
J.M.M.	*Journal of the Manx Museum*
L.C.R.O.	Liverpool City Record Office
L.R.O.	Lancashire Record Office, Preston
Lib. Canc.	Liber Cancellarii
Lib. Plit.	Liber Placitorum
Lib. Scacc.	Liber Scaccarii
M.M.L.	Manx Museum, Douglas
M.F.	microfilm
M.N.H.A.S.	*Proceedings of the Isle of Man Natural History and Antiquarian Society*
Moore, *History*	A. W. Moore, *A History of the Isle of Man* (2 vols, 1900; reprinted Douglas, 1977)
Oliver, *Monumenta*	J. R. Oliver (ed.), *Monumenta de Insula Manniae, or a Collection of National Documents relating to the Isle of Man*, Manx Society, vols iv, vii and ix (1860, 1861, 1862)
O.S.	Old Series
P.R.O.	Public Record Office, London
P.R.O.N.I.	Public Record Office of Northern Ireland, Belfast
R.D.	Manx Museum Library, Derby Receipts and Disbursements
R.S.L.C.	Record Society of Lancashire and Cheshire

Sacheverell, *Account*	W. Sacheverell, *An Account of the Isle of Man, its Inhabitants, Language, Soil, Remarkable Curiosities, the Succession of its Kings and Bishops, down to the Eighteenth Century*, ed. J. G. Cumming, Manx Society, vol. i (1859)
S.E.S.H.	*Scottish Economic and Social History*
S.H.R.	*Scottish Historical Review*
Statutes	J. F. Gill (ed.), *The Statutes of the Isle of Man, vol. i, 1417–1824* (1883)
T.C.W.A.A.S.	*Transactions of the Cumberland and Westmorland Antiquarian and Archaeological Society*
T.D.G.N.H.A.S.	*Dumfriesshire and Galloway Natural History and Antiquarian Society, Transactions and Journal of Proceedings*
T.H.S.L.C.	*Transactions of the Historic Society of Lancashire and Cheshire*
T.I.B.G.	*Transactions of the Institute of British Geographers*
T.L.C.A.S.	*Transactions of the Lancashire and Cheshire Antiquarian Society*
T.R.H.S.	*Transactions of the Royal Historical Society*
Y.L.M.	*Yn Lioar Manninagh (The Journal of the Isle of Man Natural History and Antiquarian Society)*

Note

All dates are Old Style, but the year has been taken to begin on January 1 rather than March 25. Quotations are as in the original documents, although the thorn has been abandoned, standard contractions have been silently extended and punctuation has been altered in some places.

In the interests of clarity, Manx surnames have generally been given in one standard form, based on those in L. Quilliam, *Surnames of the Manks* (Peel, 1989).

The name of the parish of Conchan has been modified since the seventeenth century. The present form is Onchan. The spelling of the name of the parish of Santan has also been slightly amended to Santon. In both cases contemporary usage has been retained in the text.

Introduction

For more than three centuries, between 1406 and 1736, the Stanleys, earls of Derby after 1485, held the title of Lord of Man. This fact is familiar enough to historians of the early modern English nobility, although the significance of the title has rarely been discussed and the history of the Isle of Man itself during this period has largely been ignored. In his study of the rise of the Stanleys from comparatively minor Lancashire gentry to prominent regional nobles and the fortunes of the family until the death of the eighth earl in 1672, Dr Barry Coward considered the implications of possession of the lordship for the Stanleys and drew attention to the place of the Isle of Man in the family's affairs,[1] but otherwise the island has generally been overlooked by early modern historians, even those concerned with society and the economy in north-west England. This is perhaps surprising, given the continuing interest in the influence of noble families and in noble estate management and the fact that the records of the Stanley administration in the Isle of Man represent the largest single extant collection of documents relating to any of the family's extensive possessions in the later sixteenth and seventeenth centuries. The present work is therefore an attempt to focus attention on the island's government and economy during the Stanley lordship, or at least that period of it which is well documented and during which the Stanleys demonstrably took an active interest in the island, that is, from about 1580 until the Manx Act of Settlement (1704). It is less concerned with the personal influence of individual Stanley Lords of Man than with how authority was exercised by the Lord's officers and how the island's economy functioned and adapted to changing circumstances.

[1] B. Coward, *The Stanleys, Lords Stanley and Earls of Derby, 1385–1672* (Chet. Soc., 3rd series, vol. xxx, 1983), *passim.*

I. THE ISLE OF MAN AND THE
PROBLEM OF PERSPECTIVE

The Isle of Man has received only limited and selective attention from historians. The settlement of the island by Norsemen from the ninth century onwards, the establishment of the kingdom of Man and the Isles in the late eleventh century and its dissolution two centuries later have ensured that the Isle of Man has received at least some attention from medievalists[2] and the growth of smuggling from Manx ports, particularly in the early eighteenth century, has inevitably drawn economic historians to examine Man's role as an entrepôt for the illicit trade in the Irish Sea.[3] The period between the acquisition of the island by Edward III in c. 1333 and the rise of the contraband trade has, however, attracted remarkably little detailed attention, even in the pages of Manx books and journals.[4]

The neglect of the Isle of Man by early modern historians can be largely attributed to the peculiar constitutional position of the island. Perhaps as a result of its small size and distance from the kingdoms which successively exerted authority over it, the island was never integrated into the Scottish or English states and retained its Norse institutions – notably the Tynwald Court and the internal divisions

[2] A. A. M. Duncan, *Scotland: The Making of the Kingdom* (Edinburgh, 1975); idem, 'The Scots' Invasion of Ireland, 1315', in R. R. Davies (ed.), *The British Isles, 1100–1500. Comparisons, Contrasts and Connections* (Edinburgh, 1988), pp. 102–3; A. Grant, 'Scotland's "Celtic Fringe" in the Late Middle Ages: The MacDonald Lords of the Isles and the Kingdom of Scotland' in *ibid.*, p. 118.

[3] R. C. Jarvis, 'Illicit Trade with the Isle of Man, 1671–1765', *T.L.C.A.S.*, vol. lviii (1947), pp. 245–67; L. M. Cullen, *Anglo-Irish Trade, 1660–1800* (Manchester, 1968), pp. 146–51; idem, 'Smuggling in the North Channel in the Eighteenth Century', *S.E.S.H.*, vol. vii (1987), pp. 9–26; idem, 'Smugglers in the Irish Sea in the Eighteenth Century' in M. McCaughan and J. C. Appleby (eds), *The Irish Sea. Aspects of Maritime History* (Belfast, 1989), pp. 85–100.

[4] There have been many popular books published on Manx history in the last twenty years, but they overwhelmingly deal with the period after c. 1750. The principal books of a more scholarly nature which deal with the sixteenth and seventeenth century in some detail are Moore, *History*; Craine, *Manannan's Isle*; R. H. Kinvig, *The Isle of Man. A social, cultural and political history* (3rd edn, Liverpool 1975).

of the island known as sheadings.[5] Even after the suzerainty of the island was secured by the English king and Man was granted to a succession of English noblemen, no attempt was made to alter the existing administrative structure of the island. The Isle of Man may have remained independent, or at least separate, in an institutional sense even though in effect it had become a part of the estates of absentee nobles, such as the Montagu earls of Salisbury in the fourteenth century and, in 1405, the Stanleys, later earls of Derby. As a consequence, it also became an element in the English polity, albeit with an attenuated connection.

The constitutional position of the island in relation to England was commented upon by contemporaries in late Tudor and Stuart Britain. John Meyrick, a Welshman who was Bishop of Sodor and Man from 1577 to 1599, noted in a letter to William Camden that the island's peculiar laws were one of the characteristics indicative of Man's 'distinct sovereignty.'[6] Sir Edward Coke judged that the Isle of Man was indeed no part of the realm of England, though an Act of Parliament could extend to the island if the latter were explicitly named in the provisions of the statute.[7] William Blundell of Crosby was in no doubt about the superior position of the English king; he observed in the mid-seventeenth century that, whatever powers the earl of Derby might wield within the Isle of Man, 'he whose authority is limited is no king but a viceroy,' and that 'a king of England is a more absolute king of Man than any other king in Man.'[8]

The fact that the island was never integrated into the territories governed by the English and British monarchs[9] has inevitably led to its isolation from the national historiographical traditions of the

[5] R. D. Farrant, *The Constitution of the Isle of Man* (Douglas, 1937, reprinted from *Law Quarterly Review*, vol. xxxiv [1909]). Cf. O. Klindt-Jensen, *The World of the Vikings* (1970), pp. 178–82. For a discussion of the administrative structure of the island, see chapter 1.

[6] Oliver, *Monumenta*, vol. i, pp. 87–9.

[7] E. Coke, *The Fourth Part of the Institutes of the Laws of England: Concerning the Jurisdiction of Courts* (2nd edn, 1648), p. 284.

[8] Blundell, *History*, vol. i, p. 111.

[9] The practical difficulties facing the English king and the limitations of English royal authority are discussed in S. G. Ellis, 'England in the Tudor State', *Historical Journal*, vol. xxvi (1983), pp. 201–12; idem, 'Crown, Community and Government in the English Territories, 1450–1575', *History*, vol. lxxi (1986), pp. 187–204.

other countries of the British Isles. Despite its place from at least the late fourteenth century as a part of the greater English state, the Isle of Man has never been regarded as part of England. This is perhaps not surprising in view of its distance from England, its unique institutions and Celtic language and culture. What is rather more surprising, however, is that the island has never been fully incorporated into the so-called 'Celtic fringe.'[10] It will be demonstrated in this book, nevertheless, that the island had close connections with adjacent parts of England, Scotland and Ireland and that it shared many of the characteristics and experiences of the upland areas of the British Isles.

2. THE STANLEYS AND THE ISLE OF MAN: STATUS AND PATRONAGE

The acquisition of the Isle of Man with its crown in 1406 was one of a series of gains in both offices and estates which Sir John Stanley (c. 1340–1414) enjoyed during the later stages of his career.[11] These were rewards for his royal service, notably in Ireland, during the reigns of both Richard II and Henry IV. The grant of the island to Stanley furthermore made strategic sense to the king. As well as rewarding distinguished service, he was placing the responsibility of protecting the Isle of Man in the hands of a man whose territorial base lay in an adjacent part of England.[12] As the Stanleys continued to accumulate estates through service to successive kings, the family's

[10] David Mathew's work on the Celtic peoples and the Renaissance, which has been praised for its imaginative sweep in dealing with aspects of the history of the British Isles from a non-anglocentric perspective, deals with all the Celtic peoples of these islands with the notable exception of the Manx. D. Mathew, *The Celtic Peoples and the Renaissance* (1933); J. G. A. Pocock, 'British History: A Plea for a New Subject', *Journal of Modern History*, vol. xlvii (1975), p. 604.
[11] For details of Stanley's career in royal service, see Coward, *Stanleys*, pp. 2–6; W. Fergusson Irvine, 'The Early Stanleys', *T.H.S.L.C.*, vol. cv (1954), p. 57; J. J. Bagley, *The Earls of Derby, 1485–1985* (1985), pp. 1–6.
[12] The implications of the disputed succession to the Stanley estates during the last decade of Elizabeth I's reign are considered in J. R. Dickinson, 'Eliza Endangered? Elizabeth I, the Isle of Man and the Security of England', *M.N.H.A.S.*, vol. x, no. 1 (1992), pp. 123–40.

territorial interests expanded but remained concentrated in the north-west, particularly in south-west Lancashire and north-west Cheshire.[13] While the Stanleys continued to increase their estates by purchase and grant, none conferred such wide-ranging powers and authority as did their possession of the Isle of Man, the lord of which wielded quasi-regal powers. Whether this state of affairs conferred additional respect on them in the eyes of contemporaries, either at national or regional levels, remains to be seen, although the title of Lord of Man – the royal title was not used outside the island after the fourteenth century[14] – may have added some social cachet to the steadily growing list of estates and honours held by the head of the family. By the end of the fifteenth century this lengthening roll of honours included the earldom of Derby, a title granted by Henry VII, stepson of the first Stanley earl.[15]

The title of Lord of Man may have added limited lustre to the standing of the Stanleys at a national level, but at a regional level it may have augmented the social and political influence of the family. The Isle of Man provided an additional pool of patronage in the form of the posts in the island's administration and in the Manx Church, control of which was explicitly invested in the Lord by the grant of 1406. As the status of the Stanleys rose, so did the numbers of lesser gentry and, later, even those of higher social standing who sought to enrich themselves in the service of the leading family in the region. Men such as Sir Charles Gerard[16] might serve as captain or governor of the island, while lesser men could fill the other principal posts in the Lord's household, and clerics seeking preferment in Stanley service might be appointed archdeacon or even bishop. It is unlikely that the positions in the island's government were particularly attractive propositions for those with ambitions and can only have been regarded hopefully as stepping stones to more important office.[17] The number of positions for men of any standing was, in any case, limited, although there were more opportunities for men of humble

[13] The territorial gains of the Stanleys in the later fifteenth century are enumerated by Coward, *Stanleys*, pp. 6–15.

[14] For a discussion of the usage of the royal title, see chapter 1, pp. 15–16, n. 14.

[15] Thomas, the second Lord Stanley, married Margaret Beaufort, countess of Richmond, in 1482. Coward, *Stanleys*, p. 11.

[16] For a list of governors of the Isle of Man, see appendix ii.

[17] The holders of the principal officers in the island's administration are listed in appendices iii–vii.

origin to gain employment as soldiers in the island and wear the badge of the Stanley Lord of Man. Throughout this period the two garrisons of the island at Castle Rushen and Peel Castle comprised between thirty and forty men, some of whom at least were Lancashire men who remained only as long as their term of service; others married Manx women and made the island their home.[18] The other places in the island's administration, such as the offices of deemster or coroner, were always held by Manxmen or members of immigrant families who had lived in the island for long enough to have become assimilated. The necessity for these office holders to speak the Manx language made it clearly impractical for such positions to be held by Stanley servants who could only speak English.[19]

While possession of the lordship of the island might not have added much to the social standing of the Stanleys, the Isle of Man did have some economic value. This did not come in the form of a large rent roll or a wealth of natural resources but rather in the position of the Isle of Man as an entrepôt in the smuggling trade, which became a problem of increasing proportions for the British government in the decades after the Restoration.[20] Until the later seventeenth century the income from the island in the form of rents and customs revenue was largely accounted for by the fees paid to the officers and soldiers and the disbursements made to workmen for repairs at the castles and other labours on the Lord's behalf.[21]

[18] The soldiers of both garrisons, and the handful of men stationed at Douglas and Ramsey, are listed for each year in the books of allowance or disbursements, sometimes bound with the books of revenue charge for the North- and Southsides of the island. M.M.L., R.D. and I.O. Even a brief examination of short runs of these lists indicates the variable rate of turnover in the soldiery and those men who decided to remain in the island.

[19] For details of the offices which unquestionably demanded a knowledge of Manx – deemster, coroner, lockman, moar and the captains of the parishes and towns – see chapter 1, pp. 43–53.

[20] The development of the contraband trade and the attempts by the British Crown to purchase the island's customs from the earl of Derby are examined in chapter 5, pp. 331–41.

[21] In the late 1640s, the rents from the Lord's tenants, the rents due in lieu of customary payments in kind and the customs revenue amounted to about £1,600. This total also includes the gross income derived from the bishopric and the abbey lands, which were then temporarily in the Lord's hands, and probably represents the maximum level of income which the Stanleys could hope to extract from the island. M.M.L., R.D. 1627–50, Books of charge,

The rise of the running trade after the 1660s, however, not only increased the island's customs revenues, particularly from the 1690s onwards, but also made the British government eager to come to some agreement with the earl of Derby by which he would surrender the Manx customs to British control. The earl was extremely unwilling to sell the customs to the Crown and was reluctant to tolerate the presence of English customs officers in the island since they represented a threat to his prerogative rights as Lord of Man,[22] but the situation did provide him with some political leverage if he wished, or were able, to exploit it.

III. SOURCES FOR EARLY MODERN MANX HISTORY

The principal sources for any study of the island's history during the early modern period are the records of the secular Manx courts. Before about 1580, the records of the principal secular courts were kept on rolls, only one of which appears to be now extant.[23] After that date, the records were split into separate series, all of which survive completely intact for the rest of the Stanley period and beyond. Of these, the most important for an understanding of the government of the island and the regulation of its economy are the records of the Exchequer Court, contained in the Libri Scaccarii (Exchequer Books), which commence in 1580. These contain orders made by the Lord, the governor and Council, the legislative proceedings of the Tynwald Court, lists of the members of the Keys, presentments, recognizances, indictments, commissions and a miscellaneous collection of material, including petitions and enrolled deeds of bargain and sale.[24]

Peel Castle, 1648 and 1649; Books of charge, Castle Rushen, 1648 and 1649; M.M.L., I.O. 1646–59, Waterbailiff's accounts, 1648 and 1649; M.M.L., R.D. 1651–70, Book of charge, abbey and bishop's revenue, 1651; Book of abbey and bishop's spiritualities and temporalities, 1651–8.

[22] The prerogative rights of the Lord of Man are discussed in chapter 1, pp. 19–23.

[23] M.M.L., MS 510C, J. Quayle, *A Book of Precedents* (n.d., *c.* 1725), p. 48; MD/401/1715/3. Court roll dated 1576.

[24] For details of the personnel and jurisdiction of the Exchequer Court, see chapter 1, pp. 67–8.

The proceedings of the other principal courts are generally less concerned with matters of government. The records of the Chancery Court, in the Libri Cancellarii (Chancery Books), which begin in 1578, do, however, contain some orders made by the governor and Council, commissions and, occasionally, lists of the Keys, but they are mainly concerned with cases in the island's court of equity. In the late sixteenth century these records contain only the barest details of the petitions brought before the court. By the 1680s, however, more detailed information is often provided about individual cases, in the form of depositions and other supporting documents bound into the books.[25] The other principal series of court records is contained in the Libri Placitorum (Books of Pleas), the earliest of which now extant dates from 1496. These books are composed of the records of the sheading courts, or courts of common law, and, from about 1580, the Court of General Gaol Delivery. As such they contain presentments for 'bloodwipes,' or assaults, general presentments and the proceedings of the island's court of criminal justice.[26]

Two uncalendared classes of documents which provide a wealth of information about the administration of the island and the Manx economy and which appear to have been scarcely used, if at all, by the most prominent Manx historian, A. W. Moore,[27] are the Derby receipts and disbursements and the ingates and outgates. The former are a collection of account books – books of charge, or revenue from the parishes; books of pension, or revenue in lieu of customary payments in kind; books of allowance, or salaries paid to officers and soldiers; and miscellaneous books of receipts and disbursements. The earliest items date from 1580 and the major series are almost unbroken during the seventeenth century. The principal account books were merged in the book of charge of the revenue for the whole island after about 1660.[28]

[25] On the Chancery Court, see chapter 1, pp. 66–7.
[26] Both the sheading courts and the Court of General Gaol Delivery are discussed in chapter 1, pp. 65–6, 68–9.
[27] A. W. Moore produced what has become the standard history of the Isle of Man in 1900, in addition to a wide range of scholarly articles and books. Moore, *History*.
[28] M.M.L., R.D. The first bundle of Receipts and Disbursements is dated 1579–98, but the earliest books actually date from 1580.

The material contained in the bundles of ingates and outgates overlaps to some extent with the receipts and disbursements series, including books of charge and disbursements, but it chiefly consists of the waterbailiff's accounts of the customs duty collected in the island's ports. These accounts begin in 1576 and, although there are a few gaps in the series, particularly before 1600, they remain extant for nearly every year in the seventeenth century. The accounts list at least the names of merchants, the goods shipped or imported and the amount of duty paid, and are of fundamental importance in a study of the Manx economy, and overseas trade in particular.[29]

Although many of the court records for the period before the late sixteenth century appear to have perished, two valuable manuscripts survive which contain extracts from such lost material. The *Book of Precedents* compiled by John Quayle, clerk of the rolls, in about 1725, comprises excerpts from the records of the courts of the Lord and the barons, essentially from the late fifteenth century until 1669,[30] while the *Abridgement* written by John Parr, subsequently deemster, in 1679, contains statements of the customary law and orders concerning a wide variety of matters.[31]

The wills and inventories recorded in the episcopal and archidiaconal registries[32] provide useful additional information for the study of Manx society in the seventeenth century. These documents, which can only be examined on microfilm, survive from 1600 onwards, but have not as yet been fully indexed. Searching for the testamentary records of an individual, even when the date of death

[29] M.M.L., I.O. The first bundle of Ingates and Outgates is labelled 1570–99, but the earliest book dates from 1576. The waterbailiff's accounts are discussed in greater detail in chapter 5, pp. 232–39.

[30] M.M.L., MS 510. C. J. Quayle, *A Book of Precedents* (n.d., c. 1725).

[31] M.M.L., MD 15,040. J. Parr, *An Abridgement or Short Tract of the most usefull Lawes Acts and Ordinances conteyned in the Statute Book of this Isle of Mann* (1679).

[32] The episcopal court sat for six months of the year, while the archidiaconal court sat for the other half of the year. On the unusual organisation of the courts in the diocese of Sodor and Man, which comprised the island alone, see A. Ashley, 'The Spiritual Courts of the Isle of Man, especially in the Seventeenth and Eighteenth Centuries', *E.H.R.*, vol. lxxii (1957), pp. 31–59. For comparison with the organisation of the ecclesiastical courts in two English dioceses, in this case Norwich and Winchester, see R. Houlbrooke, *Church Courts and the People during the English Reformation* (Oxford, 1979), ch. 2.

is definitely known, can, therefore, be a laborious task. Nevertheless, the probate records of a handful of landowners, merchants and craftsmen have been located and provide details of the standards of living among some of the more affluent members of island society. The probate inventories of those of more lowly status often record very few possessions of little value and indicate the size of the gap between the poor and the comparatively rich.

Some important sources are extant for only a part of the seventeenth century. Parish registers, which in other circumstances might be used to produce an estimate of the island's population, survive for at least part of the first half of the seventeenth century in only nine of the seventeen parishes and, even in these cases, there are years in which no entries were made. By the last decade of the century, there are extant registers for thirteen parishes, but the clear evidence of under registration, as at Andreas between 1694 and 1704, makes them unreliable sources on which to base any calculation of the Manx population.[33] A crude estimate of the island's population in *c*. 1670 can, however, be tentatively made based on the average number of burials in the nine parishes with extant registers in the decade 1665–1674 and a mean figure derived from this number supplying the totals for the remaining parishes in the island. Following the observations of the seventeenth-century demographer John Graunt, that one burial represents 32 living people, produces a total population figure for the island of 10,464, although allowance must be made for some considerable margin of error.[34] The first relatively reliable population figures for the island are contained in the 'Account of the Number of Souls in the Isle of Man,' compiled in 1726, probably at the direction of Bishop Wilson. Although figures for Marown are

[33] M.M.L., MF/PR/1. Andreas Parish Registers: Baptisms, 1691. On the criteria for using parish registers for aggregative analysis, see E. A. Wrigley and R. S. Schofield, *The Population History of England, 1541–1871. A Reconstruction* (1981, reprinted Cambridge, 1989), introduction and ch. 1.

[34] J. Graunt, *Natural and Political Observations on the Bills of Mortality* (3rd edn, 1665), p. 141. Sir William Petty arrived at the slightly lower figure of one burial for every 30 living people. W. Petty, *Another Essay in Political Arithmetick Concerning the Growth of the City of London* (1682), reprinted in C. H. Hull, *The Economic Writings of Sir William Petty* (Cambridge, 1899) vol. ii, p. 459. Both these demographers were concerned with data from London, where the rates of mortality might be expected to be considerably higher than in the Isle of Man.

wanting, Moore estimated the population of that parish to be 499; when this number is added to the figures produced by the clergy, the total population of the island in 1726 amounts to 14,426 persons.[35]

In contrast to the other countries of the British Isles, there are, in the Isle of Man, no substantial collections of family papers extant for the early modern period, although that portion of the Stanley of Knowsley papers concerning the island provides much information about many aspects of the island during the seventeenth century. These papers, which mainly span the period from the end of the sixteenth to the early eighteenth centuries, were transferred from the Lancashire Record Office in 1967 and contain commissions, copies of the Manx Books of Rates, some receivers' accounts, legal papers and a small number of leases and several bundles of letters, commencing in about 1660.[36] In addition, a small number of items relating to the Isle of Man in this period remains in the hands of the Stanley family at Knowsley Hall. These include legal papers and an early eighteenth-century copy of the Manx statutes.[37]

---

[35] R. Sherwood, *The Constitution of the Isle of Man*, Manx Society, vol. xxxi (1882), p. 284; Moore, *History*, vol. ii, p. 646.

[36] M.M.L., MD/401. Derby (Stanley of Knowsley) Papers (formerly L.R.O., DDK).

[37] Knowsley Hall, H/41. Laws of Man (n.d., *c.* 1705); H/44a. Papers relating to the Isle of Man.

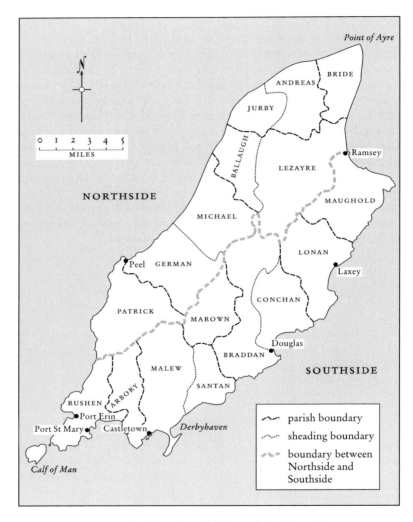

Map 1. Administrative divisions of the Isle of Man
in the seventeenth century.

1 *The Government of the Isle of Man*

The system of government existing in the Isle of Man in the early modern period was the product of the Norse settlement of the island between the ninth and late eleventh centuries and any subsequent modifications to the Norse administrative structure which may have been introduced before the fifteenth century. As such, it was quite different from the rest of the British Isles.[1] Between 1079 and 1265, the island had been the seat of a kingdom which encompassed the Hebrides and in which the king had similar powers and privileges to the English king in England.[2] The institutions established during that period formed the characteristic features of the Manx administrative system thereafter. In its original form, the chief elements of the Norse system were the king of Man and the Isles and the Tynwald Court.[3] This court was the annual assembly of all the inhabitants at midsummer to hear new laws promulgated, to present petitions and settle disputes and to deal with any other matters. It represented the Manx form of the Scandinavian *thing*.[4] The basic administrative subdivisions of the island also seem to have been established during the period of Scandinavian rule, although it is possible that they date from before the advent of the Norsemen. The principal division of the

---

[1] There is a superficial resemblance between Man and the Channel Islands, but the origins and development of the systems of government are quite dissimilar. On the government of Jersey and Guernsey, see J. Marett (ed.), 'A Survey of the Island of Jersey by Philip Dumaresq (1685)', *Bulletin of La Société Jersiaise*, vol. xii (1935), p. 422; A. J. Eagleston, *The Channel Islands under Tudor Government, 1485–1642* (Cambridge, 1949).
[2] The powers and prerogative rights of the Lord of Man are discussed *infra*, pp. 19–23.
[3] For further details of the Tynwald Court see *infra*, pp. 54, 62–4.
[4] Moore, *History*, vol. i, pp. 151–2; R. D. Farrant, *Mann: Its Land Tenure, Constitution, Lord's Rent and Deemsters* (Oxford, 1937), ch. 2. Cf. O. Klindt-Jensen, *The World of the Vikings* (1970), pp. 178–83.

island was into two parts, Northside and Southside, the line of partition following the watershed of the mountains from north-east to south-west. The island was then subdivided into sheadings,[5] of which there were six, all except one, Glenfaba, comprising three parishes (Map 1). It is widely accepted that the latter, which are thought to have originally numbered sixteen rather than seventeen, were also created during this period, in the twelfth century, though it seems likely that they were based on previously existing divisions.[6]

The establishment of English suzerainty over Man in the early fourteenth century apparently had little effect within the island on the authority of the king – or Lord, as he was increasingly known – but there were, however, changes to the administrative system. The fact that the lordship of the island was granted to a succession of English nobles meant that the Lord was now generally absent as a matter of course and that the officers who at least by this date composed the Lord's Council – the governor, comptroller, receivers, waterbailiff and attorney – assumed a prominent role in the government of the island, assisted by the two deemsters, or judges.[7] While the system of local government in the sheadings and parishes continued as before,[8] the judicial function of the Tynwald Court was modified, if it had not already been adapted before the early fourteenth century, so that specific cases could be heard before some of the officers in specialist courts, such as the Exchequer Court or the Admiralty Court.[9] The overall structure of government in the island, nevertheless, remained unchanged throughout the Stanley period.[10]

[5] The meaning of the word 'sheading' is not certain, but it seems most likely that it is derived from the Old Norse *séttungr*, 'a sixth part'. C. J. S. Marstrander, 'Treen og Keeill', *Norsk Tidsskrift for Sprogvidenskap*, vol. viii (1937), p. 431.

[6] W. Cubbon and B. R. S. Megaw, 'The Western Isles and the Growth of the Manx Parliament', *J.M.M.*, vol. v (1941–6), p. 61; Craine, *Manannan's Isle*, p. 104; Marstrander, 'Treen og Keeill', p. 427. Marown and Santan are thought to have originally formed one parish. Kinvig, *Isle of Man*, p. 13.

[7] The duties of the principal officers are examined *infra*, pp. 26–34.

[8] The officers responsible for the enforcement of law, the collection of rents and other duties in the sheadings, parishes and towns are considered *infra*, pp. 46–53.

[9] For an account of the various courts, see *infra*, pp. 62–74.

[10] The best account of the administrative structure during the Stanley period up to the end of the seventeenth century remains that by Moore, *History*, vol. ii, pp. 738–77.

I. THE CONSTITUTIONAL STATUS
OF THE ISLE OF MAN AND ITS LORD

On April 6, 1406, Henry IV granted the lordship of Man to Sir John Stanley in perpetuity in return for the provision of two falcons at the coronation of the king's successors.[11] This was the most significant of several grants of land and other property which Stanley received as reward for his services to the Crown, particularly in Ireland.[12] It endowed the Stanleys with prerogative rights which were elsewhere normally reserved to the king alone[13] and with a regal title which seems to have fallen into disuse, at least outside the island, after the annexation of the island by Edward III in *c.*1333.[14] The Stanleys

[11] Oliver, *Monumenta*, vol. ii, pp. 235–46; *C.C.R.*, *1405–9*, p. 2.

[12] For the career of Sir John Stanley, see B. Coward, *The Stanleys, Lords Stanley and Earls of Derby, 1385–1672* (Chet. Soc., 3rd series, vol. x, 1983), pp. 2–6; W. Fergusson Irvine, 'The Early Stanleys', *T.H.S.L.C.*, vol. cv (1954), p. 57; J. J. Bagley, *The Earls of Derby, 1485–1985* (1985), pp. 1–6.

[13] For the prerogative rights of the Lord of Man, see *infra*, pp. 19–23.

[14] The title 'King of Man and the Isles' originated in the Norse kingdom of that name, founded by Godred Crovan in 1079, which embraced the Western Isles until 1156, and the northern Hebrides alone thereafter. The kingdom, which had been nominally subject to Norway, was ceded to Scotland in 1266 and remained in Scottish hands until after the death of Alexander III in 1286. Man became completely separated from the Hebrides when Edward I took possession of it before 1290 and, despite temporarily successful attempts to restore Scottish control, notably by Robert Bruce, it continued as a dependent territory of the English Crown, though not of the English kingdom. Cubbon and Megaw, *Western Isles and the Growth of the Manx Parliament*, pp. 58–60; A. A. M. Duncan, *Scotland: The Making of the Kingdom* (Edinburgh, 1975), p. 547; Moore, *History*, pp. 111, 181–94. After Edward III granted the island to Sir William Montagu, later earl of Salisbury, the latter adopted the style 'Lord of Man'. See, for example, *C.P.R., 1338–40*, p. 110; *C.P.R., 1358–61*, p. 539; *C.P.R., 1364–7*, p. 169; *C.P.R., 1367–70*, p. 364; *C.P.R., 1370–4*, p. 48; *C.P.R., 1377–81*, pp. 596–7. In 1393, Salisbury's son sold the island to Sir William Le Scrope, Richard II's vice-chamberlain, who forfeited all his estates to the Crown six years later, when Bolingbroke seized the throne as Henry IV. The Isle of Man was then granted to Henry Percy, earl of Northumberland, but resumed by the king when Percy rose in rebellion in 1405. The island was temporarily entrusted to Sir John and Sir William Stanley before Henry IV made a grant of the lordship for life in October 1405. This was superseded by the grant in perpetuity to Sir John Stanley in 1406. H. T. Riley (ed.), *Chronici*

continued to be styled *Rex Manniae et Insularum* in the island's records until at least the beginning of the sixteenth century, when Thomas, second earl of Derby, called both king and Lord of Man and the Isles, confirmed former grants of property to the Manx Church in 1505.[15] Thereafter, the title disappeared from official documents, although there is evidence that the Lord of Man was still referred to as 'King of Man' in the ceremonial preamble to court proceedings in the later seventeenth century. In an anonymous account of the island dating from about 1665, it is recorded that, before the common law or sheading courts,[16] the deemster proclaimed that it was

> the kinge of Mann his pleasure, that a Court bee houlden, twise in the yeare, that poore and rich, the blinde, the poore simple or ignorant persons, the lame and mayhem'd may either come a foote, on horse backe or on carre, to learn . . . the king of Mann his minde, and his officers, and to know the old lawes of this Isle or Countrey.[17]

Despite the persistence of the title of king in such cases, the Stanleys assumed the style of Lord of Man outside the island in accordance with the practice of their predecessors since the fourteenth century. James, seventh earl of Derby, later stated that 'to be a great Lord is a more honourable Title than a petty King,'[18] but there were clearly more practical reasons for the Stanleys to drop the title. The proximity of the Stanleys to the throne after 1485 and the emphasis laid on the royal prerogative by Henry VII, stepson of Thomas, first earl of Derby, were both compelling reasons for such

---

note 14 *continued*
Monasterii S. Albani Johannis de Trokelowe et Henrici de Blaneforde, Chronica Annales (1865), p. 157; *D.N.B.*, vol. xviii, p. 1087; M.M.L., MD/401/1716/1; Oliver, *Monumenta*, vol. ii, pp. 215–19, 228–9; *C.P.R.*, *1405–9*, pp. 201–2.
[15] Oliver, *Monumenta*, vol. iii, pp. 27–31; W. Dugdale, *Monasticon Anglicanum*, eds J. Caley, H. Ellis and B. Bandinel (1846), vol. v, p. 257. There are few extant records for the island dating from the fifteenth century. In 1586, William Camden noted that the earls of Derby were called 'petty kings of Man' (*Manniae reguli*). W. Camden, *Britannia* (1586), p. 542.
[16] For details of the sheading courts, see *infra*, pp. 68–71.
[17] Cl.R.O., Nantlys MS D/NA/905, 28. See also the references to the ceremonial fencing of the Court of General Gaol Delivery in idem, 27, 53.
[18] *History and Antiquities of the Isle of Man*, p. 15.

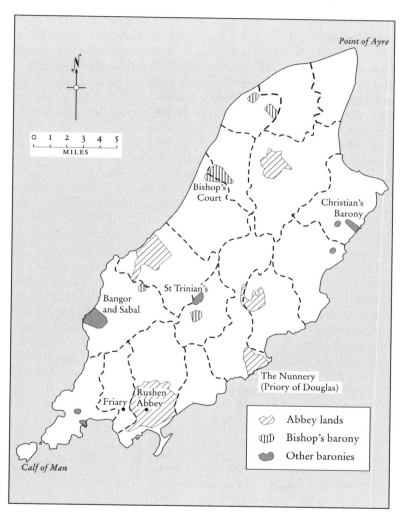

Map 2. Baronies of the Isle of Man in the Seventeenth Century.

Point of Ayre

Bishop's
Court

Christian's
Barony

Bangor
and Sabal

St Trinian's

The Nunnery
(Priory of Douglas)

Friary Rushen
Abbey

Calf of Man

N

MILES

Abbey lands

Bishop's barony

Other baronies

17

a course of action, although Earl James claimed that he did not know whether it was followed 'of Modestie or Policie.'[19]

The change in title did not affect the powers of the Stanleys as rulers of the island. William Blundell, writing from first hand experience in the late 1640s, was unable to find 'any difference at all . . . betwixt a King and a Lord of Man, but only in certain formalities and not in any realities.'[20] He observed that 'the Lord of Man is as potentially powerful, exercising *jura regalia* as fully, freely and absolutely, and in as ample a latitude as any of the precedent kings ever did or might do – for the difference of stile makes not the difference of sovereignty.'[21] This authority wielded by the Lord of Man, like that of his royal predecessors, was derived from 'the prerogative belonging unto the Island'[22] and was not dependent on the will of the king of England. This was affirmed in 1522, when Anne, Dowager Countess of Derby, had claimed the Isle of Man as part of her dower in Chancery and subsequently by petition to the king and Council. The judges and the Council ruled against her in this instance 'because the Isle of Man was no part of the Realm of England, nor was governed by the law of this Land.'[23]

This judgement was confirmed in 1598 in a dispute over the title to the Isle of Man between the heirs general of Ferdinando, fifth Earl of Derby, and William, sixth Earl of Derby. Elizabeth I referred the matter to a panel of judges, including Sir Thomas Egerton, Lord Keeper of the Great Seal, and Sir John Popham, Lord Chief Justice, who ruled not only that 'the Isle of Man was an ancient kingdome of it self, and no part of the kingdome of England,' but that no 'general Act of Parliament did extend to the Isle of Man,' although 'by speciall name an Act of Parliament may extend to it.'[24] In

---

[19] *ibid.*, p. 4.

[20] Blundell, *History*, vol. ii, p. 41.

[21] *ibid.*, p. 38.

[22] *ibid.*

[23] E. Coke, *The Fourth Part of the Institutes of the Laws of England: Concerning the Jurisdiction of Courts* (2nd edn, 1648), p. 284. Cf. idem, *The First Part of the Institutes of the Laws of England* (2nd edn, 1629), p. 9.

[24] Coke, *Fourth Part of the Institutes*, p. 284. The jurisdiction of the Court of Wards did not include the island because it was 'out of the power of the Chancery of England, and not to be bound by our Parliament of England, but by speciall name'. J. Gell (ed.), *An Abstract of the Laws, Customs, and Ordinances of the Isle of Man, compiled by John Parr*, vol. i [Notes], Manx

practice, this provision did not affect the political and legal independence of the island, since, apart from the Act confirming the grant of the lordship to Earl William and Countess Elizabeth in 1610 and that passed by the Rump conferring the lordship on Thomas, Lord Fairfax in 1649, no such Acts were passed until the time of the Revestment of the island in the Crown in 1765.[25]

Since the island lay outside the jurisdiction of English royal government and the English courts of law, the Lord of Man possessed and exercised powers which were almost identical to those of the king of England.[26] He appointed the principal officers of the island's government, who together constituted the Lord's Council.[27] He summoned the Council and the twenty-four Keys[28] to attend the Tynwald Court at which ordinances and statutes were promulgated, none of which had the full force of law without his prior assent. The courts of law were held in the Lord's name and the right of appeal from them lay ultimately to him as the supreme legal authority in the island.[29] In this capacity, he had the power to impose the death penalty, to banish offenders from the island, to mitigate their punishment or to pardon them.[30] The Lord was the proprietor from whom almost all the inhabitants held their lands, the only exceptions after the Dissolution being the tenants of the bishop and a handful of minor barons.[31]

Society, vol. xii (1867), p. 201. For the opinions of Coke, Selden, Hargrave and Blackstone on the independent status of the Isle of Man, see idem, pp. 152–64.

[25] Gell, *Abstract of the Laws*, p. 105.

[26] On the prerogative and powers of the king of England, see T. Smith, *De Republica Anglorum*, ed. M. Dewar (Cambridge 1982), pp. 85–8; G. R. Elton (ed.), *The Tudor Constitution* (2nd edn, Cambridge 1982), pp. 17–39.

[27] The individual officers of the Council are discussed *infra*, pp. 26–34.

[28] For details of the nature and functions of the Keys, see *infra*, pp. 56–62.

[29] See *infra*, p. 18. M.M.L., MD/401/1716/22. Technically, it was possible to make a further appeal to the English king in Council, but, in practice, this was rarely done. R. Sherwood (ed.), *The Constitution of the Isle of Man*, Manx Society, vol. xxxi (1882), pp. 37 n. 17, 43 n. 26, 52, 60.

[30] Offences such as felony, witchcraft, murder, treason and rebellion carried the death penalty. Cl.R.O., Nantlys MS D/NA/905, 57–9; *Statutes*, pp. 10, 21–2, 23–4, 82. Convicted felons were sometimes allowed to abjure, or forswear, the island. *ibid.*, p. 9; Craine, *Manannan's Isle*, pp. 37–8. See, for example, Lib. Scacc. 1609, 44, 48; Lib. Scacc. 1654, 9.

[31] Before the Dissolution, there were six ecclesiastical baronies: i) the bishop's barony; ii) the barony of Rushen Abbey; iii) the barony of the

He received the customs revenue from imports and exports and set the rates to be levied on goods, despite the claim of the Keys in 1608 that the Lord required their consent before any duties could be altered.[32] The Lord was entitled to all 'choice Wine,' although some

note 31 continued

priory of Douglas, in Braddan; iv) the barony of the priory of St Bee's in Cumberland, in Maughold; v) the barony of the abbeys of Bangor and Sabal in Ireland, in Patrick; vi) the barony of St Trinian's, in German and Marown, belonging to the priory of Whithorne in Galloway. The bishop's barony survived the Dissolution of the Manx religious houses in 1540, while the property of Rushen Abbey, a dependent house of Furness Abbey in Lancashire, and the priory of Douglas were vested in the English Crown. Together with the small amount of land formerly belonging to the friary of Bymaken in Arbory, these lands, collectively known as the 'Abbey lands,' were ultimately granted to Earl William and Countess Elizabeth in 1610. The Abbey lands had been previously leased to Dowager Countess Alice, the widow of Earl Ferdinando, in 1606 for a term of forty years. Gell, *Abstract of the Laws*, pp. 57–60; Coward, *Stanleys*, p. 63; Oliver, *Monumenta*, p. 87. The circumstances in which the other baronies came into secular hands are not certain, but it seems unlikely that they were seized by the Lord, as suggested by one version of the early statutes. B.L.Add. MS 4,149, ff. 331–46, printed in W. Mackenzie (ed.), *Legislation by Three of the Thirteen Stanleys, Kings of Man*, Manx Society, vol. iii (1860), p. 75. The barony of St Bee's in Maughold, subsequently known as Christian's barony, came into the possession of the Christian family of Milntown, Lezayre, probably between 1540 and 1580, when John Christian became vicar of Maughold. W. Radcliffe and C. Radcliffe, *A History of Kirk Maughold* (Douglas, 1979), pp. 158–60, 163–5; Moore, *History*, vol. ii, p. 872; R. Sherwood, *Manx Law Tenures* (Douglas, 1899), p. 16. The barony of Bangor and Sabal appears to have been taken into the king's hands in or shortly after 1540 and was later leased to the Shireburne family of Stonyhurst in Lancashire, who held it until the eighteenth century. B. R. S. Megaw, 'The Barony of Bangor and Sabal in Kirk Patrick', *J.M.M.*, vol. iv (1938–40), pp. 135–8, 160; Cl.R.O., Nantlys MS D/NA/905, 24; M.M.L., MD/401/1717/18; M.M.L., MD/401/ 1717/34. The Lord seems to have acquired the barony of St Trinian's in or shortly after 1540. In 1577, Earl Henry leased the advowson, tithes and property of the churches of 'kirkchriste in the ayre and kirk marron' (Lezayre and Marown), formerly parts of the barony to Robert Salusbury of Denbigh. B. R. S. Megaw, 'The Barony of Saint Trinian in Kirk Marown', *J.M.M.*, vol. iv (1938–40), p. 177; Oliver, *Monumenta*, vol. iii, p. 70. See Map 2.

[32] Moore, *History*, vol. ii, pp. 768–9.

might be allowed to the governor, the bishop, the archdeacon and, before 1540, the abbot.[33] He also exercised admiralty jurisdiction, which was confirmed in 1607, when it was determined that 'the Admiralty of England had not to doe in the ports of Man, but that the Earl of Derby is Lord of Man and Admirall of that Isle.'[34] He received the profits from wrecks on the coast, one-fifth of the herring catch[35] and any porpoises, sturgeon or whales caught 'within the Heads of Mann above Water or under Water.'[36] The Lord had a right to all treasure trove, deodands, waifs and strays, the goods of excommunicates and of aliens who died without having sworn allegiance to him. Any stranger who was found guilty of manslaughter lost his entire personal estate to the Lord, while a proportion of a native felon's property was similarly forfeit.[37]

Furthermore, the Lord of Man enjoyed some of the feudal dues to which English kings were entitled. These included purveyance, which was the right to purchase provisions at a price below market values, and pre-emption, which allowed the Lord to have the first choice of any goods for the supply of his household.[38] The Lord also enjoyed the exclusive right to hunt in the forest[39] and warrens of the island.[40]

[33] *Statutes*, p. 28.

[34] P.R.O., SP 14/27/39. Cf. Oliver, *Monumenta*, vol. iii, pp. 92–3.

[35] For details of the Lord's share of the herring catch, see chapter 2, p. 111.

[36] *Statutes*, pp. 5, 8.

[37] *ibid.*, pp. 9, 25, 59–60; Craine, *Manannan's Isle*, pp. 39–40; Lib. Scacc. 1692, 45.

[38] *Statutes*, pp. 10–11, 20, 27; M.M.L., MD/401/1715/5. Provisions for the garrisons, paid in kind at the Lord's price, constituted half the rent of the Lord's tenants until 1601. Thereafter, this portion of the rent was commuted to a payment in money. M.M.L., MD/401/1716/4; A. W. Moore (ed.), *The Manx Note Book*, vol. i (1885), pp. 61–4; Cl.R.O., Nantlys MS D/NA/905, 4. From March 1645, when the lease of the abbey lands made to Dowager Countess Alice in 1606 expired, the Lord received payments in kind from the abbey tenants. *ibid.*, 21.

[39] The Lord's forest comprised all the common land, principally the uplands beyond the 'Feldike' or boundary wall separating the intacks from the commons. As in England, the Lord's tenants were permitted to cut turf and graze their animals there on payment of a fee. The supervision of the forest, which covered an estimated 25,113 acres, was entrusted to a forester, whose lodge was in Ballaugh. *Statutes*, pp. 50, 76; J. R. Quayle, 'The King's Forest', *M.N.H.A.S.*, vol. iv (1932–42), p. 373.

[40] The Lord's warren covered extensive areas, especially in the northern

In addition, the Stanleys had a large measure of control over the Church in the island because the grant to Sir John Stanley had specifically included the patronage of the bishopric and all the livings in the parishes. In 1541, Edward, third earl of Derby was declared to be 'Metropolitan and Chiefe of [the] holy Church,'[41] but this was merely a confirmation of the state of affairs which had already existed in practice for more than a century. The supremacy of the Stanleys in ecclesiastical matters was only challenged once, when, in 1546, Henry VIII appointed his chaplain, Henry Man, to the bishopric, ignoring the claims of the Lord. Thereafter, it was normal practice for the bishop elect's name to be submitted to the English monarch for the royal assent.[42]

Although attached to the province of York by Act of Parliament

note 40 *continued*

lowland. There the warren extended from Cass ny Hawin in Ballaugh to Point of Ayre and southward as far as the mouth of the Sulby river at Ramsey. There was also a small area of warren at Congary, near Peel. Craine, *Manannan's Isle*, p. 40; M.M.L., I.O. 1660–71, Composition Book, 1666–73, Lease of the Lord's warren in the north to Ewan Christian of Cranstall, Bride and Edward Christian, probably of Milntown, Lezayre, April 12, 1673. In the south of the island, the boundary of the warren ran westward from Castle Rushen to Kentraugh Burn in Rushen and then northward to the Feldike; it continued north-eastward to Santan Burn, followed the river to the coast and thence back to the castle. *Statutes*, p. 61.

[41] M.M.L., MS 510C, J. Quayle, *A Book of Precedents* (n.d., *c.* 1725), p. 31; Craine, *Manannan's Isle*, pp. 41–2.

[42] Oliver, *Monumenta*, vol. iii, pp. 38–41, 42–5. In 1570, Earl Edward presented John Salesbury to the bishopric and the appointment was confirmed by Elizabeth. *ibid.*, pp. 53–7, 58–61. The same procedure was followed in the case of John Meyrick in 1576. *ibid.*, pp. 62–6. During the dispute over the Stanley estates at the end of the century, Elizabeth took possession of the island and, when the see fell vacant in 1599, she appointed George Lloyd as bishop. *C.S.P.D.*, *1598–1601*, p. 360. In 1605, John Phillips became bishop by royal grant on the translation of Lloyd to Chester. *C.S.P.D.*, *1603–10*, pp. 176, 187, 188. The whole question of presentation to the bishopric was referred to a panel of judges by Charles I at the time of the next vacancy in 1633. The right of the earl of Derby to nominate was upheld, but it was pointed out that he could not request the archbishop of York to consecrate his nominee without royal approval. The king thus retained his position of supremacy in the Church of England. The procedure was confirmed with the appointments of William Forster in 1634 and Richard Parr in 1635. Oliver, *Monumenta*, vol. iii, pp. 135–6, 137–9, 142–4.

in 1542, the diocese of Sodor and Man was more closely under the supervision of the Lord than that of the archbishop of York, and the Stanleys were able 'to chuse a Reverend and Holy Man' as bishop who was dependent on them, with little outside interference.[43]

Despite the possession of these rights and privileges, the Stanleys rarely exercised their authority in person, and, when the Lord did take ship for Man, it was usually to deal with some serious problem, such as rebellion. There are few extant records dating from before the later sixteenth century, but even after this time, the recorded visits of the Stanleys to the Isle of Man are few and far between. The first Stanley to cross the sea from Lancashire was Sir John Stanley II, the son of the original grantee, who visited the island on at least four occasions, the first of which was before his father's death in 1414.[44] His subsequent visits in 1417, 1422 and 1423 were devoted to dealing with insurrections against his governor or lieutenant, reducing the laws to writing and asserting his authority over the ecclesiastical barons, while confirming the liberties and property of the Church.[45] His work laid the foundations upon which the Stanley administration in the island was based, but its conclusion marked the beginning of a period of more than one hundred and fifty years during which the Lord was apparently never present in the island.

Although it is possible that Thomas Stanley, subsequently first earl of Derby, may have launched an attack on Galloway from the island in 1457 and that Thomas, second earl of Derby, may have landed at Derbyhaven in 1507,[46] the next adequately documented visit of the Lord of Man was that made by Henry, fourth earl of Derby in 1577. It is not clear why the earl should have visited the island at this particular time, though his presence afforded him an opportunity to assess the efficiency of the island's government and to reassert the Lord's rights and prerogatives. Earl Henry presided at the Tynwald Court in person, confirmed the first recorded Manx Book of Rates and was also present at the sheading and other courts.[47] After a second visit by Earl Henry in 1583, the reason for

[43] 33 Hen. VIII, c. 31; *History and Antiquities of the Isle of Man*, p. 14.

[44] *Statutes*, p. 4. For a list of the Stanley Lords of Man, see appendix i.

[45] *ibid.*, pp. 1–3, 8, 20.

[46] B. R. S. Megaw, 'The Scottish Invasion of Man in 1456', *J.M.M.*, vol. vi (1957–65), p. 23; Traditionary Ballad, *Mannanan Beg, Mac y Leirr*, in W. Harrison (ed.), *Mona Miscellany*, Manx Society, vol. xxi (1873), p. 45.

[47] *Statutes*, pp. 37, 47; Lib. Plit. 1577 [May 6– July 17].

which is not certain,[48] there was another lengthy interval before the Lord set foot in the island again. This was perhaps prolonged by the dispute between the heirs general of Ferdinando, fifth earl of Derby, and his brother, William, sixth earl of Derby, which commenced in 1594; the island was taken into the hands of the Crown for the duration and only came into the possession of Earl William and Countess Elizabeth in 1611 or 1612.[49]

Nevertheless, once the island had been restored to the Stanleys, it was not until June 1643 that the Manx were again favoured by the presence of the Lord, and then it was in circumstances which compelled him to make the voyage to the island. Having heard rumours that the Scots were plotting to seize the island and received letters from his officers there reporting unrest, James, seventh earl of Derby, was, in his own words, 'advised to go immediately for the Isle of Man to secure it for his Majestie's Service, as well as in Wisdome to preserve my owne Inheritance.'[50] Apart from a period of about six months in 1644, when he was instrumental in raising the siege of Lathom House, Earl James resided in Castle Rushen from June 1643 until August 1651.[51] This was the only time in more than three centuries of Stanley rule when the Lord actually took part in the government of the island, in person, for any considerable length of time. Neither Thomas, Lord Fairfax, who was Lord of Man during the Interregnum, nor Charles, eighth earl of Derby, who became Lord at the Restoration in 1660, ever visited the island,[52] but the latter's successor, William, the ninth earl, crossed the Irish Sea to

---

[48] Lib. Plit. 1583, cited in M.M.L., MS 510C, Quayle, *Book of Precedents*, p. 55; Lib. Scacc. 1583, 15.

[49] Gell, *Abstract of the Laws*, pp. 75, 136, 137.

[50] *History and Antiquities of the Isle of Man*, p. 9.

[51] Diary of James, seventh earl of Derby, in F. R. Raines (ed.), *The Stanley Papers*, pt. iii, vol. iii (Chet. Soc., O.S., vol. l, 1867), p. 4; idem (ed.), *The Stanley Papers*, vol. i (Chet. Soc., O.S., vol. lxvi, 1867), p. clxxiv. For details of Derby's movements in the 1640s, see J. R. Dickinson, 'The Earl of Derby and the Isle of Man, 1643–1651', *T.H.S.L.C.* vol. cxli (1992), pp. 39–76.

[52] Fairfax spent most of the Interregnum on his estates in Yorkshire. J. Wilson, *Fairfax. A Life of Thomas, Lord Fairfax* (1985), p. 163ff. Despite the determination of Earl Charles to punish those in the island who had betrayed his father by rising in rebellion in 1651, he was content to leave the prosecution of his policy to his officers. Moore, *History*, vol. i, pp. 375–83; Coward, *Stanleys*, pp. 178–81.

Man at least half a dozen times. While he may have come to the island in March 1681, when Richard Stevenson, the deputy governor, received 'Certeine Informacon that my Honourable Lord Intends very speedyly with his famyly to vissitt and abide in this Island for a Certaine season,' there is no doubt that Earl William landed at Douglas on midsummer's day 1686, and that he was again in the island in July 1691, when he presided at the Tynwald Court.[53] Problems arising from the presence of English customs officers in Manx ports[54] and discontent over the unsettled status of land tenure in the island[55] brought the earl back in November 1699 and February 1700; he was again in residence at Castle Rushen in September in the latter year to hear an appeal against a judgement of the Keys in a case of slander against Governor Nicholas Sankey.[56] Earl William made one further journey to the island in April 1701.[57] After his death in 1702, his brother and heir, James, tenth earl of Derby, paid much less personal attention to the island and, in fact, in thirty-four years, the last Stanley Lord of Man appears never to have crossed from England to the island.[58]

The infrequent visits of the Stanleys to the Isle of Man are not difficult to explain. From the late fourteenth century onwards, the Stanleys played an increasingly important role in local and national affairs in England, serving the Crown in both civil and military capacities and, assisted by their normally astute political judgement, acquiring a considerable amount of property from grateful sovereigns as a reward.[59] Their interests and responsibilities elsewhere

[53] Lib. Scacc. 1681, 14; M.M.L., MF/PR/18. Malew Parish Registers: Baptisms; M.M.L., R.D. 1686–95, Book of charge of Abbey temporalities, 1691; *Statutes*, p. 144.

[54] For further details of the English customs officers in the island, see chapter 5, pp. 335–36.

[55] An outline of the problems concerning land tenure can be found in Moore, *History*, vol. ii, pp. 871–88.

[56] Lib. Scacc. 1698, inter 24–5; Lib. Scacc. 1700, 8, 10–13.

[57] M.M.L., R.D. 1700–4, Book of charge of the revenue of the Isle of Man, 1700.

[58] Earl James died in 1736 without a surviving heir and the lordship of Man passed to his heir general, James Murray, second duke of Atholl, the grandson of Amelia, third daughter of the seventh earl. Bagley, *Earls of Derby*, pp. 130, 134.

[59] For the rise of the Stanleys through royal service and details of the acquisition of landed estates, see Coward, *Stanleys*, ch. 1.

therefore made it difficult for them to visit the Isle of Man in person, even had they desired to do so, and the relative isolation of the island and the inconvenience of a sea crossing doubtless acted as additional discouragements. The Stanleys were, nevertheless, jealous of their prerogative rights as Lords of Man and acted swiftly to counter any challenge to them.

II. EXECUTIVE GOVERNMENT: THE ISLAND

Executive government within the island can be divided into two levels. At the higher, national level, there were the principal executive officers – the governor, the Lord's Council and the deemsters – , and at the lower, sheading, parish and town level there were the lesser officers – the coroners,[60] the captains of the parishes,[61] the captains of the towns,[62] the lockmen[63] and moars.[64] The governor and the members of the Lord's Council – the comptroller, the receiver, the waterbailiff and the attorney general – were responsible for maintaining the Lord's rights and collecting his revenue throughout the island. With the deemsters, they were also entrusted with holding courts in the Lord's name. Both the deemsters had jurisdiction over the island as a whole, but, unless there was a reason, each usually restricted his activities to either the North- or the Southside. In the sheadings, the coroner was the chief officer and he had an assistant in each parish of the sheading known as the lockman. Captains of the parishes and the towns were appointed to organise the trained bands in the parishes and maintain order in the towns. Each parish also had a moar, who was answerable for the Lord's rent for one year.

a) The Governor

Usually styled 'lieutenant' or 'captain,' or sometimes both, before about 1650,[65] the governor was the Lord's representative and, as

---

[60] On the coroner, see *infra*, pp. 46–9.
[61] For details of the office of Captain of the Parish, see *infra*, pp. 50–1.
[62] The Captain of the Town is discussed *infra*, pp. 52–3.
[63] The lockman's duties are described *infra*, pp. 49–50.
[64] The moar's responsibilities are considered *infra*, p. 51–2.
[65] See appendix ii. The titles 'lieutenant' and 'captain' seem to have been interchangeable. John Greenhalgh of Brandlesholme, who was governor

such, was answerable to him alone. He exercised most of the
Lord's rights and privileges, even when the Lord was in the island,
and it was ordained that 'what Man offendeth to him be punished
as they that offend to the Lord.'[66] Like the other officers, the governor held his position at the Lord's pleasure.[67] He was sworn to act
'truly and uprightly' between the Lord and his people and to take
'the advice and consent' of the rest of the Lord's Council 'in all
matters that concern the state and government' of the island.[68] He
had the authority to call the deemsters, Council and Keys together,
either at a Tynwald Court or on other occasions as he thought
necessary, to deal with specific matters and was obliged to do so
by law when faced with difficult problems.[69] The main civil courts
of law could not be held without his warrant and it was normal
practice for the governor to preside over all court sessions. He
had appellate jurisdiction covering all branches of the judicature,
including the ecclesiastical courts when non-spiritual matters were
involved.[70]

The governor was responsible for the maintenance of law and
order in the island and to that end he appointed coroners in each
sheading and captains in the four towns.[71] Warrants for arrest in civil
cases could only be issued by the governor, although the waterbailiff

between 1640 and 1651, informed William Blundell that the 'titles of Governor, Lieutenant, and Captain of the Isle, did signify but one and the same
person and comand', but added that when the threat of attack existed in the
past, a captain had been appointed to assist in the supervision of the militia.
Blundell, *History*, vol. ii, pp. 62–3. Such was the case in 1532, when John
Fleming, 'captain of Man', appears on record alongside Thomas Shireburn,
'lieutenant'. *ibid.*, vol. ii, p. 59; *Statutes*, p. 29. During the wars of the 1640s,
Greenhalgh, governor and 'Captain General', was appointed lieutenant
general of all the military forces in the island by James, seventh earl of
Derby. Lib. Scacc. 1645, 54–5. After 1660, the title of governor replaced the
older styles.

[66] *Statutes*, p. 5.

[67] Sherwood, *Constitution*, p. 84; Blundell, *History*, vol. ii, p. 60.

[68] Sherwood, *Constitution*, pp. 70, 166. The oath administered to the governor under the Stanleys is given in full in *ibid.*, pp. 166–7.

[69] *ibid.*, pp. 72, 84, 147; *Statutes*, pp. 11–12.

[70] Sherwood, *Constitution*, pp. 45 n. 32, 53, 84. The procedure in appeals,
or traverses, from the courts is outlined *infra*, p. 69.

[71] *ibid.*, pp. 56–7, 133–4. In the baronies, similar functions were performed
by sergeants, appointed by the barons. *ibid.*, pp. 52, 80, 133.

was empowered to detain debtors attempting to leave the island;[72] in criminal cases, the governor shared such authority with the deemsters and the other chief officers and with the coroners.[73] The defence of the island was also in the charge of the governor. He was in command of all the military forces in the island, comprising the garrisons of Castle Rushen and Peel Castle, the soldiers of Douglas fort and the militia and supervised 'watch and ward,' the permanent watch kept in the towns and on specific hills throughout the island.[74] To prevent forestalling of the markets, the governor was to view all merchandise imported into the island and supervise the bargain struck between the merchant stranger and the four merchants appointed 'to make Bargaine for the Profitt of the Land.'[75]

When the governor was absent or the office was temporarily vacant, a deputy governor was appointed, either by the governor or by the Lord himself, and he enjoyed all the powers and privileges of the superior office. Except in the unusual circumstances when the island was in the hands of the Crown between 1595 and about 1610 and during the Interregnum, the deputy governor was almost always a member of the Lord's Council in the seventeenth century.[76] Whenever one of the main offices of the administration fell vacant, the

[72] *Statutes*, pp. 68–9; Blundell, *History*, vol. i, p. 64; Sherwood, *Constitution*, pp. 34, 102.

[73] Sherwood, *Constitution*, p. 52.

[74] *ibid.*, pp. 72, 84; Moore, *History*, vol. i, pp. 327–33. For details of watch and ward, see W. Cubbon, 'Watch and Ward in AD 1627', *M.N.H.A.S.*, vol. iii (1927–32), pp. 258–65; B. R. S. Megaw, 'A Thousand Years of Watch and Ward', *J.M.M.*, vol. v (1941–6), pp. 8–13. The governor appointed the officers and soldiers of the garrisons, subject to the Lord's approval and it was ordained that 'no Soldier be taken into either Place [castle], or put out, without knowledge of the Lord, but in needfull causes'. *Statutes*, p. 16. The Lord assigned a sergeant-major to command the militia, but the selection of subordinate officers was left to the governor, who remained in overall command. Sherwood, *Constitution*, p. 57; Lib. Scacc. 1643, inter 20–1.

[75] *Statutes*, pp. 19–20, 27. The procedure for dealing with merchant strangers and the appointment of the four merchants is discussed in chapter 5, pp. 240–42.

[76] Between 1595 and 1704, twenty-one individuals served as deputy governor. Of these, ten acted as deputy under the Crown or during the Interregnum. Of the remainder, two were deemsters and six were already members of the Lord's Council when they were first appointed. See appendix ii.

governor was at liberty to nominate a man to fill the place until the Lord either confirmed the appointment or selected a successor. All the subordinate posts in the island's establishment were at the governor's disposal.[77]

b) The Lord's Council

The Lord's Council, which assisted the governor or his deputy in the routine executive government of the island, was composed of the four principal 'household' officers – the comptroller, the receiver, the waterbailiff and the attorney general. The membership of the Council before the Revestment of the island in the Crown in 1765 has been the subject of some uncertainty, but it seems clear that these officers constituted the permanent Council and that the deemsters, the bishop and the spiritual officers – the archdeacon and the vicars general – were summoned by the governor when their presence was required. One or both of the deemsters apparently attended most meetings of the Council, at least from the end of the sixteenth century, but they were not *ex officio* members of that body.[78]

c) The Comptroller

The comptroller, whose office William Blundell considered to be 'of greatest trust' next to that of governor, was the superintendent of the Lord's revenue and household, auditing the receipts and disbursements of the receiver and the customs accounts of the waterbailiff and rendering such accounts to the Lord every year.[79] He was jointly responsible with the receiver for ensuring that the 'houses,' or garrisons, were properly victualled and that the castles were kept in good repair and, as 'judge of the houses,' he was empowered

[77] Sherwood, *Constitution*, pp. 53 and n. 47; Sacheverell, *Account*, p. 71.
[78] Sherwood, *Constitution*, pp. 4–5, 70, 72, 86–7; Moore, *History*, vol. ii, pp. 743–4. The duties of the principal officers are embodied in the oaths which they took prior to the assumption of their posts. For these oaths, see Sherwood, *Constitution*, pp. 179–80, 182–3, 185–6, 190–1; Moore, *History*, vol. ii, pp. 832–5. Although the waterbailiff's oath contains no reference to his duties in the Council, there seems to be little doubt that he was a permanent member. Moore, *History*, vol. ii, p. 743 and n. 3. For lists of the principal officers in the seventeenth century, see appendices ii–vii.
[79] Blundell, *History*, vol. ii, p. 70; *Statutes*, p. 37.

to deal with offences, capital or otherwise, committed within the garrisons.[80] In such cases, he was authorised to impanel a jury of soldiers and sit as 'sole judge, although it be in trials for life.'[81] The comptroller acted as muster master, at least in the first half of the seventeenth century, periodically assembling the garrison soldiers to check their equipment;[82] he was also the clerk of the rolls.[83] A deputy was often employed to assist him in the latter office, the duties of which included the recording of proceedings in the courts of both the Lord and the barons, the production of authoritative copies of such proceedings to be used in court, the compilation of a schedule of all fines due for the preceding year which was sent to the coroners and, most important of all, the care of the records.[84] The comptroller was, as James Chaloner observed, 'by his place Clerk of the Market' and was 'to see to the Weights and Measures of all sorts, and the Assize of Bread and Ale, that it be duly kept.'[85] He was also the 'head searcher,' with deputies in the island's ports who were to make certain that no merchant avoided paying customs duty on part or all of his cargo.[86]

[80] *Statutes*, pp. 12, 17, 18, 19, 33, 34, 35; Sherwood, *Constitution*, pp. 54, 85. Inquests concerning breaches of garrison regulations were often held before the governor, comptroller and other officers. See, for example, Lib. Scacc. 1603, 37–8; Lib. Scacc. 1650, 31.

[81] Sacheverell, *Account*, p. 71.

[82] *Statutes*, p. 19; Lib. Scacc. 1600, 17. The office of muster master later became a separate post. See M.M.L., R.D. 1651–70, Disbursements for salaries, 1673, 4.

[83] This was generally the case until the Revestment. Moore, *History*, vol. ii, p. 742; Sherwood, *Constitution*, pp. 54, 139.

[84] *Statutes*, pp. 11, 18; Sherwood, *Constitution*, pp. 35, 54, 85, 139; Sacheverell, *Account*, pp. 71–2; Cl.R.O., Nantlys MS D/NA/905, 54; Moore, *History*, vol. ii, p. 742. John Halsall had served as deputy to the comptroller for about fifteen years, at his own estimate, by November 1610. Lib. Scacc. 1611, 5.

[85] Chaloner, *Treatise*, p. 49; *Statutes*, p. 87; Sherwood, *Constitution*, p. 71. The supervision of the town market was shared with the Captain of the Town. See *infra*, pp. 52–3 and chapter 4, pp. 201–6.

[86] Chaloner, *Treatise*, p. 49; Blundell, *History*, vol. ii, p. 71; Sherwood, *Constitution*, p. 85. For further details of the office of searcher in the island, see chapter 5, pp. 226–27, 230–31.

d) The Receiver

The receiver was the officer who was responsible for the collection of the Lord's revenue from the moars, coroners and waterbailiff and who paid out the fees, wages and other, miscellaneous disbursements, subject to the scrutiny of the comptroller.[87] He was required to produce his accounts before the governor and comptroller at the end of every quarter and to deposit in the castle all the Lord's money which had been collected since the last audit.[88] His office conferred the authority to deal with any moar who neglected his duty in the collection of rents and failed to levy a distraint on a tenant who was in arrears. The receiver committed the offending moar to gaol and issued a token – a piece of slate bearing his initials – to the constable of the castle for a soldier to collect the outstanding sum or, after the third such attempt, to arrest the defaulting tenant.[89] Only in this instance could the receiver issue tokens, which served as writs of subpoena in Man; on all other occasions, they could only be given out by the governor or the deemsters, who provided them in cases arising from the courts of chancery and common law respectively.[90]

The receiver was to see that both the castles were properly supplied with provisions and was entrusted with the supervision of the garrison stores and the purchases made by the stewards. Furthermore, in consultation with the governor and the comptroller, he directed any repair work which was needed to maintain the fabric of the castles.[91]

Until the early seventeenth century, there was a receiver at both Castle Rushen and Peel Castle, the former answering for the revenue of the Southside of the island and the latter for the Northside. One or both of them attended meetings of the Council and the sessions of the courts. After the Isle of Man was returned to the Stanleys in 1610, however, a number of changes were made in the organisation of the office of receiver. Countess Elizabeth, who assumed responsibility

---

[87] Sherwood, *Constitution*, p. 85; *Statutes*, pp. 15–16, 17, 36.
[88] *Statutes*, p. 84.
[89] Chaloner, *Treatise*, p. 49; *Statutes*, p. 101; Lib. Scacc. 1662, 14.
[90] Blundell, *History*, vol. ii, pp. 72, 93–4. The jurisdiction of the various courts is discussed *infra*, pp. 62–74.
[91] *Statutes*, pp. 17–19; Blundell, *History*, vol. ii, p. 72.

for the administration of the island,[92] took a close interest in all aspects of government, attempting to ensure that the Lord's rights and privileges were enjoyed to the full. On examination of the accounts, she concluded that 'my Rentes proffittes and Revenewes of and within the Isle of Man now are, and of late yeares have beene more decayed, impayred, witholden, and detracted from me by reason of the negligence or other undue dealinge of my Officers there then formerlie they have beene to my great losse and hinderance.'[93] She believed that her officers, and the receivers in particular, were 'more greedie to take Allowance at their owne hands of their owne fees and wages then forward to pay or Cause to be payd to me my due Rents and Revenewes but Remaine in Arrerage.'[94] In August 1614, she sent Edward Rigby of Burgh to the island as her commissioner and surveyor to investigate the situation and to take appropriate measures to remedy such abuses as he found.[95] Before the end of the year, the Countess had dismissed the receivers, William Lucas and William Radcliffe, and their duties had been assumed by John Halsall, who was already comptroller, clerk of the rolls and attorney general.

When Halsall was relieved of the responsibilities of the position in 1616, there was no return to the former custom of dividing the office. Instead, Edward Fletcher of Ballafletcher, Braddan, was appointed receiver general for the whole island.[96] The appointment of a single receiver continued to be the practice under the Stanley

[92] Countess Elizabeth's son, James, seventh earl of Derby, believed that this arrangement had been made 'by certaine Agreements betweene her and my Father, and as I take it, ordered by K. James'. *History and Antiquities of the Isle of Man*, p. 29. Earl William certainly never took part in the government of the island after 1609. Orders issued to the governor and officers were invariably signed by the Countess and petitions were addressed to her alone. See, for example, Lib. Scacc. 1612, 7, 13, inter 33–4; Lib. Scacc. 1625, 5; Lib. Scacc. 1626, 35, 37.

[93] Lib. Scacc. 1614, 39.

[94] M.M.L., Rolls Office, 'Special Notes collected out of Capten Mollineux and other the officers of the Isle their letters written to the Right Honorable the Lady Elizabeth, Countesse of Derby, December 1614', cited in Coward, *Stanleys*, p. 60.

[95] Lib. Scacc. 1614, 39–40.

[96] Lib. Scacc. 1607, 17; M.M.L., I.O. 1610–19, Book of allowance, Castle Rushen, 1615; waterbailiff's accounts, 1614; book of allowance, Peel Castle, 1616.

régime except for during two periods in the later seventeenth century, between 1669 and 1673 and again from 1683 until 1700, when commissioners of revenue acted in the place of the receiver general. Generally four in number, they usually included the governor and were otherwise members of the Council or one of the deemsters.[97]

e) The Waterbailiff

The main duties of the waterbailiff and his deputies were to record 'what Goods is taken out of the Countrey and what is brought in' and 'faithfully to collect all the Customs for Ingates and Outgates of Goods' at the ports of the island – Douglas, Derbyhaven *alias* Castletown, Peel and Ramsey.[98] It was also the duty of the waterbailiff to 'order all the businesse for the Herring-Fishery,' collecting the Lord's proportion of the catch from native and foreigner alike.[99] Wrecks on the coast came under his jurisdiction and he was obliged to return an inventory of each hulk to the comptroller so that any goods and the remains of the vessel itself could be sold for the Lord's profit. Any disputes arising from maritime affairs, apart from felonies, could be dealt with by the waterbailiff, who sat as a judge in the Admiralty Court.[100]

[97] The commissioners of the revenue between 1669 and 1673 were Henry Nowell, governor; Richard Stevenson, 'major general' and 'Assistant to the Court' and former receiver; Thomas Norris, deemster; and William Qualtrough, attorney general. M.M.L., R.D. 1651–70, Book of petty disbursements, 1670; M.M.L., R.D. 1671–85, Book of receipts from the collectors of revenue, 1673. Richard Stevenson resumed the office of receiver in 1673 until his death ten years later. M.M.L., MF/PR/19. Malew Parish Registers: Burials. See appendix iv. Several combinations of commissioners served between 1683 and 1700. See, for example, the appointment of Roger Kenyon, governor, William Sacheverell, deputy governor, John Rowe, deputy governor and comptroller, and Richard Stevenson, waterbailiff in April 1692. L.R.O., DDKe 80.

[98] *Statutes*, pp. 17, 36; Chaloner, *Treatise*, p. 50. For further details about the waterbailiff and his deputies, see chapter 5, pp. 221–31.

[99] Chaloner, *Treatise*, p. 50; *Statutes*, pp. 75–6. The regulation of the herring fishery is discussed in chapter 2, pp. 109–19.

[100] For details of the jurisdiction of the Admiralty Court, see *infra*, p. 73–4.

f) The Attorney General

The main concern of the attorney general was to act on behalf of the Lord in civil and criminal cases and to prevent the infringement of the Lord's prerogative rights. He was normally present at all court sessions, both secular and ecclesiastical, to record the fines and forfeitures due to the Lord and made up an annual account of the profits arising from the purchase of pardons, the sale of forfeited goods, the fees paid by aliens for the freedom of the island, the sale of stray animals and miscellaneous 'casualtyes.' Those who were incapable of defending themselves at law, such as orphans and widows, were entitled to representation by the attorney general, who also advised the governor on questions of jurisdiction. He was furthermore responsible for setting rents on recently licensed and approved enclosed lands or intacks, a duty which he carried out at the sheading courts held in May each year.[101] The attorney general shared the duty of reporting and recording wrecks with the water-bailiff, for, as Chaloner noted, 'the businesse may be done by either of them as it lyes in their quarters or way they shall come.'[102]

g) The appointment of the governor and officers of the Lord's Council

The position of governor and the household offices were granted by the Stanleys to their clients and servants. To identify with any degree of certainty the men who served in these offices in the island's government is, however, by no means a simple task, though an attempt has been made to discover the origins of the governors and deputy governors, using family papers, manorial records and, despite their often questionable reliability, heralds' visitation records (Tables 1.1 and 1.2). Tracing individuals, even those bearing the name 'Stanley', is fraught with problems, but in doubtful cases, where there is a strong possibility that a governor or deputy governor can reasonably be identified either as a member of a branch of the Stanleys or of a family with known connections with the Stanley household, the individual concerned has been assigned to the appropriate place of origin.

[101] Sherwood, *Constitution*, pp. 55, 71, 85–6, 140; Moore, *History*, vol. ii, p. 743; Chaloner, *Treatise*, pp. 50–1; Sherwood, *Manx Law Tenures*, pp. 20–2.
[102] Chaloner, *Treatise*, p. 50.

Table 1.1 *Origins of the Governors of the Isle of Man* [103]

a) *Appointments under the Stanleys*

	1406–1594	*1612–1736*	*Total*
Lancashire	14	11	25
Cheshire	3	0	3
Anglesey	1	0	1
Flintshire	1	0	1
Isle of Man	1	3	4
Yorkshire	0	1	1
Westmorland	0	1	1

[103] Sources: L.R.O., DDSt; L.R.O., DDKe; L.R.O., DDIb; F. R. Raines (ed.), *The Stanley Papers*, pt.ii. *The Derby Household Books*, Chet. Soc., O.S., vol. xxxi (1853); idem (ed.), *The visitation of the county palatine of Lancaster, made in the year 1567, by William Flower*, Chet. Soc., O.S., vol. lxxxi (1870); idem (ed.), *The visitation of the county palatine of Lancaster, made in the year 1613, by Richard St George*, Chet. Soc., O.S., vol. lxxxii (1871); idem (ed.), *The visitation of the county palatine of Lancaster, made in the year 1664–5, by William Dugdale*, Chet. Soc., O.S., vols lxxxiv and lxxxv (1872); W. Langton (ed.), *The visitation of Lancashire and a part of Cheshire, 1533*, Chet. Soc., O.S., vol. xcviii (1876); J. P. Rylands (ed.), *The visitation of Cheshire in the year 1580, made by Robert Glover*, Harleian Society, vol. xviii (1882); E. Newton, *The House of Lyme* (1917); G. J. Armytage (ed.), *Pedigrees made at the visitation of Cheshire, 1613, taken by Richard St George*, R.S.L.C., vol. lviii (1909); J. Foster (ed.), *The visitation of Yorkshire made in the years 1584–5, by Robert Glover [and] the subsequent visitation made in 1612 by Richard St George* (1875); D.N.B.; A. W. Moore (ed.), *The Manx Note Book*, 3 vols (1885–7); Moore, *History*; Sacheverell, *Account*; J. J. Kneen, *Manx Personal Names* (Oxford 1937); T. Talbot (ed.), *The Manorial Roll of the Isle of Man* (Oxford 1924); 'An Abstract of the Earl of Derby's Governors and Officers in the Isle of Man, 1417–1570', *J.M.M.*, vol. ii (1930–4); J. Foster (ed.), *Alumni Oxoniensis* (1891); J. P. Earwaker (ed.), 'A list of the freeholders in Lancashire in the year 1600', in *Miscellanies relating to Lancashire and Cheshire*, vol.i, R.S.L.C., vol. xii (1885); idem, *East Cheshire*, vol.ii (1880); W. A. Shaw, *The Knights of England* (2 vols, 1906); W. Farrer and J. Brownbill (eds), *Victoria History of the County of Lancaster*, vols iii, iv, v, vi (1906–14); F. Parker (ed.), 'Chetwynd's History of Pirehill Hundred, 1679', *Collections for a History of Staffordshire*, pt ii, William Salt Archaeological Society (1914); *Burke's Peerage, Baronetage and Knightage* (1963).

Cambridgeshire	0	1	1
Oxfordshire	0	1	1
Not known	5	7	12
Total	25	25	50

b) *Appointments under the English Crown*

	1595–1612
Lancashire	1
Cheshire	1
Staffordshire	1
Total	3

c) *Appointments under Thomas, Lord Fairfax*

	1651–1660
Cheshire	1
Isle of Man	1
Yorkshire	1
Not known	3
Total	6

As a result, it is clear from Table 1.1 that Lancashire provided the largest single contingent of governors during the period of Stanley rule in the island. Many of these men came from the ranks of the lesser gentry of the county,[104] but some families of higher standing, such as Ireland of the Hutt, in Childwall, and Shireburne of Stonyhurst, supplied governors in the sixteenth century, as did various branches of the Stanley family, including, in 1592, William, brother of Earl Ferdinando and the latter's successor in the earldom.[105]

[104] This crude assessment of social standing is based on the recorded status of individuals in the lists of governors in Moore, *History*, vol. ii, pp. 976–7; 'Unpublished Document no. 36' [Bridge House papers], *J.M.M.*, vol. ii (1930–4), pp. 71–2 and the sources for Lancashire cited in Table 1.1. On the problems of defining gentry status, see B. G. Blackwood, *The Lancashire Gentry and the Great Rebellion, 1640–1660* (Chet. Soc., 3rd series, vol. xxv, 1978), pp. 4–11; J. E. Hollinshead, 'The Gentry of South-West Lancashire in the Later Sixteenth Century', *Northern History*, vol. xxvi (1990), pp. 82–6.

[105] See appendices i and ii.

Table 1.2 *Origins of the Deputy Governors of the Isle of Man* [106]

a) *Appointments under the Stanleys*

	1406–1594	1612–1736	Total
Lancashire	5	7	12
Isle of Man	2	6	8
Cheshire	1	0	1
Oxfordshire	0	1	1
Not known	4	2	6
Total	12	16	28

b) *Appointments under the English Crown*

	1595–1612
Lancashire	4
Isle of Man	1
Not known	1
Total	6

c) *Appointments under Thomas, Lord Fairfax*

	1651–1660
Lancashire	1
Cheshire	1
Not known	1
Total	3

Notes.

1. Nine deputy governors also served as governors. Their origins are as follows:

Lancashire	5
Isle of Man	2
Oxfordshire	1
Not known	1

2. Three deputies – Robert Molyneux, John Sharples, both from Lancashire, and Edward Ellis, of uncertain origin – served under two different régimes. Molyneux served under the Crown and the Stanleys; Sharples acted under the Stanleys and Fairfax; Ellis was in office under both the Stanleys and the Crown.

[106] Sources: see Table 1.1.

After the grant of the island to Earl William and Countess Elizabeth had been confirmed in 1610, the Stanleys continued their preference for Lancashire men, of whom they doubtless had first hand knowledge. These included men such as Robert Molyneux, probably of Melling, who was 'captain' of the island between 1612 and 1621,[107] and John Greenhalgh of Brandlesholme, who governed the island for Earl James from September 1640 until his death in the same month in 1651.[108] They occasionally cast their net further afield, as, for example, in 1622, when Sir Ferdinando Leigh of Middleton in Yorkshire was appointed 'captain.'[109] The Stanleys also commissioned a handful of Manxmen to hold the position, although apart from Edward Christian of Maughold, who assumed the responsibilities of governor in August 1627 and served for nearly seven years,[110] their terms of office were short. Edward Fletcher of Ballafletcher, Braddan, the receiver of the island at the time, was only in office for about a year, between July 1621 and June 1622;[111] Deemster Ewan Christian of Milntown, Lezayre, was lieutenant and governor for the space of only about a month or two in the early summer of 1634.[112]

The Stanleys were certainly not infallible when it came to choosing the man to govern the Isle of Man for them. Writing to his son, Charles, Earl James recalled how 'some Lords of the Court (who shall be namelesse)' recommended one Captain Edward Holmewood to Countess Elizabeth, his mother, as governor of the island. Holmewood proved to be a man who lacked 'Discretion rightly to make Use of the Occasion' and who had wasted 'a good Estate.' He was 'needie and kind-hearted,' which were, the earl added sarcastically, 'two of the most pleasing Qualities for a Governor among his People.' After

---

[107] J. P. Rylands (ed.), *Lancashire Inquisitions Post Mortem returned into the Chancery of the Duchy of Lancaster and now existing in the Public Record Office, Stuart Period, pt. i*, R.S.L.C., vol. iii (1880), p. 44.

[108] W. Harrison, 'Memoir of John Greenhalgh, Governor of the Isle of Man, 1640–51', in idem (ed.), *Manx Miscellanies*, vol. ii, Manx Society, vol. xxx (1878), p. 8; M.M.L., MF/PR/19. Malew Parish Registers: Burials.

[109] J. Foster (ed.), *The Visitation of Yorkshire made in the year 1584/5 by Robert Glover . . . to which is added the subsequent visitation made in 1612 by Richard St George* (1875), p. 45; W. A. Shaw (ed.), *The Knights of England* (2 vols, 1906), vol. ii, p. 162.

[110] M.M.L., MD/401/1716/27; Oliver, *Monumenta*, vol. iii, p. 141.

[111] Lib. Scacc. 1621, 15; Lib. Scacc. 1622, 32.

[112] Lib. Scacc. 1634, inter 32–3.

the death of the countess in 1627, Earl William entrusted the Stanley estates to James, then Lord Strange and this enabled him to make good the situation. 'The first Thing I did, to my Remembrance, was the shifting off this Gentleman; to whome I gave a good Pension for Charitie Sake, and in some Respect, to avoyde other Clamours.'[113]

As Holmewood's replacement, James chose Edward Christian, 'whom I observed soone to have Abilities enough to doe me Service.' Christian was 'excellent good Companie; as rude, as a Sea Captaine should be; but refin'd, as one that had civiliz'd himself half a Year at Court; where he served the Duke of Buckingham.'[114] After making the appointment, however, James began to realise that he might have made a mistake in choosing a man who claimed to be 'content to do Service without any [pay], or as little of it as it pleased [me].' Christian was 'ever forward to make me manie Requests' and James observed that 'the more I gave, the more he asked.'[115] Eventually, probably as a result of complaints from the Lord Deputy of Ireland to the Lords of the Admiralty in London that he had been allowing pirates to use the island as a haven, Christian was replaced by Sir Charles Gerard of Halsall in 1634.[116] He was restored to favour in 1636, when he again served briefly as lieutenant, and was given the post of receiver, which he held until 1643.[117] Earl James had sufficient confidence in Christian to appoint him as sergeant-major of the military forces in the island in January 1643, but his trust was misplaced, for Christian was one of the leaders of the 'rebellion' against the earl's authority in the summer of that year.[118]

---

[113] *History and Antiquities of the Isle of Man*, pp. 29–30.

[114] *ibid.*, p. 31. Christian had apparently made 'a good Fortune in the Indies', where he had served as an officer and subsequently as captain aboard East India Company vessels. W. Foster (ed.), *The Voyage of Thomas Best to the East Indies, 1612–1614* (Hakluyt Society, 2nd series, vol. lxxx, 1934), pp. 55, 297 n. 4. Through his connection with Buckingham, he appears to have secured a post in the Royal Navy. A. W. Moore, *Manx Worthies* (Douglas, 1901, reprinted 1971), p. 60.

[115] *History and Antiquities of the Isle of Man*, pp. 31–2.

[116] *C.S.P.Ire.*, *1633–47*, pp. 23, 32; M.M.L., Rolls Office, no. 42. Lords of the Admiralty to William, earl of Derby and James, Lord Strange, January 11, 1634; Lib. Scacc. 1635, 10.

[117] Lib. Scacc. 1636, inter 46–7; M.M.L., I.O. 1630–45, Book of charge, Castle Rushen, 1637; M.M.L., R.D. 1627–50, Book of charge, Castle Rushen, 1643.

[118] Lib. Scacc. 1643, inter 20–1; Dickinson, 'Earl of Derby and Isle of Man', pp. 42–8.

During the sixteen year period when the island was in the hands of the Crown, only three governors were appointed, and two of them came from the north west of England. Following the death of Earl Ferdinando in 1594, a dispute arose between the new earl, William, and Dowager Countess Alice over the succession to the Stanley estates, including the Isle of Man. A flaw was discovered in the original grant to Sir John Stanley – the grant had been made before Percy had been deprived of his estates by attainder – and, consequently, the island reverted to the Crown until a settlement could be reached.[119] After the death of the governor, Randulph Stanley, in 1595, Elizabeth appointed Sir Thomas Gerard of Bromley in Staffordshire to take charge 'for the better safetie and government of that place.' Gerard, whom the queen regarded as 'fittest in regard of his habitacon in those partes,' was the son of Sir Gilbert Gerard, the late Master of the Rolls, and a soldier who subsequently served as Knight Marshal of the Household, from 1597 until about 1601. In 1603, he was created Baron Gerard of Gerard's Bromley by James I.[120] Pressing duties elsewhere led to Gerard's temporary replacement by his brother in law, Peter Legh of Lyme in Cheshire, who was commissioned in July 1596, despite protests from Earl William that his rights were being infringed. Legh acted as captain for about a year;[121] thereafter, Gerard continued as governor until about late 1608, although the actual administration of the island was left in the hands of deputies.[122] John Ireland of the Hutt, a representative of a Lancashire family which had well-established links with the Stanleys, was appointed governor by James I in early 1609 and stayed in office until after the island had been restored to Earl William and Countess Elizabeth.[123]

---

[119] Coward, *Stanleys*, pp. 41–5; R. A. Curphey, 'The Background to the Disputed Derby Succession, 1594–1612', *M.N.H.A.S.*, vol. viii (1964–72), pp. 602–3.

[120] P.R.O. SP 14/253/51; Lib. Canc. 1595, 34; P. W. Hasler (ed.), *History of Parliament: The House of Commons, 1558–1603*, vol. ii (1981), pp. 184–5; *C.S.P.D., 1603–10*, p. 23.

[121] E. Newton, *The House of Lyme* (1917), p. 49; Lib. Scacc. 1596, 27–8; Lib. Scacc. 1597, 13; M.M.L., I.O. 1570–99, Book of fees and wages, Castle Rushen, 1597; B.L., Lansdowne MS 82, f. 26r.

[122] Lib. Scacc. 1608, 35.

[123] Ireland first appears on record in May 1609. Lib. Scacc. 1609, 29. He served until at least April 1612, although his duties were then being carried out by his deputy and kinsman, Thomas Ireland. Lib. Scacc. 1612, 3.

After the surrender of the Isle of Man to Parliament in October 1651, Colonel Robert Duckenfield of Duckenfield in Cheshire, the commander of the expeditionary forces, became the first governor of the Interregnum period. His other duties prevented him from remaining long in the island and, by early 1652, his authority was being exercised by deputies, including his kinsman, Captain Francis Duckenfield of Stockport.[124] Duckenfield's immediate successors have not been identified and little more has been established about them beyond their names. Major Philip Eyton was lieutenant governor of the island by December 1652;[125] Major John Wade, whom Chaloner noted as 'Lieutenant or Governor,' was appointed governor and approved by the Council of State in August 1653 and his company, together with that of his successor, Captain Matthew Cadwell, was designated as the guard for the island at the same time.[126] In 1656, William Christian of Ronaldsway, the son of Deemster Ewan Christian, who had played a leading part in the rebellion against the Stanleys five years before, became governor, although his tenure of office was relatively short, lasting only until about the middle of the following year.[127] He was replaced by James Chaloner, a Yorkshireman, and one of the commissioners appointed by Thomas, Lord Fairfax and Lord of Man during the Interregnum, in 1652 to determine the 'yearly vallue and profittes' of the island. Chaloner was still in office at the Restoration, but was removed soon after the meeting of the Tynwald Court in 1660.[128]

Of the deputy governors appointed between 1595 and 1704, about half were drawn from Lancashire. Under the Stanleys, deputy governors who not only came from the Stanley heartland but who were also related to the current or a previous governor were often chosen. Thomas Ireland, the deputy in the late spring of 1612, was a kinsman, perhaps the brother, of the governor, John Ireland of the

---

[124] Lib. Scacc. 1652, 11; J. P. Earwaker, *East Cheshire* (2 vols, 1880), vol. ii, pp. 19–20.

[125] *C.S.P.D., 1652–3*, p. 3.

[126] Chaloner, *Treatise*, p. 29; *C.S.P.D., 1653–4*, p. 74.

[127] Lib. Scacc. 1656, 3; G.R., Commissions, Fairfax to Chaloner, May 25, 1657. For an outline of William Christian's part in the rebellion of 1651 and his subsequent fate, see Moore, *History*, vol. i, pp. 265–70, 375–83.

[128] *D.N.B.*, vol. iii, pp. 1365–6; Lib. Scacc. 1652, 16, 41; Lib. Scacc. 1660, 73.

Hutt;[129] Henry Nowell, who was in charge of the proceedings against William Christian of Ronaldsway in 1662 and served both as deputy and as governor until his death in 1677, was the brother of Roger Nowell of Rede, the first Stanley appointee after the Restoration.[130] Peter Heywood, whose father, Robert, had died in office as governor in January 1691, was one of three deputies who acted jointly in 1697 and was a former member of the Lord's Council, having been attorney general from 1687 to 1694.[131]

The selection of other members of the Council to act in the place of the governor accounts for the large number of Manxmen who substituted for the Lord's representative. Edward Fletcher, the receiver, and Deemster Ewan Christian both served briefly in the superior position as well as occupying the inferior office on more than one occasion,[132] and Richard Stevenson of Balladoole, Arbory, and his son of the same name, receiver and revenue commissioner respectively, filled the post of deputy periodically, the former between 1662 and his death in early 1683 and the latter between 1691 and 1693.[133]

The deputies appointed under the Crown were almost exclusively from Lancashire. Gerard's first deputy was Robert Molyneux, probably of Melling, who later served as governor under the Stanleys. He remained in office, despite several interruptions, presumably due to absence, until about the time that Gerard ceased to be governor in 1608.[134] Cuthbert Gerrard, who was very likely from Ormskirk, had apparently occupied the governor's office briefly in 1592; he served with Molyneux and replaced him for a few months in 1596 and again acted as deputy in 1605.[135] In 1601, Edward Moore of Bank Hall, who

---

[129] F. R. Raines (ed.), *The Visitation of the County Palatine of Lancaster, made in the year 1664-5 by Sir William Dugdale*, pt. ii (Chet. Soc., O.S., vol. lxxxv, 1872), p. 165.

[130] *ibid.*, p. 221.

[131] M.M.L., MF/PR/19. Malew Parish Registers: Burials; Lib. Scacc. 1691, 13; Lib. Scacc. 1697, 49–50; Lib. Scacc. 1688, 1; M.M.L., R.D. 1686–95, Book of salaries and pensions, 1694.

[132] See appendix ii.

[133] See appendix ii.

[134] Lib. Scacc. 1608, inter 41–2. See also note 107.

[135] J. P. Earwaker (ed.), 'A List of the Freeholders in Lancashire in the year 1600', *Miscellanies relating to Lancashire and Cheshire*, vol. i, R.S.L.C., vol. xii (1885), p. 241; Moore, *History*, vol. ii, p. 976; Lib. Scacc. 1596, 13, 18, 25, 26; Lib. Scacc. 1605, 23, 40.

had been appointed as comptroller in 1599, took up the duties of deputy for several months; after the completion of his term of office, he spent little time in the island, although he held the position of comptroller until the end of 1607, his work being done by John Halsall, the attorney general.[136] Thomas Molyneux, who may have been a member of the New Hall branch of the Molyneux family of Sefton, held office briefly in 1604.[137] Of the other three deputies in this period, Edward Ellis, William Lucas and Charles Young, only Lucas can be identified with any degree of certainty. He was a Manxman and receiver at Castle Rushen, but only acted as deputy for a single month in 1597.[138] Ellis was deputy captain under the Stanleys before the Isle of Man passed to the Crown, and again in 1599; he was also steward of the Abbey lands from 1594 until at least 1604 and a servant of Dowager Countess Alice.[139] Apart from these few facts, nothing is known of his background. There are no clues to the origins of Young or to those of Captain Samuel Smith, one of the three deputies who served during the Interregnum. Captain Francis Duckenfield, of whom mention has already been made,[140] was another of the latter group, as was John Sharples, the comptroller, who was almost certainly of a Lancashire family and who died in 1652.[141]

h) The Deemsters

The only principal office in the island's government which was invariably filled by Manxmen was that of deemster. This was a matter of practicality rather than of policy since the deemster had 'to be

---

[136] Lib. Scacc. 1601, 5; Lib. Scacc. 1608, 3. The identification of Edward Moore with the Bank Hall family is confirmed by two documents pertaining to matters in the island contained in the family muniments. J. Brownbill (ed.), *A Calendar of that part of the Collection of Deeds and Papers of the Moore Family of Bankhall, Co. Lanc., now in the Liverpool Public Library*, R.S.L.C., vol. lxvii (1913), pp. 47, 166. Cf. L.C.R.O., Moore MSS L/700, L/1065.

[137] Raines, *Dugdale's Visitation*, pt. ii, p. 206; Lib. Scacc. 1604, 31, 48.

[138] M.M.L., I.O. 1570–99, Book of allowance, Castle Rushen, 1597.

[139] Lib. Scacc. 1594, 25–6, 29; Lib. Scacc. 1600, 4; Lib. Scacc. 1604, 31.

[140] See *infra*, p. 41.

[141] Sharples was probably a member of the Sharples of Freckleton family. F. R. Raines (ed.), *The Visitation of the County Palatine of Lancaster, made in the year 1664–5 by Sir William Dugdale*, pt. iii (Chet. Soc., O.S., vol. lxxxviii, 1873), p. 257.

perfect and speak the Manks language, whereby he may be able to give that charge to the juries in the courts of the sheedings, to pronounce sentence of life and death at their head courts, to give the oath to the crowner and moors, and to understand the plaintif and defendants pleading before him.'[142]

There were two deemsters, who rarely sat together 'upon any cause whatsoever for their power is distinct.'[143] One was responsible for the Northside, comprising the sheadings of Glenfaba, Michael and Ayre, and the other dealt with matters arising on the Southside, in the sheadings of Rushen, Middle and Garff.[144] William Blundell claimed that the boundary of their authority was marked 'as it were by a line crossing the island from east to west to Peeltown, in the west side of the Island, from Douglas Town in the east;' in fact, the jurisdiction of the deemsters was identical, extending over the whole of the island, although each normally acted only in the division in which he was resident.[145] The deemsters were 'in all places in the Island, where they come, Justices of the Peace'[146] and sat as judges in all the courts 'either for life or property, whether the court be held in the Lord's name or any of his barons.'[147]

Although the office was only held during pleasure, in practice it was usually held for life, for, as Blundell observed, 'they are seldom or never put out or removed.'[148] When a vacancy occurred, as in 1605, when Deemster John Curghey was suspended, a jury composed of two representatives from each parish met with the Keys to agree upon three or four 'sufficient honest men' who were in 'every way fitting to discharge the office and place of the Deemster.' The names were then submitted to the Lord or, at least in 1605, to the governor, who made the final selection.[149] The deemsters were chosen from the men 'that best know the laws and customs of the Island' and from 'the best and the most antient families,' of which,

[142] Blundell, *History*, vol. ii, p. 67.
[143] *ibid*.
[144] Sherwood, *Constitution*, p. 127.
[145] Blundell, *History*, vol. ii, p. 67; Sherwood, *Constitution*, p. 43.
[146] Chaloner, *Treatise*, p. 47. Cf. E. Moir, *The Justice of the Peace* (1969).
[147] Sacheverell, *Account*, p. 72.
[148] Blundell, *History*, vol. ii, p. 67.
[149] Lib. Canc. 1605, 33. That this was normal procedure seems to be confirmed by Bishop Meyrick's statement that the deemsters were 'elected' by the people 'from amongst themselves'. Oliver, *Monumenta*, vol. i, p. 95.

Blundell's informants assured him, 'there were not above six . . . of
note in all the Island.'[150] In fact, more than twice that number
of families provided deemsters between about 1590 and 1700.[151]

On occasion, the deemster was aided by an assistant. Since this
was generally a member of the deemster's family, it seems that he
was appointed by the deemster himself, though presumably with the
consent of the governor and Council. In the first half of the seventeenth century, for example, Deemster Ewan Christian was frequently assisted by his son, John, who acted in place of his father
when required.[152]

Before about 1660, the deemsters received 'as standing Fees for
Execution of their Offices' the sum of £7 10s. a year. This amount was
subsequently increased to £15 a year.[153] In addition, they were
allowed the rent of a part or all of their estates. In 1684, an allowance
of £2 1s.10d. was made, as usual, to Deemster Edward Christian, being
the rent of part of Milntown, Lezayre; Deemster Thomas Fletcher
was similarly allowed £1 8s. 9d. for the rent of one and a half quarters
of land in Braddan.[154] Each time the deemster granted his token – a
small piece of slate, bearing his initials – for whatever cause, he was
paid 2d., and, whenever a felon forfeited his lands and goods to the
Lord, he was to have 3d. The deemster also received a fee of 2d., called
the *croae kart*, for every verdict in a case of recovery at the sheading
courts and, more significantly, he was paid a total of £4 13s. 4d. for
serving at the barons' courts.[155]

---

[150] Blundell, *History*, vol. i, p. 55 and vol. ii, p. 67.

[151] See appendix v.

[152] See, for instance, Lib. Scacc. 1632, inter 26–7; Lib. Scacc. 1635, 54; Lib.
Scacc. 1641, 18.

[153] M.M.L., I.O. 1570–99, Book of allowance, Peel Castle, 1632; M.M.L.,
R.D. 1627–50, Book of allowance, Castle Rushen, 1632; *Statutes*, p. 84;
M.M.L., R.D. 1651–70, Book of disbursements, 1666.

[154] M.M.L. R.D. 1671–85, Book of charge of the revenue of the Isle of Man,
1684. This allowance, which in fact represented freedom from payments of
money in lieu of customary payments in kind, was briefly commuted into
an increase of the basic salary paid to the deemsters in about 1635. This was
found to be detrimental to the Lord, and the former allowance was restored.
Statutes, p. 84.

[155] R. Moore, 'The Deemsters and the Manx Courts of Law', *J.M.M.*, vol.
vi (1957–65), p. 159; Cl.R.O., Nantlys MS D/NA/905, 30, 45; Chaloner,
Treatise, p. 40.

III. EXECUTIVE GOVERNMENT: SHEADING, PARISH AND TOWN

The orders issued by the Lord and by the governor and Council were implemented in the sheadings, parishes and towns by the subordinate officers. Of these, the most important were the coroners, the captains of the towns and the captains of the parishes, for it was they who were ultimately responsible for the execution of policy, whether it concerned the assessment of the corn supply or the mustering of the parish companies.

a) The Coroner

A coroner was sworn in for each sheading at the Tynwald Court held at midsummer each year.[156] Both Blundell and Sacheverell compared the Manx coroner to the English sheriff,[157] but despite certain similarities between their offices, not least the fact that both were the chief executive officer in their divisions, there were significant differences in their respective duties. The coroners were appointed by the governor, apparently in much the same way as the king 'pricked' the sheriffs of the English counties, although the procedure for selecting coroners is far less well documented.[158]

---

[156] In 1422, it was ordered that coroners who had previously held office for two or three years in succession 'against the Law' were to 'stand in Office but one Yeare.' *Statutes*, pp. 14–15. Despite annual appointment, however, several men held the office for periods of years, such as William Radcliffe of Patrick, who was coroner of Glenfaba between at least 1604 and 1609. M.M.L. R.D. 1600–26, Book of pension, Peel Castle, 1604; M.M.L., I.O. 1600–9, Books of pension, Peel Castle, 1605, 1606, 1607, 1608, 1609. See also *infra*, p. 49.

[157] Blundell, *History*, vol. ii, p. 79; Sacheverell, *Account*, p. 73.

[158] Sherwood, *Constitution*, p. 56 n. 50. Blundell claimed that the coroners were 'elected by and out of the sheadings,' but it seems clear that they were in practice chosen by the governor from the leading landholders. See, for instance, the list of possible holders of the office in M.M.L., I.O. 1680–9, Customs book, 1684; Blundell, *History*, vol. ii, p. 79. Cf. C. H. Karraker, *The Seventeenth-Century Sheriff. A Comparative Study of the Sheriff in England and the Chesapeake Colonies, 1607–1689* (Philadelphia, 1930), p. 7. On the duties of the English sheriff, see *ibid.*, p. 15ff.; T. G. Barnes, *Somerset, 1625–1640: A County's Government during the 'Personal Rule'* (Cambridge, Mass., 1961), ch. 5.

The principal concern of the coroner was to maintain the peace. In criminal matters, he had the authority to arrest offenders for breach of the peace, felony and treason and to commit them to gaol and could call on soldiers from the garrisons, or even the local inhabitants, to assist him in the pursuance of his duty.[159] Every quarter, each coroner was to make 'a general Search' for stolen goods in 'suspected places of high wayes, mountaynes and other persons houses,' taking with him 'what company of neighbours which hee conceyves to bee honest men' and acting on information received or on his own initiative. Resistance to the coroner's search could lead to forfeiture of body and goods to the Lord.[160]

Perhaps the greater part of his work, however, was connected with the courts. The coroner impanelled various juries, including the Great Enquest of the sheading, which dealt with disputes over rights of way, boundaries and watercourses,[161] and the juries for the sheading courts, which handled all actions whether personal or relating to property.[162] The coroner summoned juries of slander to deal with cases of defamation and juries of servants to present vagrants in each parish to be put to work or punished.[163] Juries of indictment were also assembled by the coroner, either at the direction of the deemster or by virtue of his office, to establish whether or not a felony had occurred as a preliminary to the case proceeding to the Court of General Gaol Delivery.[164] The fodder jury of each parish in the sheading, comprised of 'four honest and judicious men, three of them at least to be farmers,' was sworn in under the coroner's supervision every year at Lady Day (March 25) to present those who kept more livestock than they could lawfully

---

[159] *Statutes*, p. 15; Sherwood, *Constitution*, pp. 111–12.

[160] Statutes, p. 51; Cl.R.O., Nantlys MS D/NA/905, 48. On the law enforcement duties of the English sheriff, see J. A. Sharpe, *Crime in Early Modern England, 1550–1750* (1984), pp. 30–3.

[161] Sherwood, Constitution, pp. 48, 105, 133. For further details of the Great Enquest, see *infra*, p. 70.

[162] *ibid.*, pp. 38, 104; Cl.R.O., Nantlys MS D/NA/905, 34. The business of the sheading courts is discussed *infra*, pp. 68–71.

[163] Cl.R.O., Nantlys MS D/NA/905, 46; *Statutes*, pp. 109, 133.

[164] Sherwood, *Constitution*, pp. 45–6, 112; Cl.R.O., Nantlys MS D/NA/905, 48. The personnel of the Court of General Gaol Delivery and the cases with which it dealt are considered *infra*, pp. 65–6.

put out to pasture in summer and supply with fodder in the winter.[165]

As in England, the coroner held inquests into the circumstances of sudden or violent death. A jury of six men was apparently impanelled for the purpose, as in December 1603, following the death of John Quayle of Douglas, who 'going downe a payre of stayres fell downe flatt to the ground and thereuppon sodainlye dyed.'[166] The coroner was also responsible for the enforcement of the orders and judgements of the superior courts in the sheading. He served summonses and exacted the fines imposed by the Exchequer and Chancery courts and the Court of General Gaol Delivery; furthermore, he collected the profits of minor 'casualties' in the sheading. In addition, it was the coroner's duty to supervise the execution of convicted felons, a part of whose goods, essentially any livestock, was due to him by virtue of his office.[167]

The position of coroner could be relatively profitable. Apart from his entitlement to a portion of the goods of felons and suicides, which could hardly constitute a reliable, regular income, the coroner received a fee of 4d. a year from all the Lord's tenants who held quarterlands in the sheading and a smaller payment from the occupants of intacks and other holdings.[168] For every man whom he presented who was found guilty of a 'bloodwipe,' that is, of drawing blood, the coroner received 6d.; for every woman brought before the sheading court for the same offence the sum was 3d. If the persons presented admitted their guilt immediately, however, no fee was forthcoming.[169] He was, in addition, paid 2d. for every person charged in connection with affrays.[170] The coroner, in common with the moars, was allowed the rent of one quarterland in his holding by custom, but this was, to some extent, negated by his payment of Office Silver to the Lord, also by custom. At one time, until at least

---

[165] Sherwood, *Constitution*, p. 50; *Statutes*, pp. 138–9. An Act of Tynwald of 1691 defined the duties of the fodder juries. *ibid.*, pp. 145–7.

[166] Sherwood, *Constitution*, p. 108; Lib. Scacc. 1604, 1. The deemsters could also hold inquests into sudden death. Lib. Scacc. 1692, 16. On the duties of the English coroner, see Sharpe, *Crime in Early Modern England*, p. 33.

[167] Sherwood, *Constitution*, pp. 55–6; Cl.R.O., Nantlys MS D/NA/905, 58–9; *Statutes*, p. 25.

[168] Craine, *Manannan's Isle*, p. 59; *Statutes*, p. 50.

[169] Cl.R.O., Nantlys MS D/NA/905, 47.

[170] *ibid.*, 53.

the early fifteenth century, when the coroners appear to have been called moars, this sum had been two marks, but, by the seventeenth century, the amount paid by each coroner varied from sheading to sheading, ranging from £1 6s. 8d. in Rushen to £3 os. od. in Ayre.[171]

Although there appears to have been no property qualification to hold the office, as there was for the post of sheriff, the coroner was very often, if not usually, one of the chief landholders in the sheading. Furthermore, he was frequently the holder of some other position in the island's administration. Henry Radcliffe of Gordon, Patrick, who was coroner of Glenfaba from 1615 until 1626, was at the same time a member of the Keys and subsequently, in 1627, became a deemster.[172] Nicholas Christian of Ballastole, Maughold, was also a member of the Keys from the 1680s and was coroner of Garff on several occasions between 1681 and 1693.[173] On rare occasions, a major landholder in another, adjacent sheading became coroner. Edward Fletcher of Ballafletcher, Braddan, receiver general, acted as coroner of Garff between at least 1624 and 1629, despite the fact that 'he hath noe land in the sheading,' except for a small property in Maughold.[174]

b) The Lockman

In each parish of the sheading, the coroner had a deputy known as the lockman, who was appointed annually by the coroner himself and sworn in by one of the deemsters. The lockman, whose title

---

[171] *Statutes*, p. 5; Craine, *Manannan's Isle*, pp. 57, 59. The total amount of office silver due from the coroners of the North side was £6 10s. od.; those on the South side paid £5 os. od. between them. The sums paid by individual coroners remained constant throughout the seventeenth century. See the books of charge and the books of pension and allowance in M.M.L., I.O. and R.D., *passim*.

[172] M.M.L., I.O. 1610–19, Books of pension, Peel Castle, 1616, 1618, 1619; M.M.L. R.D. 1600–26, Book of pension, Peel Castle, 1620; M.M.L., I.O. 1620–9, Books of pension, Peel Castle, 1622, 1626. Radcliffe was a member of the Keys from between 1587 and 1593 until he became deemster in late 1627. Lib. Scacc. 1587, 12; *Statutes*, p. 64; Lib. Scacc. 1627, 107. For details of the twenty-four Keys of the island see *infra*, pp. 56–62.

[173] Lib. Scacc. 1682, *ante* 1; M.M.L., I.O. 1680–9, Book of charge of the revenue of the Isle of Man, 1686; Lib. Scacc. 1688, *ante* 1; Lib. Scacc. 1691, *ante* 1; Lib. Scacc. 1693, *ante* 1.

[174] M.M.L., I.O. 1620–9, Books of pension, Castle Rushen, 1624, 1626, 1629.

apparently derived from the 'lock,' or portion of grain, due to him from every bag of meal sold in the parish, acted for the coroner at the proceedings of juries of indictment, presented offenders to the courts and carried out in person punishments such as flogging.[175] In 1641, the lockman was authorised to arrest 'all such beggars they shall find begging and wandering out of the parishes where they were borne' and 'to whippe them severely' before returning them 'from Lockman to Lockman' to their native parish.[176] He assisted the coroner at executions, often digging the grave of the convicted felon, and received as a perquisite the latter's clothes.[177] Sometimes the lockman conducted the quarterly search for stolen property in place of the coroner. He enjoyed similar powers to carry out this duty, and those who 'disobeyed his Rodde' of office, either by hindering the search or by refusing to accompany him were brought before the courts.[178] The lockman was also responsible for the proclamation of orders made by the governor and was empowered to impanel juries of inquiry in certain circumstances.[179]

c) The Captain of the Parish

The military organisation of the sheadings lay in the hands of the captains of the individual parishes. Since this position was normally held by one of the larger landholders, it was not uncommon for the coroner to be the Captain of the Parish in which he lived and, consequently, a man of considerable influence in the area. The Captain of the Parish was entrusted with the command of the militia, or trained band, of the parish, which comprised, in theory, all able-bodied men between the ages of sixteen and sixty who were permanently resident there.[180] To assist him in his duties, he commissioned subordinate officers, who were to make certain that the

---

[175] Sherwood, *Constitution*, p. 56 n. 50; Craine, *Manannan's Isle*, pp. 59–60; Lib. Scacc. 1602, 24; Lib. Scacc. 1678, 12.

[176] *Statutes*, p. 91.

[177] Cl.R.O., Nantlys MS D/NA/905, 59.

[178] Lib. Scacc. 1608, 5; Lib. Scacc. 1699, 48.

[179] Lib. Scacc. 1681, 15.

[180] Craine, *Manannan's Isle*, pp. 61, 63. Cf. L. Boynton, *The Elizabethan Militia, 1558–1638* (1967); D. P. Carter, 'The "Exact Militia" in Lancashire, 1625–1640', *Northern History*, vol. xi (1975–6), pp. 87–105.

men of the parish responded to the summons of the mustering cross, or *crosh vustha*, and attended the musters, which were generally held annually.[181]

Although in some parishes there was still a separate warden of the watch in the early seventeenth century, it seems that the burden of this office increasingly fell on the Captain of the Parish.[182] No fewer than seven of the wardens in a list of 1627 were also captains of their parish.[183] Watch and ward was kept on specified hills near the coast, both night and day, and the duty fell on four men of the parish at a time for each watch on a rota basis. By law, 'the captain, Lieutenant, Ensign [that is, the militia officers] 24 Keys men, the Moars and their Runners, the Coroners and their Lockmen, the Customers and searchers of every port, one head smith [and] one head or chief miller in every parish' were exempt from the duty unless 'in time of apparent danger.'[184]

d) The Moar

Each parish had, in addition, an officer known as the moar, or, as Sacheverell described him, 'the Lord's Bailiff.'[185] The moar had the important task of collecting the Lord's rent and other revenue and delivering it to the receiver.[186] He acted for the sheading courts, or courts of common law, as the coroner did for the superior courts,

---

[181] Sherwood, *Constitution*, pp. 57, 87; Craine, *Manannan's Isle*, pp. 65–6. In cases of emergency, a mustering drum, or *drum vustha*, was used. D. Craine, 'The Mustering Drum', *J.M.M.*, vol. v (1941–6), p. 123.

[182] It is not certain at what date the office of Captain of the Parish was created, but it may have originated in the late sixteenth century, as David Craine suggested. Craine, *Manannan's Isle*, p. 63. The earliest reference to the captains dates from March 1596, when John Stevenson, Captain of Arbory, presented the four horsemen appointed to accompany him to the Tynwald Court for refusing to do their duty. Lib. Scacc. 1596, 13.

[183] Cubbon, 'Watch and Ward', pp. 259, 264.

[184] *ibid.*, pp. 258–65; Megaw, 'Thousand Years of Watch and Ward', pp. 10–11.

[185] Sacheverell, *Account*, p. 73.

[186] Moore, *History*, vol. ii, p. 746. See also the various books of receipts from the moars, such as M.M.L. R.D. 1600–26, 'The book of moares Conteyninge aswell the particuler Receipt of Rentes heretofore accustomably payd, together with the other Rentes payable and acknowledged due in Respect of the Customes of vittle, Corne, etc., Castle Rushen, 1603'.

summoning witnesses and jurors and publishing and supervising in his parish the observation of decrees and judgements.[187] In this capacity, the moar was provided with an assistant, or runner, who also undertook such tasks as nominating four or six tenants as horsemen of the parish to serve as part of the escort for the Lord's officers in the annual midsummer progression from Castletown to the Tynwald Court, which was usually held at St John's in German.[188] Every landholder in the parish was obliged to serve, in rotation, as moar for a year, paying Office Silver to the Lord, but receiving the rent of a quarterland and fees similar in kind to those due to the coroner as recompense.[189] Like the coroner and the lockman, the moar had a rod of office, sometimes referred to as a yard, which symbolised the duty to maintain the Lord's peace.[190]

e) The Captain of the Town

The four towns 'acknowledged by the natives' – Castletown, Douglas, Peel and Ramsey – had none of the civic superstructure with which contemporary English observers, such as Blundell, Chaloner and Sacheverell, would have been familiar and, indeed, Blundell likened them to English villages in 'magnitude and bulk' as well as in their form of government.[191] Each, nevertheless, had a captain, whose authority was more extensive than that of a village constable in England.[192] He was the only officer with special responsibility for the towns, although harbingers were periodically appointed to supervise brewing and alehouses and overseers of the assize of bread

---

[187] Sherwood, *Constitution*, p. 52; Cl.R.O., Nantlys MS D/NA/905, 26, 27, 29, 30, 31, 32, 34.

[188] Lib. Scacc. 1680, inter 10–11; D. Craine, 'The Horsemen and their Successors, 1793–1825', *J.M.M.*, vol. iii (1935–7), p. 167.

[189] Moore, *History*, vol. ii, p. 746; *Statutes*, pp. 5, 26; Cl.R.O., Nantlys MS D/NA/905, 29, 47. For details of the Office Silver paid by the coroners, see *infra*, pp. 48–9 and n. 171. The moars paid smaller customary sums than the coroners, varying from 4s. 5d. in Jurby to 13s. 4d. in Patrick, German, Michael and Andreas. The total due from each sheading was two marks by 'Use and Custome of long Time'. *Statutes*, p. 5.

[190] Cl.R.O., Nantlys MS D/NA/905, 53–4.

[191] Blundell, *History*, vol. i, pp. 66, 77–8.

[192] For details of the duties of the village constable in England, see J. R. Kent, *The English Village Constable. A Social and Administrative Study, 1580–1642* (Oxford, 1986), chapters 2, 5 and 6.

and ale regulated the prices of these staple commodities from at least the end of the sixteenth century.[193]

Although there is little evidence of either the identities or the activities of the captains before the eighteenth century, it seems that they were usually the constables of Castle Rushen and Peel Castle and the commanders of the detachments of soldiers at Douglas Fort and, at least from the 1640s, at Ramsey.[194] The captain's duties, which were not set out in detail until 1769, were to maintain the peace, to assist the waterbailiff and his deputies in the collection of customs duty, to prevent any of the inhabitants from departing from the island without the governor's licence and to ensure that the market regulations were observed. The captain was also to take pains to see that the streets were kept free from 'dunghills, Filth, Lumber, Piggs or other Nuisance,' in accordance with orders made by Governor Greenhalgh in 1648 and by the command of Earl James in 1650.[195] Clearly this was a persistent problem. In March 1700, seven of the inhabitants of Douglas were fined for keeping 'their swine in Duglass streets contrary to Order,' and, in the following January, a further directive was issued by Thomas Huddleston, the deputy governor, to the effect that 'the inhabitants of the severall markett Towns of this Isle shall for the future once a weeke at least cause their streets as farr as their Rents extend to be cleanly swept and all Dung and other Rubbage there lyeing to be carried out in some convenient place without the town.'[196]

---

[193] Lib. Scacc. 1599, 26(2)–7; Lib. Scacc. 1597, 13, inter 24–5. On harbingers, see chapter 4, pp. 204–6. Orders concerning the assize of bread and ale and the appointment of overseers continued throughout the seventeenth century. See, for example, Lib. Scacc. 1649, 2; Lib. Scacc. 1695, 21. For further details of the control of the prices of bread and ale, see chapter 2, pp. 93, 99, 104.

[194] Moore, *History*, vol. ii, p. 746. David Craine asserted that the captains were assistant constables in the garrisons, but there seems to be little evidence to support this claim, at least in the seventeenth century. Craine, *Manannan's Isle*, p. 84. The first recorded captain of any of the towns appears to be Robert Calcotts, Captain of Douglas in 1627. Cubbon, 'Watch and Ward', p. 264.

[195] C. Radcliffe, *Ramsey, 1600–1800* (Douglas 1986), p. 69; Lib. Scacc. 1648, 47; Lib. Scacc. 1650, 111–12.

[196] Lib. Scacc. 1700, 16; Lib. Scacc. 1700–1, 34.

IV. LEGISLATIVE GOVERNMENT

Before the early seventeenth century, few new laws appear to have been made during the period of Stanley rule. When the governor and officers required advice or judgements on the interpretation of existing laws, the deemsters and twenty-four Keys were summoned to a meeting of the Tynwald Court. When new laws became necessary, it was, therefore, as A. W. Moore stated, 'only natural' that the Tynwald Court should formulate such legislation and 'become the supreme legislative as well as the supreme judicial body.'[197] Ordinances continued to be issued by the Lord, who retained legislative authority, but, as the seventeenth century progressed, that authority was increasingly shared with the governor and Council and the twenty-four Keys, sitting as the Tynwald Court.

a) The Lord's Council

Although the Lord's Council had a legislative as well as an executive function, this is scarcely evident before the late sixteenth century, when the records of the island's government become more plentiful.[198] Most of the laws recorded in the statute book up to this time are either judicial decisions or statements of customary law made by the deemsters in the presence of the twenty-four Keys, but, in October 1582, the deputy governor and Council issued ordinances relating to the maintenance of boundary ditches between tenements, trespass, the status of tenants and their ability to alienate their lands.[199] Although this seems to be the first instance on record, there are clear indications that it was not unknown for the Council to make such orders prior to this date. In January 1586, after failure to observe orders made at 'sundry Times by my Lord himself, as by the Councell of this Isle,' the governor, Richard Shireburne, the Council and the deemsters reaffirmed that no person 'shall shoote in his Hand Gunn or Fowling Piece at any Manner of Fowle, or hunt or course the Hare' in the Lord's warren in the south of the island.[200] It is probable,

---

[197] Moore, *History*, vol. ii, p. 759.
[198] The series of Exchequer and Chancery books, which provide most information about the island's government, commence in 1580 and 1578 respectively. See introduction, pp. 7–8
[199] *Statutes*, pp. 55–9; Lib. Scacc. 1583, 4.
[200] *Statutes*, pp. 61–2; Lib. Scacc. 1586, 7.

therefore, that ordinances of the Council were an accepted, rather than an exceptional, part of the government of the island before 1600.

From the beginning of the seventeenth century, it was normal practice for the governor and Council to consult the twenty-four Keys in matters of legislation. In June 1601, the deputy, Robert Molyneux, summoned the Keys to consider with the Council and the deemsters, who were invariably present in such cases, what action should be taken against Thomas Tyldesley of Arbory, who had defamed the Keys, claiming that 'they never did good to the Isle' and that they were 'buostin-belly churles.' Tyldesley submitted publicly at the Tynwald Court held in that month and, 'in the hope the like offence shall not be committed hereafter,' he was spared punishment; nevertheless, it was 'enacted, established and by proclamation at the Tynwald' given for law that for such an offence in the future the culprits were to be fined the sum of £10 and 'their eares to be cut of for punishment.'[201] This law was finally approved by the Lord when Earl James gave his assent in 1647 and it was again proclaimed at the Tynwald Court in that year.[202] In October 1609, 'Statutes' concerning the wages of servants and tradesmen were enacted at an assembly of the governor, John Ireland, the Council, deemsters and Keys at Castle Rushen 'for the consulting and determining of Matters concerning the State of the Land.' These, and some of the other laws passed by the Council and Keys later in the seventeenth century, do not appear to have ever received the Lord's assent, but, in spite of this fact, they still carried the force of law and were regarded as Acts of Tynwald.[203]

On several occasions in the seventeenth century, ordinances were issued by the governor and Council, such as those relating to the regulation of the herring fishery in 1613 and those designed to deal with the 'Multitude of Poore beggars . . . which wander abroad in the Countrie' in 1641.[204] In general, however, although the governor and Council could, and did, act in an arbitrary manner in certain cases, such as when the officers revised the customs duties without consulting the Keys in 1677 and 1692, it came to be accepted that

[201] *Statutes*, pp. 69–70; Lib. Scacc. 1601, 17–18.

[202] *Statutes*, p. 105; Lib. Scacc. 1601, 18.

[203] *Statutes*, pp. 72, 74, 76, 81, 111, 112, 115, 137, 139, 140, 142, 144. Eight of these twelve collections of laws are listed as Acts in *ibid.*, pp. vii–viii.

[204] *Statutes*, pp. 79–81, 91. On the regulations for the herring fishery, see chapter 2, pp. 111–18.

legislation should be made by agreement between the governor and Council and the Keys, with the assent of the Lord.[205] Promulgation of a law at the Tynwald Court in Manx and in English not only made its details public but also rendered it an Act of the island's legislature.[206]

b) The Keys

For about the first two centuries of Stanley rule in the island, the twenty-four Keys appear to have only served in a judicial capacity and it is not clear whether they were, in fact, a permanent body during that time. From at least the end of the sixteenth century, however, there is evidence to show that the Keys were a standing body and that, arising from their advisory and judicial role in the Tynwald Court, they became a part of the legislative process in the island.

The origin of the twenty-four Keys lies in the period of Norse rule in the island, although the name of the body seems to be of later date. It has been plausibly suggested that the word 'Keys' is derived from an English approximation of the Manx name for the body, *Yn Kiare as feed*, that is, 'the Four and twenty,' and from their function of 'unlocking' the solutions to questions in law.[207] The composition of the Keys, however, originated in the time of the Norse kingdom of Man and the Isles, and more particularly after the partition of the Isles in 1156, when they were 'xxiiij free Houlders, viz. viij in the Out Isles, and xvj in [the] Land of Mann.'[208] The latter are believed to have been chosen from each of the original sixteen, probably early twelfth century, parishes, Marown and Santan having formerly been, in all probability, one parish.[209] After the loss of the remaining Hebridean islands of Lewis and Skye to Scotland in 1266, the places of the 'Out Isles' were supplied by additional representatives from

---

[205] Moore, *History*, vol. ii, p. 761; P. W. Caine, 'The Story of the House of Keys', *M.N.H.A.S.*, vol. iv (1932–42), pp. 444, 445; Sherwood, *Constitution*, pp. 19–20, 72.

[206] Sherwood, *Constitution*, pp. 20–1, 146–7.

[207] Kinvig, *Isle of Man*, pp. 75–6; Moore, *History*, vol. i, pp. 160–1.

[208] W. Cubbon and B. R. S. Megaw, 'The Western Isles and the Growth of the Manx Parliament', *J.M.M.*, vol. v (1941–6), p. 61; *Statutes*, p. 11.

[209] Cubbon and Megaw, 'Western Isles and the Growth of the Manx Parliament', p. 61; Marstrander, 'Treen og Keeill', pp. 428–9.

Man, the number of twenty-four being maintained by drawing four men from each of the six sheadings and dispensing with the system of selection based on the parishes.[210]

The manner in which the Keys were chosen before 1600, and whether, in fact, they were a standing body before that date, is difficult to determine, but, from the meagre records of the fifteenth and sixteenth centuries, it appears that they were impanelled when required by the deemsters, with the approval of the Lord's officers, from the 'worthiest Men' in the island.[211] By the beginning of the seventeenth century, a slightly different method of selection was in use, which seems to have given the Keys a measure of influence.[212] In 1610, when Bishop John Phillips claimed that the governor, John Ireland, had 'placed and displaced the Keys at his pleasure,' the Council and Keys replied that Ireland had 'used no other course' in choosing the Keys 'than as ever in former times to our remembrance hath been accustomed, which is with the consent of all the officers and the rest of the Keys.'[213] This procedure, which allowed the existing Keys a voice in the selection of replacements, was modified in 1659 so that the Keys had a greater degree of control over nominations. In that year, the deemsters ruled that 'When any of the 24 Keys dye, or are removed, the rest of the number shall recommend some fit persons to supply their places,' subject to the approval of the Lord or governor.[214] In the same year, in accordance with this judgement, Governor James Chaloner approved the nomination of Charles Stanley of Ballakeighan, Arbory, James Moore of Baldromma, Lonan and John Lace of Ballavoddan, Andreas by the Keys.[215] Whenever a vacancy arose thereafter, the Keys put forward two suitable names, one of which was selected by the governor. This

---

[210] Cubbon and Megaw, 'Western Isles and the Growth of the Manx Parliament', p. 61; Kinvig, *Isle of Man*, p. 75.

[211] Caine, 'House of Keys', pp. 437–8, 441.

[212] A. W. Moore, 'The House of Keys – its Origins and Constitution', *Y.L.M.*, vol. i (1880–94), p. 250.

[213] Moore, *History*, vol. ii, pp. 769–70; Knowsley Hall, H/44a, 'A Book containing the Answeare of th'Officers Deemsters Viccars Generall and 24 Keyes to certain Articles Objected by John now Bishop of this Isle against John Ireland Esq. Lieutenant and Captaine of the Isle of Mann, February 1, 1611'.

[214] Moore, *History*, vol. ii, pp. 773.

[215] Lib. Scacc. 1659, 96.

continued to be the form of election until the reform of the House of Keys in 1866.[216]

Between the demise of the Norse kingdom of Man and the Isles and the early Stanley period, the Keys, as the deemsters and the twenty-four themselves informed Sir John Stanley in 1423, had 'not been in Certainty,'[217] and this in itself implies that there was then no permanent body of Keys. Despite the fact that some names recur over short periods of time in the few extant records of the meetings of the Keys before about 1580, there is no conclusive proof that the twenty-four were a standing body by this date.[218] It was only after the Keys began to be involved in the shaping of legislation, from 1601 onwards, that the twenty-four came to be regarded as a permanent part of the administration rather than merely as an enquest, called when judicial matters arose. Lists of Keys appear almost every year in the Exchequer books after 1598 and, though it may be stretching the evidence in view of the limited amount of material extant before 1580, this seems to reflect the greater stability of the Keys in the seventeenth century.[219]

This impression of permanence is strengthened by an examination of the annual lists of Keys, which reveals that, while membership was held during pleasure, it was often held for many years, frequently for life or until promotion to a higher office. Henry Radcliffe of Gordon, Patrick, was a member of the Keys from about 1594 until he became a deemster in 1627; George Stanley of Ballakeighan, Arbory entered the Keys in 1604 and remained a member until promoted to the position of deemster in 1631; John Barrey, probably of Castletown, was a member of the Keys for twenty years between 1671 and his death in 1691.[220] It is also clear from these lists that the system of selecting four Keys from each sheading was no longer in use by the seventeenth century. Although identification of all the

---

[216] Sherwood, *Constitution*, pp. 7 and n. 3, 8; Moore, *History*, vol. ii, pp. 788, 816–22.

[217] *Statutes*, p. 11.

[218] Caine, 'House of Keys', p. 437. See the lists of Keys in *Statutes*, pp. 2, 22, 23, 25, 26; 'Unpublished Document no. 74', *J.M.M.*, vol. ii, p. 185.

[219] The names of the Keys usually appear at the beginning of the Liber Scaccarii (Exchequer book) for most years after 1598.

[220] *Statutes*, p. 64; Lib. Scacc. 1627,107; Lib. Scacc. 1604, *ante* 1; Lib. Scacc. 1631, 55; Lib. Scacc. 1671, *ante* 1; M.M.L., MF/RB/523. Inventory of John Barrey, 1691.

Keys in a given year is often difficult, there can be little question but that they were chosen from among the representatives of the leading island families, irrespective of their place of residence. In 1620, out of a total of twenty Keys identified with a reasonable degree of certainty, six came from the sheading of Rushen and five from the sheading of Ayre, all the latter group representing the parish of Lezayre. In 1661, seven Keys came from Ayre, all but one representing Lezayre.[221]

On several occasions, members of the Keys were removed by order of the Lord. In 1612, William Tyldesley of The Friary, Arbory, was held by the rest of the Keys 'not fitting to be of our number' after a letter had been written at his instigation in which, among other allegations, 'all of us the 24 except fower were taxed as enemies' of the late governor, John Ireland.[222] In 1662, seven Keys were ejected by Charles, eighth earl of Derby, in order to obtain a unanimous decision in the Lord's favour in the case against William Christian, the former receiver general, who was held chiefly responsible for the Manx 'rebellion' of 1651.[223] In 1695, Captain John Quilliam of Marown was judged 'Unfitt and incapable of being a Member of our Societye as one of the 24 Keyes of this Isle' after committing 'severall Misdemeanours in the Lord's service' and was accordingly dismissed by Governor Nicholas Sankey.[224]

The duties of the Keys were clearly defined at the beginning of the Stanley period. Whenever a 'strange Point' arose, the governor reserved the matter 'to the Tynwald twice in the Yeare' and granted permission to the deemsters to summon to the assembly 'the best to his Councell in that Point.'[225] The Keys were, in addition, to be summoned with the deemsters when the governor needed advice in 'great Matters and high Points that are in Doubt,' 'to deem the Law

[221] Lib. Scacc. 1620, *ante* 1; Lib. Scacc. 1661, 2. William Blundell believed that the members of the Keys were required to be 'landed men, such as our freeholders in England, having 40 or 50 or more pounds of their owne'. Blundell, *History*, vol. ii, p. 77. This may well have been the case, but it was not a formal requirement.

[222] Lib. Scacc. 1612, 36–7.

[223] Lib. Scacc. 1663, ii, *ante* 1. For an outline of the 'rebellion' of 1651, see Moore, *History*, vol. i, pp. 265–70.

[224] Lib. Scacc. 1695, 39–40.

[225] *Statutes*, p. 11.

truely to the Parties.'[226] In all cases at common law, where either the plaintiff or the defendant felt himself aggrieved, the final right of appeal within the island lay to the Keys, who met at least once a year, usually in October, to deal with such matters.[227] The Keys were also to attend the Court of General Gaol Delivery 'without any Sumons, to be assistinge to the Deemsters, in any doubtfull or difficult point of Law, if any happen' and 'to pass upon the Grand-Jury for life and death, if they be suspected to digress from their Evidence or give a parciall verdict.'[228] At the same time, cases were referred to the Keys for their attention by the court or by the Lord.[229] The Keys were exempt from jury and other services. In 1605, it was ordered that they should be free 'from all common services and duties of the country,' except by the governor's order.[230] In 1629, the coroners were ordered to impanel the 'most sufficient' jurors in cases of felony, but not to trouble the Keys without specific direction.[231]

Before the end of the sixteenth century, the Keys were apparently only summoned to act in a judicial capacity, but their participation in the formulation of legislation, which evolved from their role in the Tynwald Court, developed until, by the end of the seventeenth century, they had become an accepted part of the law-making body. In 1580, Henry, fourth earl of Derby issued a commission to the governor, Richard Shireburne, the Council, deemsters, Keys and the officers spiritual for the trial of a felon and the enactment of an unspecified law. Bishop John Meyrick maintained, however, that, if the twenty-four and the other officers were assembled 'for the establisshinge of a Lawe to stand in force hereafter to bynde his successors and the whole Cuntry and not to decyde a Controversie,' the Keys 'should be elected by the whole Consent of the Cuntry, that is to saye of every shedinge an number to say for the rest,'[232] for

---

[226] *ibid.*, pp. 11, 12.

[227] Sherwood, *Constitution*, pp. 39 and n. 20, 40, 156; Cl.R.O., Nantlys MS D/NA/905, 32–3.

[228] M.M.L., MD 15,040, J. Parr, *An Abridgement or A Short Tract of the most usefull Lawes Acts and Ordinances conteyned in the Statute Book of this Isle of Mann* (1679), p. 45; Sherwood, *Constitution*, pp. 45, 101.

[229] Cl.R.O., Nantlys MS D/NA/905, 55–6.

[230] Moore, *History*, vol. ii, p. 768.

[231] Moore, House of Keys, p. 250.

[232] Lib. Canc. 1581, 5.

'noe Law is to be Enacted without the Consent of the 24 Keyes.'[233] This does not seem to have been accepted immediately, but from the early seventeenth century, the consent of the Keys came to be a necessary part of the procedure for enacting new laws. In the late 1640s, William Blundell perceived that 'their assent is soe necessary as, that without them no new law can be made nor any custome be introduced or altered.'[234] During the Interregnum, Governor James Chaloner observed that the Keys were assembled to assist the governor and Council 'in cases of doubt, and considerations sometimes taken about the ordering of the Country, for the defence and safety thereof; and propositions of good and wholesome Lawes and Orders for the Peace and Welfare of the People.'[235] By 1700, the Keys together with the governor and Council had become 'the legislative power of the nation.'[236]

On occasions when matters of importance to the whole island were to be considered, four men from each parish were sometimes chosen, 'by the whole Commons of the Isle,'[237] to provide authoritative testimony and a broader sample of island opinion. In 1608, for instance, four men from each parish joined the Keys to produce a survey of the land, rents and prices of livestock and other products of the island for Richard Hoper, the commissioner of the earls of Salisbury and Northampton, who were acting trustees for the Stanleys at the time.[238] In 1643, the four men were called to a meeting of the Lord, Council, Keys and spiritual officers to resolve the grievances of the inhabitants in general, arising particularly from a dispute with the Church over the payment of tithes.[239] It appears that the four men were last summoned in February 1652, to acknowledge Fairfax as Lord of Man.[240] They do not appear to have ever constituted a regular part of the legislative or judicial process. When Charles, eighth earl of Derby, was formulating a commission for the revision of the spiritual laws in 1667, he dismissed the idea of calling

---

[233] M.M.L., MD 15,040, Parr, *Abridgement*, p. 85.
[234] Blundell, *History*, vol. ii, p. 76.
[235] Chaloner, *Treatise*, p. 29.
[236] Sacheverell, *Account*, p. 73.
[237] *Statutes*, p. 92.
[238] M.M.L., MD/401/1715/5.
[239] *Statutes*, p. 92.
[240] Lib. Scacc. 1652, 16.

the four men as 'they having no power to settle or enact anything, I think it will be to little purpus.'[241]

V. JUDICIAL COURTS

The Tynwald Court, which increasingly became the focus of the law-making process, was also the supreme judicial body of the island and from it stemmed the other principal temporal courts of the island.[242] Each of these courts had a specific function and was comprised of a part, or all, of the Tynwald Court. The governor and at least some of the Council sat in all these courts and by themselves constituted the Staff of Government to hear appeals.[243] Criminal cases were dealt with in the Court of General Gaol Delivery, ominously known as the Head Court, where the deemsters, Keys and the jury of 'life and death' were also present.[244] Petitions and complaints were heard in the Chancery Court,[245] while the Exchequer Court handled all matters concerning revenue.[246] A sheading court sat for each of the principal administrative divisions of the island and was occupied with common law and 'manorial' business.[247] Each of the baronies of the island also had courts of common law and criminal justice in which a deemster sat along with the baron's officer or steward.[248] In addition, the deemsters held courts of general jurisdiction in their own division of the island[249] and the waterbailiff held an admiralty court with special jurisdiction in all maritime cases, with the exception of felonies.[250]

The specialist jurisdiction of these many courts emphasised the separate and institutionally independent development of government in the Isle of Man. There were, for example, few parallels between the island and England, except at national level, or perhaps, to some

---

[241] M.M.L., MD/401/1715/21.
[242] On the judicial function of the Tynwald Court, see *infra*, pp. 63–4.
[243] See *infra*, pp. 63.
[244] See *infra*, pp. 65–6.
[245] See *infra*, pp. 66–7.
[246] See *infra*, pp. 67–8.
[247] See *infra*, pp. 68–71.
[248] See *infra*, pp. 71–2.
[249] See *infra*, pp. 72–3.
[250] See *infra*, pp. 73–4.

extent, in the courts of the palatine counties of Chester, Durham and Lancaster.[251]

a) The Staff of Government

Besides their executive and legislative duties, the governor and Council exercised a judicial function. The governor, as the Lord's representative, had cognisance of all pleas, whether civil or criminal, and, with the Council acting as assessors, he sat in what appears to have been a form of supreme court, known as the Staff of Government.[252] This court, which has left scarcely any records, exercised appellate jurisdiction in all cases which had not been tried by jury, where appeal lay to the Keys.[253]

b) The Tynwald Court

Matters of greater judicial importance were held over by the governor to the Tynwald Court, which met twice a year in the early Stanley period, but only once a year in the seventeenth century.[254] The deemsters, Keys and spiritual officers were called to this court to assist and advise the governor and Council on such weighty issues. At the Tynwald Court held in June 1637, 'Laws and Ordinances' proposed by James, Lord Strange, acting Lord of Man, were considered and a judgement was issued in the case of Phillip Cannell of Michael.[255]

---

[251] Details of the national and local courts in England can be found in Elton, *Tudor Constitution*, chapters 5 and 10. For a comparison with an English county, see B. E. Harris (ed.), *Victoria History of the County of Chester*, vol. ii (1979), pp. 36–55, 61–70. On the courts of the counties palatine, see W. J. Jones, 'Palatine Performance in the Seventeenth Century', in P. Clark, A. G. R. Smith and N. Tyacke (eds), *The English Commonwealth, 1547–1640* (Leicester, 1979), pp. 189–204.

[252] Sherwood, *Constitution*, pp. 33–4, 100; Moore, *History*, vol. ii, p. 747.

[253] Sherwood, *Constitution*, p. 52. See also note 255.

[254] *Statutes*, p. 11. Between 1594 and 1687, the Tynwald Court met only on midsummer's day, June 24, at St John's, German, as was customary. In 1691, presumably at the direction of William, ninth earl of Derby, who was present at the subsequent assembly, the full court met at the end of July. Again, in 1696, and when the Ecclesiastical Constitutions of Bishop Wilson were confirmed and the Act of Settlement was passed in 1704, the Tynwald Court met at other times, *ibid.*, pp. 144, 152, 160, 161 and *passim*; Lib. Scacc. 1594–1704, *passim*.

[255] *Statutes*, pp. 86–91; Lib. Scacc. 1637, inter 23–6.

Gilbert, the latter's father and one of the farmers of the bishop's thirds in Michael, Jurby and Ballaugh, had appealed to the consistory court of York concerning the confirmation of his lease and an accompanying 'increase [in] maintenance' to the bishop awarded by Strange. This action was regarded as contrary to the laws of the island since the jurisdiction of the ecclesiastical court at York was only vaguely admitted in appeals in purely spiritual matters from the Manx church courts.[256] Cannell, who presented the appeal on his father's behalf, admitted his error and undertook to pay the outstanding rent and the bishop's expenses at the Tynwald Court; in the event, he refused and the court ordered the coroner of Michael to levy a distraint on his property to the value of £57 6s. 8d.[257]

Judicial business of a more routine character was also carried out by the Tynwald Court: petitions were presented, presentments were made and recognisances were taken.[258] In 1605, Robert Casement petitioned the court complaining that Thomas Barrie had struck him, 'as did appeare unto the court,' and requested that a jury be impanelled. The deputy, Cuthbert Gerrard, appointed two members of the Keys and a soldier to act as jurors, together with three men from Santan, and directed that the presentment was to be made at the next Chancery Court.[259] In June 1640, the Tynwald Court examined the question of the outstanding sum of rent owed by the late Henry Calcotts of The Nunnery, Braddan, and ordered that a jury of moars be sworn in to determine who was liable to make payment.[260]

The other principal temporal courts appear to have developed out of the Tynwald Court and, in fact, since they were generally composed of the same personnel, these courts were essentially the same court, sitting at different times to deal with specific types of business.

---

[256] Sherwood, *Constitution*, pp. 45 and n. 32, 110. In cases of probate, the ecclesiastical authorities claimed the right of appeal lay to the archbishop of York alone, while the deemsters maintained that it lay to the Staff of Government. *ibid.*, p. 45 n. 32.

[257] Lib. Scacc. 1637, inter 23–6.

[258] Lib. Scacc. 1644, 30.

[259] Lib. Scacc. 1605, 31.

[260] Lib. Scacc. 1640, 52.

c) The Court of General Gaol Delivery

The Court of General Gaol Delivery, or Head Court, was the superior court of criminal justice and comprised the governor, 'all the officers, if in the Isle or able to travayle,' the deemsters and the Keys.[261] The bishop and the rest of the spiritual officers were also frequently present.[262] The court was held 'without the gates of the Castle [Rushen], within the walls, in a place known for that purpose,' after the sheading courts in May and October, but occasionally at other times as necessity dictated.[263] All cases in the court were heard by a grand jury of twelve men *in camera*, following confirmation of the accusation by a six-man jury of indictment.[264] The names of seventy-two men, twelve from each sheading, were returned by the coroners, the moar of each parish having previously named '4 or 6 able persons to bee there against the Court sitting to passe upon the Jury of liffe or death or a Jury upon the felons or prisoners.'[265] The grand jury was then selected by the prisoners themselves, any of them having the right to 'make his lawfull exception against any of those persons called on the Jury,' although he had to 'shew and declare the lawfulnes of his exception, which must not bee against more then six.'[266]

Once a verdict had been reached, it was delivered to the deemster in open court by a foreman and the deemster pronounced sentence.[267] If found guilty of the theft of goods to the value of 6d. or more, of housebreaking or of murder, among other offences, the penalty was death.[268] In certain cases, such as that of William Cretney

---

[261] Sherwood, *Constitution*, pp. 45, 101; Cl.R.O., Nantlys MS D/NA/905, 53.

[262] Cl.R.O., Nantlys MS D/NA/905, 54.

[263] *ibid.*, 53. Courts of General Gaol Delivery were held, for example, in March 1641 and August 1648. Lib. Scacc. 1641, 11; Lib. Scacc. 1648, 81.

[264] Cl.R.O., Nantlys MS D/NA/905, 49, 54–6; Sherwood, *Constitution*, pp. 46–7.

[265] Cl.R.O., Nantlys MS D/NA/905, 55. In a letter to the commissioners of inquiry for the Isle of Man in December 1791, Sir Wadsworth Busk, then attorney general, stated that 'sixty-eight men, four from every parish', were impanelled for the purpose of selecting the grand jury. This was not the case in the seventeenth century, nor in the nineteenth century. Sherwood, *Constitution*, pp. 47 n. 35, 101.

[266] Cl.R.O., Nantlys MS D/NA/905, 55.

[267] *ibid.*, 56.

[268] *ibid.*, 49, 50, 57. No '*karran* man,' that is, no clergyman, was permitted

in May 1609, the convicted felon was given the opportunity to abjure the the island and go into exile; Cretney was found guilty of stealing a mutton, valued at 20d. and 'abiured into Ireland.'[269] It was also possible that the friends and relatives of a convicted felon might compound with the governor and officers for a pardon, as in 1602, when 60s. was paid for 'sparing the Arraignment of Danold Costain,' but this does not seem to have been a common practice in the seventeenth century.[270]

d) The Chancery Court

The superior civil court was the Chancery Court, in which the governor presided as chancellor and was assisted by the members of the Council whom he chose to summon and by the deemsters.[271] In 1423, the Chancery Court was ordered to meet every Monday in Castle Rushen, but it seems that, by the mid-sixteenth century, if not before, this order was being disregarded, for another directive was issued in 1561, requiring that the court should be held at the appointed time 'in the Exchequer, according to the old Laws and Statutes of this Isle,' or elsewhere in Castletown.[272] By the seventeenth century, the Chancery Court generally met every month, except for January, May, September and October, although there were often additional sittings when necessary.[273] This court dealt principally with matters in equity, but it also had jurisdiction over cases at common law. The defendant in an action at common law

note 268 *continued*
to sit in court when the sentence of death was to be pronounced, *ibid.*, 56. In England, theft of goods valued at 12d. or more constituted grand larceny and, like burglary, murder and other serious felonies, was a capital offence. C. B. Herrup, *The Common Peace. Participation and the Criminal Law in Seventeenth-Century England* (Cambridge, 1987), pp. 47, 169–172; Sharpe, *Crime in Early Modern England*, p. 24.

[269] Lib. Scacc. 1609, 40, 41, 44.

[270] M.M.L., I.O. 1600–9, Book of charge, Castle Rushen, 1602; Cl.R.O., Nantlys MS D/NA/905, 50. No instances of 'pardoninge of liffe' have as yet been found after 1602. M.M.L., I.O. and R.D., Books of charge, Castle Rushen and Peel Castle, *passim.*

[271] Cl.R.O., Nantlys MS D/NA/905, 43; Sherwood, *Constitution*, pp. 34, 102.

[272] *Statutes*, pp. 15, 37.

[273] Sherwood, *Constitution*, pp. 35, 103.

had the right to obtain the governor's token, 'a stone of blew Slate' bearing the latter's initials, to stay the proceedings before trial by jury commenced so that he might have relief 'as the Court shall find cause in Equity.'[274] If the court found the case more appropriate to the jurisdiction of another court, it was transferred from Chancery and the instigator of the action was charged with costs 'for wrongfull vexation.'[275] In cases initiated before the governor as chancellor, witnesses normally gave their evidence in court, but they were sometimes examined outside the court in the presence of the clerk of the rolls, who returned the depositions to the governor. The defendant was not compelled to answer upon oath and, when he did, his statement often went unrecorded.[276] There was, in general, no jury in the Chancery Court, though, when deemed necessary, one was impanelled and brought in its verdict to the governor in the same manner as the grand jury in the Court of General Gaol Delivery.[277]

e) The Exchequer Court

The Exchequer Court, which was composed of the same personnel as the Chancery Court, had jurisdiction over all disputes touching the Lord's rights and prerogatives and handled all questions relating to the Lord's revenues.[278] In 1648, for instance, more than two dozen inhabitants and 'strangers' were found guilty of transporting goods without licence, thus depriving the Lord of his revenue in the form of customs duty. They were fined or, like Patrick Gawne *alias* Smyth, 'beinge poore,' were imprisoned in Peel Castle.[279] The Exchequer Court also dealt with misdemeanours, lesser offences than felonies where the value of the allegedly stolen goods was below 6d., and a variety of suits where the penalty was a fine payable to the Lord.[280] Sheading court juries which did not return a verdict at the same sitting in which an action was begun had to attend the next Exchequer Court to deliver their decision. Precepts were accordingly sent to the

---

[274] Chaloner, *Treatise*, p. 43, 44; Cl.R.O., Nantlys MS D/NA/905, 42.
[275] Chaloner, *Treatise*, p. 44–5; *Statutes*, p. 76.
[276] Sherwood, *Constitution*, pp. 35, 102–3.
[277] *ibid.*, pp. 35, 102.
[278] *ibid.*, pp. 36, 103.
[279] Lib. Scacc. 1648, inter 2–3, 3, 5, 7, 9, 13, inter 13–14.
[280] Sherwood, *Constitution*, pp. 36, 46, 112; Cl.R.O., Nantlys MS D/NA/ 905, 49.

coroners to ensure that the jurors, as well as the parties involved, were present at the court.[281] The juries of slander and of indictment impanelled by the coroners returned their findings to this court, as to other judicial meetings of the officers, but it was held 'more proper' for such returns to be made to the sheading courts and to the Exchequer Court in particular.[282] There was, however, normally no jury involved in the proceedings of this court, which was held as often as occasion requires' at Peel, Douglas and Castletown.[283] This 'Circuit of the Countrey' was roughly maintained, although some meetings were held elsewhere. Ellanbane, Lezayre, the home of William Standish, a member of the Keys, provided the setting for an Exchequer Court in November 1647, and, in July 1651, the court met at the house of Phillip Corlett of Ballakoig, Ballaugh.[284]

f) The Sheading Courts

The sheading courts, or courts of common law, were, as their name implies, originally held in each sheading in the island.[285] By the seventeenth century, however, the courts had come to be held in only three places: at Peel, for Glenfaba, Michael and Ayre; at Douglas, for Garff; and at Castletown for Middle and Rushen. The courts were held twice a year and commenced within a fortnight of May Day and Michaelmas (September 29). They lasted for two calendar weeks, two days being devoted to each sheading in turn.[286] The governor, officers and the deemsters might all be present at the sheading courts 'but for the continuance in Court of the governor, Receiver, Comptroller and waterbayliffe is not soe requisite, but only for the deemsters and Attorney with the Clerke of the Court.'[287] All tenants of the Lord who paid 6d. in rent or more were required to attend on pain of fine at the governor's discretion.[288]

Once the court had been ceremonially fenced by the chief moar of

[281] Cl.R.O., Nantlys MS D/NA/905, 44.

[282] ibid., 46. See, for example, Lib. Scacc. 1641, 39–44. On juries of indictment and slander, see infra, pp. 47, 72–3.

[283] Sherwood, Constitution, pp. 36, 103; Chaloner, Treatise, p. 42.

[284] Lib. Scacc. 1647, 72; Lib. Scacc. 1651, 35.

[285] Craine, Manannan's Isle, p. 95.

[286] Chaloner, Treatise, pp. 31–2; Cl.R.O., Nantlys MS D/NA/905, 44.

[287] Cl.R.O., Nantlys MS D/NA/905, 27.

[288] Statutes, p. 51.

the sheading,[289] the moar of each parish summoned men – two from Jurby, six from Michael, Patrick and German, and four from the other parishes – to serve as the Great Enquest of the sheading.[290] The coroners and moars then presented any bloodwipes, or assaults involving the drawing of blood, within their jurisdiction. If there were any question about the incident, for sometimes 'the partie will in some manner scratt him or herself or by some other meanes bring forth some blood, out of meere malice to give losse to the other,' a jury was appointed 'to take the oath of the person accused to cleare himself if hee can' and to investigate the matter.[291]

These courts, 'in nature of a Court-Baron,' had jurisdiction over all suits between parties, unless removed by agreement of both sides to a court of a higher authority. Cases relating to real property were heard by a jury of six men from the sheading in which the disputed lands lay. Personal suits were dealt with by a jury of four men of the parish where the defendant lived.[292] In both types of case, witnesses were examined out of court and the jury's verdict was delivered at the next meeting of the court or, if expedient, to the deemster. Actions for breach of covenants and 'some tymes smaller accons upon the earnest request of [the] plaintiff or deffendant' were also heard by the sheading jury.

The verdict of the jury could only be implemented with the consent of both parties. If either felt aggrieved, he could apply to the clerk of the rolls, 'traverse' the verdict, and obtain a further trial, although no new evidence would be admitted. In real actions, the second jury was composed of twelve men; in personal suits, there was a jury of six. Further appeal was possible to the Keys, who could confirm, amend or reverse the verdict. If the Keys found just cause, they could also condemn the jurors to be fined.[293]

---

[289] The chief moars were those of German in Glenfaba; Michael in Michael; Lezayre in Ayre; Conchan in Garff; Braddan in Middle; and Malew in Rushen. Cl.R.O., Nantlys MS D/NA/905, 27.

[290] ibid., 27–8. The duties of the Great Enquest are discussed infra, p. 70.

[291] ibid., 29; Moore, History, vol. ii, p. 752 and n. 3.

[292] Chaloner, Treatise, pp. 33–4; Sherwood, Constitution, pp. 38, 104; Cl.R.O., Nantlys MS D/NA/905, 29–30, 34.

[293] Sherwood, Constitution, pp. 38–40, 104–5; Cl.R.O., Nantlys MS D/NA/905, 32–3. It was also possible, by petition to the Lord, to obtain trial of title by the Keys in the first instance, although this was 'not accounted soe legall and formal, and sutable to the lawes of this Isle'. ibid., 35.

g) The Sheading Court: The Great Enquest

After the completion of common law business, the sheading court sat as a sort of manorial court for the same area. The Great Enquest, or *Bing Vooar*, which was composed of twelve men drawn from the constituent parishes of the sheading, was responsible for making presentments concerning 'manorial' matters and was sworn in by one of the deemsters to serve for a period of six months. The main duties of the Great Enquest were set out in the charge delivered to the jury by the deemster. They were to report the presence of any outlaws or exiled felons who had returned to the island, to ensure that all 'petty Officers,' including the coroners, moars, forester, waterbailiff and their deputies, carried out their duty and to take care that foreign pedlars and chapmen 'go no further than to the next Parish Church unto the Haven wherein they doe land' before informing the governor or deputy of their business. Presentments were returned to the deemster as required or at the next Court of General Gaol Delivery.[294]

The Enquest was also to try all questions concerning pathways, watercourses and boundaries. In April 1624, for example, when Emma Stevenson sent her horses with 'Carre and Carriag' from Balladoole, Arbory, to the Calf and back, she was 'stobbed the way' by Robert Carran and Henry Corrin. She procured both the governor's token and the deemster's token for the Great Enquest of Rushen to appear 'for the fyndinge out the ancient and accustomed way.' In cases such as this, the Enquest was accompanied to the place in question by the coroner, lockman or both.[295]

h) The Sheading Court: The Setting Quest

The Setting Quest was the other jury associated with the 'manorial' court. Each parish had such a Quest, composed of four of the Lord's tenants who might serve for several years at a time, although the moar for the preceding year was always included in their number.[296]

---

[294] Craine, *Manannan's Isle*, p. 149; M.M.L., MS 510C, Quayle, *Book of Precedents*, p. 88; *Statutes*, pp. 53–5; Sherwood, *Constitution*, pp. 48–9, 105, 133, 149. On the jurisdiction of manorial courts in general, see S. and B. Webb, *English Local Government from the Revolution to the Municipal Corporations Act. The Manor and the Borough* (1908), pt. i, ch. 1.

[295] Lib. Scacc. 1624, 47.

[296] Sherwood, *Constitution*, pp. 49, 149; Moore, *History*, vol. ii, p. 902.

The main duty of the Setting Quest was to assist the governor, officers and deemsters in finding a suitable new tenant whenever a tenement fell vacant through death or alienation. No person was to be 'put upon the said rentals or Court Rolls, but such as have a good title to the same, either by tenant-right, purchase, will or otherwise.' As an incentive to the Quest to be diligent and to guarantee the regular collection of the Lord's rent, the jurors were made liable for the rent of new tenants who proved to be insolvent.[297] The Setting Quest also divided joint estates between parties and apportioned rents.[298] In 1691, the Setting Quest of Ballaugh partitioned one of the quarterlands in the treen[299] of Carmodil between Hugh and Donald Craine, dividing it into four parts.[300] The names of all new tenants were entered at the sessions of the courts held in May each year.[301]

i) The Barons' Courts

Each of the four principal baronies in the island – the bishop's barony, the barony of the former abbot of Rushen, the barony of Bangor and Sabal and the barony of St Trinian's – had its own courts of common law and criminal justice.[302] These courts had a strictly limited jurisdiction. An offence committed by a baron's tenant on the Lord's land was dealt with by a jury of indictment consisting of three baron's tenants and the same number of Lord's tenants and was tried in the Lord's court. The baron's steward did, however, have the right to demand that a prisoner indicted of felony in such circumstances appear in the baronial court before a 'grand Enquest for life and Death,' composed of twelve tenants of the barony. Although if convicted the felon might forfeit his lands and goods to the baron, 'his life is at the pleasure of the lord of the Isle.' Matters arising

[297] Moore, *History*, vol. ii, pp. 902–3.
[298] Sherwood, *Constitution*, pp. 49, 73–4.
[299] The Lord's land in each parish was divided into treens and subdivided into quarterlands. For further details of these divisions, see chapter 2, pp. 84–5.
[300] Lib. Scacc. 1691, 18.
[301] Cl.R.O., Nantlys MS D/NA/905, 31.
[302] Sherwood, *Constitution*, pp. 33 and n. 9, 40 n. 21, 41. The number of customary tenants in Christian's barony, or the barony of the Hough, in Maughold, formerly the property of the priory of St Bees, was too small to form a Setting Quest and, consequently, no court was held there.

within the baronies concerning debt, trespass, defamation and other causes not relating to the baron were heard in the Lord's courts, which had superior jurisdiction.[303] The barons' courts were held twice a year, after the Lord's courts had finished sitting, and were presided over by the proprietor, or more often his steward, with the assistance of a deemster, the comptroller and clerk of the rolls and the attorney general.[304]

j) The Debt Court

The barons had 'no voyces nor hand in the assessment of the Fines' in their courts. This duty was undertaken by the governor and the officers at the Debt Court, which sat after the Court of General Gaol Delivery at Michaelmas and assessed and levied the fines from all the temporal courts for the preceding year. The barons received the fines from their courts so long as the offenders only held land in the barony in question and had been born and lived their lives in that place. In all other cases, the Lord received the fines.[305]

k) The Deemster's Court

Courts of general jurisdiction were held separately for the North- and Southsides of the island in which the deemsters sat individually as judges. The deemster's court was held more frequently than most courts – at least once a week, and sometimes more often – and probably dealt with more business, albeit of a petty nature, than any of the other courts.[306] The deemster had the authority to deal summarily with a wide range of matters, without the necessity of calling a jury, according to the Breast Laws, or ancient common law of the island.[307] His jurisdiction embraced that of the common law courts, unless trial by jury or a higher court was requested by the parties involved in a case, and that of the criminal courts where a specific penalty was indicated by law. In cases needing a swift decision, the deemster could impanel a jury of six men, receive their verdict and order implementation of the judgement. When the offender was left to be punished at discretion, it fell to the governor and Council to

---

[303] Cl.R.O., Nantlys MS D/NA/905, 25.
[304] Moore, *History*, vol. ii, p. 755.
[305] Chaloner, *Treatise*, p. 41.
[306] Sherwood, *Constitution*, pp. 42, 107.
[307] *ibid*.

impose a fine or to have the malefactor tried at the Court of General Gaol Delivery.[308] The deemster was at liberty to summon juries of indictment, of inquiry and of trespass. The latter two were both composed of four men of the parish in which the incident had occurred and were called, respectively, to investigate reports of lost property and to examine and establish the extent of damage done by trespass.[309]

The deemster usually held his court at his own home. In 1661, Ewan Curghey, coroner of Ayre charged William Sayle to appear before Deemster John Christian at Milntown; Sayle failed to present himself at the deemster's residence and was accordingly fined 12d.[310] Sometimes, however, it seems that the deemster's court was conducted in 'petty ale houses.'[311]

l) The Admiralty Court

The waterbailiff sat as a judge in the Admiralty Court of the island which had jurisdiction over all maritime matters, apart from felonies, between the high water mark and a point three leagues from the shore.[312] Juries of six men, who were generally merchants and mariners, were impanelled at the waterbailiff's direction to assist him in arriving at a judgement in such cases.[313] The court met at a location which was most convenient for the matter in hand. After Thomas Kelly lost a pan belonging to a Mr Lowcay during the coastal voyage from Castletown to Douglas, a jury was called at Douglas in January 1661 to determine the responsibility for the loss.[314] An Admiral Quest, sworn in to present 'all offenders as any wise should be found guiltie upon proofe in relacon to this yeares herring ffishing on this side of the Island (viz the North side),' met probably at Peel in September in the same year.[315] When the jury had reached a decision,

---

[308] *ibid.*, pp. 42–3, 107.

[309] *ibid.*, pp. 43, 49, 107–8; Moore, *History*, vol. ii, p. 754 n. 5.

[310] Lib. Scacc. 1661, 47.

[311] R. Moore, 'The Deemsters and the Manx Courts of Law', *J.M.M.*, vol. vi (1957–65), p. 157.

[312] Sherwood, *Constitution*, pp. 43–4, 75, 85, 108–9; Chaloner, *Treatise*, p. 50.

[313] Sherwood, *Constitution*, p. 44.

[314] Unpublished document no. 39, *J.M.M.*, vol. ii (1930–4), p. 73.

[315] Lib. Scacc. 1662, inter 60–1.

the verdict of the Admiral Quest was either implemented by the waterbailiff or referred to the governor.[316]

The system of government which evolved in the Isle of Man was a product of the successive influences of the Norse, in particular, and of the English and was a reflection of the island's institutional independence from the rest of the British Isles. Its resemblance to national government in England is thus not so surprising, although, given the size of the island, its elaborate nature may seem remarkable. This complexity may, however, have sprung from the necessity to set the administration of the island on a firm base because of the fact that the Lord was normally absent. Officers and courts consequently had specific duties which were aimed at guaranteeing the collection of the Lord's rents and dues and maintaining order in the island. The principal offices of the island's government, and particularly that of governor, were, therefore, positions of considerable importance and were a useful medium of patronage for the earl of Derby, who could reward his servants – mainly Englishmen – by appointing them to a post in the island. Few Manxmen were chosen to serve as governor under the Stanleys, but members of prominent native families and families of English origin were regularly appointed as deemsters, to posts in the Council or to the Keys. The involvement of many of the more influential men in island society in government at this level or as sheading or parish officers helped to dissipate tensions among this group and, in theory, to make the administration more effective. Precisely how effective the government of the island was, however, it is not easy to determine. If the regular, and generally fairly complete, collection of the Lord's rents and the apparently very limited extent of popular unrest in the seventeenth century can be used as any indication, it is difficult to see the island's administration as anything other than comparatively efficient.

[316] Sherwood, *Constitution*, pp. 44, 109; Unpublished document no. 39, *J.M.M.*, vol. ii (1930–4), p. 73.

2 *Agriculture and Fisheries*

Since A. W. Moore published his detailed *History of the Isle of Man* in 1900, little work has been done on the Manx economy in the sixteenth and seventeenth centuries. This lack of attention has been in part due to the standard of Moore's pioneering contribution in the field.[1] It has also been the result of the small size and relative isolation of the Isle of Man from the adjacent countries, in physical, economic and constitutional terms. Economic historians, more concerned with developments elsewhere in the British Isles, have paid scant attention to the island during this period, only occasionally noting in passing the small scale of Manx trade, while historical geographers have been concerned with either the period down to 1266 or the Manx economy in the late nineteenth and twentieth centuries.[2] Further work on the early modern period may have been discouraged by the apparent scarcity of primary source material, an impression reinforced by Moore himself. Research in the Manx archives and elsewhere, utilising documents unknown to or little used by Moore, has, however, produced a more detailed and convincing picture of the island's economy in the sixteenth and seventeenth centuries. The most important source of information in this respect has been the almost unbroken series of waterbailiff's accounts or customs books for the island, which commences in 1576. Despite the limitations inherent in such material,[3] it provides a wealth of information, not only about the structure and organisation of Manx trade,

---

[1] See Moore, *History*, vol. i, pp. 281–340 for the period 1405–1660 and pp. 392–460 for the period 1660–1765.
[2] See, for example, D. M. Woodward, *The Trade of Elizabethan Chester* (Hull, 1970), pp. 35–6; T. C. Smout, 'The Foreign Trade of Dumfries and Kirkcudbright, 1672–1696', *T.D.G.N.H.A.S.*, 3rd series, vol. xxxvii (1960), pp. 41–2; R. H. Kinvig, 'The Isle of Man and Atlantic Britain: A Study in Historical Geography', *T.I.B.G.*, no. xxv (1958), pp. 1–29; J. W. Birch, *The Isle of Man: A Study in Economic Geography* (Cambridge, 1964).
[3] The problems in using the waterbailiff's accounts are discussed in chapter 5, pp. 244–46.

but also about Manx agriculture and the limited amount of manufacturing in the island.

Throughout the early modern period, economic activity in the Isle of Man was generally conducted at a level only slightly above that of subsistence. The principal concern of the Lord, his officers and the inhabitants themselves was to produce enough food to feed the population and, in a less than perfect environment such as prevailed in the Isle of Man, this was often a struggle. Consequently, almost the entire Manx population was engaged in farming to a greater or lesser extent, growing crops and raising cattle and sheep for consumption on the farm, the type of farming depending on the location and size of the holding. Together with the annual herring fishery, agriculture was the foundation of the Manx economy and a great deal depended on the size of the catch and the success or failure of the harvest. If either or, worse still, both failed for several years in succession, the result for the Manx was considerable hardship, as in the late 1640s, although starvation seems always to have been averted. Whenever there was a surplus of grain or fish, it could be exported, together with animals, skins and other primary products, in return for raw materials in which the island was deficient and manufactured goods which could not be readily produced in the island. In essence, therefore, the economy of the Isle of Man was colonial in nature, relying on the export of primary products in exchange for goods produced by skilled craftsmen in more industrially advanced regions, such as south Lancashire. Such manufacturing as there was in the island was purely directed towards immediate local needs and it was not until the end of the seventeenth century that any attempts were made to establish 'industries' for wider markets.[4] It was at about the same time that trade, which had always supplied the basic deficiencies of the island, began to increase markedly and the Lord's income from customs duties to rise in proportion, though this was more the result of a desire among merchants to circumvent the higher English tariffs than of a plan to encourage trade with the Isle of Man.[5] Trade and manufactures became more significant after 1700, but, both before and after that date, agriculture and herring fishing were the dominant areas of the Manx economy.

---

[4] For details of these projects, see chapter 3, pp. 175–88.
[5] Overseas trade is discussed in chapter 5.

I. AGRICULTURE

a) Relief, climate and soils

The type of farming undertaken in the Isle of Man was determined mainly by the island's topography, the climate and the nature of the soil. Physically, the Isle of Man can be divided into three regions. (Map 3). The upland or mountain region comprises all land above approximately 600 feet, a large proportion of which lies above 1,000 feet. The watershed runs from north-east to south-west through this region, following a series of relatively high mountains, from North Barrule (1,860 feet), via Snaefell (2,034 feet), the highest point in the island, to South Barrule (1,585 feet). It also served as a dividing line for administrative purposes, separating the island into Northside and Southside. This upland region naturally has the highest rainfall and the thinnest and poorest soils.[6]

The plateaux flanking the uplands constitute the second physical region, and lie between about 100 feet and 600 feet above sea level. Together with the lowland region, the plateaux comprise the land normally utilised for cultivation. The quality of the soils varies considerably from place to place on the plateaux, permitting or preventing a range of farming activity.

The lowland region consists of three distinct areas. The northern lowland stretches from the foot of the northern uplands to the Ayres, a band of shingle ridges and sand dunes along the northern coast.[7] In the seventeenth century, three marshy lakes, named by Speed as 'Balalough' in Ballaugh and Jurby, 'Lough' in Andreas and 'Malarlough' in Lezayre, occupied the lowest parts of this lowland area, which are generally known as the Curraghs.[8] Work on the drainage

---

[6] T. W. Freeman, H. B. Rodgers and R. H. Kinvig, *Lancashire, Cheshire and the Isle of Man* (1966), pp. 252, 259; N. Pye and E. Davies, *The Land of Britain. Report of the Land Utilisation Survey of Britain, part xliv: The Isle of Man.* (1941), pp. 4–5, 9.

[7] Freeman, Rodgers and Kinvig, *Lancashire, Cheshire and the Isle of Man*, p. 260; Pye and Davies, *Isle of Man*, p. 7.

[8] John Speed's map of 1605, based on a survey by Thomas Durham in 1595 is reproduced in A. M. Cubbon, *Early Maps of the Isle of Man* (Douglas 1974), pp. 24–5 and N. Nicolson and A. Hawkyard, *The Counties of Britain. A Tudor Atlas by John Speed* (1988), pp. 210–11. 'Malarlough' in Lezayre was also known as 'Mirescogh.' Oliver, *Monumenta*, vol. iii, p. 30.

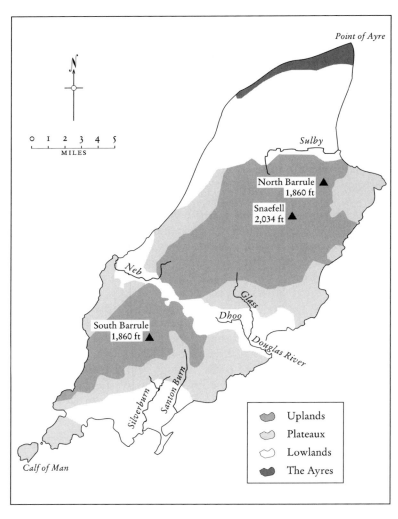

Map 3. Physical regions of the Isle of Man.

of these poorly drained areas apparently began in earnest in about 1650, following a meeting of the governor, officers and the Great Enquest of Michael in May 1648 'to view and consider of some convenient remedie and redresse for the drayning of the waters from the corraghlands.'[9] The long term result, completed before about 1700, was the cutting of the Lhen trench to the coast to the west of Blue Point in Andreas.[10] The central lowland area occupies the valley stretching from Peel in the west to Douglas in the east, cutting the upland region into two parts. Portions of this valley were poorly drained in the seventeenth century, particularly near Greeba. The southern lowland region lies in general below 100 feet in the parishes of Santan, Malew, Arbory and Rushen. The area around Castletown, mainly drained by the Silverburn, has a relatively low rainfall and soils of good quality which offer the best farmland for cultivation in the island.[11]

The climate of the island is distinguished by the lack of extremes in temperature and a generally heavy rainfall. Summer temperatures are relatively low, while winters are usually mild. In the late 1640s, William Blundell recorded that 'the air of this island is both sharp and cold in the winter months,' though he went on to say that it was 'much more mild than in Wales.'[12] Several years later, James Chaloner reported 'Frosts short and seldome,' and added that 'Snow in the Valleys by reason of its Vicinity to the Sea, will soon dissolve.'[13] Snowfalls, which are rarely heavy, occur only infrequently. No contemporary observer remarked on the island's rainfall in the seventeenth century, perhaps because it was not markedly different from that of northern England. In fact, the Lancashire plain, on which William Blundell normally resided at Crosby, received only slightly less rainfall on average than did the Isle of Man.[14]

Both Chaloner and William Sacheverell, the latter writing in the late seventeenth century, commented on the 'extraordinary high

[9] Lib. Scacc. 1648, 34.
[10] Moore, *History*, vol. ii, p. 921; Sacheverell, *Account*, p. 12.
[11] Freeman, Rodgers and Kinvig, *Lancashire, Cheshire and the Isle of Man*, pp. 252, 260–1; Pye and Davies, *Isle of Man*, pp. 5, 7–9.
[12] Blundell, *History*, vol. i, p. 40.
[13] Chaloner, *Treatise*, p. 8.
[14] Freeman, Rodgers and Kinvig, *Lancashire, Cheshire and the Isle of Man*, p. 23; Pye and Davies, *Isle of Man*, p. 11, fig. 4.

Winds' to which the island was subjected.[15] The almost complete absence of woodland noted by contemporary writers has sometimes been ascribed to the strength and frequency of such winds, but it is clear from medieval sources and from archaeological evidence that woodland existed in the island at least in the late eleventh century and that its removal was the result of human activity.[16] Blundell estimated that there 'hath been no woods in Man this 140 years past,' that is, since about 1500, and stated that he 'could not observe one tree to be in any place but what grew in gardens.'[17]

The relatively cool, damp and frequently windy nature of the climate therefore placed certain limitations on farming activity in the Isle of Man. On account of its small size – approximately 220 square miles – climatic variations within the island are minor, being in the main the result of differences in the height of land above sea level.[18] Even on the best land, however, it was, and is, difficult to produce a good crop of wheat because of the unfavourable climate.

---

[15] Chaloner, *Treatise*, p. 8; Sacheverell, *Account*, p. 11.

[16] Freeman, Rodgers and Kinvig, *Lancashire, Cheshire and the Isle of Man*, pp. 256–7. Before the battle of Skyhill, near Ramsey, in 1079, Godred Crovan concealed 300 men in a wood. G. Broderick ed., *Chronicle of the King of Mann and the Isles* (Edinburgh 1973), pp. 6, 61. Woodland also existed in the south of the island, although it may have been cleared at an earlier date. G. Bersu, 'Celtic Homesteads in the Isle of Man', *J.M.M.*, vol. v (1942–6), p. 181. Much of the woodland had consisted of oak trees, and Chaloner, Sacheverell and an anonymous writer in the 1660s all refer to the extraction of oaks from the Curraghs. Chaloner, *Treatise*, pp. 7–8; Sacheverell, *Account*, p. 14; Cl.R.O., Nantlys D/NA/905, 8. The shortage of timber for fuel, building and other purposes encouraged those unable or unwilling to buy imported wood to cut down the remaining woodland, which probably survived in the valleys. The Council and Keys passed a law to combat this problem in 1629 by which any man found cutting down 'Trees, Plaints of Trees or Quicksetts' was to be fined 10s. or 'whipped throughout all the Markett Towns of this Isle'. *Statutes*, p. 82. Little positive action appears to have been taken to remedy the situation, although Chaloner noticed 'the Plantations, which some few have made about their houses, as well of Fruit-trees as others'. Chaloner, *Treatise*, p. 8. In 1667, a further law was passed which stipulated that those cutting down or damaging trees were to plant five trees for the first such offence, ten for the second, and suffer fine, imprisonment or corporal punishment for the third. *Statutes*, pp. 133–4.

[17] Blundell, *History*, vol. i, p. 47.

[18] Pye and Davies, *Isle of Man*, p. 9.

Barley and oats are better suited to Manx conditions and these have consequently long been the most important cereal crops. The heavy rainfall of the upland region, which was mainly intack and common land, rendered it suitable only for sheep farming.

In the plateau and lowland areas, the type of farming activity was more closely determined by the quality of the soil. As has already been suggested, there is a considerable diversity of soil types. The plateaux and the bottom of the central valley are covered by slatey soils of varying depth and quality and the latter also contained areas of peat bog. Sacheverell described the northern lowland as 'poor gravel and sand' in the west and as 'a large tract of meadow called the Curragh' in the east.[19] In general, the soils of the northern lowland range from sandy loams to poorer gravels, with some patches of boulder clay and peat bog, the latter being in the Curraghs. The southern lowland has soils of similar type to those of the north, but those in the Castlerown-Ballasalla area, partly derived from the underlying limestone, are of better quality.[20]

Although there is little documentary evidence directly related to land use, it seems clear that Manx agriculture in the sixteenth and seventeenth centuries was pastoral in nature, involving subsistence corn growing and the rearing of animals, and that this farming activity was dictated solely by physical factors. Social and economic changes, such as those brought about by the rise in population in England in the century after *circa* 1540 and by the Dissolution of the Monasteries, seem to have had little, if any, effect in the island. When Rushen Abbey was dissolved in 1540, its lands were not sold off to speculators, eager to make a profit from the increasing demand for food in England or from wool. Instead, the abbey lands were ultimately leased *en bloc* by Elizabeth I, initially to Robert Ashton in 1565 and subsequently, in 1582, to Henry, fourth earl of Derby.[21] The abbey tenants continued to farm their lands, to pay their rents to the steward, and to attend the abbey court. The change in landlord occasioned by the Dissolution had not brought any noticeable change in agriculture, as might well have occurred in

[19] Sacheverell, *Account*, p. 12.
[20] Pye and Davies, *Isle of Man*, pp. 8–9; Freeman, Rodgers and Kinvig, *Lancashire, Cheshire and the Isle of Man*, pp. 254–6, 259–61.
[21] J. Gell ed., *An Abstract of the Laws, Customs and Ordinances of the Isle of Man, by John Parr*, vol. i [notes], Manx Society, vol. xii (1867), p. 57.

England, probably because of the perceived isolation of the island, its political separation from England and its unfavourable climate.

It is, in any event, unlikely that Manx agriculture could have responded to an external stimulus, such as the increased demand for food in England, since seventeenth century observers found farming techniques in the island somewhat backward.[22] According to Blundell, Governor John Greenhalgh encouraged the use of marl during the 1640s to improve arable land, 'which was never there put in practice before;' Blundell also believed that 'if the natives knew the preparation of sea-weed, whereof they have plenty,' the land could produce much higher yields of crops.[23] Marling could, however, prove to be both a difficult and an expensive undertaking, beyond the means of many, if not probably most, Manx farmers. Sacheverell noted that 'in many parts of the country there is marle; but the people have not the skill or the purses to lay it on their grounds'.[24] By the end of the century, perhaps as a result of the advice proffered by Blundell, sea weed was being used to improve the fertility of the soil, but only by those farmers who could afford to purchase it.[25] In general, soil fertility was maintained by the traditional, if relatively inefficient, practice of folding the animals on the land.[26] Conservative farming methods persisted as much from the poverty of the farmers as from any unwillingness to change.

If the impact of mainly external social and economic change on Manx agriculture was negligible, the effect of political action by the English and Manx governments was sometimes more significant. In the face of complaints from landlords in southern England, who blamed the decline in rents for their pastures on cattle imported from

[22] For further details of farming practices, see *infra*, pp. 105–9.

[23] Blundell, *History*, vol. i, p. 40.

[24] Sacheverell, *Account*, p. 12.

[25] *ibid.* In May 1683, Governor Robert Heywood, on behalf of William, ninth earl of Derby, leased the 'wrack and tang growing on the shores of this Island' to Michael Thorp of Workington. The lease ran for seven years from Michaelmas 1683 at an annual rent of 25s. 'Unpublished Document no. 148', *J.M.M.*, vol. iii (1935–7), pp. 79–80.

[26] Cl.R.O., Nantlys MS D/NA/905, 3; *Statutes*, p. 14; Moore, *History*, vol. ii, p. 921. For contemporary practices of manuring in England and Wales, see J. Thirsk, 'Farming Techniques, 1500–1640', in *idem* ed., *Agricultural Change: Policy and Practice, 1500–1750* (Cambridge, 1990), pp. 21–2.

Ireland, legislation was introduced in the form of the Cattle Acts of 1663 and 1666, which prohibited the importation into England of Irish beasts.[27] In the second of these Acts, provision was made for importing Manx cattle, but these were to be of the native breed only and numbers were limited to 600 a year. Moore believed that this had a considerable effect on Manx trade and, by extension, on Manx agriculture, but the effects of the Cattle Acts may not have been quite as severe as he suggested. Although there seems to have been a fall in cattle exports from the island in the mid-1660s, this was not entirely due to this legislation; in fact, in the years before 1660, shipments of cattle from Man to England rarely, if ever, reached the limit imposed by the second Cattle Act. Nevertheless, merchants faced some difficulties when landing Manx cattle in England as a result of this legislation.[28] English government action did not always attempt to control or exclude Manx commodities. In 1676, the English government allowed the importation of Manx corn at a time when prices had been generally much lower than average for a decade.[29] This, too, probably had only a limited effect in the island, since exports of grain in the late 1670s and 1680s remained at a low level by comparison with the amounts transported in the early seventeenth century.[30]

The island's government only took action on one occasion before 1700 to influence farming activity. In an effort to increase the island's prosperity, an Act was passed at the Tynwald Court in 1692 'for setting up a Linnen manufacture.' This Act required that all tenants should plant some flax or hemp; those occupying the better land were directed to plant half an acre, while those holding intacks were answerable for one-twelfth of an acre.[31] It seems that this scheme met with some success, though only in the long term and only with continued, official encouragement.[32]

---

[27] 15 Chas. II, c. 7 and 18 Chas. II, c. 2.
[28] Moore, *History*, vol. i, pp. 417–18. For further details of the effects of the Cattle Acts, see chapter 5, pp. 253–58.
[29] 25 Chas. II, c. 7; W. G. Hoskins, 'Harvest Fluctuations and English Economic History, 1620–1759', *Ag.H.R.*, vol. xvi (1968), appendix i, p. 29.
[30] Exports of grain from the island are discussed in chapter 5, pp. 266–68. See also Table 5.4.
[31] M.M.L., MD/401/1719/8. This Act does not appear in the official *Statutes*.
[32] Moore, *History*, vol. ii, pp. 590–1.

b) System of land holding and farming regions

An examination of the system of landholding in the Isle of Man makes it possible to distinguish, roughly, three farming regions, broadly similar in extent to the physical regions already described, each of which displays characteristics of different types of pastoral economy.

Within each parish, from an early date, possibly before the arrival of the Norsemen in the island in the late eighth century, the land on the plateaux and in the lowlands was divided into units of varying size known as *treens*. Although the origin of these divisions is not certain, it has been plausibly argued that treens represent the areas cultivated by individual families or groups and, accordingly, constituted the better, more readily worked land.[33] The number of treens in each parish varied from five in Jurby to sixteen in Andreas, but this variation bore no apparent relation either to the size of the parish or to the fertility of the soil. Santan, one of the smaller parishes, contained nine treens, whereas the largest parish in the island, Lezayre, had only eight. Near the margins of cultivation, in the higher reaches of the plateaux and in the valleys, the treens were, perhaps surprisingly, generally smaller than in the more fertile lowlands. Treens ranged in area from as little as 48 acres to as much as 970 acres, but in the main covered between 200 and 500 acres.[34] These units were used by the Norse for fiscal purposes and this function was continued throughout the period of Stanley rule in the island (1406–1736), when the treen served as part of the basic structure for the collection of the Lord's rent.[35]

Treens were subdivided into units called *quarterlands*, which formed the principal units of landholding from at least the fourteenth century, and probably from long before that time.[36] In

---

[33] Kinvig, 'Isle of Man and Atlantic Britain', p. 19.

[34] C. J. S. Marstrander, 'Treen og Keeill', *Norsk Tidsskrift for Sprogvidenskap*, vol. viii (1937), pp. 288, 289–90; E. Davies, 'Treens and Quarterlands. A Study in the Land System of the Isle of Man', *T.I.B.G.*, no. xxii (1957), p. 105. Marstrander considered that Andreas contained seventeen treens, but, since 'Balynessar' and 'kyrke Asston' are listed as one treen in the earliest records of the Lord's rent, it seems more appropriate to take the total as sixteen. T. Talbot ed., *The Manorial Roll of the Isle of Man, 1511–1515* (Oxford, 1924), p. 75.

[35] Marstrander, 'Treen og Keeill', p. 288.

[36] Fragments of the so-called 'manorial roll', more accurately the setting books or *Libri Assedationis*, compiled between 1490 and 1505, are extant

theory, each treen contained four quarterlands, as the term implies, and, in practice, nearly half of the 178 treens conformed to this pattern. Some treens, however, contained only half a quarterland, while others comprised as many as seven.[37] Like treens, quarterlands varied in size and such variations were unrelated to the size of the parish, differences in site or the quality of the soil. The average quarterland covered about 90 acres, with the majority being in the range from 50 to 80 acres.[38] Many quarterlands were in turn divided into smaller holdings, but all these farms were identified by the quarterland name, which was most often composed of the word *Balley* or *Balla* [farm] and the family name of the original or principal holder of the quarterland.[39] On the lands formerly belonging to Rushen Abbey and in the baronies,[40] the quarterlands were the only divisions of farm land since there was no treen organisation in these areas.[41] Both there and on the Lord's lands, some of the largest farms comprised several quarterlands, such as Ballafletcher in the bishop's barony lands in Braddan, Kentraugh in Rushen and Milntown in Lezayre.

The area occupied by treens and quarterlands generally lay below 600 feet, the level which marks the upper limit of arable cultivation

and display the same arrangement by treen as the published 'rolls' of 1511 (Northside) and 1515 (Southside). Although the quarterland farms are not regularly named in these records until 1703, it is clear that some of the holdings had long existed as separate farms. One branch of the Stevenson family held half of the treen of Balladoole, Arbory – that is, three quarterlands – from some time in the early fourteenth century, and probably from before that date. M. Crellin, 'An Early Manorial Roll', *J.M.M.*, vol. vii (1966–76), pp. 98–9, plates 28 and 29; Cl.R.O., Nantlys MS D/NA/905, 1; W. Cubbon ed., 'An Important Balladoole Document', *J.M.M.*, vol. ii (1930–4), pp. 168–9; Talbot, *Manorial Roll*, p. 7.
[37] Davies, 'Treens and Quarterlands', p. 107; Marstrander, 'Treen og Keeill', pp. 291–300.
[38] Davies, 'Treens and Quarterlands', p. 109.
[39] J. J. Kneen, *The Place Names of the Isle of Man* (Douglas, 1925–8, reprinted Ilkley, 1970), *passim*; Davies, 'Treens and Quarterlands', pp. 109–10.
[40] The baronies are discussed in chapter 1, p. 19, n. 31.
[41] Although treens had little significance for agricultural purposes by the seventeenth century, quarterlands were still grouped by treen for the collection of rent. On abbey and barony lands, holdings were listed by property or tenant. Talbot, *Manorial Roll*, *passim* and appendices F–J.

in the adjacent parts of England, Wales and Scotland.[42] In this region of plateau and lowland, where soils permitted, the barley and oats were grown which fed the inhabitants and which, in years of above average harvests, might yield a surplus for export. Where the land was better suited to pasture, cattle were fattened for domestic consumption and, to a certain extent, for foreign markets.[43]

The second farming region comprised the marginal lands or intacks. These lay above the treens and quarterlands, between about 750 and 1,000 feet above sea level and also in the Curraghs, the poorly drained bottoms of the valleys or glens and in some parts of the plateaux. Intacking was well established before the end of the sixteenth century, as can be seen from the records of the Lord's rentals of that date, and it continued throughout the Stanley period.[44] Many intacks were enclosed as easements to quarterlands and such 'intacks of ease' lay either adjacent to, or near, the quarterland to which they were attached. Other intacks, such as those in the Curraghs, were completely separate holdings. In both cases, however, the procedure for obtaining a licence to enclose from the Lord was the same.[45] Depending on the location and fertility of the intack, these holdings could be used to raise cattle or sheep or, in the best circumstances, to grow crops.

Above the intacks in the upland region, and beyond the *Feldike*, or boundary wall, which marked the upper limit of intacking, lay the commons, which formed the third farming region. All property holders had the right to graze their cattle, horses, pigs and sheep on the mountains on payment of 1½ d. a year to the forester and ½ d. every seven years to the keepers of the 'Lidgates' on the 'Highways to the Forest.'[46] In this region, sheep farming was probably the dominant

[42] Davies, 'Treens and Quarterlands', pp. 104–5.

[43] For details of the island's export trade, see chapter 5.

[44] See, for example, G.R., D/1. This fragment of a setting book, previously thought to date from c. 1520, has been dated to 1495–1500 by Michael Crellin, 'Early Manorial Roll', p. 99. In all probability, it represents part of one of the five such books compiled between 1490 and 1503 and mentioned by an anonymous writer in the 1660s. Cl.R.O., Nantlys MS D/NA/905, 1. Cf. Talbot, *Manorial Roll, passim*.

[45] Davies, 'Treens and Quarterlands', p. 111. The procedure for obtaining permission to enclose a parcel of intack is outlined in R. Sherwood, *Manx Law Tenures* (Douglas, 1899), pp. 20–2. Tenants enclosing common land without licence were presented by the Great Enquest at the sheading courts. See, for example, Lib. Plit. 1577, 26.

[46] *Statutes*, pp. 49, 50, 76.

farming activity since, apart from the demand in the island itself, quantities of wool were exported from Man to foreign markets.[47]

c) Crops and livestock

There is no direct evidence of the nature of Manx agriculture before the later sixteenth century. In 1577, Bishop John Meyrick informed William Camden that the 'Island not only supplies its own wants with its own cattle, fish and corn; but exports great quantities into foreign countreys every year. Yet this plenty is rather to be ascribed to the pains and industry of the natives than to the goodness of the soil.'[48] Despite his somewhat overly optimistic assessment of the size of Manx exports, Meyrick's rudimentary description of the island's agriculture does indicate the basic type of Manx farming as it can be deduced from the physical conditions in the island, namely, pastoral farming, based on cattle rearing, corn growing and sheep keeping. Cattle provided milk, butter and cheese for consumption on the farm and for sale at market, while the barley grown went to make bread and malt for brewing ale. Together with oats, which were made into bread and oatcakes, and fish, especially herring, these were the staples of the Manx diet.[49]

Information derived from the waterbailiff's accounts, whatever its shortcomings, reveals that Bishop Meyrick was correct in identifying some of the most important agricultural products exported from the Isle of Man. Cattle, barley and malt were shipped in quantity in the

---

[47] Sheep farming continued to be important in this region. In the 1790s, Basil Quayle noted that 'Few farmers keep above one hundred, except on the uplands, as [the sheep] are very difficult to prevent from climbing over the fences'. B. Quayle, *General View of the Agriculture of the Isle of Man* (1794), p. 27.

[48] W. Camden, *Britannia*, ed., E. Gibson (1695), p. 1051. The letter from Meyrick to Camden is printed in full in Oliver, *Monumenta*, vol. i, pp. 87–99.

[49] In the early 1650s, Chaloner found that oats was 'the ordinary Bread-corn of the Inhabitants'. Chaloner, *Treatise*, p. 6. Writing nearly thirty years later, Thomas Denton recorded that 'most of the inhabitants eat only oat bread'. Denton, 'Description', pp. 437–8. Barley bread was a staple of the diet for a large part of the population by the end of the eighteenth century, when it was estimated that 'more than half of the arable land was under barley each year'. B. Quayle, *General View*, p. 32.

1590s and afterwards, but the amount of fish transported, being largely dependent on the fortunes of the annual herring fishery, varied considerably.[50] Other items, which were subsequently noted in accounts of Manx farming as the produce of the island, were also exported in the late sixteenth century, including quantities of wool, hides, sheep, pigs, beans, peas and honey.[51]

The large shipments of wheat and horses from the Isle of Man in the early years of the seventeenth century probably represent re-exports rather than the shipment of grain and animals raised in the island. Manx conditions were ill-suited to wheat growing and such wheat as was grown tended to be of poor quality.[52] The type of horse transported from the island is not generally specified, but it seems unlikely that horses of the native Manx breed were exported in any numbers. Blundell believed that in 'enduring labour and hardness, they exceed others,' but he also described them as 'low and little . . . and withal frightfully poor.'[53] By the 1690s, however, some were being exported to England and Ireland, where they were 'much in request . . . to run in gentlemen's carriages.'[54] The island's government endeavoured to improve the quality of horses, stipulating, in 1577, that the inhabitants could only keep stallions worth more than 6s. 8d., and, in 1594, that such stallions must stand at least 'five quarters of a yard,' or eleven hands, in height.[55] These steps seem to have had only limited success, since, at the end of the eighteenth century, Basil Quayle noted that there was 'not due attention paid to the rearing of the live stock in this island, either horses or black cattle.'[56] Some farmers, probably the wealthier sort, purchased instead draught horses imported from Ireland.[57] Many tenants, particularly those on the smaller and upland farms,

---

[50] On the herring fishery, see *infra*, pp. 109–24.
[51] For further details of the island's exports, see chapter 5.
[52] B. Quayle, *General View*, p. 31.
[53] Blundell, *History*, vol. i, pp. 41, 42.
[54] M.M.L., I.O. 1696–1704, Customs book, 1696; B. Quayle, *General View*, p. 25.
[55] *Statutes*, p. 54; M.M.L., MS MD/15,040, J. Parr, *An Abridgement, or A Short Tract of the most usefull Lawes, Acts and Ordinances conteyned in the Statute Book of this Isle of Mann* (1679), p. 83.
[56] B. Quayle, *General View*, p. 25.
[57] *ibid.* These horses may have been used to improve the quality of the stock, but, if so, this was apparently not the practice before c.1800.

continued to rely on the native breed of horse. Many were unable to afford to keep enough horses to form a plough team and joined forces with their neighbours.[58] In such circumstances, it would seem likely that only a small proportion of the horses shipped were of the Manx breed and that a correspondingly large number were re-exported animals.

The most detailed account of Manx agriculture in the seventeenth century is that written by William Blundell after his two visits to the island in 1646 and 1648.[59] It is not certain how long Blundell spent in the island during his self-imposed retirement from the disturbed conditions of civil war in Lancashire, but, though he clearly based some of his work on literary sources and information supplied by some of the inhabitants, he obviously had some opportunity to observe Manx farming at first hand. He found that all 'parts of the Island, as well the north as the south, yieldeth store of all sorts of grain, both barley, wheat, rye, and oats (yet of the last the most), but not only of each satisfying the inhabitants' necessity, but also affording an overplus for exportation unto other parts.'[60] In his estimation, 'the corn of this Island is so purely good as that you shall not find, no, not in England, either better bread or better beer than is here commonly sold.'[61] The island also produced 'good store of flax and hemp; neither is this little bee an idle droan, but affordeth both honey and wax, not only for the use of the inhabitants, but for exportacon also.'[62] The northern part of the island had 'the most healthy [sic] and gravelly ground, much resembling the mountainous parts of Wales' and therefore offering plenty of rough grazing for sheep and cattle.[63] The southern part of the island 'is acknowledged to have good meadow and pasture ground,' but there was apparently 'not much pasture ground' and 'the most and best is in the Earl of Darby's possession, lying in the south part of the island, near unto his castle of Rushin.'[64]

[58] *ibid*; Cl.R.O., Nantlys D/NA/905, 3.
[59] M. Blundell, *Cavalier. Letters of William Blundell to his Friends, 1620–1698* (1933), pp. 19, 32–3.
[60] Blundell, *History*, vol. i, p. 39.
[61] *ibid*.
[62] *ibid*, p. 40.
[63] *ibid*, p. 39.
[64] *ibid*, pp. 39, 40.

Manx cattle were, 'by consequence, little, low, small, and poor (but not in any extremity), resembling those of Ireland, but nothing near our breed of England.'[65] This was due, in Blundell's opinion, to the fact that 'they feed for the most part in heathy ground, lying continually in the open fields both winter and summer, never housed; neither is any hay or fodder given them, but are enforced to feed on what they find.'[66] This included seaweed, which formed part of the feed of the cattle grazing by the coast. Blundell considered that 'those cows that feed on [seaweed] are far fairer, bigger-boddyed, fatter, and yield more milk than those of the inland that have not the same comodity for their saturation, sustenation and nourishment.'[67] As previously noted, he regarded Manx horses as small and rather poor.

On the other hand, Blundell observed that sheep 'thrive best in this Island.' Although Manx sheep were 'not so great of body' as English sheep, they were 'as fat and their flesh as well tasted as our mutton.'[68] Manx wool was 'very good,' but, like the wool produced in the north of England in general, it was coarse and inferior in quality to that of the Cotswolds or Leicestershire.[69] Blundell recorded that the Manx also had 'a little of a certain wool, which I accompt one of the rarities of the island.' This was the wool of the native Manx Loaghtan sheep, which 'far exceeds their other wool in fineness.'[70] The numbers of Loaghtan sheep seem to have been small

[65] *ibid*, pp. 40–1. For a brief survey of the chief English breeds, see Thirsk, 'Farming Techniques', pp. 40–1.
[66] Blundell, *History*, vol. i, p. 41.
[67] *ibid*.
[68] *ibid*, p. 42.
[69] *ibid*, p. 43; P. J. Bowden, *The Wool Trade in Tudor and Stuart England* (1962), p. 29, fig. 2; Thirsk, 'Farming Techniques', p. 44.
[70] Blundell, *History*, vol. i, p. 43. Blundell described the wool as resembling 'the dear colour, inclining to sevill mort', while Denton considered it 'a yellow tawney ffleece'. *ibid*; Denton, 'Description', p. 438. Chaloner more accurately recorded that the wool 'maketh a kind of Sand-colou'd cloth'. Chaloner, *Treatise*, p, 7. Blundell did not recognise the Loaghtan as a separate breed, believing that, since there seemed to be so few, a sheep with such a fleece had eaten a herb which produced the distinctive hue. Blundell, *History*, vol. i, p. 44. He stated that 'the rarity of this wool is very remarkable, for it is [in] no certain place to be found in all the island'. The scarcity of the wool almost certainly made it a desirable commodity, as is reflected by the fact that James, seventh earl of Derby, wore 'an entire suit made of that wool'. *ibid*, p. 43.

in comparison to other breeds,[71] although, according to Blundell, the size of the animal population in general had been exaggerated by Camden and Speed, who both followed the information of Bishop Meyrick. There were no 'mighty flocks of sheep and of other cattle.' There were, however, sufficient numbers to supply the needs of the Manx and to permit the exportation of some livestock, 'but neither of beef or sheep, or any thing else which the Island yieldeth, is there any excessive or superabundant number.'[72]

Blundell also noted that the Manx kept goats, pigs, which he described as 'hoggs of an ordinary grandure,' and poultry, including geese, ducks and hens.[73] Deer belonging to the earl of Derby as Lord of Man grazed in the mountains under the supervision of the forester.[74]

The works written later in the seventeenth century by Chaloner, Denton and Sacheverell add little to the picture of Manx agriculture provided by Blundell. Thomas Denton, of Warnell Hall in Cumberland, who wrote his *Description of the Isle of Man* in about 1681, did, however, record more details about the type of cereals grown. He observed that the Manx grew white oats, which yielded heavy grain, suitable for both bread and pottage, 'in great plenty;' 'their barley is of two sorts, with four rows in the ear, or with two, the latter is the better, whereof they make their best mault, and of it strongest ale, not inferior to Milford ale.'[75] Some efforts had been made to introduce different varieties, but without success, for Denton remarked that *bigg*, the poorest type of barley, was 'a sort of grain which doth not like this soyl.'[76] He found that Manx meadows were 'either benty or full of Rushes,' although 'some by the sides of rivers [were] much better.'[77] In Denton's view, the island 'beareth abundance of fflax and hemp;' Sacheverell, however, disagreed, stating that the 'country

---

[71] It is not clear which other breeds of sheep were present in the island in the seventeenth century, but it is likely that hill sheep from northern England had been introduced at some time in the past. On the different breeds of such sheep, see Thirsk, 'Farming Techniques', p. 43.

[72] Blundell, *History*, vol. i, pp. 42, 44. Blundell estimated that there was one Loaghtan sheep for every 50 or 100 sheep of the other breeds. *ibid*, p. 44.

[73] *ibid*, p. 45.

[74] *ibid*, pp. 45–6, 50–1.

[75] Denton, 'Description', pp. 437, 438; Thirsk, 'Farming Techniques', p. 25.

[76] Denton, 'Description', p. 438; Thirsk, 'Farming Techniques', p. 24.

[77] Denton, 'Description', p. 438.

affords . . . some small quantity of hemp and flax.'[78] Sacheverell noted that 'all sorts of grain' were grown 'in reasonable plenty' and that some farmers, 'the better sort,' were improving their cattle, sheep and horses, 'which are not yet arrived to any great perfection.'[79] He commented on the large number of pigs and was the first observer to mention the native Manx pig, 'a small mountain kind called Purs, which are admirable meat.'[80] Besides the 'small quantities of red Deer in the mountains,' some fallow deer were introduced into the Calf of Man, apparently unsuccessfully, at the end of the seventeenth century by order from the earl of Derby.[81]

d) Harvests

The diversity of Manx agriculture should not obscure the fact that, as in other pre-industrialised economies, the grain harvest was of crucial importance. Evidence for the fluctuations of the Manx harvest is somewhat patchy and is particularly thin for the years when the harvest was good, since the island's government only needed to take action when shortages were likely to occur and contemporary observers considered dearth more noteworthy than plenty. Nevertheless, the steps taken by the authorities and contemporary records form the main, indeed the only, sources of information about the harvests in the island, but necessarily provide only an impressionistic account of the fortunes of Manx agriculture. The details of the prices at which grain was sold, which were regulated from time to time and supervised by the Lord's officers, are difficult to use principally because of the unknown variations in demand and the periodic revision of the measures used in the island.[82] Clearly, factors such as these would have had a considerable impact on the price of grain. Despite the problems of interpreting the evidence, an attempt has been made to identify the years when the harvest in the Isle of Man was either deficient or bad between about 1590 and the end of the seventeenth century.

---

[78] *ibid*; Sacheverell, *Account*, p. 12.
[79] Sacheverell, *Account*, pp. 12–13.
[80] *ibid*, p. 13.
[81] *ibid*; M.M.L., MD/401/1719/6. William Sacheverell to William, ninth earl of Derby, May 23, 1692.
[82] For details of the measures used in the island in the seventeenth century, see Table 4.3.

The 1590s witnessed a series of bad harvests in England and Scotland, caused by prolonged heavy rain and frequent gales, and, although there is little direct evidence, there can be little doubt that the island experienced similar weather conditions.[83] Grain exports from Manx ports seem to have fallen in the mid-1590s, but there is scarcely any indication of dearth in the island before 1596. That year saw a disastrous harvest in England, particularly in the west, and there is every reason to believe that the Manx harvest was equally bad. This did not prevent the governor and officers from granting permission to John Stevenson of Balladoole to export eighty bolls of barley and malt in October 1596. Before sanctioning the transportation of the grain, however, the officers established to their satisfaction that 'yt may be spared without preiudice of the land or inhauncement of the marketes' and obtained from Stevenson an undertaking to supply the island's markets with another forty bolls of grain.[84]

By May 1597, the situation had changed. Within living memory, the price of wheat and barley had been as low as 2od. and 18d. per boll respectively, but, by this time, it had risen to the extent that regulations were issued, directing that wheat, barley and rye were not to be sold 'in any market, howse or other place' above the price of 15s. per boll 'the best sort' and 13s. 4d. per boll 'the worser sort.' Even oats, which had fetched 4d. per boll in the recent past, now cost the Manxman up to 3s. 4d. per boll, or ten times as much.[85] (Table 2.1). Steps were taken to ensure that the markets were supplied with grain and that barley and malt were not diverted into unlicensed brewing. To bring pressure on those without licences, it had been ordered in January that any man presented with drink in an unsealed can might lawfully 'drinke the same and pay nothing for yt.'[86] From May, the number of licensed brewers in the towns was to be limited to 'fower persons at the most,' who were to be

[83] D. M. Palliser, *The Age of Elizabeth. England Under the Later Tudors, 1547–1603* (2nd edn, 1992), p. 3 and fig. 2; H. H. Lamb, *The English Climate* (2nd edn, 1964), appendix ii, p. 197; W. G. Hoskins, 'Harvest Fluctuations and English Economic History, 1480–1619', *Ag.H.R.*, vol. xii (1964), appendix ii, p. 46. Storms are recorded as affecting the island on at least one occasion in the last decade of the sixteenth century, in 1592. 'Annals of Chester', *Cheshire Sheaf*, 3rd series, vol. ix (1913), no. 1843, p. 17.

[84] Lib. Scacc. 1597, 7.

[85] M.M.L., MD/401/1715/5; Lib. Scacc. 1597, inter 24–5.

[86] Lib. Scacc. 1597, 13.

Table 2.1. *Prices of Wheat, Barley and Oats in the Isle of Man,
c. 1580-1700 (per boll)*

Year	Oats	Barley	Wheat	
			Isle of Man	England (general average)[1]
c. 1580	4d.	1s. 6d.	1s. 8d.	—
1597	3s. 4d.	< 13s.–15s.	< 13s.–15s.	23s.
1607	1s. 2d.	4s. 6d.	5s. 0d.	17s.
1608		8s. 6d.		22s.
1628		8s. 0d.	8s. 0d.	16s.
1645		9s. 0d.	10s. 0d.	18s.
1648	< 10s. 0d.	< 14s.–16s.	< 14s.–16s.	29s.
1651		< 16s. 0d.	< 16s. 0d.	21s.
1655		6s. 0d.		17s.
1660			5s. 0d.	24s.
1696	< 9s. 0d.	< 14s. 0d.	< 14s. 0d.	22s.
1699	< 10s. 0d.	< 16s. 0d.	< 16s. 0d.	19s.
1703	< 7s. 0d.	< 9s. 0d.	< 9s. 0d.	18s.

Sources: M.M.L., MD/401/1715/5; Lib. Scacc. 1597, inter 24–5;
Lib. Scacc. 1608, 22; Lib. Scacc. 1628, 44; Moore, *Notes and Documents*,
pp. 30–1; Lib. Scacc. 1648, 65–6; Lib. Scacc. 1652, 1; Lib. Scacc. 1697, inter
32–3, 34; Lib. Scacc. 1699, 62, inter 62–3; Lib. Scacc. 1703, inter 6–7.

Note.
1. Figures from Hoskins, 'Harvest Fluctuations and English Economic
History', modified on the basis of price per boll, assuming that two bolls
are equivalent to one quarter. Prices to the nearest shilling.

appointed by the deputy governor. This was indeed a drastic move,
considering that Douglas had, on average, about thirty licensed
alehousekeepers at this time and Castletown had almost fifty.[87]

For about a decade after 1597, harvests seem to have been generally
adequate, but, in 1607, the harvest in the west of England was bad[88]
and that in the Isle of Man seems to have been at least deficient. In

---

[87] Lib. Scacc 1597, inter 24–5. For details of the numbers of licensed and
unlicensed alehousekeepers in the island during the late sixteenth and seventeenth centuries, see chapter 3, Tables 3.3 and 3.4.
[88] Hoskins, 'Harvest Fluctuations, 1480–1619', appendix ii, p. 46.

the winter of 1607–8, a boll of barley was sold in the island's markets for 4s. 6d. and a similar quantity of oats for 14d.[89] By June 1608, however, the price of barley offered for sale, with the official blessing of the Tynwald Court, was 8s. 6d. per boll. When Robert Quayle sought permission to ship a consignment of barley, it was initially refused 'because of a present dearth likely to ensue,' but was granted when he agreed to provide the inhabitants with the opportunity to buy over a two-week period.[90]

Whenever farmers wanted to export corn, it was normal practice for four men to be chosen in each parish to view every man's 'Store of Corne' and to assess how much could be spared, after due allowance 'for their seeding, housekeeping and furnishing of the markettes.' If it was deemed that there was sufficient for some 'to be sold foorth of the Cuntry,' the governor granted licence for transportation; if not, or if there were some reason to fear that the harvest would fail, the farmers had to be content to sell in the domestic market at prices set by the officers.[91]

In 1628, the shipment of grain was prohibited for the space of five weeks 'by especiall Comand from the Lord' as a result of 'the great prices of late enhaunced and demanded for the same.' [92] The Isle of Man had probably suffered from the effects of the very bad harvest which Ireland, Scotland and the north of England experienced in 1622,[93] although there seems to be no evidence that the island's authorities were compelled to take action in this particular instance, but Manx harvests in the later 1620s, if they followed the English

---

[89] M.M.L., MD/401/1715/5.

[90] Lib. Scacc. 1608, 22.

[91] Lib. Scacc. 1626, 14. The governor and officers met on a regular basis to determine which commodities might be exported from the island. See chapter 5, p. 245, n. 85.

[92] Lib. Scacc. 1628, 44.

[93] For details of the impact of the disastrous harvest of 1622 in the north of England, see A. B. Appleby, *Famine in Tudor and Stuart England* (Liverpool, 1978), pp. 146–7. For the effects in Scotland, see M. W. Flinn ed., *Scottish Population History from the Seventeenth Century to the 1930s* (Cambridge, 1977), pp. 122–5. The harvest failure of 1622 was one of several to affect Ireland in the early 1620s. See R. Gillespie, 'Harvest Crises in Early Seventeenth-Century Ireland', *I.E.S.H.*, vol. xi (1984), pp. 9–10; idem, 'Meal and Money: The Harvest Crisis of 1621–4 and the Irish Economy', in E. M. Crawford (ed.), *Famine: The Irish Experience, 900–1900* (Edinburgh 1989), pp. 75–95.

rather than the Irish pattern,[94] were probably reasonably good. If increases in the price of grain in the island can not be ascribed to harvest failure, such rises must be attributable to an unquantifiable increase in demand, manipulation of the corn supply by the larger farmers, or a combination of both. Certainly, those 'divers persons' who petitioned the Tynwald Court in 1628 had 'great quantities of Corne readie to be sould,' but, perhaps significantly, they claimed that they were unable to sell it. The governor and officers, 'tendring aswell the Case of the buyers as the sellers,' announced that any who wanted to buy corn should approach the vendors and pay 8s. for every boll of wheat, barley or malt purchased. To ensure that there was ample opportunity for the inhabitants to satisfy their needs, the embargo on exports of barley and malt was continued for another week, that on wheat for a fortnight, and that on oats and meal for a further three weeks. Perhaps surprisingly, no rates were set for oats, despite its importance, and presumably it was left to indivvduals to negotiate a price.[95] If so, this obviously allowed the more unscrupulous the chance to make a profit by charging a higher rate than was appropriate for oats, which was usually about one quarter the price of barley.[96]

In any event, complaints were made to the Lord, particularly in the early 1630s, that 'the Commons and poor Sort of Inhabitant' were 'much impoverished by Engrossers, Forestallers and Regrators.'[97] Such practices were by no means new, and may indeed have been the main reason for the revision of the island's weights and measures in 1628,[98] but, in the early 1630s, which probably witnessed harvests as bad, if not worse, than those in England, they were bound to have a detrimental effect.[99] As in the previous decade, there is

---

[94] For details of the harvests in England and Ireland in the later 1620s, see Hoskins, 'Harvest Fluctuations, 1620–1759', appendix i, p. 28; Gillespie, 'Harvest Crises', pp. 10–12.

[95] Lib. Scacc. 1628, 44.

[96] The relative prices of oats and barley were, for example, 4d. and 18d. per boll in the late sixteenth century and 14d. and 4s. 6d. per boll in the winter of 1607–8. M.M.L., MD/401/1715/5. See Table 2.1.

[97] *Statutes*, p. 92.

[98] Lib. Scacc. 1628, 89. See chapter 4, Table 4.3.

[99] *ibid*, p. 81; Hoskins, 'Harvest Fluctuations, 1620–1759', appendix i, p. 28. The limited amount of evidence from Ireland in the early 1630s suggests that harvests there may also have been poor. Gillespie, 'Harvest Crises', pp. 12–13.

scarcely any indication of harvest failure from the records of the island's government, apart from yet another attempt to control unlicensed brewing, but it is evident that there were some who not only endeavoured to corner the market in cereals and other merchandise, but also exported goods 'without Consideration [of] what may be necessary to be reserved for the Sustentacion of the Inhabitants of the Island.'[100] Following proposals made by James, Lord Strange, as a result of petitions from the Manx, it was ordered at the Tynwald Court in June 1637 that any person who attempted to forestall the markets or regrate or engross any commodities was to forfeit all such goods to the Lord or pay a fine to the equivalent value. Those who tried to transport any merchandise, particularly grain and cattle, without first obtaining licence from the governor or one of the officers, were reminded that if they did so in the future, they would face a similar punishment. In an effort to deal with one of the island's perennial problems, the system of licensing alehousekeepers was outlined again, although it continued to be ignored by many.[101]

Though the main provisions of these ordinances were doubtless flouted on occasion in the following decade, the first real test of the law against forestalling and regrating came when the Manx harvest failed several times in the late 1640s. After a succession of reasonably good harvests from 1638 onwards, England endured half a dozen deficient or bad seasons, beginning in 1646,[102] which were caused by bad weather. Ralph Josselin, vicar of Earl's Colne in Essex, noted in his diary in June 1648 that the season 'was wonderful wet, flouds every week . . . We never had the like in my memory, and that for the greatest part of the summer.'[103] Similar conditions were also reported in north-west England during the Preston campaign in August 1648 by a Lancastrian captain, who lamented that 'Such a wet time this time of the year hath not been seen in the memory of man.'[104] Since Lancashire experienced such appalling weather, and in view of the nature of the Manx climate, it seems highly likely that

[100] Lib. Scacc. 1634, 10; *Statutes*, p. 88.
[101] *Statutes*, pp. 86–8. The law concerning licences for export was restated in June 1645. *ibid*, p. 105.
[102] Hoskins, 'Harvest Fluctuations, 1620–1759', appendix i, p. 29.
[103] A. Macfarlane ed., *The Diary of Ralph Josselin, 1616–1683* (Records of Social and Economic History, New Series, iii, 1976), p. 129.
[104] Quoted in E. Broxap, *The Great Civil War in Lancashire, 1642–1651* (2nd edn, Manchester, 1973), p. 167. Source not given.

the Isle of Man shared the conditions which brought harvest failure and dearth in their wake.

Confirmation that Manx harvests followed a similar pattern can be found in the scattered evidence of Manx grain prices in the later 1640s. In the middle of the decade, barley was being sold at 9s. per boll and wheat at 10s. per boll. (Table 2.1)[105] Three years later, in July 1648, the maximum price at which wheat, barley, malt or rye were to be sold in the markets was set at 16s. per boll for the best quality grain and 14s. for the inferior grades.[106] This rise may have been exacerbated by the presence in the island of Royalist refugees from the adjacent kingdoms, but there is no way of discovering the size of this group, which was, in any case, constantly changing, or indeed of determining whether demand for food was increasing anyway because of the lack of any adequate demographic evidence.

It seems more than likely, however, that the main cause of the price increases was a poor harvest in 1647.[107] The parish clerk of Ballaugh recorded that 'there was a great scarcity of Corne' in the year ending at Lady Day (March 25), 1648,[108] and this would explain the reluctance of at least some of the inhabitants to provide corn for the provision of the garrisons and for the supply of the town markets. Already burdened with unaccustomed financial demands arising from Earl James's organisation of the island's defences,[109] which had to be paid in addition to the regular payments of rents and customary dues, the Manx found their resources stretched to the limit. William Cowle of Bride was one of nearly a dozen people presented in August 1648 for failing to supply the markets. When his house was searched, it was found that he had 'three boules of meale to spare,' besides some hidden in a bed, which he refused to bring to the

---

[105] A. W. Moore (ed.), *Notes and Documents from the Records of the Isle of Man* (Douglas, n.d.), p. 30; Moore, *History*, vol. i, p. 288.

[106] Lib. Scacc. 1648, 65. The limits for metcorn, small oats and placket were 10s., 5s. and 6s. 8d. respectively.

[107] In England, the harvest of 1647 was one of the half dozen worst during the seventeenth century. Hoskins, 'Harvest Fluctuations, 1480–1619', appendix ii, p. 46; idem, 'Harvest Fluctuations, 1620–1759', appendix i, pp. 28–30.

[108] M.M.L., MF/PR/3. Ballaugh Parish Registers: Burials, 1648.

[109] For further details of Earl James's financial demands, see J. R. Dickinson, 'The Earl of Derby and the Isle of Man, 1643–1651', *T.H.S.L.C.*, vol. cxli (1992), pp. 59–62.

markets. Another of those presented, John Skillicorn of Lezayre, brought no corn to sell in the market, despite efforts to persuade him to do so made by 'severall persons that came out of Kirk Lonnan for that purpose.'[110] The inhabitants of Castletown who petitioned Governor John Greenhalgh in December 1647 believed that the 'insufferable and insupportable rates of Corne' were not the result of 'any scarcitie of grayne in the Island,' but the product of 'the spyte and avarice of the Tennants,' 'certaine Ingrossers who for their owne privatt Lucre doe overthrowe the publicke good.' They clearly suspected 'the Richer sort of ffarmors who come to the Markett to buy corne and spare there owne, thereby indevouringe to raise the Markett.'[111] It seems, therefore, that the activities of the engrosser or regrater combined with harvest failure to drive up prices towards the limits set in July 1648, before the next harvest was brought in.

At the same time, the situation was considered serious enough to warrant the issue of orders for the regulation of the prices of other staples of the Manx diet. Greenhalgh, the comptroller, John Sharples, Deemster John Cannell and seventeen members of the Keys decided that ale and beer were not to be retailed at more than 1d. per 'sealed quarte' after Michaelmas 1648. The harbingers or market jurors in the towns,[112] who were also responsible for checking the quality of grain on sale and the accuracy of the measures in use, were to present all those who tried to make a profit by selling above the rate. The offender stood to lose his merchandise, but if the harbinger neglected his duty and failed to deliver the names of the transgressors, he was to be fined 6s. 8d.[113] The apparently more rigorous supervision of brewing and retailing ale and beer, demonstrated by the more frequent inclusion of lists of licensed brewers in the Libri Scaccarii (Exchequer Books), continued until the early 1650s, when grain supplies were more plentiful.[114]

---

[110] Lib. Scacc. 1648, inter 76–7.

[111] Lib. Scacc. 1647, inter 82–3, 83.

[112] The Market Jury is discussed in chapter 4, pp. 202–5.

[113] Lib. Scacc. 1648, 65–6.

[114] See chapter 3, Tables 3.3. After the early 1650s, lists of licensed brewers appear much less often. Although no systematic count has yet been undertaken, there does not seem to have been a marked increase in the number of presentments for unlicensed brewing in the later 1640s. See chapter 3, Table 3.4.

In an effort to protect crops and to ensure that, as far as was humanly possible, the harvest of 1648 would have a good chance of success, notice was also given that any man found cutting corn or grass on another man's land without permission would be flogged or otherwise punished at the governor's discretion. A similar fate awaited those foolhardy enough to 'bringe horses or other goodes into an other mans Corne or grasse by nighte or day without leave of the Owner.'[115]

It has already been seen that the summer of 1648 was unusually wet in England and that the Isle of Man probably experienced much the same weather conditions. As a result, the harvest in England was bad and that in the island was apparently little better. By June 1649, the inhabitants were complaining that, 'in this tyme of great dearth and scarcitie,' they could 'in noe wise bee supplyed with any maner of Corne or graine att any the Marketts of this Isle otherwise for theire monyes.'[116] Supplies of grain were also difficult to obtain for the garrisons, the requirements of which were normally filled in part during times of emergency by collecting a quantity of oatmeal or barley from every quarterland.[117]

Whereas it was possible for the officers to buy imported grain for the garrisons, such an option was not generally available to the majority of Manxmen. Accordingly, Greenhalgh ordered the coroners of the Southside to appoint four men in each parish of their sheading to establish whether any farmers had grain to spare for the markets, and, if they did, to direct them to supply a proportion from

[115] Lib. Scacc. 1648, 65.
[116] Lib. Scacc. 1649, inter 69–70 (4).
[117] Four men in each parish were sworn to assess the quantity of grain due from each tenement. This might be half a firlot or more, depending on the size of the holding and the scale of the emergency. The clergy were assessed by two of their own number. The grain was collected in April each year as necessary and stored in Castle Rushen and Peel Castle for the use of the officers and soldiers. If it were not consumed, it was returned to the farmers at or before harvest time, when a new supply would become available. If the grain were used, due allowance was made in the rents. The minimum assessment of half a firlot from each quarterland yielded, in theory, about 320 bolls of grain, which, in Blundell's opinion, was 'sufficient to furnish both these castles'. Blundell, *History*, vol. i, p. 94; Cl.R.O., Nantlys MS D/NA/905, 5. Assessments of this kind were employed on several occasions during the 1640s and 1650s. See, for example, Lib. Scacc. 1646, 7–8; Lib. Scacc. 1647, 13–14, 90–1; Lib. Scacc. 1652, 1.

time to time.[118] The returns were not encouraging. Only five parishes responded, and even they could only offer amounts which were unlikely to improve the position significantly. The assessors in Arbory named four men whom they believed 'hath some to spare,' including Richard Stevenson of Balladoole and Sir Robert Norris, vicar of Arbory, while Phillip Moore, coroner of Garff, returned a list of five men who had brought in grain in Maughold, where there were 'many needy persons.'[119] The total amount to be collected from both parishes came to less than twenty bolls, which was hardly enough to maintain even the garrisons for long.

Nevertheless, something had to be done to alleviate the worst of the shortage. Greenhalgh and the officers directed that the corn collected in Maughold and Braddan should be taken to Douglas and entrusted to four of the town's leading men; the corn from Rushen, Arbory and Malew was similarly to be delivered to four of Castletown's inhabitants. Four men in each parish and town were then to return the names of those who were 'in the most greatest neede and want for the present.' The corn was to be distributed accordingly by the men nominated in Douglas and Castletown, who were left to pay the farmers for their contributions.[120]

---

[118] A similar procedure was followed in England in the late sixteenth and early seventeenth centuries and was set out in the Book of Orders, first issued to J.P.s by the Privy Council in 1587. It was reissued in each subsequent period of dearth until 1662, after which date increased production and a reduction in population growth in England made food supply less of a problem. A. Everitt, 'The Marketing of Agricultural Produce, 1500–1640', in J. A. Chartres (ed.), *Agricultural Markets and Trade, 1500–1750* (Cambridge, 1990), p. 130; C. G. A. Clay, *Economic Expansion and Change: England 1500–1700* (2 vols, Cambridge, 1984), vol. ii, p. 228. Cf. R. B. Outhwaite, 'Dearth and Government Intervention in English Grain Markets, 1590–1700', *Ec.H.R.*, 2nd series, vol. xxxiii (1981), pp. 405–6. In early seventeenth-century Ireland, Justices of the Peace were also authorised to regulate the distribution of corn in times of dearth. Gillespie, 'Harvest Crises', p. 14.
[119] Lib. Scacc. 1649, inter 69–70 (3, 4).
[120] *ibid*, 70. The four men in Douglas were: i) William Quayle of Douglas; ii) Lt Thomas Huddleston, commander of Douglas Fort; iii) Thomas Fairbrother, customer at Douglas; iv) Hugh Moore of Douglas, subsequently waterbailiff. The Castletown men were less prominent: i) John Taubman, a soldier at Castle Rushen, Derby Fort or both; ii) William Christian, a joiner; iii) William Wattleworth; iv) James Corrin. Nothing has as yet been discovered with any certainty about the latter two men.

Those Manxmen who could afford to purchase at least a little grain sometimes found that they were being overcharged, despite the standing orders as to price limits. In May 1649, Edmund Kewne of Jurby took 9s. 3d. from William Fargher of Patrick for a firlot of meal, which was nearly twice the maximum rate set. Kewne claimed that he had sold Fargher a firlot of barley out of his only boll and that he did not do so 'in any Contempt to Commaund Butt to make himselfe a saver in respect of the hard bargaine hee had in the Tithe.'[121] Thomas Quay of Meary, Santan, sold three 'sives' of barley to John Quayle of Castletown at 9d. above the rate in April and subsequently compounded his crime by 'wilfully and obstinatly refusinge to shewe his store of Corne to the foure men apointed and sworne in that parish and the two Soldiers by Comand and warrant from the Governor.'[122]

Grain prices seem to have remained at a relatively high level until at least 1652, when, as in England, they began to fall as the yields from harvests began to improve. After the surrender of the Isle of Man to Parliament's forces at the beginning of November 1651, one of the first acts of the Parliamentarian commander, Colonel Robert Duckenfield, was to order an assessment of corn for the supply of his men, as well as for the markets, and to enquire whether any had sold above the rate of 16s. per boll of wheat or malt.[123] The price of bread, which had been set in November 1649 at 1d. for a twelve-ounce loaf of white bread or an eighteen-ounce loaf of brown bread, was reduced by increasing the size of penny loaves to fifteen and twenty-one ounces respectively in January 1654.[124] The orders regulating the maximum rates of corn had clearly become a dead letter and, by 1655, the price of a boll of wheat had dropped to 6s.[125]

The fluctuations of the Manx harvest in the later seventeenth century seem, in the main, to have continued to resemble the fortunes of the English harvest during the period. A series of bad harvests in England in the late 1650s culminated in the disastrous season of 1661, when wheat prices soared to nearly 60 per cent above the general average.[126] No evidence of a similar price rise in the Isle of Man has

---

[121] *ibid*, inter 65–6, 66.
[122] *ibid*, 62, 69.
[123] Lib. Scacc. 1652, 1.
[124] Lib. Scacc. 1650, 9; Lib. Scacc. 1653, 31.
[125] Moore, *Notes and Documents*, p. 31.
[126] Hoskins, 'Harvest Fluctuations, 1620–1759', appendix i, p. 29.

as yet been discovered, but it is likely, if the measures taken by the authorities are any indication, that the situation in the island was serious. At the Tynwald Court in June 1662, it was ordered that any who 'frequently use to make a Path-way through their Neighbours' Meddows, Corne and Grass, in the Summer and Harvest Season, to the Prejudice of the Tennant' were to be punished at the officers' discretion, although those 'of Abillity' were to be fined. The law against cutting another man's corn or grass, proclaimed in 1648, was reiterated, but punishment was henceforth to be at discretion to allow the officers to tailor the penalty to fit the offence.[127] After what was probably another bad harvest in 1662, Earl Charles himself refused to permit any merchant or farmer to export corn from the island, realising that it could not '(if not seasonably prevented) but still be the greatest occasion of Dearth and Scarcity there; introduceing a Generall inconvenience and a Calamitie unavoydable to the poorer Sort of Inhabitants for the Lucre and advantage of some few persons.'[128] Several years of at least average harvests produced 'cheape rates' and 'plentie of Corne and graine within this Isle' by 1665.[129]

When England experienced bad harvests in 1673 and 1674, the island also suffered. Writing to his kinswoman, Alice Kenyon, in May 1675, Governor Henry Nowell explained that he would not be able to visit his relations at Peel in Lancashire, because he was short of money 'by reason of every thing being so dear. There will be many poor families which will perish for want of food.'[130] Neither did the island escape the shortages brought about by six deficient or bad harvests which affected both England and Scotland during the 1690s.[131] There is some indication that harvests in the Isle of Man may have failed for several years before 1691, but there is little evidence to substantiate this claim and the source itself may be suspect.[132]

---

[127] *Statutes*, p. 113.

[128] Lib. Scacc. 1663, ii, 8.

[129] Lib. Scacc. 1665, 40; Lib. Scacc. 1666, 22.

[130] *H.M.C. Kenyon*, p. 101.

[131] Hoskins, 'Harvest Fluctuations', 1620–1759, appendix i, p. 30; Flinn, *Scottish Population History*, pp. 164–170; R. Mitchison, 'The Movement of Scottish Corn Prices in the Seventeenth and Eighteenth Centuries', *Ec.H.R.*, 2nd series, vol. xviii (1965), pp. 281–2.

[132] M.M.L., MD/401/1718/87. Ferdinando Calcott to Robert Roper, January 12, 1691. Calcott, who was both waterbailiff and steward of the abbey lands, was in arrears with the delivery of the rents and other moneys due

There is, however, no doubt that the island had to face the problems of grain shortage between 1695 and 1700. In response to petitions expressing 'great apprehencon of a Scarcity of Corne,' Governor Nicholas Sankey ordered an assessment of the store of grain in each parish in March 1696, so that the surplus might 'be sold for the publick use in the several market Townes.'[133] In June, to halt the rise in the price of grain, the Keys set the maximum rates at which wheat and barley could be sold at 14s. per boll and those for oats and rye at 9s. per boll.[134] In a letter to Earl William in September, Richard Stevenson, one of the revenue commissioners, attributed the 'great degree of Poverty' in the island to 'last sumners want of Bread,' and predicted that 'this wett harvest will not mend the last.'[135] Stevenson was proved to be right. Continued shortage led Sankey to order another assessment of corn in June 1697, barely a week after the Keys had reissued the rates for grain.[136] The harvest of 1697, which was very bad, and that of 1698, which was only slightly less so, made matters worse. In such circumstances, after at least three successive harvest failures, it can hardly be surprising that some resorted to theft to obtain corn. Ewan Corkill of Conchan was unable to explain how he had come by some straw and barley in his possession and was sentenced 'to be whipt at Duglass, and being poore noe fine imposed.'[137] Ann Fargher and Jane Quayle *alias* Fayle were caught red-handed by William Leece of Braddan in his barn at night in February 1699, attempting to steal 'a furlett of smale Oates tyed in a Canvish.'[138] William Gick of Santan tried a different method. He approached Robert Cowin, the servant of Thomas Brew of Santan, and tried to persuade him 'to steale him some corn and mault out of his masters barn,' claiming that Gilbert Corrin had done the same for him in 1697.[139]

note 132 *continued*
and it was therefore in his interest to emphasise, and perhaps to exaggerate, that 'money was never so scarce here'.

[133] Lib. Scacc. 1696, 31.

[134] Lib. Scacc. 1697, inter 32–3.

[135] M.M.L., MD/401/1719/44. Richard Stevenson to William, ninth earl of Derby, September 17, 1696.

[136] Lib. Scacc. 1697, 27–8, inter 32–3, 34.

[137] Lib. Scacc. 1698, 39.

[138] Lib. Scacc. 1699, 56.

[139] Lib. Scacc. 1698, 38.

In May 1699, 'ffor the want off the present supply off corn and meale; ass allsoe to prevent the excessive rates that any unreasonable person or persons may demand or take ffrom any such that wants,' the Keys raised the maximum prices of wheat and barley to 16s. per boll and of oats to 10s. per boll.[140] The harvest following was average in England and about the same in Scotland;[141] the island probably also enjoyed a reasonably good season, since no further measures were taken by the authorities to deal with shortages. To ease the burden on the inhabitants, particularly those who had been driven to theft because of the dearth, Earl William remitted all fines and punishments imposed in 1699 and ordered the repayment of any fines already collected.[142] The harvests in the opening years of the eighteenth century were generally good and shortages, such as that complained of in 1703, were due rather to the efforts of some farmers to force up prices than to harvest failure.[143]

e) Farming Practice

While information about the type of crops grown and livestock raised is relatively plentiful, few details concerning farming practices in the island are given by any of the contemporary writers. Moore, however, believed that the length and narrowness of many of the treens indicated that from an early date the land had been divided into strips typical of the runrig system of cultivation found in parts of Ireland and the Hebrides.[144] This involved the annual distribution of arable land between landholders.[145] As proof that a similar system was in use in the Isle of Man, Moore cited an ordinance of 1422 which directed that, 'forasmuch as the Land Setting hath not been made in due time, nor read to the People, whereby many have lost their Profitt of foulding and manuring that Year,' in future, 'the

---

[140] Lib. Scacc. 1699, inter 62–3.

[141] Hoskins, 'Harvest Fluctuations, 1620–1759', appendix i, p. 30; Flinn, *Scottish Population History*, p. 170; Mitchison, 'Movement of Scottish Corn Prices', p. 281.

[142] Lib. Scacc. 1700, 8.

[143] Lib. Scacc. 1703, inter 6–7, inter 20–1.

[144] Moore, *History*, vol. i, pp. 48–52; A. W. Moore, 'The Early Land System of the Isle of Man', *Y.L.M.*, vol. ii (1901) pp. 40–3.

[145] This system was still in existence in the Western Isles in the seventeenth century. Cf. F. J. Shaw, *The Northern and Western Isles of Scotland* (Edinburgh, 1980), pp. 88, 90–1.

Setting' should 'be made betyme before Midsomer to the People.'[146] The same ordinance provided that the lieutenant, or governor, should swear in four men in each parish, 'to deliver to every one his Pennyworth after his houlding, and spetially to new Tennants.'[147] Further evidence of a system of open fields in the island can be found in the records of the sheading courts. When several tenants who jointly held a treen were unable to reach agreement about a division of the land in 1586, it was split up into strips – termed *immyr* in Manx and butts in English – so that one tenant held 'the one Butt, and the other another Butt throughout the whole.'[148] By the sixteenth century, and probably before, the form of runrig system which apparently prevailed in the Isle of Man had been modified. Arable land was no longer reallocated each year ; instead, as an examination of the 'manorial rolls' or setting books (*Libri Assedationis*) indicates, the same tenants held the same lands from year to year.[149]

Under the runrig system, pasture land was held in common. This was also the practice on lowland pasture in the Isle of Man during the winter season, since, according to a customary law, fences were only to be kept up between Lady Day and Michaelmas (March 25– September 29).[150] From 1422 at least, however, each tenant was allowed 'to enclose his Farme Land, and keep it severall all Tymes in the Yeare'; but, as Moore pointed out, because no law was enacted to penalise those who neglected to keep up their fences, it was clearly not illegal to follow customary practice.[151] The regular

---

[146] Moore, *History*, vol. i, p. 52; *Statutes*, p. 14.

[147] *Statutes*, p. 14.

[148] Lib. Plit. 1586, cited in M.M.L., MS 510C. J. Quayle, *A Book of Precedents* (n.d., [c. 1725]), p. 60. Cf. Moore, *History*, vol. i, p. 52.

[149] Using the setting books (*Libri Assedationis*) to trace the occupation of a tenement from generation to generation is made even more difficult by the fact that the books were only periodically revised. Nevertheless, it is quite possible to do so for some estates, particularly those belonging to the more important families in the island. See, for example, the descent of Balladoole through twelve generations of the Stevenson family, summarised in Cubbon, 'An Important Balladoole Document', *J.M.M.*, vol. ii (1930–4), pp. 168–9, and the account of Ronaldsway, held for more than a century at least by the Samsburys and then passing to the Christians of Milntown by marriage, in A. W. Moore, 'The Ronaldsway Estate', *Y.L.M.*, vol. iv (1910), pp. 53–58.

[150] M.M.L. MD 15,040, Parr, *Abridgement*, p. 69.

[151] *Statutes*, p. 20; Moore, 'Early Land System', p. 43.

construction and destruction of the fences between holdings, which were generally of turf and earth,[152] was unquestionably a laborious task and it might be expected that little encouragement would be needed for the erection and maintenance of permanent enclosures.[153] Nevertheless, it seems that traditional ways persisted and that the fences which were put up, either temporary or permanent, were often found to be too poorly built to fulfil their task. In 1577, one of the 'old Customes given for Law' by the deemsters in the presence of Earl Henry was that 'all manner of Tennants, as well my Lord's as others, shall make a sufficient Ditch to defend his Goodes from his Neighbours, that is . . . such a Ditch as shall defend Horse or Cow.' In the event of livestock breaking the fences, 'a sufficient Herd' was to be employed 'to keep their Beast from doing injury one to the other.'[154]

Five years later the laws of 1422 and 1577 were re-enacted. All inhabitants 'occupieing any Lands or Tenements within the said Isle' were lawfully entitled 'to keep the same in all Winter and Summer without Prejudice, Hurt, or Gainsaying of any of his Neighbours.' To ensure that fences were of sufficient size, it was directed that 'every Ditch' should be 'of the height of four Foot and a Halfe, and in Thickness of a double Ditch, according to the antient and usual Custom.'[155] Problems clearly arose as a result of the operation of the customary law by which the tenants could remove the fences at Michaelmas. Because of the climate, the harvest in the Isle of Man was often late, which meant that many farmers could not 'have Inned their harvest at Michaelmas . . . , nor some yeares of many dayes after.' Consequently, it was ordered in 1656 that the fences were to

---

[152] Blundell did not remember 'to have seen any one hedge that parted either field or pastures, but all were either of turfs or of earth stones or of both'. Blundell, *History*, vol. i, p. 47. The construction of these fences is described by B. R. S. Megaw, 'The "Manks Spade" and the Making of Sod Hedges', *J.M.M.*, vol. iv (1938–40), p. 167.

[153] It seems unlikely, however, that an anonymous writer in the 1660s could have been correct when he asserted that 'in old tyme it may seeme there was noe boundaries betwixt tenant and tenant, ffences or high wayes for it is but since the yeare 1505 that the same were sett out and made'. Cl.R.O. Nantlys D/NA/905, 8. This claim was based on the earliest reference to 'high wayes' which the writer was able to find in the records then extant.

[154] *Statutes*, pp. 47, 49.

[155] *ibid*, p. 56.

be maintained until All Hallows (November 1).[156] Cases of trespass by cattle 'in Corne and Grass' continued nevertheless and led to numerous actions in the courts.

In an effort to reduce such disputes and to prevent land 'lying common and as Wast all the Winter Season without any Fence, contrary to the Rule of good Husbandry in other Countrys and Places,' an Act was passed in 1665 by the governor, deemsters, Council and Keys which confirmed all the former legislation and laid out the penalties for those who allowed their animals to wander, 'as well for the Trespass done or made in the Winter Season, as in the Harvest or Summer Times.'[157] Further steps to prevent such incidents were taken in 1667, when the minimum height of 'the Hedges or Fences' was set at 'five Foot at the least,' and in 1691, when it was ordered that 'all Fences for the future shall be made five Foot and a Half high, with a Trench at the Bottom of one Foot and a Half deep, and three Foot broad; or els a Fence of six Foot high in the Perpendicular where a Trench cannot be made.'[158] That the traditional practice of taking down fences continued into the eighteenth century is demonstrated by the fact that, in 1770, it was stated that 'till lately the greater part of the parish of Jurby was an open common in the winter season.'[159]

Few details are available concerning the tools and equipment used by Manx farmers before the eighteenth century. Writing in 1794, Basil Quayle observed that until 'within these few years, the instruments and geers used in agriculture were few in number, and badly constructed; of course their duration was short, and execution not complete.' The position improved towards 1800, as ploughs and other equipment, 'more firmly made, and of seasoned timber,' were imported from England and Scotland.[160] This movement of

---

[156] *ibid*, p. 110; Lib. Scacc. 1656, 8.

[157] *Statutes*, pp. 125–8. Straying cattle were to be taken to the nearest pinfold of the Lord or baron and a fine of a halfpenny 'a Foot' levied on each animal. The pinder received one half of the fine for his fee. Provision was made for the construction of a second pinfold in each parish, if deemed necessary by the local inhabitants, at the parishioner's expense. Each parish had a single pinfold, except Lezayre, which had two. P. Clague, 'Old Laws Relating to Pinfolds. A List of Manx Pinfolds', *J.M.M.*, vol. iv (1938–40), pp. 207–8, 216.

[158] *Statutes*, pp. 134, 150–1.

[159] Lib. Scacc. 1770, cited in Moore, 'Early Land System', p. 44

[160] B. Quayle, *General View*, p. 19.

agricultural implements was not, however, a recent development. From at least the late sixteenth century, ploughbeams, scythes and sickles were imported into the island on a fairly regular basis, probably in the main from England, but also on occasion from Ireland.[161] Less frequently, items such as swipples (parts of flails), harrow pins and harrow bulls were shipped to the island.[162] Many of the basic tools of husbandry, which can not be traced in the waterbailiff's accounts, were doubtless made in the island, using imported timber and metal pieces forged from imported iron.[163] In 1774, however, James Wilks, rector of Ballaugh, claimed that in his parish 'many Estates have a sufficiency [of timber] for Plows, Harrows and other Implements of Husbandry.'[164]

II. FISHERIES

Because of the relatively low yields of corn from the arable land in the island, fish played an important part in the Manx diet and much depended on the success or failure of the annual herring fishery. In a year when corn was plentiful, fish provided a supplement to the farmer's diet; when the harvest was bad, fish, and herring in particular, became a vital source of food. Blundell confidently asserted, with perhaps only slight exaggeration, that the 'sea feedeth more of the Manksmen than of the soil.'[165] He acknowledged the importance of the herring, upon which 'the less sort of Manks people of both sexes,

[161] See, for example, M.M.L., I.O. 1570–99, Customs book, 1594; waterbailiff's accounts, 1594; M.M.L., I.O. 1600–9, Ingates and outgates, 1600; ingates and outgates, 1605; M.M.L., I.O. 1610–19, Ingates and outgates, 1610; waterbailiff's accounts, 1618; M.M.L., I.O. 1630–45, Waterbailiff's accounts, 1630; M.M.L., I.O. 1660–71, Waterbailiff's accounts, 1667; M.M.L., I.O. 1680–9, Customs book, 1685; M.M.L., I.O. 1696–1704, Customs book, 1696. For a description of the tools used in arable farming in England and Wales during this period, see Thirsk, 'Farming Techniques', pp. 17–20.
[162] M.M.L., I.O. 1600–9, Ingates and outgates, 1600; M.M.L., I.O. 1610–19, Ingates and outgates, 1610; waterbailiff's accounts, 1618; M.M.L., I.O. 1696–1704, Customs book, 1696.
[163] For a discussion of the island's import trade, see chapter 5.
[164] W. Cubbon ed., 'Description of Ballaugh Parish in the year 1774', *J.M.M.*, vol. iv (1938–40), p. 17.
[165] Blundell, *History*, vol. i, p. 52.

both in the town and country, do every day constantly feed.'[166] He also recognised, however, that there was a great variety of other fish in the waters of the Irish Sea and remarked upon the 'great store of salmons, codds, haddocks, macarels, rayes, place, thornbecks and more than I can name to you.'[167]

The herring fishery had long been of prime importance in the Isle of Man, and this was reflected by the interest shown towards it by the civil and ecclesiastical authorities. Both ensured that they received a proportion of this generally abundant food supply. From at least the late thirteenth century, the Church claimed a tithe of all fish landed in the island.[168] When the spiritual laws and customs were first set down on record in the late sixteenth or early seventeenth century,[169] it was stated that 'every Master of every Fishing Boat shall cause all the Fish to be brought above the full Sea Mark, and there pay truely the Tyth.' If the master attempted to avoid payment, he was compelled to 'make five Shares of all his Fish' from which 'the Proctor shall appoint to be divided what share he will.'[170] During the herring fishing, the tithe was collected wherever the boats landed their catch; if the master took his boat to another port, he paid half his tithe there, and the remainder at his home port.[171] The bishop, archdeacon and beneficed clergy were allowed to select a fishing boat at Easter each year and a 'Herring Scoute'[172] before the 'Herring Fishing Time' and to land their catch anywhere in the island 'without

---

[166] *ibid*, p. 85.

[167] *ibid*, p. 52.

[168] The tithe on fish is first mentioned in the canons of Bishop Mark, enacted in 1291. A. W. Moore, *Sodor and Man* (1893), p. 65; Oliver, *Monumenta*, vol. iii, pp. 182–201.

[169] The date at which the spiritual laws were first set down is not certain, despite the insertion of the 'Book of Spiritual Lawes and Customes' in the Statutes between items dated 1577. *Statutes*, pp. 40–7. See P. W. Caine, 'The Story of the House of Keys', *M.N.H.A.S.*, vol. iv (1932–42), p. 438; Moore, *Sodor and Man*, p. 101 n. 1.

[170] *Statutes*, p. 44.

[171] *ibid*.

[172] A herring scout was an open, clinker-built boat, with sails and oars, of about 25 feet in length. B. R. S. Megaw and E. M. Megaw, 'Early Manx Fishing Craft', *Mariner's Mirror*, vol. xxvii (1941), pp. 92–5; E. M. Megaw, 'Manx Fishing Craft', *J.M.M.*, vol. v (1941–6), p. 15; B. R. S. Megaw and E. M. Megaw, 'The Development of Manx Fishing Craft', *M.N.H.A.S.*, vol. v (1932–42), pp. 251–2.

any Tythes paying, whether their fishing be about this Land or elsewhere.'[173] If any salmon were caught, 'either in Salt Water or in Fresh,' the fisherman paid a tithe to the Church.[174]

The Lord's share of the herring catch was probably established at a very early date, but it is not on record before the early fifteenth century. One of the earliest customary laws stated that the Lord should receive one maze[175] of herring out of every five caught by each boat.[176] This portion of the catch was known as the 'Castle Mazes' since it was destined for the provision of the Lord's garrisons. The Lord paid 6d. for each maze, but, as an incentive to the inhabitants to engage in the herring fishery, he paid, by custom, 3s. 4d. to 'the Bringers of the first Maze to Castle Rushen.'[177]

Customs duty was also payable on herring, whether it was imported or exported. This amounted to 1d. per maze or 1s. per ton for both native and foreign fishermen and merchants in the later sixteenth century.[178] In 1692, the duty payable by Manxmen on each maze shipped was halved.[179]

Although the importance of the herring fishery as part of the Lord's income, both in kind and in coin, should not be exaggerated, it was obviously in his interests to make certain that the best was made of the opportunity offered by such natural bounty. When Edward, third earl of Derby, sent commissioners to the island in 1561 to improve the efficiency of the administration there, it seems

[173] *Statutes*, pp. 40, 44.

[174] *ibid*, p. 44.

[175] A maze of herring varied in size from place to place. *O.E.D.*, *sub* maze. In the Isle of Man, a maze comprised five long hundreds of six score each; four fish were added to each long hundred, these being known as the *warp* [three fish] and *tally* [one fish], bringing the total number of herring in a maze to 620. W. Harrison ed., *Mona Miscellany*, Manx Society vol. xxi (1873), p. 226. Blundell stated that 'a meaz containeth the proportion of 500 herrings', which may be interpreted as confirmation of this calculation. Blundell, *History*, vol. i, p. 86.

[176] *Statutes*, p. 5. Landlords in England who leased fishing rights, or 'fishrooms', enjoyed similar rights to a proportion of the catch. At Burton in Cheshire in 1612, for example, it was ordained that the landlord should have the first catch on the Friday tide. P. H. W. Booth ed., *Burton in Wirral. A History* (Burton, 1984), p. 74.

[177] *Statutes*, p. 5; Blundell, *History*, vol. i, p. 86.

[178] *Statutes*, p. 38.

[179] M.M.L., MD/401/1715/20. Book of Rates, 1692.

that they found that some of the inhabitants, if not those in authority, had been evading payment of the castle mazes. To ensure that the Lord received his rightful quota, an order was accordingly issued that at 'every Herring Fishing upon the Coast of Mann, all Manner of Persons, whatsoever they be, Barrons, Officers or Soldiers, to pay the Castle Maze and Customes as hath heretofore used.'[180]

In June 1610, orders were issued for the regulation of the herring fishery. It was then acknowledged that 'the Herring Fishing is as great a Blessing as this poor Island receives, in enabling the Tennants for the better and speedier Payments of their Rents and other Impositions' and supplying all their other 'Wants and Occasions, when as all other their Endeavours and Husbandry would scarce advance any such Advantages and Gains unto them.'[181] Nevertheless, although proclamation was made at the Tynwald Court in June each year, reminding the inhabitants to have their boats and nets 'in Readiness, whensoever it pleaseth God to send them that Blessing,' many apparently failed to take notice. Governor John Ireland, the Council, deemsters and Keys therefore ordered that, each year, 'all and everye the Tennants and Fermors within this Isle, whether they be Lord's Tennants or Barons Tennants, shall have always in Rediness, prepared for the Herring Fishing, eight Fathomes of Netts furnished with Corckes or Boyes,' each quarterland being made answerable for such an amount, 'conteyning three Deepings, of nyne Score Mashes uppon the Rope.'[182] Those farmers who did not have such nets were given a month to provide them or face a fine at the discretion of the court.[183]

To ensure that the inhabitants employed boats of sufficient size, the deemsters and Keys set the burthen of the herring scouts at four tons,[184] but no mention was made of the number of boats which the

---

[180] *Statutes*, p. 34.

[181] *ibid*, p. 74.

[182] *ibid*, p. 73; Lib. Scacc. 1610, 24.

[183] *Statutes*, p. 73; Lib. Scacc. 1610, 25.

[184] *Statutes*, p. 73; Lib. Scacc. 1610, 25. Moore considered that this regulation was generally disregarded, basing his assumption on the valuation of two fishing boats seized 'for goeing to England without the lycense of the worshipful Governor' in 1676. The vessels of John Cannan and John Christian were valued at 37s. and 40s. respectively, which, Moore believed, indicated that they were too low in value to be of four tons burthen. Moore, *History*, vol. ii, pp. 947–8; Lib. Scacc. 1677, 28. In about 1720, Bishop

inhabitants as a whole were expected to provide for the herring fishery. Indeed, before the seventeenth century, there is apparently no information about the size of the herring fleet, and such data as survives for this period is fragmentary. In 1636, there were 222 Manx vessels engaged in the herring fishing; in 1672, it was reported that there were 'about 200 fishing botes in the Island.'[185] By 1697, this number had declined to 142 vessels, 'which is near three score boates less then [there] was eight or nine yeares agoe.' (Table 2.2).

Table 2.2. *Herring Boats by Sheading, Parish and Town, 1697*

Sheading	No. of Boats	Parish/Town	No. of Boats [1]
Glenfaba	23	Patrick	7
		German	4
		Peel	12
Michael	20	Michael	5
		Ballaugh	4
		Jurby	3
Ayre	29	Andreas	2
		Bride	4
		Lezayre	—
Rushen	32	Rushen	9
		Arbory	5
		Malew	4
		Castletown	—
Middle	3	Santan	—[2]
		Marown	—[2]
		Braddan	—[2]
Garff	35	Conchan	—
		Douglas	7
		Lonan	4

Thomas Wilson estimated that the average herring boat had a burthen of two tons. T. Wilson, 'The History of the Isle of Man', in W. Camden, *Britannia*, ed., E. Gibson (1722), printed in Harrison, *Old Historians*, p. 104.
[185] Megaw and Megaw, 'Early Manx Fishing Craft', p. 104; M.M.L., MD/401/1717/23.

		Maughold	—
		Ramsey	15
Total	142	Total	85

Source: M.M.L., I.O. 1696-1704, Ingates and Outgates, 1698.

Notes.

1. The discrepancy between the totals for the sheadings and for their constituent parishes is due to the number of boats which 'had nothing', that is, no herring catch, and which are only listed under the sheading. Thus, for example, twenty-three boats from the sheading of Ayre, perhaps many from Lezayre, 'had nothing.'

2. No parishes are specified for the sheading of Middle.

No reference was made to the number of men expected to crew these vessels, but Blundell's estimate, presumably based on first hand knowledge, puts it at a maximum of six. Some of these were 'such as have boats and nets of their own' and 'live and thrive with their fishing, especially of herrings;' others were 'meer mariners,' 'such as assist the former,' being 'hired by them during that time of fishing.' After the catch had been landed and the tithe fish set aside, Blundell reported that the

> rest of the fish in every boat they divide into eight parts, whereof he that furnisheth the nets hath three parts, he that is owner of the boat one part; the other four parts are subdivided among the fishermen that assisted to catch 'em, for in every boat that goeth out to fish there be four fishermen, so as if the owner of the boat be also owner of the nets, he hath the half of all the herrings that are taken in that boat and in that net.[186]

Further regulations concerning the herring fishery were recorded in 1610. These may have been embodied in an Act of Tynwald at the time, though no contemporary copy remains extant; it is perhaps more likely, however, that they were inserted in the records as a declaration of customary laws long in existence.[187] Among the

---

[186] Blundell, *History*, vol. i, p. 85.

[187] When the 'official' edition of the Statutes was compiled in the early 1880s, the original MS copy of this 'Act' could not be located. The oldest copy then extant was that supplied by George Savage, waterbailiff, to the commissioners of inquiry appointed by the British government in 1791. *Statutes*, pp. 74 n. 1, 76 and n. 1.

most important of these orders was the stipulation that no person should commence fishing for herring before July 16, which date was then taken to mark the beginning of the season.[188] The waterbailiff, who was responsible for the supervision of the herring fishery, was to be notified as soon as the shoals appeared off the coast on or after this date. It was then his duty to assemble 'all the Boats of the Island or Fleet' and to send them to the herring shoals. No fisherman was to put out to sea by day for the fishing without having first obtained permission from the waterbailiff or one of the other officers, unless 'there be a great Necessity for it.'[189] Any man found breaking this law risked losing both his boat and his nets.

A similar penalty awaited those who engaged in fishing between Saturday morning and Sunday night after sunset.[190] This suspension of fishing activity did, however, serve a practical purpose, as well as permitting the fishermen to attend church on Sunday. On every Saturday afternoon during 'the Fishing Time,' the waterbailiff held an Admiralty Court[191] at which juries of 'Enquiry,' or indictment, composed of boatmasters and fishermen, presented all who had violated the fishery regulations.[192] Any fisherman who was found to have cast his nets before the waterbailiff had given the signal to start fishing, by taking down his flag or giving 'a Watchword if the Night be dark,' was to be fined 10s. and to spend twenty days in prison.[193] If one crew were fortunate enough to come upon 'the Scul of fish' and take a good catch without informing the nearest boat, so that, by passing on the word, all might benefit, each member of the offending boat's company was to be punished by a fine of 40s., besides imprisonment.[194] Fishermen who shot their nets 'over the Netts of another' or who used 'Draw-Netts' or 'Stake-Netts' were to be fined 10s.[195] Those who mutilated another man's nets by

---

[188] *ibid*, pp. 74–5. By general consent, the same date was appointed for the fishermen 'to begin to drive for Herring' in 1613. *ibid*, p. 81.

[189] *ibid*, p. 75.

[190] *ibid*.

[191] The jurisdiction, personnel and business of the Admiralty Court are outlined in chapter 1, pp. 73–4.

[192] *Statutes*, p. 76.

[193] *ibid*, p. 75.

[194] *ibid*.

[195] *ibid*.

cutting off 'any Buoys or Corks' or who took any fish from another man's nets were liable to be indicted of felony; if the offence were serious enough, they would be sent to the court of General Gaol Delivery and possibly face the death penalty if adjudged guilty.[196] Fighting and using 'uncharitable' language within the waterbailiff's jurisdiction carried the penalty of a forty-day term in prison and a fine at his discretion. If an assault caused bloodshed, all the offender's goods were forfeited to the Lord.[197] For all his pains, the waterbailiff was entitled to 'a certain Measure called a Kybbon-full of Herrings' from every boat 'as oft as they Fish,' and to punish any master who refused to hand over the fish, or make a payment of 12d. instead, by excluding the offender from the fishery.[198]

The duration of the herring season was never fixed since the fishery depended on the presence or absence of the shoals. Once the herring appeared off the coast after the date set for the beginning of the season, it seems that fishing continued until the needs of the island, probably including a surplus, had been supplied or the herring departed. The 'Herring Fishing Time' began in July, as already noted, although the exact date varied from July 16 in 1610 and 1613 to July 1 in 1687.[199] The business of fishing often started rather later. In the late 1640s, which seem to have been years when the catch was relatively poor, Blundell recorded that the 'Manksmen begin their fishing for herrings about the latter end of August, and continue the same all the month of September.'[200] Bishop Wilson stated in about 1720 that then the 'time of fishing is between July and All-hallow's tide' (November 1).[201]

In a good year, when the herring were numerous and the fishermen had large catches, the Isle of Man was apparently self-sufficient in fish. When several Scottish merchants came to the island with herring in the spring of 1595, the governor, Randulph Stanley, 'not knowing what neede the Countrey had thereof,' consulted the four merchants of the isle appointed to deal with merchant

---

[196] *ibid*. Felony lay outside the jurisdiction of the Admiralty Court. See p. 73. On the court of General Gaol Delivery, see chapter 1, pp. 65–6.

[197] *Statutes*, p. 75.

[198] *ibid*, p. 76.

[199] *ibid*, pp. 75, 81, 141.

[200] Blundell, *History*, vol. i, p. 85. For Blundell's report of the herring catch in the 1640s, see *infra*, p. 119.

[201] Wilson, 'History', in Harrison, *Old Historians*, p. 104.

strangers,[202] 'to understand the want of the Countrey in that behalfe.' The general consensus was that the inhabitants were 'already sufficientlie provided of heyringes,' presumably after a successful fishery in the previous year, and only two men, Evan Garrett and John Stevenson, were licensed to buy herring from the Scotsmen. Garrett purchased a barque load at Ramsey of which, under the watchful eye of the waterbailiff, he was to dispose 'for the use of the Countrey;' Stevenson was told to go to Douglas, where he might have 'so manie heyringes as will satisfie his want.'[203]

After a bad year, when catches were small, surplus grain could be exported from the island to make good the deficiency. This course seems to have been taken even when there may have been a shortage of grain in the island after a poor harvest. Following perhaps several deficient or bad harvests and the apparent failure of the fishery in 1595, for example, the Keys petitioned in March 1596

> in the name and behalf of the whole Inhabitantes of the Cuntry, that they may be lycensed to exchange their barly for heringes by reason that hearinges are so necessarie a victuall for the Cuntry for mayntenance of their servantes and families that they can aswell want corne yf nede so required as victuall.[204]

The success or failure of the herring fishery was not only determined by the size of the shoals and the skill of the fishermen; it was also significantly influenced by the impositions laid on native and foreigner alike. A particular source of grievance was the payment of one maze, or 620 fish, out of every five mazes caught to the Lord. In 1613, the governor and officers reported to Countess Elizabeth that

> because of the great Imposicon by an auncyent Statute in this Isle for paying of Custom Heyrings (called Castle Mazes) in Tyme of Heyringe ffishinge, not onlie Strangers have refrayned to come to the late Fishinge of this Isle, but also the Islanders themselves being thereby discouraged, did not shewe their

---

[202] The appointment and duties of the four merchants are discussed in chapter 5, pp. 240–42.

[203] Lib. Canc. 1595, 24.

[204] Lib. Scacc. 1596, 24. The harvests in the west of England were poor in 1592 and 1593 and bad in the following two years. Hoskins, 'Harvest Fluctuations, 1480–1619', appendix ii, p. 46.

willinge Minds, nor consequentlie use their industrious Paynes in and about the Fishinge.[205]

In response, the Countess, 'desirous to have Strangers well used, and to bring Entercourse of Trafficke betwixt them and the Islanders,' directed the officers to revise the rates for the castle mazes. Taking the average size of catch into consideration, Governor Robert Molyneux and the officers ordered that 'for all the Tyme of this next Fishinge,' two mazes of the best fish were to be paid out of every small boat belonging to 'a Countriman' and four mazes out of every Manx scout; strangers were to pay one maze out of every small boat on their first night at the fishing and the same amount for each week they remained; scouts owned by foreigners paid double the rates of a small boat.[206] Fishermen who failed to enter their names with the clerk of the rolls before starting to drive for the shoals faced stiff penalties. If the offender were a Manxman, he was fined £5; if a foreigner neglected this obligation, he stood to forfeit his entire catch.[207]

The effect of these orders is difficult to assess because of the limited amount of evidence relating to the herring fishery. It seems, however, that they remained in force in succeeding years.[208] In practice, the new rates for castle mazes represented a reduction in this customary payment for Manxmen, provided that the herring fishery was a success and that each small boat owner had a catch in excess of ten mazes and each scout landed at least twice that amount. Similarly, in a good year, the stranger might do well. If the fishery proved to be a failure, for whatever reason, and the catch was small for each boat, both native and stranger would suffer.

At some point after this date and before about 1660, the castle mazes were commuted to a money payment at the rate of 5s. for every five mazes of herring.[209] In 1665, Earl Charles's income from 'the lord's Custome mazes' totalled £44 10s.[210] This imposition

---

[205] *Statutes*, p. 79.

[206] *ibid*, pp. 79–80.

[207] *ibid*, pp. 80–1.

[208] The statute book does not record that these orders 'expired,' or that they were modified or repealed, as it does in other cases where regulations were set out. *ibid*, pp. 79–81. Cf. M.M.L., MS MD/15,040, Parr, *Abridgement*, pp. 80–2.

[209] Cl.R.O., Nantlys MS D/NA/905, 21; M.M.L., MD/401/1717/23.

[210] M.M.L. R.D. 1651–70, Book of charge of the revenue of the Isle of Man, 1665.

might not weigh too heavily on fishermen selling their catch so long as the price in the market remained above 1s. per maze. When herring were abundant, however, prices could easily fall below this level. In 1667, for instance, herring could be bought in Douglas, Castletown and Peel for between 6d. and 12d. per maze.[211]

Few contemporaries give any indication of the vicissitudes of the herring fishery, despite its importance in the Manx economy.[212] Blundell and Sacheverell do, however, provide some account of the fortunes of Manx fishermen in the mid- and late seventeenth century. In the late 1640s, Blundell heard many complaints that 'of late years they have not taken half the quantity of herrings which they used to take in former times.'[213] At the end of the century, the story seems to have been much the same. Confirming Blundell's belief that 'the principal subsistence of the inhabitants is from the Sea,' Sacheverell remarked that there was a 'great variety of excellent Fish,' but that in the 1690s the fishermen did not catch 'near that quantity of fish they had in former ages.' He claimed that, at one time, herring had been so plentiful that 'five hundred have been sold for a groat,' but that now 'since their herring fails, . . . all other fish declines.'[214] In 1705, the impression of a continuous decline in the fishery was fostered when James, tenth earl of Derby, was informed by the officers that 'during the past thirty years the fishing had been a failure.'[215] The reality was somewhat less bleak.

The size of the herring catch can at present only be evaluated for two years in the later seventeenth century. This is clearly too small a sample from which to draw any useful conclusions about the fluctuations of the fishery, though it is quite possible that accounts for other years may yet be discovered which will enable this information to be viewed in its proper perspective. Nevertheless, such material does indicate the size of the herring catch in two years

---

[211] M.M.L., MF/PR/18. Malew Parish Registers: Baptisms, 1667.
[212] Little has been written subsequently on the early history of the Manx herring fishery. See Moore, *History*, vol. ii, pp. 941–59; W. C. Smith, *A Short History of the Irish Sea Herring Fisheries* (1923); *idem*, 'The Manx Herring Shoals', *Transactions of the Liverpool Biological Society*, vol. li (1938), pp. 22–70.
[213] Blundell, *History*, vol. i, p. 87.
[214] Sacheverell, *Account*, p. 14.
[215] M.M.L., MD/401/1720/11, cited in Moore, *History*, vol. ii, p. 952, n. 2; Moore, *Notes and Documents*, p. 57.

separated by more than three decades in a period which contemporaries evidently regarded as one of falling yields. The summary of the Lord's income from the custom mazes in 1665 reveals that payment was received on 178 mazes of herring, which, at the rate of one maze or 5s. for every five mazes caught, makes the total catch for that year 890 mazes.[216]

A rather more detailed account of the herring fishery is extant for 1697. (Tables 2.2 and 2.3). This lists the number of boats in the parishes and towns and the names of the masters paying the customs. It also indicates one of the reasons for a decline in the revenue from the fishery, since it was noted that 'above fiftie' of the 142 Manx boats, more than one-third of the entire native herring fleet, had been 'In Scotland at the fishing there and mist the fishing here.' This number included all fifteen boats from Ramsey, as well as perhaps about twenty-five from Andreas and Bride and others from Ballaugh, Jurby and Peel. Fishing in Scottish waters was not, however, a recent development. In 1687, it was observed that 'for some years past,'

> Some Boates (rather than they would attend the fishing about the Island to promote the good thereof) have gone over into Scotland and other places to fish for Herrings, and thereby have not only neglected the fishing at home, but also deprived our Right Honourable Lord of his Customs and other Dues arising out of the same.[217]

Governor Robert Heywood, the officers and Keys consequently issued orders that all masters should attend the fishing 'at such place as the fish is found and discovered,' after notice had been given by the coroner or lockman, and 'use all possible means to further and keep up the fishing.'[218] Those who simply absented themselves were to be presented for disobedience and fined £3 'without mitigation.' Fishermen who went over 'either into England, Ireland, or Scotland to fish there with their Boates and netts,' and neglected the fishery in Manx waters, were to pay 'all such Customs and other dutyes unto the Lord out of what fish they shall kill abroad' as if 'they had fished about the island.'[219]

[216] M.M.L. R.D. 1651–70, Book of charge of the revenue of the Isle of Man, 1665.
[217] *Statutes*, p. 141.
[218] *ibid.*
[219] *ibid.*

Table 2.3 *Herring Catch by Sheading, Parish and Town, 1697*
(1 maze contains 620 fish)

Sheading	No. of maze	Parish/Town	No. of mazes
Glenfaba	177.5	Patrick	47.5
		German	37.5
		Peel	92.5
Michael	60	Michael	27.5
		Ballaugh	22.5
		Jurby	10
Ayre	20	Andreas	10
		Bride	10
		Lezayre	—
Rushen	65	Rushen	30
		Arbory	17.5
		Malew	17.5
		Castletown	—
Middle	2.5	Santan	—
		Marown	—
		Braddan	—
Garff	431.5	Conchan	—
		Douglas	25
		Lonan	12.5
		Maughold	—
		Ramsey	394 [1]
Total	756.5 [2]	Total	754 [2]

Source: M.M.L., I.O. 1696-1704, Ingates and outgates, 1698.

Notes.

1. The Ramsey figures come from the ingates section of the accounts for 1697-8 cited above.

2. The discrepancy between the overall totals above is due to the absence of parish totals for the sheading of Middle.

In effect, this meant that Manxmen fishing in foreign waters would pay both the custom maze and an import duty on their herring catch. The evidence from the Ramsey ingates, however, seems to suggest that, in 1697 at least, only about one fifth of the native fishermen who imported herring at Ramsey paid the custom maze as well, and that even those who did paid less in custom maze than was appropriate for the size of their catch. Thomas Corlett of Ballaugh, for example, entered fourteen mazes of herring, including six mazes of salted herring from Scotland, yet only paid 2s. 6d. for custom mazes or the equivalent for a catch of two and a half mazes.[220]

The import duty on herring was, moreover, comparatively light. Manx fishermen were thus encouraged to operate in foreign waters, perhaps landing some of their fish in a Scottish or Irish port before returning to the island to pay customs duty on the remainder of their catch. Before 1692, when the Book of Rates was revised, both native and foreigner paid 1d. per maze in duty on inward shipments of herring; thereafter, the rate for Manx fishermen was halved.[221] In such circumstances, it is not surprising that a considerable number of Manx boats were prepared to risk fishing in Scottish waters. Together with the reduction in size of the herring fleet in the preceding decade, this explains the fall in the Lord's income from custom mazes, which in 1697 had declined from the level of 1665 by more than half to yield only £18 2s. 6d.; it also helps to account for the smaller number of herring landed in the island.

On the basis of the returns of the custom mazes in 1697, the catch in Manx waters came to only 362.5 mazes, while the fish imported at Ramsey, mainly, if not wholly, from Scottish waters, added another 394 mazes. The total amount of fish landed in the island during this particular season therefore came to 756.5 mazes. (Table 2.3). It would be misleading, however, to suggest that these figures provide conclusive proof that there was a decline in the herring fishery between the 1660s and the 1690s or that such a decline was gradual and continuous. There were years when the fishery was a failure. In January 1691, Ferdinando Calcott, the waterbailiff, wrote to Robert Roper, the earl of Derby's secretary, claiming that 'the Cheife things which formerly brought in money hath failed severall yeares (to witt)

---

[220] M.M.L., I.O. 1696–1704, Ingates and outgates, 1698.
[221] *Statutes*, p. 38; M.M.L., MD/401/1715/18. Book of Rates, 1677; M.M.L., MD/401/1715/20. Book of Rates, 1692. For further details of the island's customs duties, see chapter 5, pp. 235–38.

hering, corne and catle.'[222] Richard Stevenson, one of the revenue commissioners, wrote to Earl William in September 1696 concerning the 'declineing condition of your Poore People' and asserted that this was in part the result of 'the long want of Herring-fishing.'[223] There were other years when it is clear that the fishery was successful and herring were abundant. Sir Thomas Parr, vicar of Malew, recorded that 'att Fleshwicke on Sathurday the 13th of July 1667, Richard Read *cum sociis* had their boat almost loaden with herrings and on Tusday after the most were loaden; all had sufficient and soe continued with such an a boundance that they brought theire boats full to Douglas, Castletown and Peele.' The herring were, in Parr's view, 'very fatt fish.'[224]

Whether or not the herring fishery was a success, the burden of paying the tithe, the custom maze and, in some cases, the import duty encouraged Manx fishermen to attempt to evade these dues. Since only those who were discovered were presented at the courts, it is difficult to assess how widespread this offence was at any time. There were many places on the coast where a landing could be made away from the scrutiny of the Lord's officers, but there were always likely to be some in every parish, not least the lockman, who would inform the authorities if their suspicions were aroused. In 1677, Ferdinando Calcott, the waterbailiff, complained that John Cannell of Michael had concealed the Lord's 'Custome of heiringe' and uttered 'some Scurrolous Speeches' about him. Cannell was fined 6s. 8d. at the Debt Court[225] and ordered to appear at the next Chancery Court to ask forgiveness of Calcott.[226] Some offenders were quite open about their intentions. John Elsmore landed a cargo of dogfish at Castletown in 1691 but, when asked for his tithe by Sir Thomas Parr, vicar of Malew, he offered the clerk a fish and said 'I would not have you take it as tithe.' Elsmore's wife, who was also present, admonished him that 'Sir Thomas knows the law better than you do;' Elsmore, however, replied that he cared 'not a jot for him or his laws.'[227] Such refusal to pay the dues inevitably led to the offender's punishment in the courts, whether civil or ecclesiastical.

[222] M.M.L., MD/401/1718/87. Calcott to Roper, January 12, 1691.

[223] M.M.L., MD/401/1719/44. Stevenson to Derby, September 17, 1696.

[224] M.M.L., MF/PR/18. Malew Parish Registers: Baptisms, 1667.

[225] On the Debt Court, see chapter 1, p. 72.

[226] Lib. Scacc. 1677, 42–3.

[227] Craine, *Manannan's Isle*, p. 116.

Other fishermen tried to avoid payment by not attending the fishery, in spite of the standing orders to do so. At the Debt Court in November 1688, Captain William Christian of Bride and Danold Christian of Andreas and their respective boat companies were fined 10s. each for not going with their boats 'to the last herring fishing, contrary to the orders proclaimed at the Tynwald Court.'[228] For flatly refusing to appear with his crew 'in the height of the fishing,' Danold Dougherty of Jurby was punished with the lesser fine of 3s. 4d.[229] Outright non-compliance of this sort, however, was apparently comparatively rare.

Another method of evading tithes and the other dues on herring and other fish was to steal another man's catch. This approach was not without its pitfalls. In March 1630, rather more than half a maze of stolen herring, totalling 345 fish, was discovered 'hidde under Sand by Duglas.' The jurors appointed in the matter declared the herring forfeit to the Lord and vowed 'to use their best endevor by Inquisicon to detect the theef.'[230]

Although of much less importance in the island's economy, the river fishing in the Isle of Man was sufficiently good to enable the Lord to lease the fishing rights. While there are no great rivers in the island, some, nevertheless, contained salmon, as well as other fish, which made the rights desirable, though the Lord only ever received a limited income from the fines and rents.[231] (Map 3). The 'Bennifitt of the Salmon fishinge of Douglasse,' that is, in the Douglas river, was, for example, leased to Richard Joyner of Douglas in August 1660. The entry fine set by Governor Roger Nowell and the commissioners appointed by Earl Charles amounted to 40s. and the rent remained the same as that 'formerlie payd by his ancestores,' namely 13s. 4d.[232] The fishery at Douglas was the most important, as can be inferred from the fact that it bore a much higher rent than the other three salmon fisheries. At the same time as Joyner was the lessee of the Douglas fishery, James Moore of Baldromma, Lonan, and James

---

[228] Lib. Scacc. 1688, 43.

[229] *ibid.*

[230] Lib. Scacc. 1630, 13.

[231] River salmon fisheries were also important in England. Cf. A. T. R. Houghton ed., 'The Ribble Salmon Fisheries', in *Chetham Miscellanies, vol. viii* (Chet. Soc., New Series, vol. cix, 1945); A. J. L. Winchester, *Landscape and Society in Medieval Cumbria* (Edinburgh, 1987), pp. 111–112.

[232] Lib. Scacc. 1660, inter 82–4.

Bankes of The Howe, Conchan, paid 5s. for the Laxey fishery; Edward Robinson and Thomas Radcliffe of Knockaloe, Patrick, paid 3s. 4d. each for the salmon fisheries at Ramsey and Peel respectively.[233]

Rivers where the fishing was not so good could not command such high rents. In January 1694, Governor William Sacheverell leased to John Cosnahan, vicar of Santan, 'the fresh water fishing of the River of Kirk Santan afforded from the mountain to the low water mark,' to be held during pleasure rather than for a fixed term of years, for the more modest sum of 1s. per annum.[234] The rents accruing from such lesser fisheries are difficult to discover individually since very few references to leases survive. The rents from rivers in each parish were entered collectively in the books of revenue charge under the heading 'milne farm and freshwater fishing,' and it is clear from these sources that not every parish possessed fisheries. In the year ending at Michaelmas 1654, for instance, rent was received for fisheries in Patrick, Lezayre, Rushen, Braddan and Lonan.[235]

Local inhabitants were permitted to fish in the rivers by licence from the farmer of the fishery, but, inevitably, many took fish from the rivers without bothering to pay for the privilege. John Clarke and Thomas Gremshey took salmon from the Neb in 1595, but were either informed upon or discovered by the lockman of German and presented for the offence.[236] The farmer of the fishery at Peel, Silvester Radcliffe of Knockaloe, presented three men from Patrick and two from German in November 1638 for fishing 'in the Burne without lycense.' Each was fined the sum of 12d.[237] William Cosnahan, the son of one of these offenders, was in trouble for the same transgression a year later when Radcliffe's widow claimed that he 'fisheth in the burne frequently without her leave.' This was not his

---

[233] M.M.L. R.D. 1651–70, Book of charge of the revenue of the Isle of Man, 1664.

[234] W. Cubbon ed., Unpublished Document no. 20, *J.M.M.*, vol. ii (1930–4), p. 44.

[235] M.M.L. R.D. 1651–70, Book of charge, Peel Castle, 1654; book of charge, Castle Rushen, 1654.

[236] Lib. Canc. 1595, 29. The earliest extant presentments for fishing without licence appear in the sheading court roll of 1418. W. Cubbon and B. R. S. Megaw (eds), 'Our Oldest Legal Records: Extracts from the Sheading Court Rolls of AD 1417–18', *J.M.M.*, vol. v (1941–6), p. 25.

[237] Lib. Scacc. 1639, 9.

first such offence, and the court, mindful of the fact, increased the fine to be imposed from 3s. 6d. to 4s. and warned that, if he broke the law again , he would be more 'sevearely punished.'[238] In an effort to minimise the possibility of detection, some took to fishing by night. In June 1661, Thomas Radcliffe of Knockaloe complained that William Cowper the elder 'hath fished in his rented ryver before sunrise' without permission; Cowper was fined 2s. 6d.[239]

It was not only the larger and more important rivers which attracted the attention of the poachers. The farmer of Santan Burn, Caesar Patten, master gunner at Castle Rushen, protested to Deputy Governor Richard Stevenson in 1681 that 'some persons [did] presume to take and distroy the fish of the said River, viz. salmon and salmon frey, with listers, baggs, Creeles and other engiens.' Stevenson accordingly ordered the lockman of the parish to give notice in the parish church that whoever was found to be guilty of such an offence in the future would be severely fined and punished.[240] Despite the number of presentments for illegal fishing, however, there is no reason to suppose that most of the fish caught in the rivers were not taken lawfully and that they constituted a vital source of food for the inhabitants of the parishes through which the rivers flowed.

Agriculture and fishing, especially the herring fishery, were the cornerstones of the Manx economy throughout the early modern period and beyond. Nearly the whole of the island's population was involved in cultivating crops, rearing animals and, if only seasonally, in fishing. In years when the harvest was good and the herring shoals yielded plenty of fish, there was sufficient food for the island's needs. When either the harvest or the fishery failed, the Manx could, to a certain extent, compensate by relying more on the one food source than the other. If both failed, serious hardship was very likely to follow.

[238] *ibid*, 61.
[239] Lib. Scacc. 1661, 28.
[240] Lib. Scacc. 1681, 15.

3 *Manufactures*

Although agriculture and fishing formed the basis of the Manx economy throughout the early modern period, manufactures and trade had important roles to play in the economic life of the island. The limited amount of manufacturing – a term more appropriate than industry in the context of a pre-industrialised economy – was almost exclusively concerned with the processing of the primary products of the island – corn, wool and hides – to provide food, clothing and footwear for the domestic market. Despite the restricted size of this market, it is clear from the waterbailiff's accounts that the supply of such manufactures was very often insufficient to meet demand. In years of plenty, surplus grain was exported from the island in addition to cattle, sheep, herring, hides, sheepfells and wool, which regularly constituted the principal Manx exports; in exchange, the Manx obtained raw materials which were either in short supply or unavailable in the island, such as timber and iron; they also imported manufactured goods which could only be acquired from more industrially advanced regions. Manufactures and trade, therefore, played important and complementary parts in the island's economy.

I. THE NATURE AND SCALE OF MANX MANUFACTURING

Contemporary observers in the seventeenth century mentioned little about either the nature or the scope of Manx manufacturing, but what they did record clearly indicates that such activity was primarily geared to servicing the fundamental needs of the Manx population. In the late 1640s, William Blundell remarked that the Manx had 'none but the poorest trades, and such as are meerly for necessity.'[1] This assessment was confirmed several years later by

---

[1] Blundell, *History*, vol. i, p. 83.

James Chaloner, who concluded that the island 'produceth not any Commodities of value, neither is [it] improved by way of Manufacture,' the people 'being contented with such homely accomodations for dyet and clothing as their own Country affordeth.'[2] The basic need for food was largely satisfied by the tenants themselves, at least in years when the harvest was average or better and the herring catch was good. In such favourable circumstances, those whose tenements could not produce enough for their households or who could not take part in the fishery were able to purchase what they required in the island's markets.[3] The vital process of corn-grinding, however, which provided the flour for bread and oatcakes, both staples of the Manx diet, was restricted by law to licensed millers.[4] The brewing of ale for sale by retail was similarly limited to those who obtained a licence, although many attempted to evade such regulations.[5] The tenants' requirements for clothing were partially answered at home, since it was there that wool and flax were spun and cloth was usually made up into clothes, but the production of cloth itself was entrusted to weavers and fullers alone.[6] Most tenants wore *carranes*, or shoes made from untanned cow hide, which they probably made themselves, while the demand for higher quality footwear from the more prosperous farmers, merchants and officers was met, to some extent, by Manx shoemakers and, perhaps more frequently, by imports.[7] The limited variety of agricultural equipment which the farmers possessed – including ploughs, sickles, scythes and harrows, almost all of which were imported – was repaired by the small number of blacksmiths, carpenters, coopers and wheelwrights in the island, who were sometimes also members of the garrisons of Castle Rushen and Peel Castle.[8]

That soldiers and servants in the Lord's 'houses' engaged in some form of manufacturing activity in addition to their official duties serves to underline the fact that in the Isle of Man, as in England and

[2] Chaloner, *Treatise*, p. 52.
[3] The markets of the island are discussed in chapter 4, pp. 193–208.
[4] The activities of the millers are considered *infra*, pp. 152–55.
[5] For further details of licensing in the brewing trade, see *infra*, pp. 130–39.
[6] Cloth manufacture is examined *infra*, pp. 143–44, 148–50, 175–82.
[7] Moore, *History*, vol. i, p. 315; B. R. S. Megaw and H. F. McClintock, 'The Costume of the Gaelic Peoples', *J.M.M.*, vol. v (1941–6), p. 159. For details of the import trade in shoes, see chapter 5, p. 281 and Table 5.8.
[8] Cl.R.O., Nantlys D/NA/905, 4.

elsewhere in the sixteenth and seventeenth centuries, it was very common for individuals to have more than one occupation. Agriculture was the principal activity of the vast majority of the island's population, but the seasonal nature of arable and pastoral farming inevitably encouraged the farmers of quarterlands and smaller holdings, as well as those who only worked on the land as labourers, to pursue some craft or trade to ensure that they maintained an adequate level of income. These occupations were 'not accidental or subsidiary, secondary, or a miserable makeshift,' as Joan Thirsk has pointed out; they were an essential and complementary part of the pastoral economy.[9] Many farmers were thus part-time craftsmen, even if they did little more than cater for their immediate household. For others who had only a limited amount of land, particularly those who held cottages in the towns, crafts such as weaving or shoemaking could provide a sizable part of their income. Such crafts were not subject to the same seasonal demands as agriculture and could be worked at throughout the year, although fluctuations in demand, dictated by the priorities and variable financial condition of the inhabitants, and the labour requirements of the larger farmers at harvest time could cause a temporary suspension of work. Some crafts, such as brewing and milling, did experience periods of peak activity, but these occurred after the harvest, at a time when farming activity was at a low point. Consequently, few, if any, craftsmen faced a conflict of interests which prevented them from being part-time farmers, keeping livestock and, where they had sufficient land, growing crops.[10]

---

[9] J. Thirsk, 'Seventeenth-Century Agriculture and Social Change', in *idem* (ed.), *Land, Church and People, Ag.H.R.*, vol. xviii, supplement (1970), p. 172. Cf. A. M. Everitt, 'Farm Labourers, 1500–1640', in C. G. A. Clay (ed.), *Rural Society: Landowners, Peasants and Labourers, 1500–1750* (Cambridge, *1990*), pp. 190–4.

[10] The amount of time devoted to agriculture and manufacturing respectively by Manxmen depended much more on the size of their holdings and the time of year than fluctuations in market demand. In England, with its well developed cloth industry, the state of the textile market dictated the amount of time which, for instance, Lancashire weavers spent in the fields. N. Lowe, *The Lancashire Textile Industry in the Sixteenth Century*, (Chet. Soc., 3rd series, vol. xx , 1972), p. 27. Colliers in the Colne area of Lancashire may have spent about half of each year engaged in agriculture. J. T. Swain, *Industry before the Industrial Revolution: North East Lancashire, 1500–1640*, (Chet.

This pattern of occupations was further complicated by the practice of craftsmen who, like their counterparts in England,[11] often engaged in two or more generally unrelated lines of work. From the craftsman's point of view, this was a necessary state of affairs, for the well-being of the island's economy was heavily dependent on the success or failure of the harvest and the herring fishery and, in order to survive, he had to be able to turn his hand to a variety of tasks. The absence of any form of craft gilds in the island, in itself testimony to the low level and mutability of economic activity there, makes it difficult to determine the numbers of those who combined, for example, brewing and tanning on a regular or occasional basis. Craftsmen in some of the more important trades, including brewing, milling and weaving, were licensed by the island's government, but few lists of such licensees, or indeed of those presented for working without official permission, have so far been discovered.[12] Even when using such lists, it is often very difficult to identify, with any certainty, an individual named under one trade with another of the same name in the same parish or town engaged in a different trade.

note 10 *continued*
Soc., 3rd series, vol. xxxii, 1986), pp. 174–5. Many of the metalworkers of south Yorkshire and north Derbyshire earned a large part of their income from cattle rearing. D. G. Hey, *The Rural Metalworkers of the Sheffield Region*, University of Leicester Dept. of English Local History, Occasional Papers, 2nd series, no. v (Leicester, 1972), p. 21. In Kirkwall in Orkney, however, few craftsmen seem to have been involved in any significant agricultural activity. F. J. Shaw, *The Northern and Western Islands of Scotland* (Edinburgh, 1980), p. 138.

[11] In the late Tudor and early Stuart period, some of the glovers at Chester became broggers, or middlemen, dealing in the wool which they removed from the sheepskins used in their principal trade. Others were involved in trades quite unconnected with leather, dealing in commodities such as timber and wine. One Chester glover also owned an inn. D. M. Woodward, 'The Chester Leather Industry, 1558–1625', *T.H.S.L.C.*, vol. cxix (1967), pp. 80–1, 83–4. Some of the shoemakers of Worcester were also weavers or brewers, while a few of the leather workers of Manchester dealt in linen yarn. At least one glover in the latter town was engaged in the wool trade in the late sixteenth century and several linen weavers there combined textile work with shopkeeping. A. D. Dyer, *The City of Worcester in the Sixteenth Century* (Leicester, 1973), p. 122; T. S. Willan, *Elizabethan Manchester*, (Chet. Soc., 3rd series, vol. xxvii 1980), pp. 50, 59.

[12] For a discussion of these lists, see *infra*, pp. 132–39.

Such problems are magnified by the apparent reluctance of the officials who compiled the court records to set down the status of plaintiffs and defendants, creditors and debtors, except, in general, when drawing up indictments and taking depositions; this unfortunate trait was shared by the clerks who were responsible for writing out the wills and inventories of the deceased.

From the cases in which it has been possible to make at least a tentative identification of individual craftsmen, it is clear that it was by no means uncommon for such men to have up to three occupations, all of which may have been followed at the same time. For example, many of the officers and soldiers of the garrisons of Castle Rushen and Peel Castle in the 1640s had one, and in some cases two, additional occupations. In 1648, the steward, sergeant, porter and at least thirteen of the thirty soldiers in Castle Rushen obtained licences to brew and sell ale and beer in Castletown; in the same year in Peel, twelve members of the garrison there, including the surgeon and six of the twenty-four soldiers, were licensed as brewers. Among the former group were William Preswicke, the sergeant, who was described in 1644 as a saddler; Richard Halsall, who supplemented his wage as a soldier by making shoes; John Woolley, who was a soldier and a licensed weaver; George Whetstones, another soldier, who also worked as a tailor when off duty; and Matthew Postley and John Preston, both of whom were soldiers and glovers.[13] Craftsmen who were not associated with the garrisons also had diverse interests. Christopher Bridson, William Corlett and Edward Postley were glovers in Douglas in the mid-seventeenth century and, like many other craftsmen, engaged in brewing, either occasionally or on a regular basis.[14] In the 1640s, William Gell of Peel divided his time between brewing and his activities as a merchant, while William Chisnall of Castletown acted in both these capacities and, furthermore, traded as a shoemaker.[15]

---

[13] For the lists of officers and soldiers in the garrisons, see M.M.L. R.D. 1627–50, Book of allowance, Castle Rushen, 1648; book of allowance, Peel Castle, 1648. The lists of licensed brewers in both towns are recorded in Lib. Scacc. 1648, 14, 17. See also Lib. Scacc. 1644, 11; Lib. Scacc. 1645, inter 83–4 (1); Lib. Scacc. 1640, 109; Lib. Scacc. 1653, 6.

[14] Lib. Scacc. 1653, 6; Lib. Scacc. 1648, 16; Lib. Scacc. 1651, 6.

[15] Lib. Scacc. 1640, 102; Lib. Scacc. 1648, 14, 17; Lib. Scacc. 1651, 3; Lib. Canc. 1649, 96; M.M.L., I.O. 1646–59, Waterbailiff's accounts, 1647.

The extant lists of licensed craftsmen, which mainly date from the decade or so after 1640, indicate that the number of men involved in some of these trades was small and this impression is confirmed by other evidence. In January 1578, 'at the [h]umble sutte and Request of divers [h]onest parsons,' the captain and deemsters agreed that a fine should be imposed on William McCoter of Braddan, a smith, and the indictment against him for concealing a quantity of iron dropped 'because ther is no more smyth within three parishis.'[16] When the glovers of the island petitioned Governor John Greenhalgh about the activities of Irish, Scottish and Manx pedlars in November 1646, only nineteen men appended their names to the document; a similar complaint addressed to the Lord's Council by the glovers and skinners in December 1652 bore eighteen names.[17]

In the most important Manx trades – brewing, milling and weaving – in which the Lord was immediately concerned through the issue of licences and the sealing of measures, a considerably larger number of craftsmen were involved. This is clearly shown in the lists of alehousekeepers, brewers and other craftsmen with sealed measures drawn up by the island's government. One such list, compiled in 1640, reveals that there were nearly one hundred licensed websters or weavers in the Isle of Man and that at least some of the cloth which they produced on their looms was made into clothing by the score of licensed tailors. It also records that twenty-five millers brought their measures to be tested and sealed and that more than one hundred alehousekeepers obtained licences to brew and sell their product. (Tables 3.1 and 3.3). Further evidence of the island's manufacturing ability is contained in the presentments 'of all those that keepes any weights or measures unsealed, and those that Brewes without license' made in December in the same year. These show that there were almost as many weavers operating without official approval as there were weavers whose yard-measures carried the stamp of the Lord. Moreover, the number of unlicensed tailors was practically twice that of their licensed fellow craftsmen. There were also more than sixty alehousekeepers brewing illegally and fourteen millers who had failed to have their measures checked. (Tables 3.2 and 3.4).

[16] Lib. Plit. 1577, January 7, 1578.
[17] Lib. Scacc. 1647, 5; Lib. Scacc. 1653, 6.

Table 3.1 *Sealed Measures, 1640*

Parish	Firlots [1]	Websters' yards	Tailors' yards	Millers' measures
Patrick	—	3	—	2
German	4	12 [2]	4	6
Michael	1	8	1	—
Ballaugh	—	13	—	1
Jurby	6	6	—	—
Andreas	2	5	—	1
Bride	2	7	2	—
Lezayre	5 [3]	11	5	6
Rushen	2	2	—	1
Arbory	6	10 [4]	1	—
Malew	12	7	4	3
Santan	—	2	—	2
Marown	—	1 [5]	—	—
Braddan	—	1 [5]	—	—
Conchan	18	—	—	2
Lonan	—	1	—	1
Maughold	2	6	3	—
Totals	60	95 [6]	20	25

Source: Lib. Scacc. 1640, 110–111.

Notes.

1. The firlot was a standard measure for the sale and purchase of grain. See chapter 4, p. 209 and Table 4.3.

2. One of the websters' yards was granted to William Fayrebrother, walker

3. Plus one kishan. See Table 4.3.

4. One yard jointly held.

5. Unspecified yard, probably that of a webster.

6. The total number of websters was ninety-six. See note 4.

Table 3.2 *Unsealed Measures, 1640*

Parish	Firlots [1]	Websters' yards	Tailors' yards	Millers' measures
Patrick	—	—	—	1
German	—	11	3	—
Michael	—	—	—	—
Ballaugh	—	3	—	—
Jurby	—	—	—	—
Andreas	4	11	8	—
Bride	6	10	7	—
Lezayre	4	10	3	—
Rushen	3	3	—	1
Arbory	—	—	—	3
Malew	9	7	3	2 [2]
Santan	5	2	2	—
Marown	1	4	4	2 [2]
Braddan	2	3	1	3
Conchan	2	3	3	1
Lonan	4	8	—	—
Maughold	5	4	2	1
Totals	45	79	36	14

Source: Lib. Scacc. 1640, 79–98.

Note.
1. The firlot was a standard measure for the sale and purchase of grain. See Table 3.1, note 1.

2. 'Kitchins', or kishans and other measures. See Table 3.1, note 3.

Table 3.3 *Licensed Alehousekeepers and Retail Brewers*

Parish/Town		1576	1599	1609	1640	1648 (1)	1648 (2)	1650 (1)	1650 (2)	1652	1653
Patrick		20	—	—	1	2	2	6	1	4	1
German	}	4	—	—	27	6	—	3	3	1	1
Peel	}	48	—	—	—	41	16	27	18	29	24
Michael		37	—	—	2	13	3	14	9	17	4
Ballaugh		6	—	—	—	6	1	3	5	3	3
Jurby		14	—	—	—	4	—	3	1	2	—
Andreas		15	—	—	1	7	1	4	9	6	3
Bride		—	—	—	1	4	2	4	3	4	4
Lezayre		16	—	—	5	9	4	9	8	11	8
Rushen		19	—	—	3	6	2	9	7	6	5
Arbory		13	—	—	4	5	2	4	5	12	4
Malew	}	59	—	—	5	6	1	8	8	13	7
Castletown	}	—	25	—	25	49	24	47	43	49	33
Santan		6	—	—	2	5	2	4	5	3	3
Marown		—	—	—	1	3	—	3	3	5	2
Braddan		—	—	—	1	2	1	2	4	5	4
Conchan	}	—	—	—	28	5	2	3	4	5	4
Douglas	}	30	—	29	—	57	23	44	39	35	28
Lonan		9	—	—	1	5	1	5	5	4	4
Maughold	}	9	—	—	—	4	1	1	2	2	1
Ramsey	}	—	—	—	—	23	12	14	12	15	12
Totals		305	25	29	107	262	100	217	194	231	155

Sources: Lib. Plit. 1577 [Feb.1576]; Lib. Scacc. 1599, inter 26–26(2); Lib. Scacc. 1609, inter 36–7; Lib. Scacc. 1640, 100–111; Lib. Scacc. 1648, 14–18; Lib. Scacc. 1649, 11–13; Lib. Scacc. 1650, 15–16; Lib. Scacc. 1651, 3–7; Lib. Scacc. 1652, 6–10; Lib. Scacc. 1653, 13–16.

Note. Where there is no number given for one of the towns, it is to be assumed that it has been included in the parish with which it is bracketed.

Table 3.4 *Unlicensed Alehousekeepers and Retail Brewers*

Parish/Town		1640	1647	1650	1651	1654	1663	1682	1696	1699
Patrick		—	2	5	—	25	9	—	—	—
German	}	7	8	5	—	21	7	—	1	—
Peel	}	—	—	—	—	—	3	—	3	10
Michael		3	7	—	5	17	—	—	—	—
Ballaugh		—	1	—	3	8	—	—	—	—
Jurby		—	1	—	2	2	—	—	—	2
Andreas		5	1	2	—	—	13	—	—	—
Bride		1	—	—	—	—	7	—	—	—
Lezayre		—	9	9	—	6	15	—	—	—
Rushen		9	2	—	—	13	—	17	3	—
Arbory		4	10	—	—	—		11	—	—
Malew	}	5	18	—	9	—	—	7	—	—
Castletown	}	—	6	14	—	21	—	—	6	—
Santan		—	4	—	3	18	—	—	3	—
Marown		—	2	1	—	—	—	—	2	—
Braddan		—	8	12	—	—	—	—	1	—
Conchan	}	11	6	1	4	14	—	—	—	—
Douglas	}	—	5	—	—	18	—	—	—	2
Lonan		2	8	1	2	29	—	—	—	—
Maughold	}	15	2	—	—	—	—	—	—	—
Ramsey	}	—	1	—	—	—	—	—	—	—
Totals		62	101	50	28	192	54	35	19	14

Sources: Lib. Scacc. 1640, 79–98; Lib. Scacc. 1647, 84–9; Lib. Scacc. 1650, 17, 30, 33, 40, inter 40–1, 41, 57; Lib. Scacc. 1651, 11, 16, 17; Lib. Scacc. 1654, 1, 2, inter 2-3 (5, 6, 9, 10, 11), 7; Lib. Scacc. 1663, inter 35–6 (1, 3, 4), 49; Lib. Scacc. 1682, inter 15–16 (1–4); Lib. Scacc. 1696, 27–8; Lib. Scacc. 1699, 51, 53, 55, 64.

The reliability of these figures may be challenged on the grounds that such presentments do not accurately reflect the full extent of the problem of unsealed measures and unlicensed brewers since they only record unlawful activities which came to the attention of the authorities. It is clearly impossible to establish how many offenders, if any, escaped the notice of the coroner, lockman, moar and the various other officers in the island, but it is tempting to believe that, in the relatively small parish communities, it would have been difficult to conceal illicit undertakings of this nature for long and that, consequently, the number would be low. The surviving lists of licensees and offenders for the 1640s may represent an isolated attempt to improve the effectiveness and profitability of the licensing system, in the same way that leet officials in Lancashire turned alehouse licensing into a sort of local 'business tax,'[18] but equally they may be part of a series of such efforts, only a very few of which remain extant. There can be little doubt that the figures for unlicensed alehousekeepers and brewers would be significantly higher in 1640 if returns had been forthcoming from – or had survived for – all seventeen parishes. In the event, only nine appear to have submitted lists. When compared with the records for 1647, when it seems that only Bride failed to respond, the possible scale of the discrepancy becomes apparent. (Table 3.4).

A similar problem may be detected in the figures for craftsmen's measures, although on a much more modest scale. Weavers using both sealed and unsealed yards were recorded in every parish in the island in 1640, and it seems likely that the overall total of these craftsmen, derived from both lists, is probably fairly accurate. Tailors, however, were only noted in twelve parishes; there were apparently none in Patrick, Ballaugh, Jurby, Rushen or Lonan. In view of the numbers presented for working without the sanction of the Lord's officers and the fact that it was easier to hide the tools of the tailor's trade than it was to conceal a weaver's loom, it is difficult to resist the suspicion that some tailors must have avoided detection. The number of millers' measures recorded further suggests that some of the lessees of the Lord's mills or their appointees had managed to evade the efforts of the officers. Although the exact number of corn mills operating in the island in 1640 is difficult to determine, there

[18] W. J. King, 'Regulation of Alehouses in Stuart Lancashire: An example of discretionary administration of the law', *T.H.S.L.C.*, vol. cix (1980), pp.36–7.

were probably more than the total implied by the appearance of thirty-nine millers in the lists for that year. No miller at all was entered for the parishes of Jurby or Michael, despite the fact that there were two mills in the former and five, or perhaps six, in the latter.[19] (Tables 3.1 and 3.2). Nevertheless, even after taking into account the shortcomings of this evidence, there seems little reason to doubt that these lists offer a broadly accurate impression of the numbers of Manx craftsmen in four important trades in the early 1640s. Unfortunately, no comparable lists for the later seventeenth century have as yet come to light.

While considering the size of the manufacturing 'community' in the island, it should be borne in mind that the number of men and women involved in the various trades fluctuated, to a greater or lesser degree, from year to year, depending on the prevailing economic climate and other, less tangible, factors. This was evidently the case in the retail brewing trade, as can be seen from the lists of licensed and unlicensed alehousekeepers and brewers in the 1640s and early 1650s. (Tables 3.3 and 3.4). In trades in which more than merely the most basic equipment was required and which were more than simply limited extensions of production for a single household, such as weaving, variations in the numbers involved were likely to be considerably smaller. A reduction in demand or the short term lack of necessary raw materials for certain trades, such as bark for tanning, doubtless encouraged some to abandon one craft, albeit temporarily, to try their hand at another.

Whatever the reasons for such changes, the island's government did not look favourably upon tradesmen who embarked on a different line of work without licence. In 1611, for example, several weavers were presented 'for neglecting to do the Countrys work and betakeing themselves to do other work they ought not to do.'[20] In

---

[19] The mills in Jurby were both on the Killane river. The mills in Michael were: Mullen e Kelley, Mullin Harry, Mullengaw, Borodall [Borodaill], Ballagawne Mill and, probably, the mill in Glen Wyllin which was 'wast' in 1703. M.M.L., MF/RC/1. Lord's Composition Book, 1703. Cf. appendix viii. For a convenient list of the mills in the island in the early sixteenth century, see T. A. Bawden, L. S. Garrad, J. K. Qualtrough and J. W. Scatchard, *The Industrial Archaeology of the Isle of Man* (Newton Abbot, 1972), appendix vi, pp. 245–6.

[20] Lib. Plit. 1611, cited in M.M.L., MS 510C, J. Quayle, *A Book of Precedents* (n.d., [c. 1725]), p. 93.

1647, Thomas Quayle of Malew, a tailor by trade, was presented by William Clague, coroner of Rushen, for brewing and selling ale and beer without licence and, two years later, Robert Crowe of Lezayre, a shoemaker, faced a similar charge brought by Edmund Crowe, coroner of Ayre.[21] Some appear to have changed trades frequently, though not necessarily neglecting to obtain a licence to do so, and to have acquired at least a basic knowledge of several trades, such as Thomas Woods, a resident of Malew in 1683, who bore the nickname 'all traid.'[22] Until further and more comprehensive lists of craftsmen, both licensed and unlicensed, are discovered, if any indeed survive, it will not be possible to calculate either long-term variations in numbers or the frequency with which they combined or changed trades.[23]

II. THE DISTRIBUTION
OF MANX MANUFACTURING

The limited amount of extant evidence makes it difficult to draw any definite conclusions about the distribution of manufacturing activity in the island. Of seventeenth-century observers, only William Blundell, writing in the late 1640s, touched upon the subject, and he restricted his comments to the extent of such activity in the island's four towns. He claimed that there was 'an ordinary taylor, shoemaker, a weaver, and a smith' in each town, but, to emphasise the small scale of these trades, stressed that 'of every one of these there is but one in every of the said towns.'[24] The lists of craftsmen compiled in 1640 and references in the records of the Exchequer and

---

[21] Lib. Scacc. 1647, 88; Lib. Scacc. 1650, 13.

[22] M.M.L., MF/PR/18. Malew Parish Registers: Baptisms, 1683; A. W. Moore ed., *The Manx Note Book*, vol. iii (1887), p. 138.

[23] Although there are extant lists of both the Lord's and the barons' tenants, which were updated at irregular intervals throughout the sixteenth and seventeenth centuries, none systematically records the occupations of the inhabitants, either in the parishes or in the towns. Even the lists drawn up in 1703, prior to the Act of Settlement, generally only give the name of the tenant or tenants, the nature of the tenement and the name of the holder of the property at the 'Great Fining' in 1643. M.M.L., MD/401/1715/4; M.M.L., MF/RC/1. Lord's Composition Book, 1703.

[24] Blundell, *History*, vol. i, p. 83.

Chancery courts and other sources tell a somewhat different story and indicate that Blundell clearly underestimated the number of craftsmen working in the towns. During the 1640s, Castletown, for example, had at least two tailors, two, or possibly three, shoemakers, the same number of weavers and one, or perhaps two, blacksmiths.[25] Information concerning the other towns is less complete, and consequently appears to substantiate Blundell's statements, but, where at least some details are available, it is clear that the number of craftsmen was greater than he suggests. There were, for instance, four weavers resident in Peel in 1640, none of whom were in possession of a licence, while there were three, all licensed, living in Ramsey in the same year.[26]

Trades other than those mentioned by Blundell were also to be found in the towns, which, despite their small size,[27] represented a

[25] The craftsmen were as follows: i) tailors: Thomas Moore and George Whetstones, a soldier. Lib. Scacc. 1640, 109; M.M.L., MF/PR/18. Malew Parish Registers: Baptisms, 1653; M.M.L. R.D. 1627–50, Book of allowance, Castle Rushen, 1648; ii) shoemakers: Richard Halsall, a soldier, William Chisnall and William Wattleworth. Lib. Scacc. 1645, inter 83–4 (1); M.M.L. R.D. 1627–50, Book of allowance, Castle Rushen, 1648; Lib. Canc. 1649, 96; P.R.O. SP 29/67/150/I. iii) weavers: Thomas Norris, Peter Robinson, a soldier, and Anthony Corrin. Lib. Canc. 1637–8, 33; P.R.O. SP 29/67/150/I; M.M.L. R.D. 1627–50, Book of allowance, Castle Rushen, 1648; M.M.L., MF/EW/17. Inventory of Anthony Corrin, 1663. iv) blacksmiths: Robert Wattleworth and Tobie Massie. Lib. Canc. 1650, inter 40–1 (2); Lib. Scacc. 1645, inter 60–5 (2).

[26] The weavers in Peel were Hugh Colbin, a soldier in Peel Castle, William Gell, Henry Thomason and John Woods. Lib. Scacc. 1640, 84; Lib. Scacc. 1648, 17; M.M.L. R.D. 1627–50, Books of allowance, Peel Castle, 1648 and 1649. The Ramsey weavers were Philip Cowle, John Christian and John Costain. Lib. Scacc. 1640, 104; Lib. Scacc. 1648, 16.

[27] The earliest population 'figures' for the island's towns are the totals of 'souls' in the ecclesiastical 'census' of 1726. According to this probably reasonably reliable source, Douglas then had a population of 810; Castletown contained 785 persons; Peel had a population of 475; and Ramsey, marginally the smallest town, had 460 'souls'. R. Sherwood ed., *The Constitution of the Isle of Man*, Manx Society, vol. xxxi (1882), appendix B, no. 89, p. 284. The population of the towns was subject to short term fluctuations, but may have been generally growing in the early eighteenth century. For a preliminary assessment, see J. R. Dickinson, 'The Population of Douglas, Isle of Man, in 1730', *Liverpool University Archaeology Newsletter*, no. iii (1987), pp. 15–16.

larger market than the parishes. This was not so much because of a higher population density or the greater affluence of their inhabitants in general, but rather because of the presence of the Lord's officers and soldiers, a handful of relatively prosperous merchants who lived in the towns, especially Douglas and Castletown, and a varying number of transient strangers who might be merchants, mariners, passengers or refugees.[28] Although some of the demands of these groups in particular were supplied by imported goods, many of their basic requirements were answered by local tradesmen, a fact which is reflected by the consistently higher number of licensed alehousekeepers and brewers in the towns. (Tables 3.3 and 3.4). Besides the weavers, tailors, shoemakers and blacksmiths already mentioned, there were, in Castletown and Peel at least, slaters, glaziers, coopers, carpenters and joiners who served the needs of the Lord's garrisons[29] and probably also offered their talents to the inhabitants of the towns and the surrounding countryside, or at least to those who could afford them. Edward Wycliffe, for example, the slater who worked in Peel Castle in the late 1640s, also accepted commissions from individuals, such as Richard Coard of Castletown, whom he sued for failure to pay for 'worke and slates' in July 1649.[30] Twelve of the eighteen glovers in the island in the early 1650s were also based in the towns; six seem to have operated in Douglas, four in Castletown, and one each in Peel and Ramsey.[31] In the 1640s, Castletown furthermore boasted a saddler and one, or perhaps two masons.[32] Four decades later, Douglas

[28] Refugees were particularly in evidence in the island during the wars of the 1640s and William III's campaigns in Ireland between 1688 and 1691. See, for example, *C.S.P.D.*, *1645–7*, pp. 242–3; Lib. Scacc. 1649, inter 24–5 (3), inter 48–9; *H.M.C. Kenyon*, p. 255; P.R.O.N.I., Waring MSS D695/155.

[29] M.M.L. R.D. 1627–50, Books of allowance, Castle Rushen, 1648 and 1649; books of allowance, Peel Castle, 1648 and 1649.

[30] M.M.L. R.D. 1627–50, Book of allowance, Peel Castle, 1648; Lib. Canc. 1649, 104.

[31] Lib. Scacc. 1653, 6. Provisional identification of individual glovers has been possible by comparison with the lists of licensed brewers for the towns and petitions from the inhabitants. See the sources for Table 3.3; Lib. Scacc. 1642, post 36 (2); Lib. Scacc. 1650, inter 40–1 (2, 3).

[32] Lib. Scacc. 1644, 11; Lib. Scacc. 1651, 3; M.M.L., MF/EW/17. Will of Lt. William Huddleston, September 15, 1663; M.M.L., MF/PR/19. Malew Parish Registers: Burials, 1659.

was at least the temporary residence for a goldsmith, William Saunders, who was described as 'of Duglass' in February 1688.[33] The same town had also been the home of a pewterer in the early years of the seventeenth century.[34]

No lists comparable to those for 1640 have as yet been discovered for the later seventeenth century, but the information contained in the Lord's Composition Book of 1703 provides at least an indication of some of the craftsmen working in the towns. There can be little doubt, however, that, since most, if not all, such men worked at their craft on a part-time basis, the occupations of many of the inhabitants, both in the towns and the countryside, went unrecorded, and that the picture of manufacturing offered by this source is inevitably partial. According to the Composition Book, Douglas, for example, had only two blacksmiths, three glovers and a joiner,[35] while Castletown was credited with the same number of blacksmiths, two tailors, one, or possibly two, hatters, a weaver and a mason.[36] Ramsey, the smallest of the island's towns in the seventeenth century, possessed one, or perhaps two, blacksmiths, a weaver, a cooper, a glazier and a shoemaker.[37]

In spite of the shortcomings of Blundell's assessment of manufacturing in the island, he nevertheless correctly identified the most important trades. Weavers and tailors were evidently among the most common of all craftsmen in the countryside, as indeed they were in the Hebrides, Orkney and Shetland.[38] Their importance is demonstrated not only by their numbers in the parishes, but also by the efforts of the island's government to regulate their activities, extracting fees for sealing their yards and fining those who attempted to work without permission. (Tables 3.1 and 3.2). Shoemakers were perhaps less numerous in the Isle of Man than they were in the northern and western islands of Scotland, for, besides those in the towns, only four have so far been discovered in the parishes – one

[33] M.M.L., MD/401/1718/58.

[34] Lib. Scacc. 1606, 19.

[35] M.M.L., MF/RC/1. Lord's Composition Book, 1703, Conchan, ff. 25, 26, 37, 43, 45. The joiner, Arthur Bridson of Malew, may well have been non-resident. *Ibid*, f. 26.

[36] *ibid*, Malew, ff. 23, 34, 37, 39, 41, 42, 43, 48, 49.

[37] C. Radcliffe, *Ramsey, 1600–1800* (Douglas, 1986), pp. 116, 120, 130, 146.

[38] Shaw, *Northern and Western Islands*, pp. 132–4.

in Lezayre and three in Malew.[39] The number of blacksmiths outside
the towns is by no means certain, but, although further research may
well bring more to light, an extensive search has to date only revealed
three – in Ballaugh, Malew and Marown.[40]

Apart from these trades and the inevitable brewing activity, which
was to be found throughout the island, the parishes were also the
scene of a wide variety of manufacturing operations. Tanning, for
example, seems to have been largely confined to the countryside,
while tawing, the process used by glovers in the preparation of
skins, was mainly located in the towns.[41] At least five tanners, and
perhaps more, were at work in the island in the mid-seventeenth
century, one in Ballaugh, one possibly in Lezayre, one, or perhaps
two, in Rushen and one in Malew.[42] Coopers, who made the barrels
for storing herring, ale and other commodities, may well have been
as common as they were in Orkney and Shetland, where they were
among the half dozen or so most numerous craftsmen, and yet, to
date, only three have been identified – one in Bride, another possibly
in Rushen and one in Arbory.[43] Much of the cloth produced, and in
particular that destined for the domestic market, seems not to have
been fulled or tucked, but there were, nevertheless, some who engaged in this stage of cloth manufacture in, for instance, German,

---

[39] *ibid*. The shoemakers were: i) Lezayre: Robert Crowe. Lib. Scacc. 1650,
13; ii) Malew: Robert Shimmin, cobbler, William Harrison and Henry
Quayle, cobbler. P.R.O. SP 29/67/150/I; M.M.L., MF/PR/19. Malew Parish
Registers: Burials, 1662; Lib. Scacc. 1661, 48; Moore, *Manx Note Book*, vol.
iii (1887), p. 76.
[40] The blacksmiths were: i) Ballaugh: Philip Cowley; ii) Malew: Martin
Stowell; iii) Marown: John Moore. Lib. Scacc. 1644, 70; Lib. Scacc. 1649, 66;
Lib. Canc. 1648, 39.
[41] See *infra*, p. 141. The 'tann-house' on the North side, perhaps at Peel, was
'gone to decay' by 1652. M.M.L. R.D. 1651–70, Book of charge, Peel Castle,
1652: Casualties and venditions.
[42] The tanners were: i) Ballaugh: John Killip; ii) Lezayre [?]: John Curghy;
iii) Rushen: Robert Gawne and John Clucas; iv) Malew: John Caesar. Lib.
Scacc. 1656, 68; Lib. Canc. 1650, 83; Lib. Canc. 1649, 96; Lib. Canc. 1644,
post 29.
[43] Shaw, *Northern and Western Islands*, p. 132. The coopers were: i) Bride:
John Lace; ii) Rushen [?]: Richard Watterson; iii) Arbory: Patrick Kelly.
'Lord's Composition Book, 1703', printed in W. Radcliffe and C. Radcliffe,
Kirk Bride. A Miscellany (Douglas, n.d.), pp. 196, 199; Lib. Scacc. 1643, inter
10–11 (1); Lib. Canc. 1647, 58.

Lezayre and Rushen.[44] Cloth made from the brown wool of the native Loaghtan sheep was generally not dyed, but other woollen and linen cloth often underwent the process. Those who did such work have not been easily identified. There was, however, a dyer working in Malew in the 1670s, and it is clear that he was not alone in the practice of the profession, for in 1616, William Fairbrother of Douglas, described as 'gentleman,' died in possession of a 'panne for dyeinge' and the Lord's 'dye house' on the North side, perhaps at Peel, was rented out for 3s. a year during the late 1640s and early 1650s at least.[45] Two brickmakers, Thomas Moore and Samuel Greene, termed separately either 'breekelayer' or 'breekeman,' worked in Malew, almost certainly in the vicinity of Castletown, between about 1650 and about 1680, some years before the first documented brickworks was established in the island, probably in that part of Red Gap Farm which is still known as 'The Brickfield,' about half a mile outside Castletown, in or shortly before May 1692.[46] There were, in addition, a couple of hatters outside the towns. Redman Kewney of Malew and John Norris of Andreas supplied those inhabitants who could afford to purchase headwear with hats and caps at the time of the restoration of the Stanleys as Lords of Man in 1660.[47]

[44] Moore, *History*, vol. i, p. 315. The individuals involved in this stage of cloth production were: i) German: William Fairbrother, walker; ii) Lezayre: John Crowe, walker; William Christian of Sulby, tucker; iii) Rushen [?]: Thomas Wood, walker. Lib. Scacc. 1640, 101 (2); Lib. Scacc. 1621, 41; Lib. Canc. 1650, 83; Lib. Canc. 1649, 96.

[45] John Cottier of Malew, dyer, was buried on December 27, 1677. Moore, *Manx Note Book,* vol. iii (1887), p. 76; P.R.O. SP 29/67/150/I; M.M.L., MF/EW/2. Inventory of William Fairbrother, July 1616; M.M.L. R.D. 1627–50, Book of allowance, Peel Castle, 1648; M.M.L. R.D. 1651–70, Books of charge, Peel Castle, 1652, 1653, 1654: Casualties and venditions.

[46] M.M.L., MF/PR/18. Malew Parish Registers: Baptisms, 1656, 1664, 1667; Bawden *et al.*, *Industrial Archaeology*, p. 132; M.M.L., MD/401/1719/6. William Sacheverell to William, ninth earl of Derby, May 23, 1692. An inventory of Castle Rushen, the governor's house, Derby Fort and the Lord's bath house, Bagnio House in West Street (now Arbory Street), Castletown, drawn up in *c.* 1694 implies, by its internal arrangement, that the brick kiln was near the latter. Unpublished Document no. 4, *J.M.M.,* vol. ii (1930–4), p. 13.

[47] Lib. Scacc. 1661, 47, 48. It is possible that John Norris moved to Castletown during the 1660s in search of a more promising market, since a hatter

III. THE REGULATION
OF MANX MANUFACTURING

In the Isle of Man, as in England during the late Tudor and Stuart periods, the government shouldered the main responsibility for the supervision of manufacturing practices. Indeed, in the absence of any craft gilds, the island's government was the sole regulatory body. In corporate towns in England, each gild governed its respective trade, ensuring, at least in theory, that apprentices bound to master craftsmen learned their craft for a period which was widely accepted as being of seven years' duration before this became the statutory minimum in 1563.[48] The gilds were consequently able to control, on paper at least, the supply of skilled labour. They also maintained the standards of work and watched over the rates of pay. In the face of the increase in the labour supply brought about by the rising population of England in the sixteenth and seventeenth centuries and the consequent spread of manufacturing into rural areas, the influence of the gilds declined gradually, though not uniformly, as the English government relied on Justices of the Peace to oversee craftsmen working outside the towns.[49] If perhaps somewhat less energetic in this direction, if the handful of orders and the meagre amount of legislation extant are any indication, the island's government was nevertheless always ready to ensure that the inhabitants received 'fair dealing' from craftsmen by fining those who attempted to work without having served an adequate period of apprenticeship or who demanded more than the accepted rate for their labour.

of that name worked in the town from c.1668 to c. 1688. Moore, *Manx Note Book*, vol. ii (1886), p. 185.

[48] Palliser, *Age of Elizabeth*, p. 279. In 1552, an Act of Parliament required that all weavers should serve a seven year term of apprenticeship. 5 and 6 Edw. VI, c. 8. In 1563, the Statute of Artificers extended this requirement to all those engaged in 'any Arte, Mysterye or Manuell Occupation . . . nowe used or occupied within the Realme'. 5 Eliz., c. 4; Lowe, *Lancashire Textile Industry*, p. 84. Neither Act refers to the Isle of Man by name and since, as Sir Edward Coke stated, it was only 'by speciall name [that] an Act of Parliament may extend to it', these regulations did not necessarily affect the period of apprenticeship served in the island. E. Coke, *The Fourth Part of the Institutes of the Laws of England: Concerning the Jurisdiction of Courts* (1648 edn), p. 284.

[49] D. C. Coleman, *Industry in Tudor and Stuart England* (1975), pp. 20–2.

a) Apprenticeship

Before the middle of the seventeenth century, there do no seem to have been any regulations in the island concerning the leng h of time for which an apprentice was required to serve before he vas considered to have qualified as a craftsman. If such rules w re made before the records of the Stanley administration become elatively plentiful, from about 1580 onwards, it may well be that t ley have long since perished; conversely, it seems possible that th general practice of a seven-year term of apprenticeship which op rated in England and elsewhere was adopted without any formal legi lation.[50] Whatever the case, the Lord's officers were quick to tal e action against any who tried to set up in business before they had nastered a craft, as in 1595, when a weaver was presented 'for useing he trade of a Webster being not sufficiently Instructed in the same ind fined for his trouble.'[51] This problem continued in the sevente 1th century, doubtless fostered by the fact that those who attaine(l le status of tradesman were exempt from yarding, the system by w hich the Lord's officers had the right to choose any man or woman as their servant, except for those labouring for the members of the l eys and the clergy.[52] In 1665, the 'great Scarcity both of Servant and of honest and able Tradesmen in the Isle' which resulted led C overnor Bishop Isaac Barrow and the officers to propose that

> no Person or Persons within this Isle shall for the future after Proclamation hereof, take or entertaine any Apprent :e to learn any Science or Trade, without such Apprentice, with sufficient Surety, do first enter into a Penalty by Bond t o the Lord's Use in the Sum of tenn Pounds at the least to ser e for the Time, Term, and Space of five Years.[53]

---

[50] There is a suggestion in the charge administered to the Great Inquests that such regulatory legislation did exist before the seventeenth century. *Statutes*, p. 53. The seven-year term of apprenticeship had long b en compulsory in some English towns and was increasingly being adop ed elsewhere even before it became law by the Statute of Artificers of 156 3. M. G. Davies, *The Enforcement of English Apprenticeship, 1563–1642. A Study in Applied Mercantilism* (Cambridge, Mass., 1956), p. 10.

[51] Lib. Plit. 1595, 10; M.M.L., MS 510C, Quayle, *Book of Precede ts*, p.70.

[52] Moore, *History*, vol. i, pp. 290–1; Craine, *Manannan's Isle*, p. 47; *Statutes*, p. 50.

[53] *Statutes*, pp. 128–9.

The draft legislation was approved by Charles, eighth earl of Derby, on June 16 and promulgated at the Tynwald Court held eight days later.[54]

In addition to the provisions stipulating the duration of apprenticeship, other regulations were made at the same time to control the conduct of newly qualified craftsmen. They were 'inhibitted, forbidden, and barred to receive and entertaine any other Apprentice or Apprentices with, unto or under [them] for the Space and Terme of one Year' after the completion of their apprenticeship and could only then do so 'upon the Approbation of three of the same Faculty at least for the Sufficiency to take and teach an Apprentice for the Terme of Years.'[55] In order to give them time to establish themselves in their chosen craft and to prevent any extra financial drain which would mean that they would be forced to 'live meanly and poorly, and turning Cottlers and Inclosurers on some Highway Side,' they were furthermore not to be allowed to marry 'for one Year's Time and Space' without special licence from the bishop or another of the spiritual officers and a certificate from their parish priest and two 'sufficient Neighbours' concerning the craftsmen's 'Condition, Honesty, and Abillity, according to their Knowledge and Common-Feme and Report.'[56] The customary payment of 2d. a year, which was made by 'all Men of Occupation, what Science soever they be,' as a tithe on their trade, was apparently regarded as a relatively insignificant burden in comparison to a wife, but one from which, nevertheless, as apprentices they had been exempt.[57]

[54] *ibid*, p. 131.
[55] *ibid*, p. 129.
[56] *ibid*, pp. 128, 129.
[57] *ibid*, p. 45; M.M.L., MS MD/15,040, Parr, *Abridgement*, pp. 141–2. No indentures of apprenticeship appear to have survived in the island from this period. There is, however, an extant acquittance, dated April 9, 1692, made by Richard Moore of Douglas, joiner, for the receipt of 20s. and a boll of corn from Thomas Quay of Ballavilla, Santan, on behalf of the latter's brother, Patrick, 'for instructing and teaching him perfect in the Trad and art' which Moore professed. A further payment of 10s. was to follow at Christmas, 1692. Unpublished Document no. 95, *J.M.M.*, vol. ii (1930–4), p. 220. Some Manxmen were sent abroad to be apprenticed to foreign craftsmen or merchants. In 1602, for example, Thomas Halsey [Halsall] of Ballasalla became apprenticed to Danold Callister of Chester, merchant, who was himself of Manx origin. J. H. E. Bennett ed., 'Chester Apprentices, 1557–1646', *Cheshire Sheaf*, 3rd series, vol. vii (1909), no. 1488, p. 99. John,

b) Standards

Besides endeavouring to formalise the procedure by which untrained young men became skilled workers, the island's government also took pains to ensure that all craftsmen maintained an adequate standard of work and that none were permitted to charge excessive rates. This was achieved primarily through the agency of the Great Enquest[58] in each sheading. At the beginning of their six-month period of service, the members of each Enquest were charged to 'enquire whether all petty Craftsmen doe execute their Occupation justly; that is to say, Shoemakers, Coblers, Taylors, Websters Women, Weavers and Smithes.' If any were found to 'do otherwise then the old Lawes of this Isle will permit,' they were to be presented forthwith.[59]

Poor workmanship on the part of the craftsmen, especially in the most important trades, if unchecked, could have a certain destabilising effect on the Manx economy. If widespread, it would inevitably lead to discontent among the inhabitants, who had little choice in many cases but to use the services of local craftsmen. Consequently, the island's government, as concerned as the government of any early modern state to maintain social order, was quick to take action against those who had failed to deal justly with the people. In 1534, for instance, several weavers were presented for not doing their work and some others for cheating the Lord's tenants.[60] In a similar case in 1573, when a single weaver was brought before the officers 'for deceiveing the Tennants diverse Wayes,' the offender was fined and it was ordered that he should not thereafter be allowed to practise his trade.[61] Weavers were also brought to book for more specific

note 57 *continued*
the son of William Standish of Lezayre, was bound as an apprentice to the London skinners' company in 1635. D. Mathew, *The Age of Charles I* (1951), p. 197, n. 2. Cf. D. Hollis ed., *Calendar of the Bristol Apprentice Book, 1532–1565, pt i, 1532–42*, Bristol Record Society, vol. xiv (1949), pp. 68, 177, 179; J. A. Twemlow ed., *Liverpool Town Books, vol. i, 1550–1571* (1918), p. 529; *ibid, vol. ii, 1571–1603* (1935), pp. 922–3, 944, 946; J. H. E. Bennett (ed.), 'Chester Apprenticeship Indentures, 1603–1684', *Cheshire Sheaf*, 3rd series, vol. viii (1910), no. 1641, pp. 44, 53.
[58] For details of the Great Enquest, see chapter 1, p. 70.
[59] *Statutes*, p. 53. Cf. M.M.L., MS MD/15,040, Parr, *Abridgement*, p. 48.
[60] M.M.L., MS 510C, Quayle, *Book of Precedents*, p. 29.
[61] *ibid*, p. 43.

transgressions, the most common of which was the detention or concealment of a web or yarn which had been delivered for weaving by a farmer. A number of weavers were fined 12d. each in 1608 'for keeping Webbs for a year,' and in 1616, John Fargher of Malew was presented 'for keeping a Webb in his House a whole year un-woven.'[62] William Teare, a weaver in Lonan, was presented by a jury of six men of the parish in May 1651 for having 'deteyned and concealed one hundred threeds of yarne from Donald Qualtrough which hee gave to the said webster in a webb to weave,' and was punished with a fine of 12d.[63] In 1660, John Craine was fined 2s. 'for detaining a Webb of William Craines two years till the same was spoiled' and another 6d. for failing to appear at the sheading court to answer the charge.[64] Weavers were also found to be defrauding their customers by retaining the thrums, the loose threads or tufts remaining on the loom after the web was removed, and, probably in the wake of some such complaints, the Great Enquest of Ayre petitioned the governor and officers in 1659 that 'Websters be sworn to deal truly with the tennants as accustomed, and to restore the tennants thrums.'[65]

Weavers were not the only craftsmen whose activities attracted the attention of the authorities. In 1703, members of the Keys, perhaps acting on information received, reported to the deputy governor and officers that 'there have been severall parcels of woolen cloth sent of the Isle which have not been sufficiently wrought or fulled, whereby the vent of that sort of comodity is wholy disencouraged to the great prejudice and obstruction of the Trade of the Island.' As a result, the walkers or fullers were in future required not to 'presume to deliver out any cloath from their milnes, untill the four of the Great Enquest of the parish wherein they live have first viewed the same,' and found 'the said cloath to be sufficiently fulled or dressed.' Any fuller contravening this order could expect to be presented by the Great

---

[62] *ibid*, pp. 87, 102; Lib. Plit. 1608, 43.
[63] Lib. Scacc. 1651, 26.
[64] M.M.L., MS 510C, Quayle, *Book of Precedents*, p. 181.
[65] *ibid*, p. 175. It was not always the weavers who were at fault, however, for, on some occasions, the tenants failed to supply them with the necessary yarn, despite prior arrangement. In 1614, for example, John Kelly, a weaver, complained that he had lost time at his work because Thomas Quane had not sent him the yarn for the weft and was awarded 6d. by the court. *Ibid*, p. 98.

Enquest and heavily fined at the court's discretion. A plea of ignorance of these instructions would be of little use as a defence, since, although the order was issued in October, at the beginning of the fulling 'season' and would not be promulgated until the Tynwald Court in the June following, the coroners were directed to make sure that, like many other orders, it was published in the parish churches of the island 'that all persons concernd may take notice thereof, and conforme themselves thereunto accordingly.'[66]

Protests about the quality of leather manufactured in the island, in particular from shoemakers and cobblers, raised questions about the standards maintained by the craftsmen involved in its production. It seems that tanners and glovers were often found selling leather which was 'not thoroughly tanned' or which was in some other way 'unmarchantable.' Recognising that the standard was 'very much abused to the damage and delusion of the inhabitants,' Governor Matthew Cadwell, the officers and Keys took steps in 1655 to guarantee the quality of the leather produced in the island by directing that four 'sufficient persons' were to be appointed and sworn in by the deemsters 'to examine all tanned leather in the island before it be cut to use or made sale of.' If the leather viewed by one or more of these men was considered to be 'sufficiently wrought and marchandable,' they were 'to sett a stamp or mark thereon of the three leggs of Mann with the letters T.F.,' signifying the approval of Thomas, Lord Fairfax, Lord of Man during the Interregnum (1651–1660). A fee of ½d. was payable for each hide which was passed. Should any tanner or glover be unwise enough to try to sell any leather 'without the approbacon of the said foure men or any one of them,' his goods were to be seized and divided equally between the Lord and the informant who brought the matter to light. If, however, one or more of the four men were found to be abetting the sale of substandard leather, he, or they, were to be 'severely punished' for the first offence and 'the second tyme to be proceeded against as in the case of perjurie,' which meant that they would be handed over to the spiritual courts for trial.[67]

When these orders came to be 'revised, rescribed, and enlarged' in 1664, after the restoration of the Stanleys as Lords of Man, further

---

[66] Lib. Scacc. 1703, 37.
[67] Lib. Scacc. 1655, 80; *Statutes*, pp. 107–8; M.M.L., MS MD/15,040, Parr, *Abridgement*, p. 60. Cf. Woodward, 'Chester Leather Industry', pp. 98–9.

details about the system of supervising standards of leather manufacture were included. In all probability, these additions were merely a record of existing arrangements rather than modifications, but they do make it clear, nevertheless, that the four leather sealers were appointed for specific areas. One was to be sworn in for each of the 'four Quarters of this Isle,' each quarter being centred on one of the four towns, and was to be solely responsible for the leather stamped within that quarter.[68] At the same time, the penalties imposed on these men for passing leather 'not thorowly tanned' and 'unmerchantable' were altered, so that for a second offence the leather sealer in question was liable to a fine as well as punishment; only a recidivist who broke the law for a third time would be delivered to the ecclesiastical courts.[69]

It is not possible to determine the success of this system because no records of the proceedings of the leather sealers appear to have survived. Indeed, were it not for the fact that the names of the 'sufficient persons' appointed to the post are recorded in one instance, in 1693,[70] it could easily be assumed that the office of leather sealer had quickly fallen into abeyance. It is certainly true that there were no more major complaints about the poor standard of Manx leather and that no further legislation was introduced in the seventeenth century, but this is perhaps testimony to the

[68] *Statutes*, pp. 115, 117. The Northside was divided into the West Quarter, comprising the parishes of Patrick, German, Michael and Ballaugh and centred on Peel, and the North Quarter, consisting of Jurby, Andreas, Bride and Lezayre and centred on Ramsey. The Southside was similarly divided into the East Quarter, consisting of Maughold, Lonan, Conchan and Braddan and centred on Douglas, and the South Quarter, composed of Santan, Malew, Arbory and Rushen, with Castletown as its centre. For a convenient map of these divisions, see R. Kissack, *Seed of Isaac. A Family History of the Kissacks of the Isle of Man* (Douglas, n.d.), p. 4. Cf. R. Sherwood (ed.), *The Constitution of the Isle of Man*, Manx Society, vol. xxxi (1882), p. 260.
[69] *Statutes*, p. 118.
[70] Lib. Scacc. 1693–4, 40. The leather sealers were: i) Peel: Caesar Wattleworth, a member of the Keys between 1693–4 and 1699–1700. Lib. Scacc. 1693–4, *ante* 1; Lib. Scacc. 1700, 1; ii) Ramsey: John Wattleworth, probably also a member of the Keys (1688–9 – 1741?), Captain of Ramsey in *c*. 1703. Lib. Scacc. 1689, *ante* 1; W. Radcliffe and C. Radcliffe, *A History of Kirk Maughold* (Douglas, 1979), pp. 241, 320, 336, 357; Radcliffe, *Ramsey, 1600–1800*, p. 144; iii) Douglas: David Gray; iv) Castletown: Thomas Caine.

effectiveness of the office rather than an indication that it had become redundant.[71]

The monopolistic position of the island's millers inevitably led to suspicions about their dealings with the inhabitants. All landholders were bound as tenants to a particular mill, where they were required to have their corn ground. The 'owners' of the mills, who paid an annual rent to the Lord, delegated the responsibility for operation to millers, who were obliged to take an oath every year to serve the tenants justly. The fact that the millers were entitled to take only one twenty-fourth of the corn ground as *foilliu*, or mulcture, did little to reassure the tenants that they would be dealt with fairly, especially since the latter had long experience of the devious practices of many of the former.[72] Among the earliest extant records of the Manx courts there is, for example, a case dating from 1418, in which William Causee was presented by the Great Enquest of Garff for keeping an illegal measure at Cornaa Mills in Maughold and demanding extortionate amounts of mulcture.[73] By the seventeenth century, little had changed. The most common offence committed by millers seems to have been the use of an unsealed, and therefore illegal, measure, doubtless smaller than the standard required by law. (Table 3.2). There were, however, many others, not the least of which was the failure to grind the tenants' corn sufficiently, thus producing lumpy, partially ground meal or *groblagh*. In 1659, the Great Enquest of Garff presented the current miller at Cornaa, Danold or David Cowle, 'for giving ill grinding' to John Kerruish, and the court fined

---

[71] For a general comparison with the English leather trade, see L. A. Clarkson, 'The Organisation of the English Leather Industry in the Sixteenth and Seventeenth Centuries', *Ec.H.R.*, second series, vol. xiii (1960–1), pp. 245–56; idem, 'The Leather Crafts in Tudor and Stuart England', *Ag.H.R.*, vol. xiv (1966), pp. 25–39.

[72] Craine, *Manannan's Isle*, p. 163; J. K. Qualtrough, 'An Introduction to Manx Watermills', *M.N.H.A.S.*, vol. vii (1964–72), pp. 253–4. For a comparison with the similar system in England and Scotland, see H. S. Bennett, *Life on the English Manor* (Cambridge, 1937, reprinted 1967), pp. 129–30; Coleman, *Industry in Tudor and Stuart England*, p. 38; Whyte, *Agriculture and Society*, pp. 32–3.

[73] M.M.L., MS 510C, Quayle, *Book of Precedents*, p. 4. The level of mulcture was clearly set at an early date – in the fifteenth century or, more likely, before. It does not appear in the printed Statutes, but it is recorded by Deemster John Parr. M.M.L., MS MD/15,040, Parr, *Abridgement*, p. 98.

him 3s. 4d. for the neglect of his duty. Kerruish was evidently angry at his shabby treatment at the hands of the miller, for he was brought before the sheading court 'for spoiling and abuseing the said Milne and materials thereunto belonging' and punished with a fine of 12d.[74] William Qualtrough, the miller at Kentraugh, Rushen, was faced with a fine of 2s. in 1700 after he had been presented for failing to grind the tenants' corn adequately. For some reason, which is not apparent but which must have been compelling, he also refused to take the obligatory miller's oath in the same year and was fined 2s. 6d.[75]

Some millers were guilty of committing a comprehensive range of offences. In 1655, discontent among the inhabitants of Castletown with the activities of Robert Gelling, miller at the 'wheele mill' near the town belonging to Thomas Moore of the Abbey, Ballasalla, reached such a level that a detailed list of complaints was submitted to Governor Matthew Cadwell and the officers. The townspeople claimed that the mill itself was 'nott maintained in sufficient repaire wherby . . . corne is greatly wasted to the beniffitt of the said owner and Miller by reason much of the best of the tenants flower is gaithred in . . . through the want of repaire;' they further complained that Gelling 'doth keepe the rimm or wheele aboutt the mill stones att such an unreasonable distance that the tenants are greately damnified, for much of their flower is received therein and espetially after [the] mill stones are newley pickt.' Gelling was said to be absent from the mill and not to have assigned a deputy 'to see every on receive their due griste, wherby divers quarrells [and] abusses . . . hapen betweene neighbours and servants, and to see that the mill bee in good order for grindinge.' Neither did he employ a servant to take the tenants' corn to the mill, as the townspeople believed he should, and he would only agree to collect wheat or malt with his horse if there was less than a firlot[76] to carry; the tenants were consequently 'forced to carry mettcorn on their backes (if otherwise they can nott procure horses) unto the said mill.'

Cadwell and the officers ordered a full enquiry. They directed Henry Watterson, coroner of Rushen, to appoint two townsmen to assist two garrison soldiers who had experience in such matters. On

---

[74] M.M.L., MS 510C, Quayle, *Book of Precedents*, p. 175.
[75] Qualtrough, 'Manx Watermills', p. 254.
[76] A standard measure for grain. See Table 4.3.

viewing the millstones, the latter, Edward Redferne and John Bennett, '(sometymes Millers),' reported that 'they found the same to be insufficient or not fitt for grindinge, for that the undermost was broken and peeced.' Together with the townsmen, they further stated that 'the Milne itselfe is out of repaire for thatch and stayes, and also the wales thereof to bee out of repaire to the prejudice of the Tenants.'[77]

Statements concerning Gelling's dealings with the tenants were taken from more than a dozen of his customers, all of whom confirmed some of the charges levelled at the miller. Margaret Beale, for example, sent a boll[78] of wheat to be ground at the mill and, 'when it came home,' she discovered that she had 'but twelve kitchins [kishans][79] out of the boule, where formerly she was wont to have eighteen or nineteen kishans.'[80] It seems that Gelling made no bones about the fact that he was defrauding the tenants. When Elizabeth Corrin, Margaret Beale's servant, complained angrily that some of her corn had 'runn by the milne to her losse,' the miller retorted : 'why should hee not have some to feede his horse, and there upon the miller swept about the milne, and gave the sweepinges to his horse.'[81]

In another case the fraud was even more plain. Richard Skerrett and his wife sent their maidservant to the mill with a half firlot of wheat 'in a bagge,' having first measured it in a sealed measure. When the maidservant returned to grind the wheat a few days later, she 'mistrusted some corne to have beene taken out of the bagge' and refused to grind it until the Skerretts had been informed. Taking the sealed measure with them, the Skerretts went to the mill and confronted Gelling. They found that there was 'seaven quartes full awantinge of their measure' and demanded an explanation. Gelling alleged that 'the ratts had eaten the corne,' but when it was pointed out that the bag and the remaining wheat showed no evidence of any such damage, the miller's wife 'fell a cursinge and swore many oathes.'[82]

<hr>

[77] Lib. Scacc. 1655, 59–60.
[78] A standard measure for grain. See Table 4.3.
[79] See note 78.
[80] Lib. Scacc. 1655, 60.
[81] *ibid*.
[82] *ibid*, 62. For the other statements, see *ibid*, 61–2, 64–5.

At the Court of General Gaol Delivery in May, the evidence was submitted to the governor and officers, who ordered Gelling to make 'reparation and satisfaccon to the severall persons . . . that appeares to have sustayned losse in their corne by and through his meanes or default.' Gelling and Thomas Moore were each fined 20s. – subsequently mitigated to 6s. 8d. – 'ffor not keepinge the Milne in good order and repaire' and for not carrying the townspeoples' corn, contrary to custom; for the future, the miller was to perform his duties to the letter or, together with Moore, face such fine and punishment as the court thought appropriate.[83]

c) Wages and Prices

In spite of the importance attached to such breaches of the largely unwritten code of 'fair dealing,' the government of the island was equally, if not more, concerned with the level of wages demanded by craftsmen. As in the case of the regulations for apprenticeships, however, there is no evidence extant for the setting of wage levels in the island before the seventeenth century. There can be little question that, prior to 1600, the Isle of Man was buffeted by the same economic trends which affected neighbouring countries, but no indication has yet been found of the existence in the island before that date of any system of wage control akin to that which operated in England from the late fourteenth century. It is not known whether the island was afflicted by the Black Death, which brought about the acute shortage of labour and the 'outrageous and excessive hire' demanded by servants and labourers in England, leading to the statutory legislation concerning maximum wages in 1388.[84] A. W. Moore believed that, even if the plague had reached the island, the effects, so far as the labour market was concerned, would have been limited because of the co-operative system of cultivation, which persisted in Man until the sixteenth century, and the consequently small number of agricultural labourers.[85] Due to the paucity of evidence, it is clearly not possible to substantiate Moore's theory, yet it is worth noting that it fails to take account of the number of artificers and craftsmen in the island and their effect on wage rates. While it would be

---

[83] *ibid*, 67–8.
[84] 12 Ric. II, c. 4; C. G. A. Clay, *Economic Expansion and Social Change: England, 1500–1700* (2 vols, Cambridge, 1984), vol. ii, p. 229.
[85] Moore, *History*, vol. i, pp. 284–5 and n. 2.

impossible to demonstrate that the presence of such men was an important factor in driving up wages, it is perhaps significant that Moore felt constrained to acknowledge that it was 'almost certain that the causes which were at work in England to augment the value of labour were, in a greater or lesser degree, operative in Man also.'[86] The only piece of evidence which Moore was able to produce to reinforce his assertion of inflationary pressure, however, was the statement of John Hugh, vicar of Malew, in 1368, perhaps of doubtful reliability, that a previous incumbent had been able to live better on six marks than he was then able on twenty.[87]

All that can be said with any certainty in relation to wage levels in the island before 1600 is that, by the second half of the sixteenth century, the Isle of Man was experiencing a rise in prices similar in scale to that in England[88] and that, whether a regulatory mechanism existed or not, this unquestionably hit hardest those who depended on crafts or labour for a significant part of their income. The number of such people in the island must have been very small and they were probably in practice only to be found in the towns. The vast majority, who had more than one occupation, probably weathered the inflationary storm reasonably well, except in the worst years of the 1590s, but there can be little doubt that, whether they lived in a town or in the countryside, all the inhabitants felt the impact of the increase in prices, particularly of foodstuffs, and that this in turn must have fuelled demands for higher wages.

Although those who lived on relatively large holdings could produce much of their own food, they, like the smaller landholders and towndwellers, depended to some extent on the fairs in the parishes

---

[86] *ibid*, vol. i, p. 285.

[87] P. A. Munch and Dr Goss (eds), *Chronica Regum Manniae et Insularum. The Chronicle of Man and the Sudreys*, vol. ii, Manx Society, vol. iii (1874), p. 387.

[88] E. H. Phelps Brown and S. V. Hopkins, 'Seven Centuries of the Prices of Consumables, Compared with Builders' Wage Rates', *Economica*, no. xcii (Nov. 1956), new series, vol. xxiii, reprinted in P. H. Ramsey, *The Price Revolution in Sixteenth-Century England* (1971), especially fig. 1. Although this figure is based on data from southern England, it is evident that the same upward trend in prices affected the rest of England and, indeed, the rest of Europe. Palliser, *Age of Elizabeth*, pp. 152–4. Cf. R. B. Outhwaite, *Inflation in Tudor and Early Stuart England* (1969); H. Phelps Brown and S. V. Hopkins, *A Perspective of Wages and Prices* (1981).

and especially the markets held in the towns to supply their needs.[89] Evidence for the prices paid for foodstuffs in these markets is scarce, but, from the fluctuations in the rates for grain already examined and other sources, it is clear that there was a sharp increase in some commodity prices towards the end of the sixteenth century. When, in 1608, the Keys and four men from each parish were questioned by Richard Hoper, the commissioner for the earls of Salisbury and Northampton, trustees of the island during the later stages of the dispute over the Stanley estates including Man (1594–1609), they answered that, 'in Respecte of alteracon of tyme and Casualties which have and may happen,' they could 'not Certenlie lay downe a directe price of Cattell, Corne and other provisions.'[90] Accordingly, the 'ancientest men' in the island were sworn 'to deliver the Certen prices of thiese provisions in there tymes.' Casting their minds back perhaps thirty or forty years, these men testified that they had sold, 'in open markett,' a beef for 4s. 6d., a mutton for 6d. and 12d. 'the deereste,' a lamb for 2d., a goose for the same price, a hen for 1d. and a year-old 'swyne-purre,' or Manx pig, for 6d.[91] By Michaelmas, 'the best and deerest tyme,' in 1607, the Keys and men from the parishes stated that a beef was sold for 16s.; a mutton at midsummer cost 2s. 6d.; a lamb in May retailed at 8d.; a goose at Michaelmas went for 4d., whereas a hen cost 2d. 'at all tymes;' and a 'swyne purre' was sold at midsummer for 18d.[92]

[89] For details of the frequency and location of the fairs and markets, see chapter 4, pp. 193–98.

[90] M.M.L., MD/401/1715/5.

[91] *ibid*. It is clearly not possible to test the accuracy of these figures, nor to determine to which year, or years, they might relate. Assuming that these men were unlikely to be less than fifty and that they were recalling, perhaps accurately, their earliest market transactions, the prices can not date from after c. 1578.

[92] *ibid*. The general increase in prices was by no means constant during the sixteenth century. In 1540, young cattle at Rushen Abbey were valued at between 5s. 3d. and 6s., the latter being the price for an adult animal. Sheep and pigs were priced at 8d., lambs at 4d. and goats at 6d. Moore, *History*, vol. i, p. 286. The effects of the upward movement of prices were made worse by the system of customary payments in kind made by the inhabitants to the Lord. The rates at which these were calculated had been fixed before they were first recorded in 1422 and had not been raised to take account of inflation. Consequently, while the market value of cattle and corn increased, the allowances for payments in kind remained static and the inhabitants

The general increase in the prices of foodstuffs, as well as of raw
materials and manufactured goods, fostered demands for higher
wages, which were, in turn, intensified by periodic harvest failure. It
may not, therefore, be a coincidence that the first recorded instance
of wage regulation in the island occurred in 1609, a year which
probably witnessed an average harvest, but which had been preceded
by years when the harvest was very likely deficient, in 1607, and bad,
in 1608.[93] The timing of this move may also have been influenced by
the efforts of the trustees of the island, Salisbury in particular, to
improve the financial administration of the island before it was delivered to William, sixth earl of Derby, and his wife, Countess Elizabeth, Salisbury's niece.[94] Whatever the circumstances in which the
regulations were set down in October 1609, it was clearly considered
necessary to establish, or at least record, the maximum wage levels
for servants in husbandry and the most numerous craftsmen in the
island. Governor John Ireland, the officers and Keys accordingly
directed that every ploughman was to receive 13s. 4d. 'by the Yeare'
for his wages, 'and not above;' similarly, a driver was to be paid 10s.
and a horseman the sum of 8s. Before any of these servants were
permitted to work, however, they had to be 'reputed sufficient' and
approved by the deemsters and the jury for servants in each parish.[95]

note 92 *continued*
received credit for an ever-dwindling proportion of the current value of
their produce. See, for example, the position regarding cattle, in chapter 5,
pp. 249–50.
[93] In general, Manx harvests followed the pattern of English harvest success
or failure. See chapter 2, pp. 92–105.
[94] For details of the dispute over the Stanley estates, including Man, precipi-
tated by the death of Ferdinando, fifth earl of Derby, in 1594, see R. A.
Curphey, 'The Background to the Disputed Derby Succession, 1594–1612',
M.N.H.A.S., vol. vii (1964–72), pp. 602–17; Coward, *Stanleys*, chapter 4.
[95] *Statutes*, p. 70; Lib. Scacc. 1610, 39. The 'Jury for Servants' was composed
of four men, sworn in at the deemster's direction, who were responsible for
setting vagrants to work and ensuring that the Lord's tenants were not 'desti-
tute of Servants', even if it meant making those on smaller holdings serve
the larger landholders. In all cases, the deemster had the final word as to the
ability of the servant. Cl.R.O., Nantlys MS D/NA/905, 3; *Statutes*, p. 55.
A similar function, as far as the employment of paupers was concerned, was
performed in England from 1597 by the overseers of the poor. J.F. Pound,
Poverty and Vagrancy in Tudor England (2nd edn., 1976), pp. 52–3; A. L.
Beier, *The Problem of the Poor in Tudor and Stuart England* (1983), p. 25.

The latter, together with one of the deemsters, was responsible for determining the amount paid to every female servant, who was given as much 'as she shall be thought to deserve.'[96] Although not stated in these regulations, it appears to have been normal practice in the Isle of Man, as elsewhere in the British Isles, for agricultural servants who had been hired by the year to live with their masters and receive their meat and drink in addition to their money wages.[97]

Craftsmen, though they, too, received part of their wages in the form of victuals, were not 'live-in' servants and were paid at a daily rate. Tailors were henceforth to be paid a maximum of 4d. a day and their apprentices half that amount, except when they were working for servants themselves, when the rates were 2d. and 1d. respectively. Masons, carpenters, shipwrights, joiners, hoopers, slaters and thatchers 'thatching after the English fashion' all received the same daily rate as head tailors, with the same proviso, that they were deemed 'sufficient Workmen.' Any craftsman who refused to work at the rate specified, or who declined to come, 'being sent for by the Farmer (except he be in other Men's work),' was to be 'put to be a Servant.'[98]

The wages of other craftsmen were set on the basis of a piece rate, without meat or drink. Woollen weavers, for example, were to receive a halfpenny for every yard of cloth to be made up into a 'Blankett' or mantle, ¾ d. for 'every four great Hundred Breadth of Keare,' a dark grey cloth, and 1¼ d. for every yard of medley or ¼ d. for every great hundred of the same cloth. Linen weavers were to be paid according to the old Custome after, as the Yarn shall be in Smallness or Greatness.'[99] This customary rate, mention of which strongly suggests some previous wage regulation in the island, appears from later seventeenth century evidence to have been 2d. for every yard of linen cloth of one great hundred breadth, with an additional ¼ d. 'for every Great Hundred according to the fineness

[96] *Statutes*, p. 101; Lib. Scacc. 1610, 39.

[97] Moore, *History*, vol. i, p. 289. This practice was common in England, Scotland and Ireland. See, for example, M. H. B. Sanderson, *Scottish Rural Society in the Sixteenth Century* (Edinburgh 1982), pp. 44–5; Shaw, *Northern and Western Islands*, pp. 191–2; Everitt, 'Farm Labourers', pp. 202–3; E. MacLysaght, *Irish Life in the Seventeenth Century* (Cork, 1939, abridged edn, reprinted Dublin, 1979), p. 175.

[98] *Statutes*, p. 71.

[99] *ibid*.

or courseness of the Yarn.'[100] Walkers or fullers were paid ½ d. for every yard of blanket cloth properly fulled, ¾ d. for every yard of keare, 1d. for every yard of white cloath and 1½ d. for every yard of medley. Smiths were entitled to charge 1d. for the 'laying' or fixing of every coulter, the vertical blade in front of the ploughshare, and 2d. for casting it; they were to receive 2d. for each new sock, or ploughshare, made and ½ d. for making and fixing a transverse blade, or wing, to the ploughshare. Any farmer or other person who made use of the craftsmen's skills or hired agricultural labourers and offered wages above the levels set was to be punished by forfeiture of the whole amount paid, whether it was for several days' work or only one.[101]

d) Coinage

Any comparison between the wage rates set in the Isle of Man and those in force elsewhere is rendered more difficult because it is not known to what extent payments were made in kind rather than in coin, of which there seems to have been a shortage in the island throughout the seventeenth century, and also because it is not clear what value was assigned to the currency of account in the island in relation to sterling. No coinage was issued by the Stanley administration before 1709, but, before that date, a wide variety of coinage circulated, principally of English, Scottish and Irish origin, though also including Flemish ducketoons and Spanish reales or pieces of eight.[102] A. W. Moore was of the opinion that, before the later seventeenth century, 'the island had suffered from the absence of genuine specie of any kind,' except for a time during the 1640s, when

[100] *ibid*, p. 148.

[101] *ibid*, p. 71.

[102] C. Clay, *Currency of the Isle of Man*, Manx Society, xvii (1869), pp. 27, 45. The Flemish ducketoon, as a coin, was worth 5s. 6⅛d. in 1622, whereas its value as bullion was 5s. 4d. In November 1646, the value of these coins in the island was set by proclamation at 5s., 'beinge of lawfull weighte, one of them in a payment of 20s. and not otherwise.' Lib. Scacc. 1647, inter 6–7. Two years before, in November 1644, it was ordered that 'Spanishe monys peecs of eight may passe and bee currante paye in this Islande without preiudice to the Comon welth, viz. That in payment of every Twentie shillings One peece of eighte may passe after the rate of ffoure shillings ffoure pence provyded yt bee of the weighte of 4s. 9d. sterlinge.' Lib. Scacc 1645, inter 7–8.

Royalist refugees brought money with them.[103] This is, however, refuted by Blundell, who found that the currency in the island was 'almost all English,' but that 'the Scottish 13½ d., and their twopence, and their 5 shilling pieces minted at Dublin, do freely pass there.'[104] It is also contradicted by an examination of the island's court records for the period, which contain numerous references to payments made in money, sometimes explicitly in sterling, and suits brought for cash debts.[105]

Moore further believed that the island's economy, and trade in particular, was greatly encouraged by the 'introduction of an independent coinage' in 1668, when 'John Murray's Pennies' were issued.[106] These were merely tradesman's tokens issued by one of the leading Douglas merchants and they circulated in the island along with others, particularly from Ireland, until such 'Copper and Brass Money,' with the exception of the king's farthings and Murrey's

---

[103] Moore, *History*, vol. i, p. 414 and n. 4. Moore's statement concerning the money brought in by Royalists is derived from an early eighteenth-century observer, George Waldron, *A Description of the Isle of Man*, ed., W. Harrison, Manx Society, vol. xi (1864), p. 71.

[104] Blundell, *History*, vol. i, p. 60. It is likely that the Irish coins, to which Blundell alludes, were silver crowns, minted under the authority of the lords justices in Dublin between 1642 and 1644. R. H. M. Dolley, 'The Irish Coinage, 1534–1691', in T. W. Moody, F. J. Byrne and F. X. Martin (eds), *A New History of Ireland, vol. iii: Early Modern Ireland, 1534–1691* (Oxford, 1976), p. 416. Some of the coinage in the island had clearly been in circulation for a long time by the 1640s, since, in an order regulating the value of 'Monys diminishte by Clipinge or ffylinge', any 'olde monys' were excluded 'which are aparente not to bee Clipte or otherwise unlawfully diminishte but only growne lighte by wearinge and wastinge by longe passinge ffrom hande to hande'. Lib. Scacc. 1648, 26.

[105] See, for example, the deeds of bargain and sale enrolled in the records of the Manx courts. In the majority of a random sample of such deeds, the consideration was paid in sterling. In May 1600, for instance, John Standish of Lezayre sold half a quarter and a fourth part of a quarter called 'Conder's ground' in Andreas to Danold Christian of Bride for the sum of £4 'English money'. Lib. Scacc. 1603, 13–14. John Qualtrough of the 'Mylne' (Kentraugh), Rushen, and his wife sold a fourth part of a quarter to William Gawne in November 1621 for 50s. sterling. Many other examples could be given. For suits brought for money debts, see Lib. Canc. *passim*.

[106] Moore, *History*, vol. i, pp. 413–14.

Pence, was declared illegal at the Tynwald Court in 1679.[107] Because of the scarcity of any sort of money, a fact remarked upon at the time by William, ninth earl of Derby,[108] and the necessity for such tokens to pass for currency in everyday transactions, this order was generally ignored and half pennies from Scotland, 'stamped with a Thistle, of the worst or basest sort of Copper,' and from Ireland, 'stamped with the Harpe,' were 'brought in and disposed through the island.'[109] As a consequence, in 1682, Deputy Governor Richard Stevenson and the officers ordered that from the beginning of July in that year, such coins should, '(for the necessity of change only),' pass for a farthing and no more. At the same time, it was directed that 'Rixum Groates or any other false or counterfeitt Coyne' were to be destroyed and only 'good old Silver Groates' were to be accepted as legal tender.[110] The shopkeepers and other inhabitants, however, resisted this change and refused to accept the groats, passing the half pennies and farthings as current money. In 1687, therefore, the order was reissued with instructions that all such money not issued by the king was to be withdrawn.[111]

---

[107] Lib. Scacc. 1679, 33; *Statutes*, p. 137. The money specifically referred to in the order was called 'Butchers half pence' and 'Patricks half pence'. The latter, which do not appear to have been coins or tokens of the usual type, evidently originated in Ireland, although nothing further seems to be known about them. 'Butchers half pence' were tokens issued by one, or possibly several, such tradesmen, perhaps including, as Charles Clay suggested, Michael Wilson of Dublin, whose half penny was dated 1672. Clay, *Currency of the Isle of Man*, pp. 51–4. Cf. S. Marrinan, 'Limerick Tokens of the Seventeenth Century', *North Munster Antiquarian Journal*, vol. ix (1987), p. 35.

[108] M.M.L., MD/401/1717/56. Derby to Robert Heywood, governor, and the officers of the Isle of Man, April 20, 1680.

[109] Lib. Scacc. 1682, 33; *Statutes*, pp. 139–40. The importance of some form of 'small money' to the inhabitants had been recognised more than thirty years before. In March 1648, the island's government banned the importation of clipped money, only permitting it to pass in payments in the island at the rate of 1s. in every 4s., or 5s. in every 20s.; nevertheless, it was provided that all such coinage 'under twelve-pences' were to pass at the current rates in transactions up to 12d., because 'the poorer sorte of this Islande canott subsiste without passinge of smale monys in smale payments'. Lib. Scacc. 1648, 26–7.

[110] Lib. Scacc. 1682, 33; *Statutes*, pp. 139–40.

[111] Lib. Scacc. 1687, 61; *Statutes*, p. 142.

While it is evident that there was a certain amount of 'small moneys' in circulation, much of it in the form of tokens and coins of inferior quality, the problem of the shortage of sound specie was exacerbated by the transportation of good coinage out of the island, a movement encouraged by the relatively high silver content of English money and the rising price of silver in Europe. Fearing that the influx of base coins and the outflow of good money would rapidly lead to the ruination of the island, William Sacheverell, the deputy governor, the officers and Keys passed an Act in 1692 'for prevention of such inconveniencyes and for the future encouragement that the current money and Coyne of England may more freely circulate within this Isle.'[112] Before this time, there is no definite indication of the value of the currency of account in the island in relation to sterling. Although apparently similar – both shared the same units – a differential clearly existed, as demonstrated by the addition of the words 'sterling' or 'English' after totals in various Manx court records and elsewhere.[113] It is not certain whether this Act ever came into force, since there is no conclusive evidence that it received the Lord's assent,[114] but it does nevertheless mark the first apparent attempt to fix the value of the Manx currency of account, taking into consideration the enhanced intrinsic value of English coinage at the time.[115] According to the Act's provisions, gold English guineas of 20s. were henceforth to pass for 22s., silver crown pieces of 5s. were to be taken as 5s. 4d. and half crowns were to be accepted as 2s. 8d. In short, sterling was to circulate in the island at approximately one-tenth more than its face value when calculated in

[112] M.M.L., MD/401/1719/8. This Act is not included in the printed Statutes.
[113] See note 105.
[114] M.M.L., MD/401/1719/8. Although the only extant copy of this Act lacks Derby's name and is merely dated 'the [blank] day of July 1692,' the words 'Bee it enacted as is desired' have been appended. It is clear that when Sacheverell discussed the matter with the earl in early August, the Act had still not received the Lord's assent. M.M.L., MD/401/1719/13. Sacheverell to Derby, August 3, 1692.
[115] C. H. V. Sutherland, *English Coinage, 600–1900* (1973, reprinted 1982), pp. 174, 177. Between 1688 and 1694, as the value of English gold increased, the English guinea of 20s. lost its fixed face-value stability and its value rose until it was worth nearly 30s. Thereafter its value fell until, by the end of 1698, it was worth 21s. 6d. Moore wrongly assumed that the guinea was valued at 21s. in the early 1690s. Moore, *History*, vol. i, p. 415.

the Manx currency of account. The export of coinage for its value as bullion was further discouraged by a restatement of the customary law that prohibited the shipment of sums in excess of £5 from the island on pain of forfeiture; this was, however, no longer directed solely at the barons, but applied to all who attempted 'to carry away silver or gould out of this Isle.'[116]

In another effort to control the stability and supply of coinage in the island and to assist the project for the establishment of a linen manufactory there,[117] proposals were made for the coining of money in 'a base metal, not exceeding the value of 10,000*l.*,' probably during the latter part of 1692. The negotiations with the English government were conducted at least in part by Sacheverell and seem to have reached a critical point in March 1693, when, having secured the consent of William III to the plan, so long as it did not prove prejudicial to the Crown, the matter was referred by the earl of Nottingham, the Secretary of State, to the Commissioners of the Treasury.[118] Despite Sacheverell's belief that 'the request seems so modest I think they are ashamed to refuse,' the scheme appears to have run into trouble at this stage and to have been shelved. The first coins issued by the Stanley administration, consisting of pennies and halfpennies, did not appear until 1709.[119]

Concern about the draining away of sound coinage from the island and the value of the Manx money of account in relation to sterling continued throughout the 1690s and into the first decade of the eighteenth century. On April 24, 1703, the Keys petitioned Deputy Governor Robert Mawdesley about several matters, including the rates at which English money should be accepted in the island. They requested that 'all crown peeces after this day by pubblick consent bee allowed to pass for 5s. 10d. a peece and half one at 2s. 11d. a peece, a shilling at 14d., and sixpences at 7d. a peece, and guyneys to pass for 24s. 6d. a peece.' This was clearly an attempt to combat the outflow of English money by raising its value against the Manx currency of account, so that sterling would circulate at one-sixth above its face value when computed by the island's standards. This

[116] M.M.L., MD/401/1719/8; *Statutes*, p. 15.
[117] For details of this project, see *infra*, pp. 176–82.
[118] *C.S.P.D.*, 1693, p. 54; M.M.L., MD/401/1719/21. Sacheverell to Derby, March 4, 1693.
[119] M.M.L., MD/401/1719/21; Clay, *Currency of the Isle of Man*, pp. 59–63; Moore, *History*, vol. i, p. 415.

is confirmed by the Keys' additional request that the earl 'may be pleased to take those severall peeces of money and gold at those values in his Rent,' but that 'all Rents due to his Lordshipp till the 25th of March last be paid at the value which the said peeces of silver doe now pass for.'[120]

The importance attached to the establishment of definite rates of exchange between sterling and the Manx currency of account in the decade or so after 1690 strongly suggests that specie had already assumed a vital role in the Manx economy. It could be argued that the moves to stem the flow of good money out of the island are indicative of the small amount of such currency in Man, but the same concerns about the draining away of silver coinage in particular are evident at the same time in England, a country with a far greater amount of money in circulation.[121] There are, however, signs that there was a considerably greater quantity of specie in the island than has hitherto been supposed. Rents, for example, which had previously been paid partly in kind, were, after 1601, paid wholly in money, although in exceptional circumstances, the earl was prepared to accept a portion of his rents in the form of grain or livestock.[122] Property was almost always purchased and sold for sums in sterling and only very occasionally for a combination of cash and commodities.[123] In fact, in Man during this period, as in Ireland, little trace can be found of barter as a means of exchange,[124] although it was probably adopted for some

[120] Lib. Scacc. 1703, inter 6–7.

[121] Sutherland, *English Coinage*, pp. 176–9.

[122] Moore, *Manx Note Book*, vol. i (1885), pp. 61–4; *Statutes*, pp. 83–4; M.M.L., MD/401/1717/56. William, ninth earl of Derby to Governor Robert Heywood and the officers, April 20, 1680. In 1680, the earl was ready to accept cattle 'because money is not very plentifull in the Island', but would take only 240 animals.

[123] Out of a random sample of thirty-three deeds of bargain and sale of parcels of land made between 1593 and 1654 and enrolled in the Chancery and Exchequer books, there were only three cases in which commodities formed part of the payment. In March 1624, for instance, Danold Cowley of Ballaugh sold half the quarter of Ballaterson in that parish to his neighbour, John Corlett of Ballakinnag, for £7 10s. and half a firlot of barley. Lib. Scacc. 1625, 19–20.

[124] The apparently limited use of barter was one of many similarities between the Irish and Manx economies, not the least of which was the real or imagined shortage of coin, the subject of frequent, and perhaps exaggerated, complaints from Ireland in the early seventeenth century. M. MacCarthy-

dealings, particularly away from the markets. The majority of transactions, however, involved cash, as can be seen by even a superficial
examination of the suits brought for debt in the Chancery Court, and
the lists of debts appended to the wills and inventories of the deceased
are almost always quoted in this medium.[125] Furthermore, the governor, officers and soldiers, together with all the labourers and craftsmen who worked in the garrisons and elsewhere for the Lord, were
paid in coin, as the lists of fees and payments in the books of allowance
and subsequently the books of charge make clear.[126] Much of this
money was derived from rents and other incidental domestic sources,
but a relatively small, though generally increasing, proportion came
from customs revenue. This brought specie into the island, which also
benefited from the fact that, until about 1680, the value of exports
regularly exceeded that of imports.[127] The presence of larger amounts
of coinage than previously accepted, therefore, makes it highly probable that payments to craftsmen outside the Lord's employ would
frequently have been made at least partly in cash rather than wholly
in kind.

e) Trends in Wages and Prices

A comparison between the wage levels set in the Isle of Man and those
in other parts of the British Isles in the early seventeenth century
reveals that in many occupations the differences may not have been

note 124 *continued*
Morrogh, 'Credit and Remittance: Monetary Problems in Early Seventeenth-Century Munster', *I.E.S.H.*, vol. xiv (1987), pp. 5–10; R. Gillespie,
'Peter French's Petition for an Irish Mint, 1619', *I.H.S.*, vol. v (1987), pp.
413–20. Cattle were used as 'commodity money' in the Hebrides because
of the limited amount of coinage in circulation. Shaw, *Northern and Western
Islands*, p. 158.
[125] Lib. Canc., passim. For lists of debts in cash, see, for example, the following inventories: M.M.L., MF/EW/6, Richard Stevenson of Balladoole,
Arbory, 1623; M.M.L., MF/RB/517, John Black of Ramsey, 1665; M.M.L.,
MF/EW/20, Edward Shimmin of Ballasalla, Malew, 1674. For debts including items in kind, see, for example, the short list appended to the will of
Alice Scarisbrick, 1602. M.M.L., MF/EW/1.
[126] The books of allowance for Castle Rushen and Peel Castle are often
bound with the respective books of charge. After *c.* 1660, the former are
incorporated in the latter series. M.M.L., I.O. and R.D.
[127] See appendix viii.

as great as might be expected. It is not clear whether the rates set in the island in 1609 were calculated in sterling, but, even if they were not, it may well be that the differential between the Manx money of account and English currency was then as small as it was at the end of the century, and that, accordingly, any problems arising from rates of exchange may be discounted.[128] On the assumption that this was the case, and that Manx wage levels may be compared at face value with those set in sterling elsewhere, it is evident that Manx craftsmen, such as masons, carpenters, joiners, slaters and thatchers, received payments which were in some cases the same as those made to their counterparts in England and in others only slightly lower. (Table 3.5). The wages paid to slaters and thatchers in the island were actually marginally higher than the winter rates paid in at least one English county, Wiltshire, in the early seventeenth century. Although it would be unwise to generalise from the very limited evidence available, it seems that wage rates in Ireland were somewhat higher than in Man, both in rural areas and, as might be expected, in the towns.

Table 3.5 *Comparison of Wage Rates in the Isle of Man,*
England and Ireland, 1594–1612
(daily rate, with meat and drink unless stated)

Occupation		Wage					
	I. of Man		England			Ireland	
						Co.	
		Chester	Lancs.	Wilts.	Rutl.	Tyrone	Youghal
	1609	1594	1595	1604	1610	1608	1611
Ploughman	13s. 4d. p.a.	—	—	—	—	26s. 8d. p.a.	—
Driver	10s. 0d. p.a.	—	—	—	29s. 0d.[4] p.a.	20s. 0d. p.a.	—
Horseman	8s. 0d. p.a.	—	—	—	—	—	—
Tailor	4d.	—	2–3d.[1]	26s. 8d–40s. p.a.	4d.	—	—
(working for servants)	1d.	—	—	—	—	—	—
Apprentices	2d.	—	2d.	2–3d.[3]	2–4d.[5]	2d.	—

[128] See *infra*, pp. 163–64.

	Chester	Lancs.	Wilts.	Rutl.		Co. Tyrone	Youghal
(working for servants)	1d.	—	—	—	—	—	—
Mason	4d.	2d.	3–4d.[1]	5–6d.[3]	4–5d.[5]	6d.	6d.
Carpenter	4d.	3½d.	3–4d.[1]	5–6d.[3]	4–5d.[5]	6d.	6d.
Joiner	4d.	1½d.	3–4d.[1]	5–6d.[3]	4–6d.[5]	—	—
Shipwright	4d.	—	—	—	—	—	—
Slater	4d.	1½d.	3–4d.[1]	3–4d.	4–5d.[5]	—	—
Thatcher	4d.	1d.	3–4d.[1]	3–4d.[3]	4–5d.[5]	—	—
Hooper	4d.	1½d.	3d.	26s. 8d.–40s. p.a.[1]	—	—	—
Weaver	—	—	—	—	—	4d. per slatt[6]	—
(wool)	½d. per yard	1d.	—	26s. 8d.–40s. p.a.	3–4d. + meal[7]	—	—
(linen)	2d.[8]	1d.	—	—	—	—	—
Walker	½d. per yard	1d. per yard	—	—	—	—	—
Fuller (blanket)	½d. per yard	1d.	—	26s. 8d.–40s. p.a.[1]	—	—	—
Fuller (keare)	¾d. per yard	—	—	—	—	—	—
(medley)	1½d. per yard	—	—	—	—	—	—
Blacksmith	—	1½d.	—	26s. 8d.–40s. p.a.[1]	—	—	—
(making coulter[9])	2d.	—	—	—	—	18d.[10]	—
(laying coulter)	1d.	—	—	—	—	—	—
(making sock[9])	2d.	—	—	—	—	—	—
(making and laying wing[9])	½d.	—	—	—	—	—	—
Labourer	—	—	—	—	—	2d.	4d.
(agricultural)	—	—	2–4d.[2]	3–5d.[2]	2–5d.[2]	—	—

Sources: Isle of Man: *Statutes*, pp. 70-1, 148; England: Chester: R. H. Morris, *Chester in the Plantagenet and Tudor Reigns* (1894), pp. 367-8; Lancashire and Rutland: J. E. T. Rogers (ed.), *A History of Agriculture and Prices in England, vol.vi, 1583-1702* (Oxford 1887), pp. 690-1, 692-3; Wiltshire: *H.M.C. Various Collections, vol.i* (1901), pp.162-7; Ireland: Co. Tyrone: *Calendar of the Carew Manuscripts, 1603-24* (1873), p.29; Youghal: R. Caulfield (ed.), *The Council Book of the Corporation of Youghal* (Guildford 1878), p.15.

Notes.

1. The lower rate applies to craftsmen who were not masters or apprentices, that is, journeymen.

2. Wages varied according to the ability of the labourers and the task in hand.

3. The lower rate was to be paid between Michaelmas and Lady Day (September 29–March 25), the higher rate during the rest of the year.

4. 'A mean-servant which can drive, plough, pitch, cart, and thresh, but cannot expertly sow.'

5. The lower rate to be paid between Michaelmas and Easter, rather than Lady Day, as in Wiltshire. See note 3.

6. For every weaver's slatt, containing three market slatts, 4d. and 8 quarts of meal. Cloth such as frieze was measured by the slatt of fifty inches in length and between twenty and twenty-three inches in width. *O.E.D., sub* slatt.

7. For weaving a mantle, 3d. and a medder or two gallons of meal. For weaving 'the best caddowe' or rough woollen blanket, 4d. and a medder of meal.

8. One great hundred breadth, with an additional farthing for every great hundred, according to the fineness of the yarn. *Statutes*, pp. 71, 148.

9. Coulters, socks and wings are all parts of a plough.

10. 'For making a plough iron, the owner making finding iron.'

In the same way that Justices of the Peace in some English counties issued the same wage rates every year, regardless of increasing prices,[129] the official rates in the island remained essentially static

---

[129] Clay, *Economic Expansion and Social Change*, vol. ii, p. 230. For a comparison with the movement of wages elsewhere in the British Isles during this period, see P. J. Bowden, 'Agricultural Prices, Farm Profits and Rents, 1500–1640', in *idem* ed., *Economic Change: Wages, Profits and Rents, 1500–1750* (Cambridge, 1990), pp. 19–20 and appendix E, table xliv; L. M. Cullen, T. C. Smout and A. Gibson, 'Wages and Comparative Development in Ireland and Scotland, 1565–1780', in R. Mitchison and P. Roebuck (eds), *Economy and Society in Scotland and Ireland, 1500–1939* (Edinburgh 1988), pp. 105–116.

throughout the seventeenth century. Payments to craftsmen working for the garrisons suggest, however, that these levels may have been exceeded, although there is no explicit provision in the regulations of 1609 limiting the rates paid to those in the Lord's service.[130] Some of these men were retained as members of the establishment at Castle Rushen or Peel Castle, and were probably the more highly skilled craftsmen, receiving a fee or salary in addition to the day-rate for their craft. Others were clearly outsiders, but even if the payments to both sorts of craftsmen did not include meat and drink, usually reckoned at between 3d. and 6d.,[131] the rates which they received were apparently above statute levels. In 1637, for example, two masons were paid on the Peel Castle accounts at the rate of 1s. per day.[132] Twelve years later, carpenters were employed on the same accounts at rates of 10d. and 1s. per day.[133]

There is also some evidence that, by the early 1660s, agricultural servants were demanding and obtaining wages considerably in excess of the statute levels of 1609, probably as the result of a shortage of labour.[134] In 1667, it was observed that 'Servants will not of late Yeares hire for double the Wages [set], unless they may receive what Wages they please' and, in fact, in that year, farm labourers were receiving between £2 and £4 a year.[135] In the view of the officers and Keys, among whom were many, if not most, of the island's larger farmers, each with a vested interest in holding down wage levels, the farmers had been better able to pay the official rates in 1609 than 'of late Times.' Since 'the enhancing of the Wages,' 'the Farmer is far more unable now

---

[130] It appears from a memorandum of James, tenth earl of Derby, dated 1705, that it had been normal practice to pay at least some workmen employed on the Lord's behalf at half the official rate. After protests that 'they could not subsist on halfe wages as formerly', a clause stating that this custom was to cease was apparently included in the regulations for wages introduced in 1691, but it must have been discarded before the Act was proclaimed at the Tynwald Court in July that year. Moore, *History*, vol. i, p. 290–1, 395 n. 1; *Statutes*, pp. 148–50.

[131] See the sources for Wiltshire and Rutland in Table 3.5.

[132] M.M.L., I.O. 1630–45, Book of allowance, Peel Castle, 1637: Reparations and works.

[133] M.M.L. R.D. 1627–50, Book of charge, Peel Castle, 1649: Reparations and works.

[134] *Statutes*, pp. 128–9. See *infra*, p. 146.

[135] *Statutes*, p. 132; Lib. Scacc. 1667, cited in Moore, *History*, vol. i, p. 393. Maid servants were paid between 30s. and £2 a year. *ibid*.

than formerly to pay the same, in respect of the scarcity of Money and the cheap Rates both of Corn and Cattle.' It was also objected that servants were then 'in a better Condition to subsist, by the Cheapness of Cloath, both Woolen and Linnen, and all other Comodities they stand in need of.'[136] Some servants seem to have justified their demands by claiming that the existing rates applied only to those put to service by the juries for servants[137] or those who had been yarded, or arbitrarily chosen to serve the Lord or one of the officers.[138] This was an understandable conclusion drawn from a law passed in 1665, which stipulated that those put to service were to be paid according to the rates set in 1609.[139] This claim was firmly rejected by the governor, Bishop Barrow, the officers and Keys, who maintained that 'the Statute is plain to the contrary, being for the Wages Generall of Servants' and ordered that 'there be a Restraint of such Exorbitancy in the Servants.' Though recognising that prices might well rise in the future and 'so continue for some Time,' they took 'the Cheapness of all Comodities at present' as their guide line and issued wage rates for servants in husbandry with only minor changes from those of 1609. Ploughmen were henceforth to receive a maximum of 15s. a year; maid servants of ability were to be paid up to 9s., while the wages of those of 'meaner Capacity' were to be determined by the deemster, with the jury for servants, if necessary. The wages of shepherds and other lesser servants were to be assessed by the same method. Household fishermen, who had not been noticed in the former statute, were to be paid 13s. a year. The other rates remained unchanged and, as in 1609, it was directed that 'no other certain Wages' were to be paid above these levels 'unless it be by Way of Bounty.'[140]

---

[136] *Statutes*, p. 132.

[137] See note 95.

[138] *Statutes*, p. 132.

[139] *ibid*, p. 123.

[140] *ibid*, pp. 132–3. These rates were considerably lower than those in English counties, such as Essex, as might be anticipated. In 1651, for instance, a 'best ploughman' in Essex was to receive £4 10s. in wages and 10s. in livery, whereas in the island, a ploughman was officially to receive no more than 13s. 4d., with board and lodging. J. E. T. Rogers, *A History of Agriculture and Prices in England, vol. vi, 1583–1702* (Oxford 1887), p. 696; *Statutes*, p. 71. At Castle Waring, County Down, a driver was paid £2 a year in 1640, while his Manx counterpart received only 10s. *H.M.C. Egmont*, p. 122; *Statutes*, p. 71.

An addition to the regulations governing the rates paid to agricultural servants was made in 1679, when the wages of mowers were fixed. It was alleged that such men had been in the habit of taking 'extraordinary wages' and of failing to pull their weight, so that three men were needed to do the work of two. Consequently, the governor, officers and Keys ordered that every mower 'doing his work sufficiently' and cutting a 'daymath,' or half an acre, was to receive 4d. per day with meat and drink and 12d. otherwise, at the farmer's discretion. Any mower who refused to work at these rates was to be put to service or fined and punished as the court thought fit; farmers paying more than the official levels forfeited the day's wages to the Lord.[141] Although the wages of Manx mowers may have been held down, they were only slightly lower than those paid in some English counties, such as Warwickshire, where the rate was 6d. per day with meat and drink in the early 1680s.[142]

That the rise in prices in the island followed a similar pattern to that in England, where the upward trend levelled off after about 1650,[143] seems quite likely, although it is not possible to draw any significant conclusions from the very limited amount of price data available. The problem of detecting any movement in Manx prices over a long period from such meagre information is rendered even more intractable by the haphazard survival of price data, an incomplete record of Manx harvest failures and consequently an inability to distinguish short term variations in the prices of foodstuffs and other commodities from an underlying trend. At the time of the restoration of the Stanleys in the Isle of Man in 1660, for example, the price of wheat stood at the relatively low level of 5s. per boll,[144] while a beef retailed at 24s. and a mutton was sold for 3s., both of the latter being sizable increases over the market values of half a century before; the rates for poultry showed no change.[145] Writing during the series of bad harvests which afflicted the island in the 1690s, driving the price of wheat and barley up to a maximum of 16s. per boll in 1699, William Sacheverell recorded prices for some items

---

[141] Lib. Scacc. 1679, 33; *Statutes*, p. 137.
[142] Rogers, *History of Agriculture and Prices*, vol. vi, p. 699.
[143] On the price rise in England, see Clay, *Economic Expansion and Social Change*, vol. i, chapter 2; Bowden, *Economic Change*, passim.
[144] See Table 2.1.
[145] Moore, *Notes and Documents*, p. 31. For beef and mutton prices in 1607, see *infra*, p. 157.

which were slightly higher again. A 'fat Goose,' for instance, could be purchased for 6d. and hens and ducks at 3d. a piece.[146]

Whether these rises were the product of increased demand for food, brought on by harvest failure, or an indication of a general trend it is not possible to tell, but there can be no doubt about the marked increase in prices in the island during the late sixteenth and the first half of the seventeenth century. The failure of the island's government to adjust the wages of craftsmen in the light of this price rise meant that those who depended on such work for most of their income and who were paid at the official rate set in 1609 – perhaps the great majority – inevitably experienced a considerable degree of hardship, particularly in years, such as the late 1640s, when successive bad harvests forced up the price of corn. Craftsmen who managed to obtain wages above the official rates were obviously less seriously affected, but it is clear that the authorities had no intention of allowing such practices to become widespread. At the Tynwald Court in July 1691, in the presence of William, ninth earl of Derby, an Act 'for establishing of Wages to Artificers, Tradesmen, and other Workmen and Labourers' was passed which simply reaffirmed the wage levels of 1609. As far as wages were concerned, the only new regulations were the rates paid to linen weavers and common labourers, but the former had been in operation for some time, since they were fixed 'according to the old Custome,'[147] and the latter were merely a record of generally accepted levels. Labourers, who had not been mentioned in the statute of 1609, were to be paid at the same rates which seem to have generally applied before 1690.[148] 'Gardeners, Hedgers, Reapers of Corn, Haymakers and such like' were to take 2d. per day with meat and drink or 4d. without board,[149] rates

---

[146] Sacheverell, Account, p. 13. For poultry prices in 1607, see *infra*, p. 157.

[147] See *infra*, pp. 159–60.

[148] Labourers employed on the accounts of the castles in the 1640s appear to have been paid 2d. per day, probably without food. Moore estimated that this would have been the rate in the early seventeenth century, and it was apparently the day-rate paid in 1663. M.M.L. R.D. 1627–50, Book of allowance, Peel Castle, 1648; Moore, *History*, vol. i, pp. 289, 393 n. 4.

[149] *Statutes*, p. 149. This Act also set out the hours to be worked by craftsmen and labourers. Between Lady Day and Michaelmas (March 25– September 29), a 12-hour day, beginning at 6 a.m., was to be worked; in the winter half of the year work was confined to daylight hours. Tailors and shoemakers were to work until 8 p.m. every night all year round. *ibid*, pp. 149–50.

which were lower than in many parts of England, but similar to those in Ireland in the late seventeenth century.[150]

In an effort to foster the development of manufacturing in the island, the Act of 1691 made special provisions 'for the Encouragement of such Artificers, Handycraftmen, and Labourers, as do come over here out of England, Ireland and other Places from beyond Seas to reside and work.' Such craftsmen were not to be bound by the wage levels laid down, but were to 'have and receive for their Work and Wages by the Day so much as the Governor and the Lord's Councell shall think fitt.'[151] The refusal of the authorities to raise wages in general and the preferential treatment to be given to outsiders combined to encourage some Manxmen to consider leaving the island, with or without licence from the governor. Among these was Charles Crowe, the son of a former vicar of Jurby, who, in 1693, was prepared 'to goe out of the Cuntrey to try [his] fortune.'[152] The problem of the emigration of craftsmen and labourers was clearly regarded seriously by the Keys, who, seeing their interests threatened by a reduction in the labour supply, petitioned Deputy Governor Robert Mawdesley in April 1703 to make it much more difficult, if not in practice impossible, for such men to leave the island. Mawdesley granted their request and ordered that no servant would in future be permitted to depart without a certificate from the parish priest, the Captain of the Parish and the jury for servants 'that it will be no determent to the Island by such servant going out.'[153] Nevertheless, the process continued to some extent, and, in fact, even before this order was included in an Act of Tynwald in 1713, the increased demand for labour, arising in

[150] Reapers in Warwickshire in 1684, for example, were paid 6d. per day with meat and drink, or 1s. without board, during the summer half of the year. Female reapers and haymakers received 4d. and 8d. respectively, while the rates for mowers of corn and grass were 6d. and 1s. All these labourers received 1d. less during the winter. Rogers, *History of Agriculture and Prices*, vol. vi, p. 699. According to Sir William Petty, labourers in Ireland were paid 4d. per day in the 1670s. The Marquess of Lansdowne ed., *The Petty Papers* (2 vols, 1927), vol. ii, p. 58.

[151] *Statutes*, p. 150.

[152] M.M.L., Lezayre Old Deeds, 1692–3, bundle 2/43.

[153] Lib. Scacc. 1703, inter 6–7 (2), inter 20–1 (3).

Moore's opinion, from the spread of smuggling, had begun to drive up wages and the regulations of 1691 soon became outdated.[154]

f) Projects

By the early seventeenth century, schemes for the development of new industries and the reinvigoration of those long-established had become an integral part of the English economy. Originating in the mid-Tudor period as a result of the English government's concern to reduce the country's dependence on foreign imports and to provide employment for the rapidly growing population, particularly the poorer sort, by encouraging the establishment or reintroduction of industries, the notion of projects, plans for the exploitation of human and material resources, quickly took hold. By the early Stuart period, as Joan Thirsk has observed, 'Everyone with a scheme, whether to make money, to employ the poor, or to explore the far corners of the earth had a "project."'[155]

Projects designed to stimulate domestic manufacturing were usually sited in areas where the necessary raw materials and expertise were already available, although the latter was less significant as a determining factor if skilled workers could be induced to settle in the appropriate location. Relative isolation from the principal markets, and London in particular, appears to have been a much less important consideration.[156] There was, therefore, no reason why the Isle of Man, which was, after all, not so very much more distant from the English capital than Lancashire, with its burgeoning textile industry, should not benefit from such schemes. In the 1650s, James Chaloner reported that, though the inhabitants were 'ingenuous in learning of Manufactures,' a 'Manufacture of their Wools might here be profitably erected; for we see Jersey, that hath no Wooll within itself, considerable; yet it maintaineth a great Trade with the Wools there wrought, and brought from other Countries.'[157] Nothing came

---

[154] Moore, *History*, vol. i, pp. 397–8; *Statutes*, p. 191.

[155] J. Thirsk, *Economic Policy and Projects* (Oxford, 1978), pp. 1–12, 26–7, 158–61.

[156] *ibid*, pp. 2, 26.

[157] Chaloner, *Treatise*, pp. 11, 52–3. For a brief assessment of the Jersey wool trade, see J. C. Appleby, 'Neutrality, Trade and Privateering, 1500–1689', in A. G. Jamieson ed., *A People of the Sea. The Maritime History of the Channel Islands* (1986), pp. 71–3.

of Chaloner's tentative suggestion and, apart from some vague proposals for attracting Frenchmen to settle in the island in the early 1670s, there were no further moves to develop manufacturing before the last decade of the seventeenth century.[158]

The architect of the ambitious plan for the establishment of linen and other manufactories and the expansion of the island's trade drawn up in July 1691 was William Sacheverell. Although he had had some connection with the Isle of Man in 1688,[159] Sacheverell held no office at the time, and it may be that his project was an attempt to gain favour with William, earl of Derby. If so, it appears to have succeeded, because, in April 1692, he was one of four revenue commissioners for the island appointed by the earl, and the next month he was sworn in as deputy governor.[160] Sacheverell urged that 'all sorts of manifacture be sett up and some advantagious laws made in favour of all Artisans as smiths, showmakers, Taylors, Weavers, Bricklayers, Carpenters, Tanners [and] Chandlers.' Strangers were to be encouraged to settle 'by appointing them wast lands and obligeing all persons to be assisting to them in their clereing and fencing.' Sacheverell suggested that this might also be achieved by offering very long leases of properties at very low rents and fixed fines, 'that they may be convinced they improve for themselves and their familys and not for the Lord.'[161]

One of the two main goals of the project was the foundation of a linen 'manufactory' and Sacheverell outlined his plans in this direction at some length. Every woman in the island, he maintained, 'without distinction of quallity,' was to be required to spin 'some small quantity of wooll or flax as suppose twenty pound' and to receive set rates of payment on delivery. Prizes of spinning wheels were to be offered for the finest spun yarn and for the greatest amount of cloth made in every parish. Sacheverell further proposed that, if a woman won the prize a second time, 'the Magistrates [sic] should offer her a sutable husband' or 'some reasonable reward towards her portion.' The parish in which the prize-winner

---

[158] M.M.L., MD/401/1717/32.
[159] Sacheverell, *Account*, p. 109.
[160] L.R.O., DDKe 80. Appointment of commissioners of the revenue and to set lands in the Isle of Man, April 18, 1692; Sacheverell, *Account*, pp. ix-x.
[161] L.R.O., DDKe 80. Articles for erecting a company for the Isle of Man (1691?). Cf. Knowsley Hall, Box H/44a. Sacheverell's Proposals to Lord Derby for erecting a Company for the Isle of Man (n.d.).

for the best cloth lived was to receive a 'publick marke of esteem,' such as a 'Whittsun Ale, where the young woman would be taken notice of by strangers of neighbouring parishes.' This might not only lead to matrimony, with the proceeds from the ale and household goods to the value of £5 awarded to the woman for her portion as added inducements to single men; the spectacle would also inspire others to greater efforts.[162] Sacheverell believed that if the manufactures were to be a success, an adequate supply of labour was essential. The best way to achieve this, in his opinion, was through population growth, by encouraging all people to marry at the age of twenty-five. Industrious people were to be rewarded, but all 'publick beggars, lazy persons, theeves, fellons, drunkards [and] swearers' were to be consigned to a workhouse, which was to be built for the purpose.[163]

The second principal objective of Sacheverell's plan was the creation of a company, with the backing of the Lord and the support of legislation, to handle the island's trade. Sacheverell envisaged that this company would comprise the earl of Derby and the leading men of the island, financed by voluntary subscriptions of between £100 and £1,000 per person. Any man born in the island could invest in the company, within these limits, at any time. He could, if things went well, treble his money 'within the compas of five years,' after which period the first dividends would be paid, but nobody with less than £600 invested would have a voice in the running of the company. It was Sacheverell's suggestion that the Lord should issue £10,000 in silver and brass coinage 'for the present management of affairs.' This money, which was to be lent to the company for seven years, was to be employed for the construction of a 'publick brewhouse, bakehouse for biskett, stillhouse, storehouse, miln and tanyard,' the buildings being 'tyed' to the Lord as security for the loan. Committees were to be selected to supervise the linen manufacture and the planting of flax, the fishery, and husbandry, each having the authority 'to censure all sutch as are not industrious.' They were to be empowered to direct what crops should be planted – corn or flax – to inspect the work of fishermen, weavers and other craftsmen, to ensure that parishes delivered 'their proportions of linen,' and to set the rates for all commodities and craftsmen's

---

[162] *ibid.*
[163] *ibid.*

wages. A clerk was to be engaged to record the receipt of commodities and disbursements on behalf of the company, but he was to be the only salaried official, 'this being the publick interest.'[164]

Sacheverell had chosen a propitious moment to submit his plan to Earl William, as the island was apparently experiencing a series of harvest failures and low yields from the herring fishery.[165] In the circumstances, such a scheme was likely to find a ready audience, offering, as it did, the possibility of alleviating to some extent the island's economic problems. Some of Sacheverell's proposals were accordingly incorporated in an Act of Tynwald passed in July 1692 'for setting up a Linnen manufacture.'[166] This set out, in some detail, the way in which the enterprise was to be conducted. All those who held quarterlands were directed to plant half an acre of hemp or flax 'in a husbandlike manner, and soe proportionable to greater and lesser houldings,' from the following Michaelmas; tenants occupying intacks of 6d. rent or more were to plant the twentieth part of their land. When the crop was ready, the tenants were 'to gather, water and hatchell' [heckle] the flax, retain what was necessary for their family needs and deliver the rest to the moar[167] of the parish, for which the Lord '(out of his speciall regard to the welfare of his people) will deduct soe much of the said persons Rent as the flax or hemp shall amount unto, according to the marketable price of flax or hemp at that time in the Island.'[168] Refusal to cultivate these crops carried the penalty of a fine of 3s. 4d. for every half acre which

---

[164] *ibid.*

[165] On the fortunes of the Manx harvest and the herring fishery, see chapter 2.

[166] M.M.L., MD/401/1719/8. This Act is extant only in the form of a copy. Moore maintained that it was 'duly signed and approved' by the earl, but the copy bears no signature. Moore, *History*, vol. i, p. 426 n. 1. That the Act was passed in 1692 is confirmed in a letter written by Sacheverell to Richard Norris of Speke, dated July 4, in which he stated that on 'Midsummer day I held the Tynwald Court . . . when I passed two Acts – one for setting up a linen manufacture, another for regulating moneys'. L.C.R.O., 920/NOR/1/6.

[167] The office of moar is discussed in chapter 1, p. 51–2.

[168] M.M.L., MD/401/1719/8. Quarterland tenants who could convince the parish priest and four of the 'ablest men' there that their land could not support such crops 'by any reasonable Improvment' were exempted from this order. The preparation of flax for weaving is described in Lowe, *Lancashire Textile Industry*, pp. 43–4.

should have been planted, the money arising from fines being used to support the workhouse.[169]

Sacheverell's proposals concerning the employment of women for spinning and the establishment of a system of rewards for achievement were also included in the Act, though with slight modifications. All able women between the ages of fifteen and fifty, whether natives or immigrants, whether their condition was 'very necessetous' or not, 'without distinction of quality, state or condicon,' were to spin as much linen yarn as would make twelve yards of cloth and were to bring it to the sheading courts in May each year. There, two weavers, one chosen by the governor and officers and the other by the deemsters and Great Enquests, were to set a just price for the yarn; the revenue commissioners, acting in the place of the receiver, would then pay 'unto every person the true and just vallue of the Cloath or yarne.' Whoever produced the finest yarn or cloth was to receive, in addition, the sum of 20s. as a reward. The yarn or cloth was to be taken to the following Tynwald Court, 'where shee that hath spunne the finest yarne or Cloath in the whole Island by the Judgment of the two weavers and the approbation of the Court shall as a further encouragement for her Industry receive the further summe of ffour pounds.' If she were a maid or servant, she was to be freed for life from yarding and from being put to service by juries for servants. Those who, for whatever reason, could not produce or obtain sufficient hemp or flax were to apply to the moar, who supplied any deficiencies from the quantity already delivered to him by other tenants. Failure to obey these instructions was to be dealt with in the first year by an admonition to the offender 'to doe their duty better for the future,' on the second occasion, by imprisonment or consignment to 'the publick house of Correction' and further punishment at the discretion of the governor and officers.[170]

When it was clear that his project had received at least the tacit approval of the earl, and before the draft legislation had been submitted to the Tynwald Court, Sacheverell approached John

---

[169] M.M.L., MD/401/1719/8. Sacheverell's proposal that every town in the island should have 'a Matronlike woman who should teach a schoole for Girles to read and spin and nedle-worke' was adapted in the Act, which provided that there should be 'roome sufficient' in the workhouse for such a woman 'to teach children to spinn, and for a weaver to teach [them] to weave and dresse flax gratis'.

[170] *ibid.*

Scanfield, a clothier, sending him some 'patterns' of cloth worked up in the island.[171] The latter expressed himself 'not only well disposed, but in a fair Prospect of being greatly instrumentall in the good and prosperity of the Island.' He promised to meet the earl in London 'in Company of an Eminent ffreind of mine, and to propose such beneficial matters as tend not only to the Linnen Manufacture, but to give the Island a sure and speedy improvement in most (if not all) things wherein Art or Nature do or can befreind it.' Assuring Sacheverell that the project would profit the earl, the island's government and the Manx people in general, 'perhaps by degrees in some measure to every individual with regard to their several Circumstances and Qualifications,' Scanfield, a prudent speculator, was nevertheless reluctant to commit himself until he had obtained detailed information about the island. The size of the island and its population, the fertility of the soil and the products of the land, the nature of the island's government and laws, the disposition of the people, the number of harbours and the prospects for manufactures were all subjects on which he requested particulars from Sacheverell at the latter's first convenience.[172]

Sacheverell responded promptly and encouragingly in early July 1692, by which time the Act for organising the linen manufacture had been passed. He informed Scanfield, not without a hint of pride, that he had 'established by a Law that every wooman in the Isle shall spin twelve yardes of Linnen Cloth, which, if we have 3000 woomen in the Isle fitt for spining, is not an inconsiderable advancement towards the work proposed, especially if you will consider how much more above halfe that number will spin voluntarily.'[173] He also endeavoured to answer Scanfield's questions about the island as fully as 'the shortness of the time I have resided in the Island (which is not yet two months) will permit.'[174] Perhaps not surprisingly, the impression of the island which he conveyed contained little likely to deter the potential investor. Soils were generally good; farming methods were 'neer the same with England,' the land producing all sorts of crops; the island was governed 'by a wise body' and laws

---

[171] M.M.L., MD/401/1719/7. John Scanfield to [William Sacheverell], June 13, 1692.
[172] ibid.
[173] M.M.L., MD/401/1719/21a. Sacheverell to John Scanfield, July 5, 1692.
[174] ibid.

were made 'in a parliamentary way.' Most importantly, so far as the
project in hand was concerned, the 'Genius of the peeple Crafty, and
the men generally disposed to fishing, the woomen to spining.'
Having had his hopes raised 'beyond the Linnen manifacture,' Sacheverell reported that the commodities then produced in the island –
cloth, shoes, hats, stockings, soap and beer, among other items –
could, in most cases, 'be improved to great perfection, especially
earthen potts which will turn to great profit in Ireland.'[175] In his
view, in spite of shortages of timber, iron, coal and 'all sorts of
merchantdyce,' the Isle of Man only required 'a present stock of
mony to make it one of the most florishing Islands in Europe.' The
other prerequisite was a number of skilled craftsmen, who could
instruct the Manx in various trades.[176]

Negotiations with Scanfield concerning his part in the project
continued, but appear to have broken down as a result of his
insistence that two conditions be fulfilled before he committed
himself. In return for his promotion of manufacturing in the island,
he desired – and, it seems, had been promised – that a house and
land amounting to between 400 and 500 acres should be granted to
him and his heirs, 'that they may reap some part of the Benefit of
my improvements.' He further required freedom of worship for
himself and 'any other Artists that may come over to promote so
good a work' and sought an undertaking that no such craftsmen
would be 'molested in [their] persons or estates as in relation to the
worship of God whilst [they] live peaceably under the Government.'
One or both of these demands proved to be a stumbling block, and,
at the beginning of September, Scanfield attempted to enlist the
support of the countess of Derby 'to prosecute these things effectu-
ally with the earl in order to give [him] the greater encouragement
to proceed in this weighty concern.'[177] It is not certain to which
denomination Scanfield belonged, although he was almost certainly
a Dissenter. It seems unlikely, however, that Earl William would
have refused to guarantee his religious liberty, since, though he was
an Anglican Tory himself, he was frequently in the company of

---

[175] *ibid.* Cf. L.R.O., DDKe 80, 'Mr. Sacheverells computacons about the Isle
of Man' (n.d.).
[176] M.M.L., MD/401/1719/21a. Sacheverell to Scanfield, July 5, 1692.
[177] M.M.L., MD/401/1719/24. Scanfield to Elizabeth, countess of Derby,
September 1, 1692.

nonconformist gentry in Lancashire and Cheshire when it suited his interests.[178] The allocation to Scanfield of a large estate, by island standards, may well have been the greater obstacle. Certainly the tenants occupying the best land, some of which the speculator undoubtedly intended to secure if possible, would have resolutely opposed any attempted dispossession, assuming the earl ever considered such a rash course of action. Any confrontation with the leading men of the island was clearly to be avoided, especially at a time when there was already a considerable amount of discontent over the uncertainty of land tenure.[179]

Whatever the circumstances, the fact remains that Scanfield did not come to the island. The wide-ranging, if somewhat vague, plans which he had discussed with Sacheverell did, nevertheless, have some practical results. Some form of linen manufactory seems to have started and, in about 1700, seems to have received encouragement to continue, perhaps from Earl William himself. A soap boiling operation appears to have been set up by the end of the seventeenth century and the construction of a brewhouse and a malthouse was then under consideration. The failure of the Scanfield project to materialise served as a stimulus to the search for other 'projectors' who were willing to come to the island to instruct the inhabitants in their skills and to supervise the venture, particularly woollen clothiers, tanners and curriers.[180]

The last decade of the seventeenth century also witnessed renewed, if not continuing, interest in other areas of manufacturing. Brickmaking, which may have already been undertaken on a limited scale in about 1650, was promoted by the establishment of a brickworks in the vicinity of Castletown in the spring of 1692, possibly on the initiative of the earl.[181] From the outset, the enterprise was plagued by the same difficulties which had beset earlier attempts – clays which were less than perfect for brickmaking and an absence of

---

[178] B. Coward, 'The Social and Political Position of the Earls of Derby in Later Seventeenth-Century Lancashire', *T.H.S.L.C.*, vol. cxxxii (1983), pp. 147–50.

[179] For an outline of the problems relating to land tenure, see Moore, *History*, vol. ii, pp. 871–888.

[180] M.M.L., MD/401/1719/63. An undated list of tasks to be undertaken, probably drawn up in *c.* 1700. The author is not known. One of the priorities was to 'Continue the linnen Manufacture'.

[181] See *infra*, p. 144.

locally available fuel of the right type. Shortly after his arrival in the island to assume the post of deputy governor in May 1692, Sacheverell reported to Earl William that there was an acute shortage of coal, not only in the garrisons, but also 'for your brick, which will require great quantitys.'[182] Supplies may not have been immediately forthcoming, but preparations for firing the bricks continued, and, later in the month, the deputy governor informed the earl that 'we have all reddy a kiln reddy and Brick enough for one burning.'[183] By early August, John Rowe, the comptroller, was able to send Earl William the news that 'there are now a hundred thousand of Brick burnt in the Ovens; the workmen say that they are as good as those made at Knowsley, but the great Rate of cole here makes them deare.' He estimated the cost of the bricks at 15s. per thousand 'in cole and workmanship, besides costing up the clay and other charges, which if not done by your Lordships tennants for boone services would make the brick dearer.' Rowe suggested that costs could be reduced by 'the other way of burning in Clams [which] if your Lordship thinks fitt would save 5 *li* in every 40 thousand.'[184] At the end of August, after the production of bricks to the number of '150 thowsand in Ovens and 20 thowsand in the Clamp,' the brickmaker, who had been brought to the island, almost certainly from England, to supervise the operation, returned home 'by reason of the winter season.' Rowe noted optimistically that he had 'promised to be here againe in ffebruary next in order to sett up a Pottery' and to produce tobacco pipes,[185] but, apart from a vague indication that there was a working pottery kiln in operation about 1700, no further references to the brickmaker or his operations have as yet been discovered.[186]

Throughout the seventeenth century, efforts were made to exploit the known mineral wealth of the island and to discover additional sources. Mine working had a long, if somewhat sparsely documented history, stretching back at least to the middle of the thirteenth

---

[182] M.M.L., MD/401/1719/23. Sacheverell to Derby. This letter is not dated, but, from internal evidence, must have been written soon after Sacheverell took his oath of office on May 9. Sacheverell, *Account*, p. ix.

[183] M.M.L., MD/401/1719/6. Sacheverell to Derby, May 23, 1692.

[184] M.M.L., MD/401/1719/11. John Rowe to Derby, August 3, 1692.

[185] M.M.L., MD/401/1719/15. Rowe to Derby, August 30, 1692.

[186] M.M.L., MD/401/1719/63. See note 180. This list includes a reference to 'The Pottery', but it is not possible to determine whether this relates to an established manufactory or a project for the future.

century, when Harald, king of Man and the Isles, granted full mineral rights and three acres of land for a smelting works at Ronaldsway to Furness Abbey, of which Rushen Abbey was a dependent house. The monks processed lead, possibly from mines in Rushen or at Foxdale, and may even have extracted silver from the lead.[187] When Sir John Stanley and his heirs were endowed with the lordship of Man by Henry IV in 1406, the rights to 'mines of lead and iron' were included, and not long afterwards, in 1423, the governor and officers were directed to 'sett forward' the Lord's mine and to 'see the Miner doe his Duty.'[188] All the iron and lead mines in the island remained in the Lord's hands except for those which might be opened on the bishop's estates, which were granted by Thomas, second earl of Derby, to Bishop Huan Hesketh and his successors in 1505.[189] No record of any mine workings in the early Stanley period seems to have survived, but, by contrast, there is a considerable amount of material extant relating to seventeenth-century mining projects.

The first significant operation during this period began after a grant by letters patent from Charles I to James, Lord Strange, the son and heir of William, sixth earl of Derby, of full mineral rights in the island for a period of twenty-one years in May 1627.[190] Strange, who in practice became Lord of Man on the death of his mother, Countess Elizabeth, in the preceding March, was eager to improve the income from the island and saw the short-term leasing of the mineral rights as a way of securing a modest return for several years, with the possibility of greater rewards in the future, when the lease came to be renewed, should further deposits be found.

Among the men in the north of England best qualified to search for and exploit mineral ores, perhaps the most highly skilled were the German miners who had settled in small numbers in Cumberland and Westmorland in the sixteenth century,[191] and it was with members of

---

[187] B. R. S. Megaw. '"Bakenaldwath" and the Medieval Lead Mines', *J.M.M.*, vol. vi (1957–65), pp. 105–7.

[188] Oliver, *Monumenta*, vol. ii, p. 236; *Statutes*, p. 19.

[189] Oliver, *Monumenta*, vol. ii, pp. 27–31.

[190] M.M.L., MD/401/1725/3. The term of the grant ran from March 25, 1627.

[191] For details of the settlement of German miners in these counties and their activities, see L. Bouch and G. P. Jones, *A Short Economic and Social History of the Lake Counties* (Manchester, 1961), pp. 119–127; J. F. Crosthwaite,

this community that negotiations were opened for such a project in the Isle of Man. The result was that, in July 1628, Strange leased the mineral rights in the island to Daniel and Joseph Höchstetter of Keswick and Richard Tickell of Thornthwaite for a period of seven years at an annual rent of £30, which commenced in the second year of the term.[192] The lessees were empowered to 'search, digg, open, roast, melt, stamp, wash, draine water and otherwise in any kind whatsoever to worke, gett and provide for all and all manner of mynes and Oares of Gould, Silver, Copper, Lead houlding Silver or mixed with Silver, and Quicksilver and all mynes of [Copper], Tynne and Lead' throughout the island. Buildings were to be erected, if necessary, near any workings which they might establish, so that they could 'trie out and convert' copper or lead ore and refine the silver and gold contained in it.[193] Workmen and their families could be brought to the island to run the mines, but the lessees had to ensure that all 'such workefolks and servaunts, with theyre wives and children' left the island at the end of the term of the lease.[194]

There are no further references to this project and it is most probable that, after a preliminary survey, the Höchstetters and Tickell decided that the difficulties in working the mines outweighed the likely profits and took advantage of the clause which allowed them to surrender the lease by June 1629 without incurring any great expense.[195]

There was, however, at least one other mining enterprise under way at about the same time, or shortly after, this scheme was abandoned. According to James Chaloner, Captain Edward Christian of Maughold, who was appointed governor in August 1627,

---

'The Crosthwaite Registers', *T.C.W.A.A.S.*, O.S., vol. ii (1874–5), pp. 226–7; *idem*, 'The German Miners at Keswick', *Transactions of the Cumberland Association for the Advancement of Literature and Science*, vol. viii (1882–3), pp. 111–126; W. G. Collingwood, 'Germans at Coniston in the Seventeenth Century', *T.C.W.A.A.S.*, New series, vol. x (1910), pp. 371–2, 385–6.

[192] M.M.L., MD/401/1725/3.

[193] *ibid.* If any of the mines established by the lessees produced more than sixty ounces of silver for every ton of lead, so attaining the standard of a mine royal of silver, a tenth of the profits was payable to the king. *Ibid*; Bawden et al., *Industrial Archaeology*, p. 51. Cf. H. Hamilton, *The English Brass and Copper Industries to 1800* (2nd edn, 1967), pp. 54–5.

[194] M.M.L., MD/401/1725/3.

[195] *ibid.*

'experimented' with the 'Ore of Lead, at, or neer unto the Sea-Crag, called Mine-hough,' or Bradda Head in Rushen, which was reputedly found 'to hold much silver.'[196] It is not certain for how long these deposits were worked, although Chaloner's comments suggest that it was only briefly. At the end of the century, Sacheverell recorded that 'the rocks called the Mine-haugh give very probable signs of other minerals' and that he was informed that 'they have found iron, lead and copper.'[197] These observations are ambiguous as far as the operation of the mines is concerned, but the suspicion that they may have ceased production by about 1700 at the latest would seem to be confirmed by a report to the Company of Mine Adventurers of England in 1740. This states that the mines at Bradda had been out of use for such a long time that it was not possible to discover the nature and extent of the workings underground.[198]

After the restoration of the Stanleys in the Isle of Man in 1660, Charles, eighth earl of Derby, sought a further grant of the 'Mynes Royall of Gould and Silver' from Charles II, 'as there is some Probabilitie of findinge some Mines in the said Isle with silver in them.'[199] A warrant for such a grant was finally issued several months later, in September 1666, and, within about two years, the earl had leased all the mines in the island to three merchants, two from London and one from Liverpool.[200] They were given permission 'to erect a smelting mill, or more than one, for the smelting of the oar,' chiefly copper and lead, and were apparently to deliver one-fifth of the output to the earl.[201] The fate of this operation is not clear, but its inception may have encouraged Earl Charles, 'being by good reasons persuaded that there is plenty of coales' in the island, to order a search for deposits in the following year, 1669.[202] Fostered by a realisation that the discovery of a local fuel source would remove one of the disincentives to mining projects in the island, the earl's optimism was, however, misplaced, for the Isle of Man has no coal.

---

[196] Chaloner, *Treatise*, p. 8. Cf. Blundell, *History*, vol. i, p. 49.
[197] Sacheverell, *Account*, p. 14.
[198] Bawden et al., *Industrial Archaeology*, p. 52.
[199] P.R.O., SP 29/159/22.
[200] *C.S.P.D., 1666–7*, p. 123; Moore, *Notes and Documents*, p. 2.
[201] Moore, *History*, vol. ii, pp. 961–2.
[202] *ibid*, p. 962.

In spite of a record of apparently limited success, efforts continued to be made by the earl and his officers to attract mining speculators to the island. The search for new mineral deposits was maintained and, to avoid the possibility of disputes with the Crown, William, ninth earl of Derby, petitioned Charles II in 1679 for a grant of the mines royal in the island, in case any workings which might be opened began to yield significant quantities of gold or silver.[203] In May 1692, Sacheverell reported to Earl William that he had recently found some 'perites' [pyrites] which, he hoped, 'are good signs of a mine under them.'[204] Nothing further is heard of Sacheverell's discovery, however, so it can be safely assumed that the deposits were either non-existent or proved to be too small to be worth working. At about the beginning of September 1696, Richard Stevenson, one of the revenue commissioners, sent some unspecified Manx ore, probably lead, to a certain Mr Beller in Ireland, who was 'experimentally knowen and reputed there to be a most knowing and Ingenious Person in the discovery and working of Miniralls.'[205] Beller replied by sending proposals for a project in which he was ready to bear all the charges if the earl would accept 'an eight Part cleare' or, if Earl William was prepared to supply half the necessary capital, to share the profits equally. Alternatively, Beller was willing to take a salary for supervising the operation. Stevenson advised the earl not to hesitate in making a decision 'least the Undertaker languish and grow cold by delay.'[206] It seems, however, that Earl William may have been guilty of procrastination, for there are no further references to Beller.

The mines in the island were, nevertheless, in production at this time. In 1699, the Lord's percentage of the output, which seems to have been twenty per cent, amounted to 32 tons and thirteen hundredweight of copper and lead,[207] the total production of these metals being, therefore, 163 tons and five hundredweight. In the following year, 227.5 tons of iron ore were shipped from the mines at 'Daunane' [Dhyrnane] in Maughold.[208]

[203] *ibid.*

[204] M.M.L., MD/401/1719/6. Sacheverell to Derby, May 23, 1692.

[205] M.M.L., MD/401/1719/44. Richard Stevenson to Derby, September 17, 1696.

[206] *ibid.*

[207] Moore, *History*, vol. ii, p. 962.

[208] *ibid*; Radcliffe and Radcliffe, *History of Kirk Maughold*, pp. 178–9.

Projects were not neglected, however, for, in April 1700, Earl William leased all the copper mines in the island, probably at Glen Chass and elsewhere in Rushen, to Middleton Shaw of Uttoxeter, Staffordshire, for twenty-one years. Shaw was to deliver a quarter of all the processed copper ore from the mines to the earl, who reserved the right to become a partner in the venture and to receive, in addition, one-sixth of the profits. Shaw agreed to spend at least £400 on workmen and equipment during the first two years 'in searching, digging, trying and working in and about the said mines,' while Earl William gave the customary permission for the construction of buildings and granted £15 towards making 'a Piere for the safety of Boats' at a place of Shaw's choosing. If, after two years had elapsed, Shaw could demonstrate that he had fulfilled his part of the bargain, he was free to surrender the lease,[209] and this was, in fact, what seems to have happened. In 1703, William Ross, the waterbailiff, wrote to James, tenth earl of Derby, informing him that the lease was no longer in force, 'Shaw being broke and having left the mines.'[210] At about the same time as the lease to Shaw was made, Earl William also leased the iron mines in Maughold to Captain John Price of Dublin, but, beyond this fact, few details of this operation appear to remain extant.[211]

The manufacturing projects of the last decade of the seventeenth century were attempts to broaden the base of the Manx economy and thus, in the long term, reduce the island's almost total dependence on the success of the harvest and the herring fishery. Efforts were made to attract skilled craftsmen, especially clothiers, and mining speculators to the island, but met with only limited success. In the seventeenth century as a whole, however, manufactures remained a minor, though by no means unimportant, part of the island's economic activity. Practically the whole population was engaged in some form of manufacturing, even if the end products were only for household consumption, but only a relatively small number appear to have earned a significant part of their income from the island's most important trades, such as milling and weaving. Many of those involved in manufacturing, both in the towns and in the countryside, followed more than one occupation in order to

[209] M.M.L., MD/401/1719/67.
[210] M.M.L., MD/401/1720/6, cited in A. M. Harrison, 'Economic Opportunities, 1700', *J.M.M.*, vol. vii (1966–76), p. 82.
[211] Lib. Scacc. 1700–2, 59. The lease was in force by August 29, 1701.

provide themselves with an adequate living, but, whichever of the principal trades they plied, the wages which they could demand and the standards which they were expected to maintain were set down by the island's government. As William Blundell rightly observed, the only trades in Man in this period were those which were necessary to supply the inhabitants' basic needs and it was not until after 1700 that manufacturing with wider markets in mind began to assume a greater degree of importance in the Manx economy.

The prospect of Castle Rushen in the Isle of Man, on ye south side.

1. Castle Rushen, Castletown.

The Prospect of Peel Caſtell, in y̆ Iſle of Man on y̆ West ſide.

A. Ireland
B. Wales

2. Peel Castle, St Patrick's Isle, Peel.

3. Douglas, with the mouth of the Douglas River in the foreground.

The Prospect of Bishops Court in the Isle of Man on the East side.

4. Bishopscourt, Kirk Michael, the residence of the Bishop of Sodor and Man.

The Prospect of Balfaly Abby, on the South Weft side.

5. Rushen Abbey, Ballasalla, Malew.

4 *Internal Trade*

Trading activity within the Isle of Man, although inevitably poorly documented, had undoubtedly always been a fundamental part of the Manx economy.[1] Certainly, any impression that most Manx farmers, except for those on the smallest and poorest holdings, were generally self-sufficient in food and clothing would be quite misleading. While many of the larger farmers were able to some extent to feed and clothe themselves and their families from the products of their own land, at least in years of plenty, even they had to obtain their outstanding requirements in the markets and fairs of the island. The great majority of the inhabitants, smaller farmers and town dwellers in particular, were necessarily even more dependent on such gatherings. The scale of this domestic trading activity is impossible to determine, especially in the absence of any reasonably reliable population figures before the early eighteenth century, but it may have been more than ten times greater than the amount of overseas trade.[2]

[1] For a discussion of the characteristics of internal trade in England, see J. A. Chartres, *Internal Trade in England, 1500–1700* (1977); A. M. Everitt, 'The Marketing of Agricultural Produce, 1500–1640', in J. A. Chartres (ed.), *Agricultural Markets and Trade, 1500–1750* (Cambridge 1990); J. A. Chartres, 'The Marketing of Agricultural Produce, 1640–1750', in *ibid*; *idem*, Introduction, in *ibid*. On internal trade in Scotland, see I. D. Whyte, *Agriculture and Society in Seventeenth-Century Scotland* (Edinburgh 1979), pp. 178–192.
[2] England's overseas trade was probably of similar importance, in comparison to the country's internal market, in the early sixteenth century. W. G. Hoskins, *The Age of Plunder, 1500–1547* (1976), p. 10. This differential may have decreased by the late seventeenth century, when Gregory King estimated that the home market was four times the size of foreign trade. G. King, *Of the Naval Trade of England* (1688).

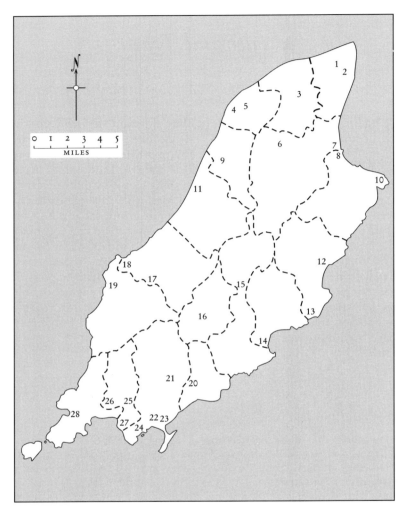

Map 4. Fairs in the Isle of Man in the Seventeenth Century.

1. Bride	2. Ballavarkish	3. Andreas	4. West Nappin
5. Jurby	6. Sulby	7. Ballakillingan	8. Ramsey
9. Ballaugh	10. Maughold	11. Kirk Michael	12. Laxey
13. Kirk Lonan	14. Douglas	15. Baldwin	16. Kirk Marown
17. St Johns	18. Peel	19. Patrick	20. Santan
21. St Mark's	22. Cross Four Ways	23. Ballasalla	24. Castletown
25. Balladbeg	26. Colby	27. Poyll Vaaish	28. Rushen

I. THE LOCATION, NUMBER AND FREQUENCY
OF MARKETS AND FAIRS

The degree to which the Manx people relied on internal trade is indicated in some measure by the number and frequency of markets and fairs in the island. Each of the four towns – Castletown, Douglas, Peel and Ramsey – had a market, which appears to have been held twice weekly.[3] The town markets drew people from the surrounding countryside, where, it seems, there were no weekly markets. These town markets were supplemented by regular annual fairs, both in the towns and in rural areas, many of those in the parishes being held on 'Patron Days' to commemorate the saint to whom the parish church was dedicated.[4] At a conservative estimate, there were probably forty-three fairs during the year in the island in the seventeenth century. (Tables 4.1 and 4.2).

Table 4.1 *Fairs in the Isle of Man in the Seventeenth Century* [1]
(Dates: Old Style. P: Patronal fair)

Date		Location/Parish	Festival
Jan.	5–6	St Mark's, Malew	Epiphany (Fiddlers' Fair)
Feb.	1	Kirk Bride, Bride	St Bridget (P)
	6	Poyll Vaaish, Arbory	St Dorothy[?] (Periwinkle Fair)
	7 → 2[2]	Kirk Marown, Marown	St Ronan → Purification of the Virgin (P)
	24	Cross Four Ways, Malew	St Matthias
March	16	Baldwin, Braddan	St Abban
	17	Peel	St Patrick (P)
	28[3]	Patrick	St Patrick
April	5	Jurby	St Patrick's first baptism in Ireland/Annunciation of the Virgin (P)

[3] Craine, *Manannan's Isle*, p. 85.
[4] The feasts of the Celtic saints were replaced, probably long before the Reformation, by those of saints more familiar to the English Church, which fell on or about the same day. The patronal fair of Marown, for example, held originally on the feast of St Ronan, or *Marooney* in Manx, February 7, was transferred to February 2, the Purification of the Virgin. J. J. Kneen, 'Manx Fairs and Festivals', *M.N.H.A.S.*, vol. iii (1927–32), pp. 39, 60.

Month	Day	Place	Dedication
	6[4]	Rushen	Holy Trinity (P)
	25	Ballasalla, Malew	St Mark
	25	Ballavarkish, Bride	St Mark
	28?/May?[5]	Douglas	St Conchan (Christopher) (P)
May	3	Castletown	St Mary[6]
	3	Douglas	St Mary[6]
	3	Ballaugh	St Ronican
	9	Santan	St Sanctan (Anne?) (P)
	12	St Mark's, Malew	
	18	St John's, German	*Spitlhin Souree* [Hospitals of St John in summer]
	24	Douglas	St Brennan (Braddan) (P)
June	—[7]	Sulby, Lezayre	Holy Trinity (P)
	9 → 11[2]	Ballabeg, Arbory	St Columba → St Barnabas (P)[8]
	24	St John's, German	[Tynwald Court] St John Baptist
	24	Sulby, Lezayre	St John Baptist
July	13	Peel	St German (P)
	25	Cross Four Ways, Malew	St Malew (Lupus) (P)
	31	Kirk Maughold, Maughold	St Maughold (P)
Aug.	5	Kirk Lonan → Laxey, Lonan	St Lonan (Mac Laisre)[9] (P)
	15	Ballaugh	St Mary (Nativity of the Virgin) (P)
	24	Ramsey	St Bartholomew[10]
Sept.	29	Ballasalla, Malew	St Michael
	29	Kirk Michael, Michael	St Michael (P)
Oct.	11 → 28[2]	Ballabeg, Arbory	St Cairbre (P) → SS Simon and Jude
	15[11]	Castletown	St Michael (?)
	28	Ramsey	SS Simon and Jude[10]
	29	Kirk Michael, Michael	St Michael
Nov	9	West Nappin, Jurby	St Cecilia
	15	Ramsey	St Maughold in winter
	18	St John's, German	*Spitlhin Geuree* [Hospitals of St John in winter]

	25	Colby, Arbory	St Catherine
	30	Kirk Andreas, Andreas	St Andrew (P)
Dec.	12	Ballakillingan, Lezayre/Ramsey[12]	St Fingan (Finnian) → St Thomas
	27	Kirk Andreas, Andreas	St John Evangelist

Sources: J. J. Kneen, 'Manx Fairs and Festivals', *M.N.H.A.S.*, vol. iii (1927–32), pp. 59–80; R. Airey (ed.), *Feltham's Tour Through the Isle of Man in 1797 and 1798*, Manx Society, vol. vi (1861), pp. 66-7.

Notes.

1. Only markets for which references exist before 1797-8 have been included in this table.

2. Fairs held at festivals of Celtic saints were transferred to an adjacent feast of a saint more familiar to the English Church, probably before the Reformation. See the notes by P. M. C. Kermode appended to Kneen, *Manx Fairs and Festivals*, p. 81.

3. This fair may only have been held on this date since the Gregorian calendar was adopted in 1752, as, taking into account the eleven day difference in the Old Style Julian calendar, March 28 could also be taken as St Patrick's Day in the New Style. *ibid.*, p. 63.

4. The only record of this fair dates from 1733. The date of the patronal fair was variable as it fell within the octave, or seven or eight-day period, after Easter. *ibid.*, p. 64.

5. The feast of St Christopher fell on April 28, but in the nineteenth century the fair was held on the variable Ascension Day. *ibid.*, p. 70.

6. May 3 was the feast of St Mary at Rome. *ibid.*, p. 65.

7. Variable date. The fair was held on the Tuesday after Trinity Sunday in the nineteenth century. *ibid.*, p. 70.

8. The parish of Arbory was dedicated to two saints, Cairbre and Columba. *ibid.*, pp. 71, 77.

9. There were several saints named Lonan, but the feast of Lonan mac Laisre (August 2) is the nearest to the date of the fair. *ibid.*, p. 74.

10. This fair was appointed to be held by the authority of James, seventh earl of Derby in November 1646. Lib. Scacc. 1647, 4.

11. Held on variable dates between October 3 and 15, as in 1732–3. Kneen speculated that as it sometimes lasted for 2 or 3 days, it might merely be an extension of the Michaelmas fair in Ballasalla, which was also occasionally held in Castletown. *Manx Fairs and Festivals*, pp. 76, 77.

12. By the late eighteenth century, this fair was held in Ramsey. Airey, *Feltham's Tour*, p. 67.

Table 4.2 *Distribution of Fairs in the Isle of Man in the Seventeenth Century (by parish and town)*

Parish/Town	Total
Patrick	1
German	3
Peel	2
Michael	2
Ballaugh	2
Jurby	2
Andreas	2
Bride	2
Lezayre	3[1]
Rushen	1
Arbory	4
Malew	6
Castletown	2
Santan	1
Marown	1
Braddan	1
Conchan	0
Douglas	3
Lonan	1
Maughold	1
Ramsey	3
Total	43

Sources: See Table 4.1

Note.

1. The fair held at Ballakillingan, Lezayre, on December 12 had been transferred to Ramsey by the end of the eighteenth century, but the date of transfer is not certain. In the absence of evidence that it was being held in Ramsey before 1700, it has been included under Lezayre. Kneen, *Manx Fairs and Festivals*, pp. 79–80.

There was at least one fair every year in each of the seventeen parishes, the patronal fair, held on or about the appropriate saint's day, though not on a Sunday,[5] but some areas enjoyed a considerably larger number. For example, two fairs were apparently held annually in Castletown, but, with a little effort, the townspeople could easily attend a further six during the year within a two-mile radius of the town – two at Ballabeg, Arbory, two at Cross Four Ways, Malew and two at Ballasalla, Malew. (Map 4). Those tenants who lived in places less well provided almost certainly travelled to fairs in neighbouring parishes or to those held at Castletown and Douglas in May and October at the time of the sheading courts, attendance at which was theoretically compulsory for all those in the sheading who held land of 6d. rent or more from the Lord.[6] There is little evidence to show that any of these fairs specialised in particular types of goods, such as cattle, and it is most likely that a variety of items from a wide area, perhaps including foreign wares, were traded at each fair.[7]

The number of fairs and markets in the island was strictly controlled, despite the apparent informality of a system in which no charters were granted. All fairs and markets were held by the authority of the Lord, and any of the inhabitants were at liberty to petition for a new market, an alteration of the date of an existing fair or market or a change of location. Only one such petition dating from before 1700 has, however, so far come to light. In 1646,

[5] In 1594, it was ordered that 'no Markettes be kept on the Lord's Day' on pain of fine and imprisonment, and a similar order, specifically including the Tynwald Court and its associated fair, as well as 'all other Faires and Markets throughout the Year', was issued in 1610, the Monday following being set as the time for such fairs or markets. *Statutes*, pp. 65, 72. By the early eighteenth century the patronal fair for Braddan seems to have been held in Douglas, which, in the seventeenth century, lay wholly in Conchan. Kneen, 'Fairs and Festivals', p. 69.

[6] Cl.R.O., Nantlys MS D/NA/905, 43. The sheading courts were held at Douglas for Garff and at Castletown for Middle and Rushen. For details of the sheading courts, see chapter 1, pp. 68–71.

[7] Kneen, 'Fairs and Festivals', p. 57. Foreign pedlars were, in theory, only allowed to proceed as far as the parish church nearest the haven where they landed; this was often the site of the patronal fair. *Statutes*, pp. 53–4. Cf. Everitt, 'Marketing of Agricultural Produce', pp. 81–6.

forty-two of the inhabitants of Ramsey complained to Governor Greenhalgh that the two fairs near Maughold church were adversely affecting their trade and requested that the officers consider the transfer of both fairs to Ramsey.[8] The matter was referred to the Keys, who declared that the fairs at Maughold should be retained and that fairs might be held at Ramsey on August 24 and October 28. With the earl's consent, this was accordingly proclaimed at the Tynwald Court in June 1647.[9]

II. REGULATION OF THE MARKETS AND FAIRS

The need to secure an adequate supply of food at reasonable prices was a priority for all local authorities.[10] In the Isle of Man, the dependence of the townspeople upon supplies of food from the surrounding countryside was underlined by the fact that farmers were prevented from selling their produce wherever they chose and directed to deliver it to the market in a specific town. For example, the inhabitants of the parishes of Rushen, Arbory, Malew, Santan and Marown were permitted to sell their goods only at Castletown; similarly, the people of Patrick, German, Ballaugh and Michael had to bring their 'Victuall, Corne, Wares, and other Merchandize' to Peel.[11] It is not certain at what date this order was first issued, the original being no longer extant, but it had clearly been in force for some time when it was repeated in June 1594 and again in October 1595,[12] during a series of poor or bad harvests. These later reissues of this order, which are essentially identical, only seem to refer to

[8] Lib. Scacc. 1647, 3.

[9] *ibid*, 4.

[10] Cf. J. H. Thomas, *Town Government in the Sixteenth Century* (1933), reprinted New York, 1969), ch. 8; P. Clark and P. Slack, *English Towns in Transition, 1500–1700* (Oxford, 1976), p. 95.

[11] *Statutes*, p. 65; Craine, *Manannan's Isle*, p. 86. Such restrictions, which were unknown in England, were perhaps more readily understandable in the context of a relatively small island community. Cf. Everitt, 'Marketing of Agricultural Produce', pp. 47–51.

[12] *Statutes*, pp. 65–6; Lib. Canc. 1595, 17.

Castletown and Peel, yet there can be little doubt that the same system applied to Douglas and Ramsey.[13]

Failure to obey the order to supply the town specified carried the penalty of imprisonment and a fine to the Lord, although if farmers were unable to sell their goods, they were granted liberty to 'bring it to anie other markett in the Countrey.'[14] Some were prepared to flout the regulations and take their corn and other produce to whichever market they desired, especially when there was the prospect of obtaining a higher price in times of dearth. In March 1596, Thomas Griffith swore on oath that John Fargher, Gilbert Costain and Thomas Cowley, all of Santan, had 'brought corne to the market at Duglas before they had presented the same at the market at Castletowne where they ought.'[15] Eighty years later, in 1676, some of the people of Castletown complained to Governor Henry Nowell that the inhabitants of the sheading of Rushen – the parishes of Rushen, Arbory and Malew – who 'were enjoyned to bring what Commodities soe ever they had to sell at any time to the Market of Castletown,' did 'of late carrie theire goods to other townes.'[16] In 1703, the townspeople petitioned the deputy governor, Robert Mawdesley, that 'most of the Inhabitants and Farmers of the several Parishes that are by law obligd to supply the markett do constantly sell their corn and other provisions att other markets . . . [so] that this Metropolis . . . scarcely appears to be a markett Town, which exposes us to the contempt and ridicule of all strangers.' Deprived of 'all manner of necessarys,' the people of the town claimed that they were compelled to break market regulations and 'repair to Farmers houses where they in vain Importune for such Goods as they very much want.'[17] Mawdesley, the officers and Keys consequently directed that no sales should be made in private, a practice which not only stopped produce reaching the open market, but also forced up the price of remaining stocks.[18] Farmers who were accustomed to sell corn from their houses

---

[13] The division of the island into quarters, each centring on a town, was clearly conceived for the purpose of supplying the town markets. For details of the quarters, see chapter 3, p. 151, n. 68.

[14] *Statutes*, pp. 65–6; Lib. Canc. 1595, 17. Cf. Lib. Scacc. 1653, 4.

[15] Lib. Scacc. 1596, 14.

[16] Lib. Scacc. 1676, 46.

[17] Lib. Scacc. 1703, inter 6–7 (1).

[18] *ibid*, inter 6–7 (3). For petitions and regulations against forestalling and regrating in England, see A. E. Bland, P. A. Brown and R. H. Tawney (eds),

to the inhabitants near the market towns, without bringing the grain to market, were allowed to continue this practice during the 1650s, but others who attempted to forestall the market were to be punished according to law.[19]

Such breaches of market regulations were considered particularly serious by the authorities when they involved corn, since, as has already been seen, the markets were the medium through which the supply of grain was controlled in times of dearth.[20] Dealings in other items outside the confines of the market were regarded as only slightly less important. In July 1609, for instance, the Great Enquest of Middle presented Edward Fletcher of Ballafletcher, Braddan, one of their own number, because he 'did contrarie to the orders provided for observance of the markett sell certen oxen at his house and served not the markett with them according to law.'[21] The activities of pedlars, both native and foreign, were periodically a source of concern, especially when it seemed likely that, as a result, the inhabitants might be defrauded or the markets destabilised. Many such foreign pedlars were found to be using weights and measures which were different from those officially sanctioned in the island, 'to the great Annoyance of many of the ignorant People,' and doubtless to the advantage of the trader. Consequently, in June 1645, steps were taken to enforce the use of the official standards and any pedlar failing to observe the law was to be fined, punished at the officers' discretion and forbidden to trade in the island.[22] Charges of engrossing were also levelled against Irish, Scottish and Manx pedlars by the glovers of the island in 1646. These craftsmen claimed that the pedlars bought the sheep and goat skins, which they needed to make their living and which they usually purchased in 'open faires..both in the Townes and Countrey, at men's houses, without the bringinge of them to any faires or markettes.'[23] The skinners of the island

---

note 18 *continued*

English Economic History (1914, reprinted 1933), p. 388; R. H. Tawney and E. Power (eds), *Tudor Economic Documents* (3 vols., 1924), vol. i, pp. 144–6; Chartres, *Internal Trade*, pp. 49–50, 58–60; Chartres, 'Marketing of Agricultural Produce', pp. 247–8.

[19] Lib. Scacc. 1653, 12.

[20] See chapter 2, pp. 92–105.

[21] Lib. Scacc. 1609, 69.

[22] *Statutes*, p. 102.

[23] Lib. Scacc. 1647, 5.

joined the glovers in making a similar complaint in 1652, alleging that they were being impoverished by 'the subtiltie of some who imployes certaine petlers through the whole Iland to buy all sheepe skins and such like under hand, before they come to the markett place.'[24] In both cases, the order that merchandise was to be brought to the markets to be sold was reissued, but the problem of such illegal transactions not surprisingly persisted.

Supervision of the town market was one of the responsibilities of the Captain of the Town or constable.[25] As a deputy clerk of the market,[26] he appointed a market jury, composed of two or four residents of the town, who were sworn in by the coroner of the sheading and normally served for the period of a year.[27] The jurors acted in much the same capacity as the 'market lookers' appointed in many Lancashire towns to keep a watchful eye on the market in general.[28] They checked on weights and measures to ensure conformity to the official standard, examined all merchandise brought to the town for sale to make certain that it was of merchantable quality, and presented those who attempted to sell goods below that standard. In September 1691, John Norris, Thomas Looney, George Woods and John Quilliam the younger, 'sworn to examine all such corn and other goods as are brought to the markett of Castletown, whether the same are markettable or not,' presented John Quayle of 'Clycurr' [Clougher], Malew, for a sack of 'metcorn,' which they

[24] Lib. Scacc. 1653, 6. In January 1656, it was ordered that no skins were to be sold before they had been viewed by the Captain of the Parish or the coroner to establish that they bore the mark of the vendor. Lib. Scacc. 1656, 8.

[25] For details of the duties of the Captain of the Town, see chapter 1, pp. 52–3.

[26] The comptroller acted as clerk of the market. On the duties of the clerk of the market, a post which was revitalised in England in the early seventeenth century, see Everitt, 'Marketing of Agricultural Produce', pp. 127–8. Cf. R. J. Hunter, Ulster Plantation Towns, 1609–41, in D. Harkness and M. O'Dowd (eds), *The Town in Ireland*, Historical Studies, vol. xiii (1981), p. 67.

[27] Craine, *Manannan's Isle*, p. 85. Two men were appointed as jurors in Douglas and Peel in late 1648 and four men in both Castletown and Ramsey. Their term of service was 'for one whole yeare or untill further [notice] bee given'. Lib. Scacc. 1649, 2.

[28] G. H. Tupling, 'Lancashire Markets in the Sixteenth and Seventeenth Centuries', *T.L.C.A.S.*, vol. lviii (1947), 20–1.

found to be 'not well dryed, loomed nor cleaned,' and quite unfit for sale.[29]

The market jury acted swiftly to curb sharp practices, such as forestalling and engrossing,[30] and, under the supervision of the Captain of the Town, to enforce market regulations. Particular care was taken to make sure that 'noe commodetyes bee sold in [the] markett before the markett bell bee runge' at ten o'clock in the morning.[31] In 1611, for example, two men were presented for selling a pig in the market place before the bell was rung and consequently forfeited half the price to the Lord and the other half to the poor. During the Interregnum, after the island had been surrendered to the Parliamentarians in November 1651, the responsibility for presenting such offenders seems to have been temporarily delegated to officers of the 'occupying' force. In April 1656, Sergeant William Cockes, who was 'authorised to see good orders att the markett in Castletowne,' presented a total of seven individuals who had tried to conclude some business before the stipulated time; these included William Callow, who had purchased a mutton from Thomas Gell of Rushen 'three quarters of an houre before the bell did ringe.'[32]

The jurors were also entrusted with the task of ensuring that the orders concerning brewing and the price and standard of bread and ale were properly observed. This aspect of their duty was of greatest importance in times of dearth, when additional, usually temporary, regulations were issued. In January 1597, after what had probably been several bad harvests, the governor, Peter Legh, and the officers directed that only those who had brewing cans sealed were to be allowed to make ale or beer and that it was to be lawful for 'everye man unto whome a canne is presented with drinke, unsealed, to drinke the same and pay nothing for yt.' The 'foure men of every towne,' as the jurors were called, were to serve as aleconners or ale tasters, checking that those who 'breweth twoe sortes of drinke' sold the better quality brew for 1d. per quart, and no more, and did not try to pass off the lesser at the same rate. They were to view the drink 'without collusion' to determine its quality and to present those found to be in breach of the regulations, fines of 3s. 4d. being

---

[29] Lib. Scacc. 1691, 32.
[30] The measures taken by the authorities to combat forestalling and engrossing are also discussed in, pp. 96–8, 104–5, 204, 207, 215, 218.
[31] Lib. Scacc. 1653, 4.
[32] Lib. Scacc. 1656, 38(2)–39; Lib. Scacc. 1653, 12.

imposed for such offences. To counter any claims of ignorance of these orders, the jurors were instructed to 'give warning to every alehouse keeper.'[33] Four months later, as the grain shortage grew worse, the maximum price for wheat, barley and rye was set and customers making purchases in the market were required to take an oath before the 'fower men appointed for the markettes' that the corn was 'for their own provision and necessary sustenance.' Only four people in each town, nominated by the deputy governor, were to be permitted to brew and none were to be allowed to make any malt, except by special licence. The jurors were to examine the corn brought to market, as usual, and 'to estimate [the value of] the same according to the goodness thereof;' they were furthermore required to 'looke to the assize of the Cannes' and to present any resident of the town who was brewing illegally. Any member of the market jury who could be shown to have failed in this duty was to be punished by a fine of 6s. 8d.[34]

Another series of bad harvests, in the late 1640s, also produced a number of short-term measures to control the prices of bread and ale,[35] but, in this instance, no such strict limitations were placed on brewing. Provided that individuals were in possession of a licence, which meant that they had entered into the usual bond with sureties, they were entitled to brew ale and beer for sale by retail. It was left to the jurors in the towns to enforce the orders stipulating the rates at which both bread and ale were to be sold and to present towns-people who were brewing without licence. In May 1651, William Chisnall, a shoemaker, John Taubman, a soldier and glover, Thomas Taubman and George Whetstones, a tailor, the four men appointed 'to looke to the assize of breade in the Towne of Castletowne,' presented the wife of one Birkett for selling a loaf of brown bread weighing 25 ounces for 2d.; by order, such a two-penny loaf should have weighed 36 ounces.[36] George Whetstones was also a member of the jury in the previous year which presented eleven men and three women for unlawfully retailing ale and beer in the town.[37] The two jurors appointed for Peel in 1649, Henry Thomason, a weaver, and

---

[33] Lib. Scacc. 1597, 13. For the activities of ale tasters elsewhere, see Thomas, *Town Government*, pp. 80–3; Tupling, 'Lancashire Markets', pp. 25–6.

[34] Lib. Scacc. 1597, inter 24–5.

[35] See chapter 2, pp. 99–102.

[36] Lib. Scacc. 1651, 25.

[37] Lib. Scacc. 1650, 57.

Thomas Lecke, a labourer, took quick action to draw up a list of sixteen townspeople, including two women, who 'sould alle contrarie to the order' in January of that year.[38] During the Interregnum, this task seems to have fallen to the soldiers appointed as constables of the towns.[39]

On occasion, the presentments made by the jurors could reveal negligence or complicity on the part of other market officers. In 1694, the Castletown jury seized seven pairs of shoes which had been offered for sale by one of the town's shoemakers when they discovered that the leather from which the footwear was made had not been properly tanned. It seems that Thomas Caine, the leather sealer or searcher of the town,[40] had either failed to examine the leather or had connived with the shoemaker to profit at the expense of the townspeople. Instead of following normal procedure in such cases by dividing the goods between the Lord and the informant who exposed the fraud, the jurors decided in this instance that the market would be best served by the sale of the shoes at the reduced rate of 1s. 6d. per pair, or about half the current market rate.[41]

One of the principal duties of the market jury of the town, the prevention of forestalling or engrossing, may have been shared with officers known as harbingers. No explicit reference to harbingers has yet been found after about 1610, and, since there seem to have been generally four of them in the towns, at least in Castletown and Douglas,[42] and their duties, as laid down for Douglas in 1592–3,[43] were not unrelated to supervision of the town market, it seems likely that the market jurors and the harbingers were, in fact, the same

---

[38] *ibid*, inter 40–1 (1).

[39] Lib. Scacc. 1655, inter 23–4. A constable was also appointed for Ballasalla, Malew. *ibid*.

[40] The appointment and duties of the leather sealers are described in chapter 3, pp. 150–52. Cf. Tupling, 'Lancashire Markets', pp. 22–3.

[41] Craine, *Manannan's Isle*, p. 85.

[42] There were generally four harbingers in Castletown and Douglas and probably the same number in Peel and Ramsey. The only reference to such officers in Peel, in 1576, seems to list only three, while no mention has been found of harbingers in Ramsey. See Lib. Plit. 1577, [Feb. 1576]; Lib. Scacc. 1599, 26(2)–7; Lib. Scacc. 1609, inter 36–7(2), 49, 68.

[43] Lib. Scacc. 1609, inter 36–7. The orders were issued by William Stanley, subsequently sixth earl of Derby, during his term as governor in 1592–3. See appendix ii.

officers. If they were not, the duties of the latter must have been assumed by the former some time in the early seventeenth century. The comparatively few references to either market jurors or harbingers and the ambiguity of orders directed to the 'four men of the towns' make it very difficult to arrive at any definite conclusions as to the exact number of market officers in the towns.

Whether or not they were one and the same with the market jurors in the late sixteenth century, the harbingers were primarily responsible for seeing that strangers, mariners and merchants were adequately lodged in the town. They were ordered 'to bee carefull and see that none brewe to sell and kepe allhowse but suche as are sufficiently able to lodge straungers or ells that they have especiall lysence for to kepe allhowse.' Those who wished to brew for retail purposes were to enter into bonds, with sureties, in 40s. sterling to observe these regulations.[44] In June 1609, the harbingers of Douglas charged eight men with keeping alehouses, 'having noe bedding to lodge strangers, after they were warned not to brewe.'[45] Two months later, five of these offenders were again presented and another, William Hutchin, entered into a bond that he would not brew or sell ale at his house until he was 'sufficientlie provided to keepe two ffether bedes furnished with clothes for lodging of strangers.'[46] The harbingers were required 'to see good order, Rule and behaviour in the towne,' especially at night, by preventing any drinking in houses after ten o'clock in the evening between the beginning of February and the end of September and nine o'clock during the remainder of the year.[47] They were to make certain that none of the townspeople sold ale during the time of church services on Sundays. Furthermore, they were directed to send the owners or masters of ships to the governor, so that the latter could be advised of the nature of the cargo, a procedure which the merchant stranger was obliged to follow in accordance with laws recorded in 1523.[48] As previously indicated, the harbingers were also answerable

[44] Lib. Scacc. 1609, inter 36–7; Lib. Plit. 1577 (February 1576). The amount of the bond was increased to £3, at least in the towns, in July 1609, and later, if not at that time, in the rest of the island. For the form of these bonds, see Lib. Scacc. 1648, 14 (2).

[45] Lib. Scacc. 1609, 49.

[46] *ibid*, 68.

[47] *ibid*, inter 36–7; Lib. Plit. 1577 (February 1576).

[48] Lib. Scacc. 1609, inter 36–7; *Statutes*, p. 37. For further details of the procedure of dealing with the merchant stranger, see chapter 5, pp. 240–42.

for presenting 'any that doth hinder or forestaull the market etc. by byinge of corne and other wares.'[49]

Outside the towns, supervision of the periodic fairs and other internal trading activity lay in the hands of various jurors and officials. Chief among these were the members of the market juries and, if indeed they were officers with a separate existence before the early seventeenth century, the harbingers in each parish as well. Most parishes had four of the latter in the late sixteenth century – the same number, it seems, as in the towns – but, in one instance at least, in 1576, Malew apparently had only two, whereas Lezayre, the largest parish in the island, and Marown, one of the smaller parishes, could boast five harbingers each.[50] These market officers were almost certainly identical with the ale tasters mentioned in several parishes among the surviving fifteenth century court records[51] and with the market jurors in each parish during the seventeenth century.

Few references to either parish harbingers or market jurors in the countryside have as yet been found, but, from the evidence available, there seems to be little doubt that their duties were similar to those of their counterparts in the towns. In November 1633, for example, the governor, Captain Edward Christian, the officers and Keys issued an order concerning brewing in the parishes which was similar in nature to the instructions directed to the harbingers of Douglas about forty years earlier. No farmer or any other person 'not dwelling in some of the ffoure Townes' was to be permitted to brew for retail, 'excepte such as shalbe comended by ffoure men in every parishe to bee worthie soe to doe.' Those deemed acceptable were to enter into the customary bond to maintain good order in their houses and 'in especiall that they shall not entertaine mens servantes to bee drinckinge in their howses in the night tymes or at any other unseasonable tymes.'[52] Besides acting as ale founders, they were also 'to make enquiry for all manner of ffelony and misorder' and to supervise the slaughter of livestock, ensuring that no sheep, cattle, pigs or other 'victualls' were killed until the owner's brand or mark had been checked by several neighbours.[53]

[49] Lib. Scacc. 1609, inter 36–7.
[50] Lib. Plit. 1577, (February 1576).
[51] M.M.L., MS 510C, J. Quayle, *Book of Precedents* (n.d., c. 1725), pp. 3, 4, 13. Cf. Craine, *Manannan's Isle*, p. 224.
[52] Lib. Scacc. 1634, 10.
[53] M.M.L., MS 510C, Quayle, *Book of Precedents*, p. 35.

In November 1648, four men who appear to have comprised the market jury of Bride attempted to prevent what was, in their opinion, a case of forestalling at a time of dearth. John Christian, probably of Ballafayle, Ewan Christian of Ballaghennie, John Lace of Ballacowle and William Casement of Ballavair, being sworn 'to present by virtue of our oaths all Brogers,' or middlemen, stated that they found that Donal McSorell or Soreley 'goeth up and downe buyinge of corne for stollinge of the marketts,' and claimed that he had purchased eighteen bolls of barley and a boll of malt. Soreley denied the charge, asserting that he had supplied the markets with ten bolls of barley, according to the order 'for as much as hee could spare ffrom the reliefe off himselfe and poore smale familie, being eight in number.' The officers accepted Soreley's argument that the corn had been purchased solely to support his family and that his only other means of relief was 'his shifts by dealinge.'[54]

Some of the responsibilities of the market jurors in the towns were undertaken in the countryside by the Great Enquest,[55] by the coroners of the sheadings,[56] and by the latter's deputy, the lockman,[57] in each parish. This was particularly the case in the supervision of brewing. Orders directing that all who brewed without licence were to be presented, such as that made by Deputy Governor Henry Nowell in May 1665,[58] were addressed not to the market juries or the 'four men of the parish,' but to the coroners, lockmen and Great Enquests of the sheadings. Indeed, it was normal practice for the coroner or lockman to make such presentments at the Exchequer Court,[59] even when the breaches of regulations governing the trade were connected with parish fairs. In the latter cases, however, no fines were imposed on the offenders, although their names were put on record. In December 1647, William Stevenson, coroner of Glenfaba, submitted to the court the names of eight men from German and two from Patrick, all of whom had been brewing for retail without licence, but, since they 'only brewed against the Patron

[54] Lib. Scacc. 1648, inter 56–7.
[55] The composition and duties of the Great Enquest are discussed in chapter 1, pp. 68–71.
[56] On the office of coroner, see chapter 1, pp. 46–9.
[57] For details about the lockman of the parish, see chapter 1, pp. 49–50.
[58] Lib. Scacc. 1665, 40.
[59] There are many examples of such presentments. See, for instance, Lib. Scacc. 1634, 25–9; Lib. Scacc. 1696, 27–8.

dayes of their parish,' all were spared from beinge fined for that reason.[60] Perhaps surprisingly, none of those presented at the same time by the coroners of the other sheadings were excused on the same grounds.[61] Despite this fact, it is clear from other lists of offenders that presentments of this nature were not uncommon. When Thurstan Tyldesley, coroner of Rushen, and William Comish, lockman of Arbory, drew up their respective lists of illegal brewers in the latter parish in 1682, they managed to name between them eleven individuals who had broken the regulations, but who were not to be penalised 'by reason they brued none but at faires.'[62]

By the end of the seventeenth century, the coroner had assumed the principal role in supervising brewing activity, both in the countryside and in the towns. In fact, this was a position which he already held in practice, since he was ultimately answerable for presenting transgressors within his jurisdiction, but his responsibilities were confirmed by an order issued by Deputy Governor William Sacheverell and the officers in October 1692. The coroners were henceforth to deliver to the Lord's Council the names of the people whom they considered fit to brew in the towns and parishes and from these a certain number would then be chosen by the officers 'to be lycensed and qualified to keep publick houses of intertainment.' The coroners and lockmen were directed to bring lists of those who brewed without licence to the Chancery Court and were reminded that they would be fined if they failed to carry out their duty diligently.[63]

III. WEIGHTS AND MEASURES

To ensure that licensed brewers and all other tradesmen dealt justly with their customers, it was clearly essential for the authorities to make certain that the weights and measures used in the fairs and markets conformed to the official standards. This proved to be difficult to achieve, in spite of the comparatively small size of the island and the fact that public transactions were, at least in theory, easily monitored. Problems were created not so much by the regulation of

[60] Lib. Scacc. 1647, 87.
[61] *ibid*, 84–9.
[62] Lib. Scacc. 1682, inter 15–16 (3,4).
[63] Lib. Scacc. 1692, 41–2.

the weights and measures ordered by the officers in the late sixteenth and early seventeenth centuries, but by the constant use and consequent deterioration of the official standards and the similar fate of the sealed standards used by tradesmen.[64] The situation was made worse by traders who risked incurring a fine through the use of unsealed weights or measures, which doubtless often differed, to the owner's advantage, from the official standards, and by foreign merchants and pedlars who came to the island to sell their goods by measures which, in many cases, bore the same names as those familiar to the inhabitants, but which were of a different, frequently smaller, size.

Attempts to set and enforce official standards were probably made before the advent of the Stanleys, but the first move in this direction of which there is any record dates from the lordship of Sir John Stanley II (1414-37). At a Tynwald Court held in March 1429, the governor and Keys ordered that 'all Measures of [the] Land of Mann be made all after one, that is to say, Firlett and Quart be justly and truly ordained and made.'[65] The firlot (Manx *farlane*) and boll (Manx *bolley*), which had very likely been introduced into the island from Scotland in the later thirteenth century,[66] continued to be the measures by which all sorts of corn were bought and sold in the fairs and markets, but the inevitable confusion for both natives and merchant strangers caused by the multiplicity of such measures in Scotland and the north of England, as well as Ireland, was compounded by differences in the generally accepted relationship between these units of measurement in the island. In Scotland, it was widely held that four firlots constituted one boll, whatever the precise volume ascribed to these standards by local custom, whereas in the Isle of Man, the number of firlots to the boll varied from two to three, depending on the type of corn being measured.[67] In practice,

---

[64] The deterioration of standard weights and measures through everyday use was a general problem. R. E. Zupko, *British Weights and Measures. A History from Antiquity to the Seventeenth Century* (Madison, Wisconsin, 1977), p. 31.

[65] *Statutes*, p. 22.

[66] After the death of the last king of Man and the Isles in 1265, the Isle of Man and the Hebrides were ceded by Norway to Scotland. English suzerainty was finally established after c. 1333. Moore, *History*, vol. i, pp. 136, 181–95.

[67] Whyte, *Agriculture and Society*, appendix ii, p. 268; Shaw, *Northern and Western Islands*, appendix, p. 203; W. Harrison (ed.), *Mona Miscellany*, 2nd

since the Manx and Scottish bolls seem, in most cases, to have been of approximately the same size, that is, between four and six Winchester bushels, this discrepancy only caused difficulties for merchants and their customers when transactions involved smaller quantities.[68]

Most of the corn which was bought and sold in the fairs and markets was very probably purchased in such limited amounts by the occupants of smaller and poorer holdings and by the inhabitants of the towns. For these people, who were dependent on these sources for a significant proportion, if not all, of their food, the possibility of being defrauded through the use of unofficial measures was a cause of no little concern. Disputes arising from suspicions of underhanded dealing were probably more frequent than the relatively small number of surviving cases of this type on record would suggest and were made even more complex by the apparent uncertainty of the exact size of standard Manx measures. In April 1582, following 'some controversie emongest the comon people of the Isle of what quantitie the sellinge and buyinge measures of the cuntry ought to be,' Governor Richard Shireburne and the officers determined to clarify the matter once and for all by restating 'the auncient order of the Isle for measures.' The inhabitants were reminded that every firlot was to be made 'of the Quantitie of thirtene pottels, measured with wheat, stricken measure, every pottel conteyninge thre wyne quartes, Chester measure.'[69] Wheat, rye, peas, beans and vetches

---

note 67 *continued*
series, Manx Society, vol. xxi (1873), p. 210; Lib. Scacc. 1628, 89. An indication of the variations in the size of the boll in Scotland and northern England can be gained from W. W. Skeat and J. Britten (eds), *Reprinted Glossaries and Old Farming Words*, English Dialect Society, vol. iii (1879–80), p. 168; R. E. Zupko, 'The Weights and Measures of Scotland before the Union', *S.H.R.*, vol. lvi (1977–8), pp. 124–6. Cf. G. V. Harrison, 'Agricultural Weights and Measures', in P. J. Bowden (ed.), *Economic Change: Wages, Profits and Rents, 1500–1750* (Cambridge, 1990), pp. 307–17.

[68] Shaw, *Northern and Western Islands*, appendix, p. 203; Zupko, 'Weights and Measures of Scotland', pp. 124–6; A. Cregeen, *A Dictionary of the Manks Language* (Douglas, 1835 [1838], reprinted Ilkley, 1984), p. 16. In some parts of Scotland, the boll was not only somewhat larger than average, but also varied with the season. Skeat and Britten, *Reprinted Glossaries*, p. 168.

[69] Lib. Scacc. 1582, 11. Like its English and Irish equivalents, the Manx pottle seems to have usually contained two quarts, a fact which is demonstrated

were to be sold by stricken measure, that is, in vessels in which the contents were not allowed to rise above the rim of the measure, while barley, oats and malt were to be traded by upheaped measure, where some grain was permitted to rise above the rim of the container. In an effort to convince market customers that they could purchase goods without fear of deception, Shireburne and the officers also announced that a standard firlot and pottle were to be made, sealed and 'kept within eyther of the castels to the entent that from tyme to tyme the cuntry measures may be reformed and sealed as occasion shall require.'[70]

The same standard measures were in use in the early seventeenth century when Richard Hoper, servant of Robert Cecil, earl of Salisbury, surveyed the island during the closing stages of the dispute over the succession to the Stanley estates.[71] In 1608, Hoper observed that 'every Boule of wheat and Rye conteyneth nineteen gallons and a half and the boule of Barly and otes twenty-nine gallons and a quarter, all of this contry measure.'[72] His statement accords well with the regulations set down in 1582, since the Manx firlot of wheat was equivalent to 39 quarts, or 9.75 gallons, exactly half the size of the boll noted by Hoper. It also reveals that barley and oats were measured by a different standard, the firlot in this case containing 14.625 gallons. (Table 4.3).[73]

Table 4.3 *Manx Weights and Measures*

i. Weights (Avoirdupois), after 1670.[1]

16 ounces	=	1 pound
14 pounds	=	1 stone
8 stones	=	1 hundredweight (cwt)
20 cwts	=	1 ton

by its name in Manx, *podjal daa chaart* (jug of two quarts). Harrison, *Mona Miscellany*, p. 211; Zupko, *British Weights and Measures*, p. 152; *O.E.D.*, *sub* pottle.
[70] Zupko, 'British Weights and Measures', p. 22 n. 10; Lib. Scacc. 1582, 11.
[71] The dispute included the lordship of Man, as well as the Stanley estates in England and Wales. See Coward, *Stanleys*, ch. 4. Salisbury acted as a trustee of the island between 1608 and 1612.
[72] M.M.L., MD/401/1715/5.
[73] These standards are confirmed by a note written on the back of the waterbailiff's accounts for 1623. M.M.L., I.O. 1620–9, Waterbailiff's accounts, 1623.

a Miscellaneous Weights

2.5 pounds	=	1 quart (butter)
7 pounds	=	1 quart (wool)
21 pounds	=	1 stone (wool)[2]
256 pounds	=	1 wey (cheese)
4 firlots	=	1 ton (salt)
2 barrels	=	1 hogshead (herring)
8 barrels	=	1 ton (herring)

ii. Linear Measure

12.5 inches	=	1 foot
3 feet	=	1 yard (37.5 inches)
2 yards	=	1 fathom

iii. Area Measure

37.5 square inches	=	1 sq. yard
5,042 sq. yds	=	1 acre

iv. Dry Capacity Measure

a) Wheat and Rye, before 1628[3]

3 wine quarts (Chester measure)	=	1 pottle
13 pottles or 9.75 gallons }	=	1 firlot
2 firlots	=	1 boll

b) Barley, Oats, Malt, Peas, Beans, Vetches, before 1628

2 pints	=	1 quart
8 quarts	=	1 kishan (or peck)
4 kishans or 7.312 gallons }	=	1 bushel or 1 lioarlhan (half firlot)
14.625 gallons	=	1 firlot
3 bushels	=	1 windle
2 firlots or 4 bushels }	=	1 boll

c) All Corn, after 1628[4]

2 pints	=	1 quart
8 quarts	=	1 kishan (or peck)
4 kishans or 8 gallons }	=	1 bushel or 1 lioarlhan (half firlot)
16 gallons	=	1 firlot
3 bushels	=	1 windle
2 firlots or 4 bushels }	=	1 boll (barrel)

v) Liquid Capacity Measure

4 noggins	=	1 pint
2 pints	=	1 quart
2 quarts	=	1 pottle
2 pottles	=	1 gallon
63 gallons	=	1 hogshead (wine, brandy)
4 hogsheads	=	1 tun

Sources:, *Statutes*, pp. 32, 81, 102, 138; Lib. Scacc. 1582, 11; Lib. Scacc. 1628, 89; Lib. Scacc. 1671, 17, 18; Lib. Scacc. 1700, 11; M.M.L., I.O. 1620–9, Waterbailiff's accounts, 1623; M.M.L., I.O. 1680–9, Customs book, 1685; M.M.L., MD/401/1715/5; M.M.L., MD/401/1715/20; W. Harrison (ed.), *Mona Miscellany, second series*, Manx Society, vol. xxi (1873), pp. 210–14; R. E. Zupko, *British Weights and Measures* (Wisconsin, 1977), pp. 152, 156; *idem*, 'The Weights and Measures of Scotland before the Union,' *S.H.R.*, vol. lvi (1977), list 1; D. R. Hainsworth (ed.), *The Commercial Papers of Sir Christopher Lowther, 1611–1644*, Surtees Society, vol. clxxxix (1977), pp. 104–6.

Notes

1. In 1670, an order was issued, directing that the avoirdupois standard was to be adopted for the future. It is not certain what system had been previously in use. Lib. Scacc. 1670, cited in Moore, *History*, vol. i, p. 419.

2. According to a record of the customs duties payable in the island made by, or for, Christopher Lowther of Whitehaven, dated November 1633, the stone of wool contained 20 pounds. The Book of Rates, drawn up in 1692, however, states that this unit comprised 21 pounds. Hainsworth, Commercial Papers of Sir Christopher Lowther, p. 106; M.M.L., MD/401/1715/20.

3. For the purpose of clarity and to avoid repetition, only the units of measurement for wheat and rye laid down in 1582 are here listed. It should be remembered, however, that these grains were also measured by the pint, quart, kishan and bushel in the same way as barley, oats and other cereals.

4. This system of measurement seems to have remained unchanged until the early nineteenth century. See Moore, History, vol. ii, p. 590 n.1; A. Cregeen, *A Dictionary of the Manks Language* (Douglas 1835 [1838], reprinted Ilkley 1984), p. 16.

In July 1628, however, a significant change was made in the system of measuring corn and salt. The circumstances in which this was brought about remain unclear, but it seems that, despite the interest he displayed in promoting the island's trade at a later date, James,

Lord Strange, who became in effect Lord of Man in 1627,[74] was not behind the reform. It may instead have been the result of pressure from native merchants, some of whom were also members of the Keys, to make trading activity less complicated by achieving greater uniformity between Manx and English measures. Whatever the background to this move, it was agreed by the general consent of the governor, Edward Christian, the deemsters, officers and Keys that 'the measures wherewith corne or salt are comonly bought or sould throughout the cuntrey be Reformed to a certentie.' For the future, it was ordered that two firlots, stricken measure, were to contain 'a Bristoll band barrell' of 32 gallons, 'That is to say, the fferlett sixteen gallons, wherewith all sortes of graine shall be bought and sould by strike.'[75] This meant a substantial increase in the size of the Manx firlot of wheat and a very much smaller rise in the same measure for barley and oats. (Table 4.3). New measures in accordance with this order were to be made at the Lord's expense, probably in England, and despatched to each of the island's towns. Those who brought their corn to be measured by the Lord's standard paid a pint for each firlot measured; others might choose to have their old measures altered, inspected and sealed by 'him that keepeth the Lordes measure' at the cost of a penny.[76]

Problems with the measures seem to have arisen almost immediately. In March 1629, after he had been 'very much moved and importuned by divers of the Inhabitantes and Tenantes . . . to have licenses granted unto them for the transportacon of corne,' Governor Christian directed the deemsters and Keys to investigate the matter. They agreed that licences should only be granted in return for an undertaking to supply the markets with the same amount of corn as that to be exported, although exceptions could be made if the inhabitants were given the opportunity to purchase salt or other necessary commodities in the place of corn. Those with mercantile interests in the Keys were keen to make certain that none of their rivals in the export trade flouted the regulations by measuring their shipments by the old standards, thus transporting significantly greater quantities of wheat in particular than appeared in their licences. They complained to Governor Christian about 'the greatnes of the new

---

[74] See appendix i.
[75] Lib. Scacc. 1628, 89; *Statutes*, p. 81.
[76] *ibid.*

measures lately made' and secured his consent to the appointment
of two men in each town 'iustly to measure the said measures by the
size quarte.' If any individual's measure were found to be larger than
the new standard, it was to be 'cutt and made of the size of 32
gallons,' 'the like course [to] be taken with the other lesser measures.'
The old measures were to be broken and fines imposed on those who
were caught using them.[77]

Inevitably, this action failed to prevent the use of unsealed, non-
standard measures and, consequently, orders prohibiting such measures and confirming the official standards continued to be issued
periodically throughout the remainder of the seventeenth century. In
1637, as part of a comprehensive programme against forestalling,
regrating and engrossing proposed by Strange as a result of 'great
Complaints' from 'the Commons and poor Sort of Inhabitants of the
Island,' it was ordered that all weights and measures should be
brought to the comptroller for inspection. Weights and measures
which agreed with the Lord's standard were to be sealed and the fee
of a penny paid for the examination. A fine of £3 was to be levied on
recalcitrant individuals who disregarded this order and kept unsealed
measures in their houses after the beginning of November in that
year.[78] The use of non-standard measures by foreign pedlars, which
has already been noticed,[79] led the Keys to request in 1645 that 'there
may be Measures for all Manner of Graine made after the Winchester
Bushell, every Barrell to contain four Bushells, and Measures of lesser
Soarts agreeable.' This was granted, but seems to have made no
difference to the official standard, since, after 1628, each barrel contained four bushels, whatever the corn being measured. Measures
were to be made and kept in each market town, where the comptroller,
as clerk of the market, or his deputy, was to test all measures brought
in by the inhabitants, as stipulated in the law of 1637. A period of
about five weeks was allowed to farmers and tradesmen with unlawful
measures so that they could have them adjusted; if they failed to take
the appropriate steps, they were to be fined.[80]

The Act of 1645, in common with previous orders and legislation of
this nature, was passed at a time when there was no apparent shortage
of corn in the island. This may seem surprising, as reliable measures

[77] Lib. Scacc. 1629, 22, 24.
[78] *Statutes*, pp. 86–8, 89–90.
[79] See *infra*, p. 200.
[80] *Statutes*, p. 102.

were particularly necessary to deter fraudulent dealing in times of dearth, but, when regulations concerning weights and measures were issued on subsequent occasions, it was sometimes in the wake of harvest failure. In October 1649, following probably three bad harvests, Governor John Greenhalgh and the officers ordered that all corn measures were to be tested, and sealed if they conformed to the official standard. Four men were appointed in each town and two in each parish to bring those who ignored this directive before the court. The Captain of the Town, as deputy clerk of the market, was at the same time authorised to send soldiers to seize any unsealed measures.[81] This move was, however, more than merely a response to the practices arising from a temporary grain shortage in the island's markets; it was also another attempt to tackle the persistent problem of illegal measures by the appointment of men specifically chosen for the task.

The sealers of weights and measures seem to have been appointed for limited periods, although the exact duration of their term of office is far from certain. That they were selected only when an examination of the weights and measures in the hands of the inhabitants was deemed necessary by the authorities is strongly suggested by the fact that they are not mentioned in the court records, except in orders requiring such inspections, and also because, nine months before the 1649 survey was set in motion, their duties appear to have been carried out by the Great Enquest. In January 1649, Thomas Thompson of Ballaugh complained to Governor Greenhalgh that he and some others had purchased a firlot of salt from John Gawne 'by Phillipe Corlett and his mothers ferlett, which ferlett was unlawfull wherby your peticoner and many others were damnified.' Significantly, Greenhalgh referred the matter to the Great Enquest of Michael, who were to view the measure and present the offenders if it were 'not agreable to the Lord's measure.'[82]

Since the unscrupulous were ready to take any opportunity to make a profit at the expense of buyers at the markets and fairs, sealers of weights and measures were appointed in times of plenty as well

---

[81] Lib. Scacc. 1649, 103. For details of Manx harvests in the 1640s, see chapter 2, pp. 97–102. William Blundell recorded that 'a furled of oatmeal' was 'but a 3d or 4th part of a barrel', but this observation may rather be attributed to his unfamiliarity with the island's weights and measures than to either a faulty memory or the prevalence of non-standard measures which he may have found on his visits in 1646 and 1648. Blundell, *History*, vol. i, p. 94.

[82] Lib. Scacc. 1649, inter 14–15.

as in times of dearth. At the sheading courts held in Peel in January 1654, for example, after two harvests which had very likely been good or better,[83] Governor Matthew Cadwell and the officers appointed two 'sufficient' men in each of the towns 'to try and seale all measures and weights in their townes and the parishes next adiacent, both of ffarmors, tradsmen, marchants and Inkeepers, that the same may bee made agreable to the lords measures and weights.' At the same time, the prices of ale, beer and bread, staples of the Manx diet, were lowered and the usual command that all persons should observe these regulations was added.[84]

This injunction seems to have met with a degree of success similar to that of previous orders, for, in April 1656, the deputy governor, the officers and Keys were still struggling to see that all corn measures in the island accorded with the Winchester bushel standard, as laid down by the Act of 1645.[85] Continuing uncertainty about the lesser measures led Governor William Christian, the officers and Keys to issue a declaration in April 1657 to clear up the confusion. They stated that 'the barrell for the measure within this Isle to buy and sell with shall contayne thirty two gallons, strike measure, every gallon to contayne foure quarts, every quart to hould two pound weight of water, and every pound to bee sixteen ounces in weight.' An official standard of each measure was to be provided, at the Lord's charge, and kept in each market town by the waterbailiff and his deputies, the customers. These standards were to be used to check the measures of the inhabitants and, to avoid disputes in the future and to guarantee impartiality, such examinations were to be carried out in the presence of the Great Enquest of the sheading. The accustomed fee of 1d. was paid for the inspection and the stamping of the Lord's seal on each measure in private hands and, as before, a fine of £3 was to be exacted from the holders of unsealed firlots or quarts. Perhaps somewhat optimistically, it was ordered that this procedure should be completed within a month.[86]

---

[83] W. G. Hoskins, 'Harvest Fluctuations and English Economic History, 1620–1759', Ag.H.R., vol. xvi (1968), appendix i, p. 29. In general, Manx and English harvests seem to have followed a similar pattern. See chapter 2, pp. 92–105.
[84] Lib. Scacc. 1653, 31.
[85] Lib. Scacc. 1656, 37.
[86] Lib. Scacc. 1657, 19–20. According to this order, liquid capacity measures, which are not listed in detail, were to remain unchanged.

The use of non-standard weights proved to be as great a problem, both for the authorities and the inhabitants, as the use of illegal measures. In June 1660, Governor James Chaloner and the officers received a petition at the Tynwald Court from some of the people of Rushen sheading, who claimed that, although there was supposed to be 'a certaine measure and true and just weights in everye markett towne' to ensure 'upright and impartiall dealinge' for all, the laws in this respect were not being observed. As a result, the parishioners of Rushen, Arbory and Malew were '(of late) much damnifyed both in measure of salt and weight of Pitch, Iron, etc.,' but, they maintained, 'by whose meanes they are ignorant of.' To prevent cases of fraud in future, they requested the court 'to make such order that all weights and measures may (forthwith) be made equall to the lords, according to the statute.' Chaloner and the officers consequently directed that the order of 1657 should be implemented and that the receiver, Arthur Squibb, 'doe take course to have a standard of weights and measures made and provided in every markett towne of the Isle.'[87]

Efforts were probably made to put this order into effect, despite the fact that both Chaloner and Squibb were removed from office shortly after it was made, on the arrival of commissioners from Charles, eighth earl of Derby, who regained possession of the Isle of Man after the Restoration. Nevertheless, the abuse of official standards continued. After complaints in early 1665 that, though corn was plentiful and sold 'at very low rates,' alehousekeepers were not selling their drink at 'a ratable measure,' Governor Bishop Isaac Barrow and the officers appointed one man in each of the towns 'to seale all weights and measures of all merchants, chapmen or tradsmen, and of ffermers and aylehousekeepers, according to the standard and assize already appointed and nominated.' These men, each of whom was assisted by Thomas Norris, deputy clerk of the rolls, were authorised 'to breake, burne or otherwise dispose' of any measures which deviated from the official standard and to present those who kept and used any unofficial measures. The Great Enquests, coroners and lockmen, who were also entrusted with the responsibility of bringing such offenders to the notice of the court, were criticised in this instance for their lack

---

[87] Lib. Scacc. 1660, 73.

of diligence and reminded 'to performe their duties both in towne and countrey.'[88]

It is not clear which system of weights was in use in the island before the late seventeenth century, but it seems likely that, in line with developments in England during the Tudor period, the avoirdupois system was adopted for general use by about 1600.[89] When, therefore, in 1670, it was ordered that all weights were to be 'after the rate of haberdupoize of 16 ounces,'[90] it was probably more of an attempt to enforce standards with which the inhabitants, and merchants in particular, were already familiar than a move to introduce a novel system of weights. With the significant exception of bread, staple commodities were, however, sold by volume rather than weight, a fact emphasised by the number of orders relating to measures for ale and corn, but, nevertheless, weights were employed in many transactions, notably when items such as butter, cheese, hemp, hops, tobacco and wool were bought and sold.[91] Protests about unlawful weights were doubtless as numerous as those concerning illegal measures, although almost no detailed presentments for such offences appear on record, and, perhaps as a result of 'all the petty complaints of fals weights and mesure' with which Governor Sacheverell refused to trouble him in 1693, Earl William took the step in November 1699 of ordering brass weights and measures to be 'sent for out of England to remaine in the custody of the clerke of the markett as standards for the Island.' These weights and measures, which were to be paid for out of the profits of the iron mines in Maughold, comprised a Winchester quart, presumably the standard quart mentioned in an order of 1695 as containing two 'large Winchester pints,' a pint, a boll or barrel of four Winchester bushels, and a set of weights ranging from a quarter ounce to a twelve pound weight.[92]

---

[88] Lib. Scacc. 1666, 22–3. A year later, in May 1666, Deputy Governor Henry Nowell was forced to issue another, similar order to the coroner and Great Enquest of Glenfaba, 'seeing my former presepts of this kind hathe beene heretofore neglected'. 'Unpublished Document no. 99', *J.M.M.*, vol. ii (1930–4), pp. 221–2.

[89] Zupko, *British Weights and Measures*, pp. 78–81.

[90] Lib. Scacc. 1670, cited in Moore, *History*, vol. i, p. 419.

[91] See M.M.L., I.O., Waterbailiff's accounts, *passim*.

[92] M.M.L., MD/401/1719/26. Sacheverell to Derby, August 2, 1693; Lib. Scacc. 1695, 21; Lib. Scacc. 1700, 11. On the iron mines, see chapter 3, pp. 183–87.

The fragile nature of the Manx economy, which was heavily dependent on the grain harvest and the herring fishery, meant that the island's markets performed a vital function in the distribution of foodstuffs, especially in times of dearth. This accounts for the stringent regulations governing the supply of the markets and the division of the island into four quarters, each assigned to provide food and other necessaries to one of the four towns. This system guaranteed that, when shortages occurred, the inhabitants would have the opportunity to buy such grain as was available in the island at a price which was subject to control by the authorities. Efforts were made to stamp out 'private bargaining' in commodities and to confine most trading activity to the open market, where transactions could, at least in theory, be monitored by the clerk of the market and his deputies. The apparent difficulties which the island's government encountered in enforcing the use of standard weights and measures and the repeated orders requiring observance of the Lord's standard reflect the crucial importance of the market as a mechanism of exchange and the problems which could arise from widespread use of illegal measures. The town and parish fairs, where livestock, cloth and other items were traded, served a less vital function, but, nevertheless, offered craftsmen the opportunity to sell their wares to people from all over the island. To most farmers, markets and fairs offered the opportunity to dispose of their surpluses and obtain manufactured goods, whether native or foreign; to the town dweller and small landholder, who depended to varying extents on others for their food, the markets in particular were of far greater importance.

5 *Overseas Trade*

While most of the basic needs of the farmers and town dwellers were provided for at the markets and fairs, the requirements of the inhabitants for raw materials which were either in short supply in, or absent from, the island in addition to the general demand for manufactured goods and other items could only be satisfied by way of trade with neighbouring countries. In exchange for grain, livestock, especially cattle, fish and other primary products, the island obtained timber and iron, which were vital to the domestic economy, footwear and clothing to supplement the output of Manx craftsmen, and wine and other luxury items for the Lord's officers, higher clergy, more affluent merchants and farmers. Overseas trade was, therefore, quite as important for the economic well-being of the Isle of Man as internal trading activity, although, as already suggested, the amount of the latter very probably far exceeded the level of the former.

I. CUSTOMS ADMINISTRATION: PERSONNEL

It is not certain at what date customs duties were first collected in the island. The practice of levying duties, whether in kind or in money, on goods imported or exported by merchants may have originated in the period when the island was the seat of the Norse kingdom of Man and the Isles (1079–1265), during the troubled years when the overlordship of the island alternated between Scotland and England (1265–1333), or in the relatively more settled period which followed the establishment of English suzerainty over Man in 1333.[1]

---

[1] Customs duties were by no means unknown to the Scandinavians in the twelfth century and were regularly collected in England from the late thirteenth century and in Scotland from at least the early fourteenth century. P. G. Foote and D. M. Wilson, *The Viking Achievement* (1970), pp. 230–1; N. S. B. Gras, *The Early English Customs System* (Cambridge, Mass., 1918), p. 59; *E.R.S., 1264–1359*, p. xcviii.

At whatever time a system of regular customs collection was set up, there can be little doubt that it was erected on authority derived from the prerogative rights of the Lord of Man in much the same way as the English customs system is thought to have developed.[2] Since there are no documentary references to the island's customs before the early fifteenth century, however, the origins of the Manx customs system must necessarily remain obscure. Nevertheless, it is clear that the machinery for the collection of duties on imports and exports was already in place by this time, for the grant of the island made by Henry IV to Sir John Stanley in 1406 included the 'sea ports and all things pertaining to a port' and the 'free customs.'[3] The first references to customs officers occur shortly after this date.

The officer in the Lord's Council responsible for the collection of customs duties and the supervision of the movements of cargo and shipping was the waterbailiff,[4] who is first mentioned in the island's records in 1423.[5] Apart from the fact that he seems to have held office for life rather than during pleasure, the waterbailiff operated in much the same way as the customer or collector at a head port in England.[6] He was entrusted with a brass seal of office, bearing the *triscellis* or 'three legs of Man' and the motto *Dieu et ma foue* [*sic*], with which he stamped the cockets or receipts for payment of customs duty and was answerable for this and all other revenue received from merchants and shipmasters at the periodic audit of the Lord's accounts.[7]

[2] Gras, *Early English Customs System*, pp. 13–15.

[3] *C.P.R.*, *1405–8*, p. 201–2; Oliver, *Monumenta*, vol. ii, pp. 235–46.

[4] For further details of the office of waterbailiff, see chapter 1, p. 33.

[5] *Statutes*, p. 17.

[6] There is insufficient evidence to establish conclusively whether it was normal practice for the waterbailiff to hold office for life. In at least one case, however, this was clearly the intention, for, in 1630, James, Lord Strange issued a commission to Fermor Coote to hold the post for life. Lib. Canc. 1630. The impression that this was not an isolated instance is strengthened by the observations of Robert Roper, secretary to William, ninth Earl of Derby, who noted three waterbailiffs – Coote (d. *c.* 1643?), Richard Calcott (d. 1665?) and Hugh Cannell (d. 1670) – who died in office. B. L. Add. MS 33,589, f. 222r. At least one other waterbailiff, James Hey, was still carrying out his duties when he died in May 1607. Lib. Scacc. 1607, 20. For details of the responsibilities of the customer at a head port in England, see N. J. Williams, *The Maritime Trade of the East Anglian Ports, 1550–1590* (Oxford, 1988), pp. 13–20.

[7] Lib. Plit. 1577, 44; Williams, *Maritime Trade*, p. 17; *idem* (ed.), *Descriptive*

The waterbailiff's activities were supervised in general by the comp-troller,[8] to whom he delivered his accounts every year for scrutiny.[9] On a number of occasions, generally when the holder of the office was an absentee, the comptroller himself acted in the capacity of waterbailiff until a deputy was appointed. In 1622, for example, John Halsall, who not only served as comptroller and clerk of the rolls, but also as attorney to the Lord, was 'Accomptant for the water-balifes office' and continued to carry out the necessary duties of the post even after the appointment of Fermor Coote in 1623–4. Unlike most of the other officers of English origin who secured a place in the island's government through a connection with the Stanleys, Coote seems never to have crossed the Irish Sea. According to Robert Roper, secretary to William, ninth earl of Derby, he 'for 30 or 40 yeares lived constantly in the family in England and dureing his life acted in the Island by a Deputy.' In these circumstances, it is not surprising to find that Halsall continued to serve until George Squire was 'sworne to execute the waterbalifes office' in October 1624.[10]

Whether or not the waterbailiff carried out the duties of his office in person or through a deputy, it is clear that it would not have been

List of Exchequer, Queen's Remembrancer, Port Books, Part I, *1565–1700* (1960), p. vi; *Statutes*, p. 36. The term 'cocket' was generally applied to both the seal and the document, but it is not known whether the word was first used to describe the former or the latter. The origins of the term are not certain, although it may be a corrupted form of the last three words of the English customer's receipt: *quo quietus est*, 'by which he is discharged'. *O.E.D.*, *sub* cocket. Cf. R. W. K. Hinton (ed.), *The Port Books of Boston, 1601–1640*, Lincoln Record Society, vol. l (1956), p. xvii n. 1. The form of cocket issued by the waterbailiff was somewhat different, at least by the late sixteenth century. See the cocket printed in *Statutes*, p. 40.

[8] The duties of the comptroller are discussed in chapter 1, pp. 29–30.

[9] The waterbailiff was certainly required to deliver a copy of his accounts to the comptroller every year from 1561 onwards. *Statutes*, p. 36. The early fifteenth century order directing that he present his accounts to the bishop and 'Auditors for the Time being' every quarter does not appear to have been followed. *ibid*, p. 13; Knowsley Hall, Box H/44a, 'A Book containing the Answeare of th'Officers, Deemsters, Viccars Generall and 24 Keyes to certain Articles Objected by John now Bishop of this Isle against John Ireland, Esq., Lieutenant and Captaine of the Isle of Man, February 1, 1611'.

[10] Lib. Canc. 1622,1; M.M.L., I.O. 1620–9, Book of allowance, Castle Rushen, 1624; B.L., Add. MS 33,589, f. 222r; Lib. Scacc. 1625, 5.

possible for him to fulfil his responsibilities without the assistance of subordinate customs officers at each of the main harbours of the island. Such officers had very probably existed for as long as the duties on imported and exported goods had been collected, but, to emphasise their importance as a regular part of the machinery of customs administration, it was ordained in 1423 that the waterbailiff was 'to have his deputys or Customers in every Haven or Sea Poart within this Isle, to execute his Charge and duty there.'[11] These deputies were normally called customers until 1693, when they began to be termed deputy searchers, and there was one such officer at each of the four port-towns of the island.[12] Until about 1615, there were also customers at the lesser harbours of Derbyhaven or Ronaldsway and Port Erin, but after that date their duties were undertaken by the customer of Castletown. The latter, like his colleagues at Douglas, Ramsey and Peel, was responsible for the collection of customs duties and other revenue along a roughly defined length of coastline which in this case stretched from Port Erin in the west to Derbyhaven in the east.[13] The customer of Douglas seems to have supervised the east coast of the island at least as far north as Laxey, while the western side, perhaps including Jurby, was entrusted to the officer at Peel. The remaining coastline, between the mouth of the Lhen trench in Andreas and the precipitous cliffs south of Port Cornaa in Maughold, lay within the jurisdiction of the customer of Ramsey.[14] Each customer was required to

---

[11] M.M.L., MS MD/15,040, Parr, *Abridgement*, p. 51. Cf. *Statutes*, p. 17.

[12] M.M.L., I.O., Waterbailiff's accounts, 1594–1693, *passim*; M.M.L., I.O. 1690–5, Book of salaries and pensions, 1694: Christmas quarter, 1693; M.M.L., I.O. 1690–5, Customs book, 1695.

[13] After about 1615, the same customer served for Derbyhaven and Port Erin as well as Castletown and the minor landing places along the southern coast of the island, such as Port St Mary and Poyll Vaaish. See, for example, M.M.L. R.D. 1600–26, Book of charge, Castle Rushen, 1617: 'extract' of ingates and outgates, 1617 and M.M.L., I.O. 1672–9, Ingates and outgates, 1677: summary of the charge of Robert Shimmin, customer of Castletown, Derbyhaven and 'the Ports adjacent', 1677.

[14] Only a very small proportion of the maritime trading activity of the east coast of the island was conducted at Laxey. The references to this harbour are generally included in the accounts for Douglas, although sometimes there is a separate list of entries. See M.M.L., I.O. 1570–99, Ingates and Outgates, 1594: 'owtgates at the port Laxe'; M.M.L., I.O. 1610–19, Waterbailiff's accounts, 1618: Douglas ingates; M.M.L., I.O. 1630–45, Waterbailiff's

keep a record and 'to write what Goods is taken out of the Countrey, and what is brought in.'[15] When disputes concerning some aspect of trade or shipping arose, the customers were authorised to arrest the alleged offender or his vessel 'for one tyde-water' while the complainant sought the governor's consent to extend the period of detention until the case could be heard. Efforts were made to expedite such matters, which were theoretically dealt with inside a week, but, in the interim, the customer was charged with securing the defendant.[16] In 1628, the customers were empowered to remove the sails and rudder of a vessel under arrest and ordered 'to see that she procure noe other Sayles and Rudder, wherby She might make her Escape, untill the Law be fulfilled.'[17] If the defendant nevertheless managed to abscond and it appeared that his escape was a result of the customer's negligence, the latter was compelled to pay the debt owed or to face the action brought by the complainant.[18] Most of the men who were appointed to carry out these duties during the late sixteenth and seventeenth centuries were otherwise employed as soldiers in the garrisons at Castle Rushen and Peel Castle or in the smaller detachments at Douglas Fort and, from the late 1640s onwards, at Ramsey. In the year ending at June 24, 1602, for example, only four out of the eight men serving in the office were also soldiers, but, after the number of customers in the island had been reduced from six to four in the early seventeenth century, it was usual for each post to be occupied by a member of the local garrison, in some instances for long periods.[19]

accounts, 1631: 'extracte' of the ingates and outgates. The landing places at Kirk Michael and Ballaugh were apparently the responsibility of the customer at Peel, since entries for both appear in his accounts. See, for example, M.M.L., I.O. 1610–18, Waterbailiff's accounts, 1618: Peel ingates. The 'other Poarts on the north side,' which included the exposed anchorage at the Point of Ayre, comprised a part of the charge of the customer of Ramsey. See *ibid*: Ramsey ingates; M.M.L., I.O. 1660–71, Waterbailiff's accounts, 1660: abstract.

[15] *Statutes*, p. 17.

[16] M.M.L., MS MD/15,040, Parr, *Abridgement*, p. 52.

[17] Lib. Scacc. 1628, cited in *ibid*.

[18] *ibid*. In 1605, Danold Christian, customer of Ramsey, was ordered to pay such a debt. Lib. Canc. 1605, cited in M.M.L., MS 510/C, Quayle, *Book of Precedents*, p. 84.

[19] The customers who served at the various harbours in the island in 1601–2 were: i) Douglas: John Quayle, the waterbailiff. M.M.L., I.O. 1600–9,

In addition to the customer, there was another officer subordinate to the waterbailiff in each port who was called the searcher or undersearcher.[20] Although mentioned only infrequently in the customs records, there is no doubt that he performed the same duties as his counterpart in English ports, ensuring that the goods carried in each ship tallied with the cocket issued to the merchant by the waterbailiff or his deputy and that no merchandise was being transported without paying the appropriate duty. If, during his examination of the cargo on the wharf or aboard ship, he discovered that the merchant was attempting to ship more than the quantity declared, the searcher was authorised to seize the concealed goods.[21] Since, like the customer, the searcher was generally a soldier, he was well placed to call on the garrison for assistance, should the need arise, in such cases. To enable him to be on hand at all times to

note 19 *continued*
Ingates and outgates, 1602; ii) Castletown: Edward Lucas and subsequently John Tetlowe, soldier and gunner respectively at Castle Rushen. *ibid*; M.M.L., Ellesmere Papers 244/C/2, 106; Lib. Scacc. 1593, 20; M.M.L., I.O. 1610–19, Book of allowance, Castle Rushen, 1612; iii) Ramsey: Danold Christian. M.M.L., I.O. 1600–9, Ingates and outgates, 1602; iv) Peel: Phillip Cross, soldier at Peel Castle. *ibid*; M.M.L., Ellesmere Papers 245/D, 104; v) Derbyhaven: William Pedley, soldier at Castle Rushen. M.M.L., I.O. 1600–9, Ingates and outgates, 1602; M.M.L., Ellesmere Papers 244/C/2, 106; vi) Port Erin: Robert Watterson and John Nelson. M.M.L., I.O. 1600–9, Ingates and outgates, 1602. There is no evidence to indicate that these subordinate positions were held other than during pleasure. Nevertheless, a number of soldiers acted as customer in their respective port-towns for long periods. William Curleod served at Douglas for about twenty-five years between 1616–17 and the early 1640s and Robert Shimmin, sergeant at Castle Rushen, was customer at Castletown between late 1665 and 1688. M.M.L. R.D. 1600–26, Book of charge, Castle Rushen, 1617: abstract of ingates and outgates; M.M.L., I.O. 1630–45, Waterbailiff's accounts, 1642; M.M.L., I.O. 1660–71, Waterbailiff's accounts, 1666; M.M.L., I.O. 1680–9, Customs book, 1688.
[20] The earliest reference to a searcher that has yet been discovered dates only from 1655 at Castletown, but it seems very unlikely that there would have been no such officers before that time.
[21] Most references to searchers relate to such cases of forfeiture. See, for example, M.M.L., I.O. 1620–9, Book of charge, Castle Rushen, 1629. On the duties of the searcher at an English port, see Williams, *Maritime Trade*, pp. 13–14; Hinton, *Port Books of Boston*, p. xv.

perform his duties, he was exempted from watch and ward service.[22]
Only half a dozen searchers have as yet been identified, but of this
number, four were soldiers.[23]

To serve as a check on the accounts drawn up by the waterbailiff
and the customers, an official known as the clerk of the ships was
appointed and directed to record the movements of shipping and the
nature of the goods imported and exported. It is not certain when
this officer, who may also have been known as 'the Captaine's
Clark', was first commissioned, but the earliest reference to the clerk
of the ships in the island's records dates from 1523.[24] It was at that
time that the role played by the clerk in the process of striking a
bargain with the 'Merchant Stranger' for goods 'for the Commonwealth of this Countrey,' which will be examined later, was set
down; it was not until nearly forty years afterwards, however, in
1561, that his duties in connection with the administration of customs revenue were outlined. The commissioners sent over to the
island by Edward, third earl of Derby, to improve the efficiency of
its government, ordered that the clerk 'do make a perfect Book of all
such Wares as the Merchant Stranger shall bring into the Country . . .
and what Wares he shall carry out of Mann, and how much Custome
is due for the same.'[25] This directive, however, would appear to have
been a statement of existing, or at least desired, practice, since the
Book of Orders, of which it formed a part, also reiterated – albeit
with a greater degree of elaboration – the ordinances of 1423

[22] Lib. Scacc. 1595, 12. A day and night watch was kept in the ports and on
certain hills in the island and all the inhabitants were liable for such service
on a rota basis. W. Cubbon, 'Watch and Ward in AD 1627', *M.N.H.A.S.*,
vol. iii (1927–8), pp. 258–265; B. R. S. Megaw, 'A Thousand Years of Watch
and Ward', *J.M.M.*, vol. v (1941–6), pp. 8–13, especially the map, p. 10.
[23] The following searchers have been identified: i) Ramsey: Thomas Christian. M.M.L., I.O. 1610–19, Ingates and outgates, 1610; ii) Douglas: Silvester
Stevenson, undersearcher and soldier. M.M.L. R.D. 1627–50, Waterbailiff's
accounts, 1634; M.M.L., I.O. 1570–99, Book of allowance, Peel Castle 1632;
iii) Ramsey: Ferdinando Fox, soldier at Douglas (?). *ibid*; Lib. Scacc. 1635,
inter 20–1; iv) Douglas: Richard Carter, undersearcher and soldier at
Douglas. M.M.L., I.O. 1630–45, Book of charge, Peel Castle, 1637; v) Peel:
William Cowper. Lib. Scacc. 1647, inter 83–4; vi) Ramsey: William Kewley,
searcher and soldier at Ramsey. M.M.L., I.O. 1680–9, Customs book,1688;
M.M.L. R.D. 1686–95, Book of charge of revenue of the Isle of Man, 1687.
[24] *Statutes*, pp. 27–8.
[25] *ibid*, p. 36.

concerning licences for exports and the duties of the waterbailiff, a fact which suggests that the commissioners were merely issuing a reminder of the responsibilities of the clerk rather than increasing the burden of the office.[26] Although only a few other references to the clerk of the ships have so far been discovered, it is clear that this officer also served as a soldier. Silvester Stevenson, who occupied the post from about 1630 until his death in 1636, was one of the complement of half a dozen men stationed at Douglas Fort and furthermore acted as 'undersearcher' in the harbour there; his successor at Douglas, Richard Carter, assumed all these duties.[27] John Wood was 'clerk for keeping the Custome house book' for more than twenty years before his death in 1693, as well as being a soldier in the garrison of Castle Rushen.[28]

Of all the customs officers in the island, it would appear that only the waterbailiff and the customer of Douglas received regular wages throughout the period under consideration. In the late sixteenth century, the waterbailiff was paid £6 13s. 4d. a year and £5 for his 'diet' 'in regard of his seldome coming to the houses' [castles].[29] When James Hey was appointed to the office in January 1603, this subsidiary payment was increased to £20, but was abruptly abolished altogether in 1605, without explanation.[30] From 1610 onwards, the waterbailiff was paid out of the general revenue rather than directly from the money collected by his deputies. His wage was set at £20 a year and, with the exception of a nine year period beginning in 1645, when the waterbailiff was allowed one-tenth of the customs

[26] *ibid.* Cf. *ibid*, pp. 15, 17. As far as the waterbailiff was concerned, the most significant difference between the ordinance of 1423 and the Book of Orders of 1561 was that the latter directed that he should be responsible for keeping a record of imports and exports rather than his deputies.

[27] M.M.L. R.D. 1627–50, Book of allowance, Castle Rushen, 1630; Lib. Scacc. 1631, 46; M.M.L., I.O. 1630–45, Book of allowance, Peel Castle, 1637; Lib. Canc. 1637–8, 32. See also note 23.

[28] M.M.L., MD 401/1719/10. Roger Kenyon to William, ninth earl of Derby, July 10, 1692 (?); M.M.L. R.D. 1671–85, Book of salaries, pensions and petty disbursements, 1683; M.M.L., I.O. 1690–5, Book of salaries and pensions, 1694.

[29] M.M.L., I.O. 1570–99, Ingates and outgates, 1598.

[30] M.M.L., I.O. 1600–9, Ingates and outgates, 1603; Ingates and outgates, 1606.

revenue 'for his ffee for wages,' it remained at this level until after 1704.[31] The customer of Douglas was inevitably the most important of the waterbailiff's deputies, since he presided over maritime affairs in the island's busiest port.[32] His pre-eminent position in relation to the other customs officers was emphasised by the fact that he was the only such officer to receive a separate salary before about 1617, when the wages paid to his colleagues in the other ports, except Ramsey, first appear on record. While the latter were paid 10s. a year each in addition to their salaries as soldiers, the customer of Douglas received 13s. 4d. and, at least in the late 1620s, a supplementary payment of 20s. 'for his extraordinarie paynes in executinge the office.'[33]

The only significant alteration to these wage levels before the late seventeenth century was made in the decade after the restoration of

[31] The last reference to the waterbailiff's wages in the customs accounts occurs in 1609. M.M.L., I.O. 1600–9, Ingates and outgates, 1609. After that year, the waterbailiff appears in the list of officers in the books of allowance of both castles. As in the case of the other officers, half his salary was paid from the revenue from the Northside, the other half coming from Southside revenue. See, for example, M.M.L., I.O. 1610–19, Book of allowance, Castle Rushen, 1615; book of allowance, Peel Castle, 1615. The decision to convert the fixed salary of the waterbailiff into a proportion of the customs revenue may have been taken in an effort to improve the collection of duty or to save a little money. Since the total income from customs revenue had only ever exceeded £100 on two occasions in the fifty years preceding 1645, and it would need to be twice that amount for the waterbailiff's salary to retain even its face value, the net result was that the salary of the chief customs officer was reduced by at least half, even in a good year for trade. See appendix ix. The salary of £20 a year was restored in 1654. M.M.L., I.O. 1646–59, Waterbailiff's accounts, 1655; M.M.L., I.O. 1696–1704, Book of salaries and pensions, 1704.

[32] For details of the number of anchorages in the island's ports, see Table 5.15.

[33] M.M.L., I.O. 1570–99, Ingates and outgates, 1598; M.M.L. R.D. 1600–26, Book of charge, Castle Rushen, 1617. Probably the first reference to wages paid to the customer of Ramsey occurs in 1623. M.M.L., I.O. 1620–9, Book of charge, Castle Rushen, 1624. For accounts of the wages paid to the customers, see, for example, M.M.L., I.O. 1620–9, Waterbailiff's accounts, 1627. Mention of the supplementary payments to the customer of Douglas in the 1620s is made in M.M.L. R.D. 1627–50, Book of charge, Castle Rushen, 1630: Rewards.

the Stanleys as Lords of Man in 1660. Robert Shimmin, customer of Castletown, petitioned Governor Bishop Isaac Barrow in July 1668, claiming that he was unable to subsist on the allowance of 10s. a year which he was paid and that he had incurred considerable loss as a result of holding his office.[34] Accordingly, Bishop Barrow, with the consent of the other officers, increased the wages of the customers of Castletown and Peel to 20s. each.[35] The wages of the other customers, who were not mentioned in these proceedings, were also raised at some point, but, because the sums paid to the customer at Douglas from 1635 and to his opposite number at Ramsey from 1663 were included in the salaries which they received as soldiers, it is difficult to determine exactly when this took place. It seems, however, that, by about 1670, all the customers received 20s. a year.[36] By the end of the century, probably as a consequence of the increase in the overall level of the island's trade during the 1690s, a relatively large rise in some customs duties in 1692, and the greater burden of their offices, the wages of the customers of Douglas and Castletown had been raised so that the former received £6 and the latter was paid £3 a year.[37]

The other customs officers, the searchers and the clerk of the ships, seem to have depended in general on the fees paid to them by merchants to supplement their salaries as soldiers or other income. The earliest extant list of such fees is appended to the Book of Rates of 1692 and shows that the waterbailiff and the customer each received 12d. for every cocket for a ship, 6d. for a cocket for a small boat, 6d. for an 'entry Inward' and 4d. for a 'Lycence outward.' A certificate or bond cost the merchant 6d., as did the execution of 'an Arreast against any person,' while a post entry, that is, an entry subsequent to the initial declaration, 'if admitted,' was charged at 3d. If the merchant's vessel called at more than one port in the island, he was liable to pay unspecified 'extraordinary charges.' The searcher

[34] M.M.L., I.O. 1660–71, Waterbailiff's accounts, 1668.

[35] M.M.L., I.O. 1660–71, Book of charge of revenue of the Isle of Man, 1668: abstract of ingates and outgates.

[36] See, for example, M.M.L., I.O. 1660–71, Book of waterbailiff's accounts, 1671; M.M.L. R.D. 1671–85, Book of disbursements of salaries, 1673. The amount paid to the customers of Douglas and Ramsey is not certain, but, in view of the wages given to other soldiers, it seems likely that it was the same as that which their fellow customers received.

[37] M.M.L. R.D. 1700–4, Book of charge of the revenue of the Isle of Man, 1702: disbursements of salaries and pensions.

was paid 6d. for listing cargo which could not be easily carried into the Lord's storehouse and a further 6d. for holding goods 'that are not fully entered and admitted in a post entry.'[38] The clerk of the ships, or 'Captain's Clark,' extracted a fee of 1d. for each entry he made in his book[39] and, at least during the sixteenth century, he was also entitled to a certain small proportion of cargoes of salt, wine and 'small wares' landed by foreign merchants.[40] In 1631, however, it was declared that the clerk should 'receive noe pondage for any goods bartered from the Merchant Stranger,' this element of the latter's dues belonging instead to the Lord, though if he did 'any duty to the Stranger, he [was] to be rewarded for the same by him, and what is allowed him by the Statute.'[41] Besides the fees which he was paid, the searcher received the benefit of half the goods justly seized by him, the other half being sold for the Lord's profit.[42] He does not seem to have normally received wages in this capacity in addition to his other income, although John Taylor, searcher at Castletown between at least 1655 and 1660, was paid 10s. a year during this period.[43]

[38] M.M.L., MD/401/1715/20, Book of Rates, 1692. Cf. *Statutes*, pp. 225–32. English customs officers received much higher fees at an earlier date. At Lynn in Norfolk in the late sixteenth century, the customer received 5s. for each cocket issued to an English merchant, while the controller and the searcher were paid 3s. 4d. each. Such fees varied between ports and were slightly higher for foreign merchants. Williams, *Maritime Trade*, p. 15 and n. 22; Hinton, *Port Books of Boston*, p. xxx, n. 1.

[39] *Statutes*, p. 39. This was acknowledged by the deemsters and Keys in June 1609, not 1669, as stated in Gill's edition of the *Statutes*. Knowsley Hall, H/41, Laws of Man (n.d. [1705?]), p. 55.

[40] *Statutes*, pp. 27–8.

[41] M.M.L., MS MD/15,040, Parr, *Abridgement*, p. 44, summarising Lib. Scacc. 1631, 46.

[42] M.M.L., I.O. 1610–19, Ingates and outgates, 1610: loose slip, concerning goods forfeited by William Christian after seizure by Thomas Christian, searcher at Ramsey.

[43] M.M.L., I.O. 1646–59, Waterbailiff's accounts, 1656, 1657, 1658, 1659; M.M.L., I.O. 1660–71, Waterbailiff's accounts, 1660.

II. CUSTOMS ADMINISTRATION: RECORDS

Records of the inward and outward shipment of goods must have been kept from the time when customs duties were first imposed, some time before c.1420, but the earliest accounts now extant date only from the late sixteenth century. The series of surviving water-bailiff's accounts, generally entitled as such, but sometimes labelled 'Customs Book,' 'Port Customs,' or 'Book of Ingates and Outgates,' begins in 1576 and constitutes the most important source of information for the history of the island's maritime trade. Although there are some gaps in the series, particularly in the late sixteenth century, the accounts are almost complete for the period after 1600.[44] These books of accounts normally cover a period of one year which, before 1700, ends at June 24, and are usually divided into sections for each of the four main ports; the sections for each port are then subdivided into ingates and outgates. After June 1700, the accounting period was changed to a year ending at Michaelmas and, following the practice begun in 1694, the entries in the books were only divided into ingates and outgates, with a note in the margin to identify the port to, or from, which shipments were made.[45] In accordance with the Book

[44] For the waterbailiff's accounts, see M.M.L., I.O. 1570–99, 1600–9, 1610–19, 1620–9, 1630–45, 1646–59, 1660–71, 1672–9, 1680–9, 1690–5, 1696–1704. The waterbailiff's accounts for 1642 and 1646 can be found in M.M.L., Folder of miscellaneous excise records. The accounts for 1580, 1595, 1596, 1627, 1634, 1652 and 1700 are in M.M.L. R.D. 1579–98, 1627–50, 1651–70 and 1700–4. No accounts survive for the years 1577, 1578, 1581, 1584, 1585, 1590, 1591, 1593, 1616, 1622, 1633, 1635 or 1662.

[45] Before 1700, only six books cover a different accounting period: i) M.M.L., I.O. 1570–99, Customs book, 1588 (June 12, 1587–June 1, 1588); ii) M.M.L., I.O. 1570–99, Customs book, 1592 (May 31, 1591–May 31, 1592); iii) M.M.L., I.O. 1570–99, Customs book, 1594 (June 1, 1593–January 22, 1594); iv) M.M.L., I.O. 1570–99, Waterbailiff's accounts, 1594 (January 22–June 22, 1594); v) M.M.L., I.O. 1620–9, Comptroller's accounts of ingates and outgates, 1625 (June 24, 1624–October 26, 1624); vi) M.M.L., I.O. 1620–9, Waterbailiff's accounts, 1625 (October 26, 1624–June 24, 1625). It is difficult to determine the reasons for the adoption of the unusual accounting periods in 1588 and 1592, but the breaks in the accounts for 1594 and 1625 can be explained by the fact that in both the latter years a new waterbailiff was appointed: in January 1594, John Quayle replaced Henry Radcliffe in the office and in October 1624, after the comptroller, John Halsall, had been performing the waterbailiff's duties for some time, George Squire

of Orders of 1561, the waterbailiff was to record 'every Shipp,
Pickard and Boat that bringeth any Wares into the Countrey, and
the Day when she cometh, and what Wares she brings into the Land
and what Wares she taketh out of the Land, and what Custome is
due for the same.'[46] In fact, the waterbailiff's accounts usually record
a date, the name of a merchant or shipmaster, the nature of the cargo
and the amount of customs duty collected, but, until the last decade
of the seventeenth century, provide no information on a regular basis
about the vessel carrying the goods, save, in some instances, for the
fact that it belonged to the individual named in the entry, nor its port
or country of origin or destination.

The entries in the waterbailiff's accounts may, therefore, seem to
conform fairly closely to the directions given by the commissioners
of Earl Edward in the mid-sixteenth century; on further examination,
however, problems of interpretation become apparent. As in English
or Welsh port books, the date noted beside an entry may be, in some
cases, that on which a vessel arrived or departed, but, in others, where
the entries relating to cargo unloaded from a single ship occur on
more than one day, it clearly indicates the time at which the customs
duty was received.[47] The latter method of dating entries was probably normal practice, in spite of the injunctions of the earl's commissioners, since the waterbailiff's accounts were essentially a record of
the revenue collected by the chief customs officer and his deputies
rather than a register of the movement of shipping in the island's
ports. This assumption seems to be substantiated by a comparison
of the dates in the accounts and those recorded in the books of

was sworn in to take over the position. M.M.L., I.O. 1570–99, Customs
book, 1594 and waterbailiff's accounts, 1594; Lib. Scacc. 1594, 7, 25; Lib.
Scacc. 1625, 5.

[46] *Statutes*, p. 36.

[47] Some English port books, especially those compiled by the searchers,
record the actual date of a vessel's arrival or departure; in the Boston
searcher's book for 1601–2, even the time of day is noted. Other port books,
such as that for London in 1567–8, evidently record the date on which the
duty was paid, as can be seen from entries referring to individual ships.
D. M. Woodward, 'The Port Books of England and Wales', *Maritime
History*, vol. iii (1973), p. 152; Hinton, *Port Books of Boston*, p. xx; B. Dietz
(ed.), 'The Port and Trade of Early Elizabethan London', *London Record
Society*, vol. viii (1972), *passim*. If records of the activities of the searchers
in the Manx ports were ever kept, they are no longer extant.

licences and entries, the other principal source for the history of
Manx overseas trade in this period,[48] which shows that many merchants were issued with 'tickets of entry' before their names were
entered in the ingates. In most cases, the interval between the dates
of the entries in the respective books is only a few days, although on
occasion it is somewhat greater; William Walles of Ayr, for example,
obtained his 'ticket' on April 27, 1594, but did not pay the duty on
his cargo of white salt, linen cloth, shoes, alum, argol and hops until
May 16.[49] Some merchants who imported goods appear in entries of
the same date in the books of licences and entries and the waterbailiff's accounts, as do the great majority of those who were granted
a licence to export from the island, but this can not obscure the fact
that the former evidently offer a much more reliable indication of
the time of a ship's arrival and departure than the latter.[50]

Although the commissioners' directions stipulated that every
vessel carrying commodities to, and presumably from, the island
should be entered in the waterbailiff's accounts, no guidance was
given as to whether the name of the 'very owner' of the cargo or that
of the master of the ship were to be noted. In practice, there are
almost no references to vessels of any sort in the outgates before
about 1690, the entries containing only the most basic information
of a name and the details of the items licensed for export, and it is
by no means clear whether the individual named is the merchant, his
factor or agent, or the ship's master. Entries in the ingates occasionally record the name of the ship and its home port[51] before about

---

[48] For details of the books of licences and entries, see *infra*, pp. 238–39.

[49] M.M.L. R.D. 1579–98, 'Custome Book,' 1594 (Captain's book of licences
and entries, 1594–5); M.M.L., I.O. 1570–99, Waterbailiff's accounts, 1594.

[50] See, for example, M.M.L., I.O. 1610–19, Book of licences and entries,
1618.

[51] The difficulties of identifying vessels in the waterbailiff's accounts are
increased by the fact that, even after 1690, the name of the master, who was
in many cases probably also the owner, is not normally recorded. Details
of the ship's burthen or tonnage were never included in the entries, as they
were in at least most late sixteenth and early seventeenth century English
and Welsh port books. Since many vessels shared the same name, it is
hazardous to attempt to identify them by this means alone, but, in view of
the fact that it is unlikely that there would be two Manx vessels with
identical names in the same home port, this problem is less acute as far as
the island's ships are concerned. The home port is taken to be the place at
or near which the chief or full owner of the vessel was normally resident

1690, after which date such information was included in the ingates, as well as the outgates, as a matter of course; a much larger number of such entries in the earlier part of the seventeenth century – approximately one-third of all ingates in the accounts for 1618, for example – records an unnamed vessel which was apparently owned by the person whose name appears at the beginning of the entry, since it is described as his barque or boat. In cases in which goods are listed in the same entry, it is likely that this individual was the 'very owner' of the merchandise as well as of the ship which carried it. Similarly, the men, and very occasionally the women, named in succeeding entries as importing goods 'there,' that is, in the same barque or boat, were probably the owners of the commodities recorded. Entries which state that one man brought in goods in another man's barque suggest that it was generally the name of the merchant which was recorded, though there is evidence to indicate that at least some of the names in the ingates represent factors or agents, acting on behalf of the owners of the cargo.[52]

The total amount of customs duty paid by each merchant or factor was recorded after every entry in the accounts, the sum levied on individual commodities being laid down in a Book of Rates similar in form to that which was used in the ports of England and Wales. The specific duties imposed on Manx imports and exports were, however, very substantially lower than those which merchants shipping through an English or Welsh port had to pay, but they were increased on occasion during the seventeenth century. Some sort of schedule of rates must have been in existence from at least the early fifteenth century, when customs duties are first mentioned,[53] but the earliest extant list of duties for the island dates from 1577.[54] This 'Book of Rates' includes nearly one hundred items, against each of which a certain or specific duty is noted for a definite quantity of the commodity. This duty was apparently paid on both imports and

and to which the vessel would most often return. Woodward, 'Port Books', pp. 153, 154; Hinton, *Port Books of Boston*, p. xxi.

[52] The role of the factor in Manx overseas trade is considered *infra*, pp. 315–17.

[53] *Statutes*, p. 17.

[54] *ibid*, pp. 37–9; Knowsley Hall, H/41, Laws of Man, pp. 52–5. The low level of the island's customs duties can be readily demonstrated by a comparison between the Manx Book of Rates of 1577 and the English Book of Rates of 1582. T. S. Willan (ed.), *A Tudor Book of Rates* (Manchester, 1962).

exports and it seems that it was levied at the same rate on cargoes shipped by both Manx merchants and strangers, with the exception of consignments of tanned leather, for which the foreigner paid almost double the native's rate. The duty on certain goods – coal, lime, timber, salt and wine – could be, and frequently was, paid in kind as a proportion of the cargo, especially in the case of timber, which was always in considerable demand in the island.[55] In addition, large cargoes of wine were subject to prisage; this amounted to half a tun on shipments of ten tuns or more and one tun on cargoes of twenty tuns or more.[56]

The rates established or merely confirmed in 1577 remained largely unchanged until well into the seventeenth century, in spite of the continuing rise in prices which, while lightening the already limited burden of the merchant, reduced the value of the customs revenue in real terms. An unofficial list of 'Customes in the Ile of Man' drawn up by, or on behalf of, Christopher Lowther of White-haven in 1633 clearly shows, if accurate, that the levels of duty then levied on imports and exports were almost identical to those set or recorded more than half a century before, the only major difference being that, at some time in the interim, the rates on sack and wine had been doubled. This list also provides evidence that differential rates were being paid by natives and strangers on commodities other than tanned leather. It is not certain when these rates for foreign merchants were introduced, but, significantly, they were imposed on quick beeves (live cattle), hides and wool, three of the island's most important exports. The merchant stranger then paid half as much again as his Manx counterpart for every stone weight of wool and twice the amount of duty the latter paid for live cattle, hides and tanned leather. He may also have had to pay a higher rate of duty on shipments of wheat, malt and oats, as was the case in the later seventeenth century, but, as there are blanks in the manuscript where the duty should be recorded, it is not possible to be certain.[57]

---

[55] On timber in the island, see chapter 2, p. 80.

[56] *Statutes*, p. 39.

[57] D. R. Hainsworth (ed.), *Commercial Papers of Sir Christopher Lowther, 1611–1644*, Surtees Society, vol. clxxxix (1977), pp. 104–6. A. W. Moore is quite incorrect in suggesting that differential rates were introduced with the Book of Rates of 1677. Moore, *History*, vol. i, p. 441.

Increases seem to have been made in the duty levied on shipments of wheat in 1642 and on cargoes of sack in 1647,[58] but no review of the rates in general took place until 1648. A new Book of Rates was then issued and, although no copy of it remains extant,[59] it is clear from an examination of the waterbailiff's accounts for the following years that it must have contained higher duties on commodities such as coal, malt, tanned hides and sheep. This book was in turn 'revised, rectified and inlarged' in July 1677, when the duty imposed on coal, raw hides, horses and other items was raised. The Book of Rates of 1677, which lists nearly two hundred commodities, also reveals the range of goods on which native merchants were charged lower duties than foreigners. Merchant strangers paid heavier duties than Manxmen on nineteen types of goods, in all but five cases rendering double the amount which the islander delivered to the customer or waterbailiff.[60] In 1692, there was a further review of the duty levied on imports and exports and a revised Book of Rates was drawn up as part of a plan to stimulate native manufactures and to encourage trade.[61] The duty on imported cloth of various sorts was consequently substantially increased, though it remained very low by English standards, and considerably higher rates were set for a number of commodities, notably ale, brandy, wine, butter and pigs. Duties which Moore regarded as 'practically prohibitive' were imposed on imports of wheat, barley, malt and oats when the price of corn in the island was relatively low and on exports of these grains when prices rose above a certain level. In both cases the merchant stranger paid twice the amount of customs duty demanded from the Manxman. The rates levied on herring were also adjusted so that they were more favourable to the native than to the foreigner.[62] Fears that the importation of cattle, horses, tanned leather, shoes and other items from Ireland and cloth from Scotland and elsewhere would be

[58] According to Moore, *History*, vol. i, p. 322 n. 1. Moore does not give a source for this statement and no evidence has yet come to light to substantiate it.

[59] The only reference to the Book of Rates of 1648 is to be found in the two surviving copies of the Book of Rates of 1677. M.M.L., MD/401/1715/18, MD/401/1715/19.

[60] M.M.L., MD/401/1715/18, MD/401/1715/19.

[61] M.M.L., MD/401/1719/6. William Sacheverell, deputy governor, to William, ninth earl of Derby, May 23, 1692.

[62] M.M.L., MD/401/1715/20; Moore, *History*, vol. i, p. 442.

damaging to domestic manufactures and the 'cause of having the money exhausted out of the Country' led to the introduction of prohibitive duty on such goods in 1702 and 1703, but such measures were only temporary.[63]

While the interpretation of the waterbailiff's accounts thus presents several problems, there are few difficulties in using the books of licences and entries, the other main source for a study of Manx maritime trade in the late sixteenth and seventeenth centuries. These books, which are sometimes confusingly called books of ingates and outgates like some of the waterbailiff's accounts, only survive for the period from 1578 to 1653; a mere half dozen books are extant for the years before 1600, and there are many other gaps in the series. Most of the books list, in separate sections and in chronological order, the export licences and tickets of entry issued by the governor or his deputy and recorded by the clerk of the ships during the period of a year ending at June 24. The information provided is broadly similar to that which appears in the waterbailiff's accounts except for the fact that, as in the searcher's book for an English port, the amount of duty payable is omitted. The official copy of a ticket of entry records the date on which the entry was made, the port at which the goods were to be unloaded, the name of a merchant, factor or shipmaster and occasionally the place with which he was associated, an indication of the ownership of the vessel carrying the merchandise and details of the cargo. The section of each book devoted to export licences contains much the same information, but makes no reference to the barque or boat in which the goods were transported.[64]

Unlike the waterbailiff's accounts, the books of licences and entries were working copies, written up at the time the warrants were issued by the clerk of the ships. There is some evidence to suggest that there were two such similar books, one in the hands of the latter and another, containing the same details as well as information concerning anchorages, which was held by the governor or deputy and kept up to date by a clerk. Since there is only one year for which two books of licences and entries survive, namely 1622, this must, however, remain conjectural.[65] By contrast, it is clear that

[63] Lib. Scacc. 1701–2, inter 69–70 (2); Lib. Scacc. 1703–4, 39–41; Moore, *History*, vol. i, pp. 421, 442.

[64] See, for example, M.M.L. R.D. 1600–26, Book of licences and entries, 1604 ('The deputyes booke for Ingates and Outgates', 1604).

[65] M.M.L. R.D. 1600–26, Book of licences and entries, 1622 [March 21,

the waterbailiff's accounts were made up only periodically, in many, if not most, cases only at midsummer, or shortly afterwards, before the annual audit. The customers apparently rendered their accounts '(at soonest) but once [a] year,' delivering the export licences, tickets of entry and, most importantly, the customs duty which they had collected to the waterbailiff or his deputy.[66] A clerk[67] was then set to the task of compiling the accounts from the loose slips of paper, which doubtless explains the occasionally erratic chronological order and duplication of some entries and the insertion of lists of anchorages among the ingates in many books. It is possible that the entries were dictated to the clerk as this would most readily account for the often considerable variations in spelling between the books of licences and entries and the waterbailiff's accounts.[68]

1621–June 24, 1622]; Book of licences, 1622 (Incomplete. September 24, 1621– April 29, 1622); M.M.L., I.O. 1620–9, Book of licences, 1622 (fragment covering July–September 1621). Taken together, the latter two items constitute a now incomplete book of licences and entries, the entries having apparently become separated and lost. The unusual circumstance of having two extant books for approximately the same period may have some connection with the fact that John Halsall, the comptroller, who normally supervised the clerk of the ships, was also acting as waterbailiff at the time; it may have been considered necessary for another officer, probably the governor, Edward Fletcher, to keep a second book as a check on Halsall's accounting. See *infra*, p. 223. References to the 'Capt[ain's] booke' which occur from time to time in the waterbailiff's accounts may indicate that this was a regular practice or may simply relate to the book kept by the clerk of the ships, which recorded entries and licences issued under the governor's hand. See, for example, M.M.L. R.D. 1627–50, Waterbailiff's accounts, 1634; M.M.L., I.O. 1660–71, Waterbailiff's accounts, 1671.

[66] M.M.L., MD/401/1719/65. 'A new Method proposed for the levying and manageing of our honorable Lord's Customes of Outgates and Ingates etc. within the Isle of Man for the future.' (n.d., *c.* 1692?) Cf. M.M.L., MD/401/1719/9.

[67] The waterbailiff's clerk is regularly mentioned in the accounts until 1609, in which year he received 20s. in wages and £5 for 'dyatt'. M.M.L., I.O. 1600–9, Waterbailiff's accounts, 1609. Thereafter, his duties were probably carried out by one of the soldiers in the garrison at Castle Rushen, although this is nowhere explicitly stated.

[68] The manner in which the waterbailiff's accounts were drawn up was not dissimilar to the way in which English port books were compiled. See Hinton, *Port Books of Boston*, pp. xxxi–xxxii; Williams, *Maritime Trade*, pp. 17–18.

The procedures which gave rise to these records are well documented in both official and unofficial sources. As early as 1523, 'the Merchant Stranger his Duty' on arrival in one of the island's ports was set down and entailed his personal appearance before the governor or the latter's deputy in Castletown 'to shew him what his loading is, and to tell him Newes from whence he came.' The merchant requested 'an entry of his goods,' which was granted if the governor or his deputy considered 'that the Wares he hath [were] for the Commonwealth of this Countrey.' The merchant was then directed to go to the 'Captain's Clark' '(who keeps the Custom book) to make his entry,' a copy of which he returned to the governor for the latter's signature. The ticket of entry was then delivered to the customer of the port where the merchant's goods were waiting to be unloaded, but the actual supervision of the landing of the cargo was the responsibility of the searcher.[69]

Before the merchandise could be brought to market, a bargain had to be struck with the merchant stranger to ensure that the island was adequately supplied and to preclude any possibility of profiteering. This procedure was somewhat in the nature of the 'common bargain' made for a cargo between a merchant and the mayor of a town, such as Liverpool or Chester, with the consent of the town council.[70] In the early fifteenth century, the activities of speculators who made 'privy Bargaines' with merchants arriving at Manx ports and bought up goods, either 'carrying them forth for their own Gaine' or 'selling the same to the Countrey by their Prices,' had led Sir John Stanley II to order that 'noe Manner of Person bargaine or buy any such Merchandize before it be seen and allowed by the Lieutennant and Councell.' The latter were directed to appoint 'six or four discreet Men of the Country to be solemnly sworne to [be] the ... Merchants [of the Country]' and 'to endeavour them truely to make Bargaine for the Profitt of the Land, soe that the Buyers of the Countrey shall have the Preferment thereof.'[71] These merchants, who always seem to have been four in number, two each representing Northside and Southside,[72] were summoned by the clerk of the ships to negotiate a

[69] *Statutes*, p. 27; M.M.L., MD/401/1719/65.
[70] J. H. Thomas, *Town Government in the Sixteenth Century* (1933, reprinted New York, 1969), p. 70.
[71] *Statutes*, p. 19.
[72] It was presumably originally intended that a merchant should be chosen for each of the six sheadings, but there is little evidence to show that this

price with the merchant stranger and to attempt to improve upon
any deal proposed to him by the governor or his deputy. Once terms
were agreed, the clerk wrote out the bargain and a copy was sent to
the governor. The latter then consulted the comptroller and the
officers responsible for the supply of the castles[73] to determine the
needs of the garrisons, and after the necessary goods had been
allocated, the clerk recorded the amounts taken up by each merchant
'in his Quarter,' setting down 'every Man's Name that hath taken

plan was ever put into effect. In the late seventeenth century, John Parr
recorded that 'in ancient time the Countrey-Merchants were to be chosen
and appointed by the Great Enquests within the severall Divisions [i.e.
sheadings] of the Isle', but, by the beginning of the sixteenth century at
least, four merchants only were being selected and they were nominated by
an enquest of twenty-four 'of the Cuntrey'. M.M.L., MD/15,040, Parr,
Abridgement, pp. 95–6; Unpublished documents, no. 74, *J.M.M.*, vol. ii
(1930–4), p. 185. This enquest may have been identical with the Keys,
although this is nowhere specifically stated. By the end of the sixteenth
century, it had apparently become usual for the merchants to be commissioned by the governor or his deputy and this continued to be the method
of appointment throughout the seventeenth century, although, in 1653,
James Chaloner, one of the Lord's commissioners, claimed that they were
'ever chosen by the Country'. M.M.L., MD/15,040, Parr, *Abridgement*, p.
96; Lib. Scacc. 1663, inter cover–1(2); Chaloner, *Treatise*, p. 53. The merchants so chosen probably represented the four Quarters of the island
described in chapter 3, p. 151, n. 68. In 1653, Chaloner recorded the names
of the four merchants of the island and each can be identified with a different
Quarter: i) *South*: John Stanley (Ballakeighan, Arbory?); ii) *East*: Phillip
Moore, (Baldromma?) Lonan; iii) *West*: Thomas Crellin; iv) *North*: David
Christian, Cranstal, Bride and Ballacurry, Jurby. Chaloner, *Treatise*, p. 53.
The connection between the merchant and the area for which he served was
not always so clear. The four merchants chosen in June 1502, for example,
were: *Southside*: i) John Stevenson, Ballakeighan, Arbory; ii) Gibbon
McFayle, Ballaquayle, Conchan; *Northside*: i) Finlo Skillicorn, (Ballaker-
meen?) Conchan; ii) Edmund McCorkell, Ballavinch, Conchan. Unpublished Documents no. 74, *J.M.M.*, vol. ii (1930–4), p. 185; Talbot, *Manorial
Roll*, pp. 7, 30, 33, 98, 100; W. Cubbon, 'Maritime Commerce at the End
of the Sixteenth Century', *M.N.H.A.S.*, vol. iv (1932–42), p. 613.
[73] Before *c.* 1614, there was a receiver at both castles; thereafter, a receiver-
general assumed their duties. Between 1669 and 1673 and again between
1683 and 1700, the office was held in commission by several of the Lord's
officers. See chapter 1, pp. 31–3, and appendix iv.

Wares, and how much every Man hath taken.'[74] The four merchants were 'to distribute [the goods] according to every Man's holdinge,' that is, to ensure that nobody acquired more than his fair share, payment being generally made by an exchange of goods with the merchant stranger. In 1653, Chaloner observed that it was normal practice for 'the Country . . . to bring in their Commodities of Wooll, Hides, Tallow, and such like, and for the same have their equall proportions of the Commodities of Salt, Wine, Iron, Pitch, etc. so brought in and compounded for.'[75] If the produce of the country did not match the value of the foreigner's commodities, the four merchants were authorised to 'assesse the rest of the Commodities upon the Country every one his equall proportion; for which they are to pay ready moneys as the four Merchants had agreed for them.'[76] These transactions could not commence, however, until the cargo had been unloaded from the merchant stranger's vessel under the watchful eye of the searcher, although they were not delayed by the activities of the other customs officers.

The customer was primarily concerned with the collection of customs duty, which, it seems, was not generally obtained from the merchant until some time after the latter's shipment was landed. Native merchants, who were also required to apply for a ticket of entry when importing their merchandise, were sometimes permitted to delay payment until the customer settled his accounts with the waterbailiff. A similar course of action was followed by merchants, both Manx and foreign, who desired to export goods, although the customers could hardly afford an equally leisurely approach to the

[74] *Statutes*, p. 27. Cf. Knowsley Hall, H/41, Laws of Man, p. 41.
[75] Chaloner, *Treatise*, p. 53. There is some evidence to suggest that such exchanges were carefully organised. In May 1663, Deputy Governor Henry Nowell appointed John Standish of Ellanbane, Lezayre, to be 'one of the foure merchants of this Isle' and ordered 'all persons in that division [i.e. the North Quarter] . . . to take notice and give there appearrance at Duglas on Munday next to take there proporcon of salt'. Those who failed to turn up were 'lyable to pay demurrage', which Nowell promised to 'see performed on the merchant strangers behalf'. Lib. Scacc. 1663, inter cover–1(2).
[76] Chaloner, *Treatise*, pp. 53–4. Cf. Blundell, *History*, vol. i, p. 79. According to Bishop Thomas Wilson, writing c. 1720, this method of bargaining with merchant strangers was by that time 'entirely laid aside'. Bishop Wilson's History, in W. Harrison (ed.), *The Old Historians of the Isle of Man*, Manx Society, vol. xviii (1871), p. 105.

collection of duty from merchants, especially strangers, who very often received their licences and departed the same day.[77]

The inconvenience and inefficiency of this system were quite evident to any merchant who, after landing at Douglas, Peel or, worse still, Ramsey, had made the tiresome journey to Castletown to request an entry, only to find that the governor was either absent or too busy with official duties to see him. It was not until the end of the seventeenth century, however, that any significant effort was made to reduce the delays which often faced those requiring entries or export licences, to ensure that all goods shipped were first adequately checked by the searcher and to see that customs duty was paid promptly. Proposals for the reform of the customs were made by commissioners of the revenue appointed in April 1692 by William, ninth earl of Derby, who was then under some pressure from the English government to take action against merchants and others using the island as a base for smuggling operations. These commissioners, who included William Sacheverell, the energetic and indefatigable author of numerous schemes for the improvement of the island, were given the authority to put into effect any measure 'for the good, profitt and advantage' of the earl.[78] They recognised the difficulties facing the merchants in the conduct of their business, but were equally, if not more, concerned about late payment or evasion of customs duty and the possible loss of revenue due to the Lord. As a result, they produced a 'new Method . . . for the levying and managing' of the island's customs in the future and this plan was approved at a meeting of the Lord's Council in July 1692. Accordingly, a 'Custome Office' was to be established within Castle Rushen, where the waterbailiff and one customer were to be in attendance daily for a period of two hours from 9 a.m. onwards. During these sessions, all entries and licences were to be issued and signed by them and the duty payable was to be collected at the same time. A storehouse was to be built in each port and equipped with weights and measures to check all cargoes shipped to or from the island. Merchants importing coal, timber, salt and other bulky goods which could not be easily put into the storehouse were to make a declaration to the searcher in the port,

[77] *Statutes*, p. 27; M.M.L., MD/401/1719/65.

[78] L.R.O. DDKe 80. Appointment of commissioners of the revenue and for setting lands, April 18, 1692. Cf. G. R., Lib. Irrotulamentorum, 1691–1709. For Sacheverell, see chapter 3, pp. 175–83. Smuggling in the island is considered *infra*, pp. 331–41.

who was to stay aboard the vessel during unloading and was empowered to seize any unentered cargo until the offending native or foreigner made a second, or post, entry and paid the outstanding duty. The searcher was similarly authorised to detain goods which merchants attempted to export over and above the amount recorded in their licences. To enable the searchers to carry out their duties, it was ordered that merchandise could only be loaded or unloaded during the hours of daylight at specified havens, namely Castletown, Port St Mary, Port Erin, Peel, Ramsey and Douglas. Goods were liable for customs duty according to their value, the valuations being given on oath by the merchant or taken from his 'Bill of Parcells,' and no vessel was to be permitted to leave the island before the merchant or master had obtained a cocket, or receipt for the payment of the duty.[79] Earl William gave his assent to this plan, directing the Council in 1694 to implement regulations 'about the levying and collecting of the Customes and Dutyes payable and arising upon all goods and merchandizes;' he also confirmed the revision of the Book of Rates made at the same time in 1692.[80]

III. THE WATERBAILIFF'S ACCOUNTS
AS SOURCES FOR THE STUDY OF
MANX OVERSEAS TRADE

It has already been observed that the waterbailiff's accounts are fiscal records, which detail the customs revenue received by the waterbailiff and customers,[81] and consequently it would be unwise to accept without qualification the commercial data which can be extracted from them. It is generally agreed that English and Welsh port books do not provide a full record of the amount of trade conducted at a particular port[82] and there can be little doubt that the Manx

[79] M.M.L., MD/401/1719/9.
[80] G.R., Lib. Irrotulamentorum, 1691–1709, cited in Moore, *History*, vol. i, p. 430; M.M.L., MD/401/1715/20. The duties of the searcher were underlined by orders addressed to this official in each port in 1698. G.R., Lib. Irrotulamentorum, 1691–1709, cited in Moore, *History*, vol. i, p. 430 and n. 3.
[81] See *infra*, p. 233.
[82] Woodward, 'Port Books', pp. 157–8; *idem*, 'Short Guides to Records: 22: Port Books', *History*, vol. lv (1970), pp. 209–10; Williams, *Maritime Trade*,

waterbailiff's accounts, which were compiled in much the same manner, share some of the same shortcomings. Some probably minor inaccuracies may have resulted from errors made by the clerk in writing up the accounts, but more significant was the deliberate omission by the officers from their returns of part or all of a cargo in order to supplement their meagre wages by retaining the duty which they received from the merchant. Few cases of concealment of duty by Manx customs officers seem to have been recorded, but this should not be taken as proof that such practices were absent from the island; the successful embezzler of customs duty, who diverted only small amounts from time to time, could well go undetected and unpunished for a long period, if indeed his activities ever came to light. This could be achieved relatively easily since, as already noted, the customers submitted their accounts to be copied into the waterbailiff's book only once a year.[83]

The smuggling of goods, with or without the connivance of the customs officers, was a problem of equal, if not greater, importance, one of which it is impossible to gauge accurately the extent at any particular time, and another reason for approaching the waterbailiff's accounts with caution. It has been argued that smuggling is usually a response either to the prohibition of certain types of trade or to high duties.[84] Although it is true that shipments from the island of certain commodities, especially corn and cattle, were restrained in times of shortage, the movement of goods was not generally restricted[85] and

pp. 48–9; T. S. Willan, *Studies in Elizabethan Foreign Trade* (Manchester 1959), p. 65; Hinton, *Port Books of Boston*, p. xxxii.

[83] M.M.L., MD/401/1719/65. See *infra*, p. 239.

[84] Willan, *Tudor Book of Rates*, p. xlviii; Woodward, 'Port Books', p. 158; R. C. Jarvis, 'Illicit Trade with the Isle of Man, 1671–1765', *T.L.C.A.S.*, vol. lviii (1945–6), pp. 246–8; G. D. Ramsay, 'The Smugglers' Trade: a neglected aspect of English commercial development', *T.R.H.S.*, 5th series, vol. ii (1952), pp. 136–8.

[85] The governor and officers met when necessary to determine whether or not certain commodities could be exported, but trade was only restrained when it was thought that the island's population would otherwise suffer from shortages. See, for example, M.M.L., I.O. 1570–99, Book of licences, 1578; Lib. Canc. 1595, 6; Lib. Scacc. 1628, 44, 87; Lib. Scacc. 1632, inter 38–9; Lib. Scacc. 1663, 8. Two merchants, Robert Lawson and David Murrey, leased the exclusive right to export skins in 1611, but this proved to be a short-lived experiment, lasting only one year. M.M.L., I.O. 1610–19, Waterbailiff's accounts, 1611, 1612. See *infra*, p. 262.

the customs duties levied were low by English standards. Neverthe-less, there is ample evidence in the island's court records and elsewhere to show that smuggling took place throughout the period and, since recorded instances probably represent only an uncertain and doubt-less variable proportion of the actual illicit trade, it may well have been more extensive than these sources indicate.[86]

It is perhaps overstating the matter to suggest that 'if a merchant's first concern was the safe arrival of his cargo at its port of discharge, his second was the evasion of the customs,'[87] yet there can be no question that the waterbailiff's accounts under-record the amount of the island's trade to some extent. The degree to which this occurred can never be ascertained, and therefore the data derived from the accounts can only be regarded as a partial record of the volume of trade passing through Manx ports. The following account of the island's trade is necessarily based largely on these accounts, for they are the main primary source for any study of the subject, but it is important to bear in mind that, while the range of goods traded in the island, the names of the merchants and shipmasters and, from the later seventeenth century, the country of origin or destination of the merchandise are probably reliably recorded, the figures extracted from the waterbailiff's books are not commercial statistics; at best, they provide a reasonably accurate record of Manx overseas trade; at the very least, they represent the minimum level of commercial activity in the island. Some figures should be viewed with more suspicion than others, especially those for commodities such as tobacco, which could be profitably smuggled from the Isle of Man into any of the countries bordering on the Irish Sea; however, without these figures, whatever their potential deficiencies, it would be scarcely possible to come to any conclusions about the nature and scope of the island's trade in the early modern period.

IV. THE EXPORT TRADE OF THE ISLE OF MAN

Throughout the sixteenth and seventeenth centuries, Manx com-merce largely retained its colonial characteristics. Primary products, especially cattle, hides, fish, corn and wool, were exported to the

---

[86] For details of smuggling in the island, see *infra*, pp. 331–41.
[87] N. J. Williams, 'Francis Shaxton and the Elizabethan Port Books', *E.H.R.*, vol. lxvi (1951), p. 387. Cf. Williams, *Maritime Trade*, p. 25.

other countries of the British Isles, and England in particular, in return for the raw materials and manufactured goods which could not otherwise be obtained in the island. As the seventeenth century progressed, however, the relative importance of the commodities in the island's export trade changed, partly as a result of external pressures, such as the legislation limiting the number of cattle imported into England from the Isle of Man after 1666,[88] and partly as a result of the commencement of the manufacturing projects in the island which have already been described.[89] By the end of the century, cattle, and livestock in general, as well as corn were much less significant as elements in the export trade than they had been in 1600, whereas woollen and linen cloth had assumed a position of some importance for the first time, most of the cloth previously shipped having been 'raw' or unfinished. By the end of the century, it was also apparent that the island's trade was being affected by the Navigation Acts of 1660 and 1671 and the increases in English import duties after the outbreak of war with France in 1689. The cumulative effect of this legislation was the expansion of Manx trade in general and the growth of contraband trafficking from the island in particular, in commodities such as brandy, wine and tobacco.

a) Cattle

At the end of the sixteenth century, however, the island's export trade was not hampered by such regulations and was firmly based on the shipment of agricultural produce and livestock, especially cattle. The export trade in cattle, which involved the transportation of 'quick beasts' or live animals as well as carcases in barrels, was probably long established by then, although the earliest evidence of shipments of beef from the Isle of Man to an English port dates only from 1566.[90]

[88] The effects of the Irish Cattle Acts of 1663 and 1666 on Manx exports are discussed in chapter 2 and in the following pages.

[89] See chapter 3, pp. 175–88.

[90] In March 1566, Thomas Lea of Castletown imported into Chester from the island three hogsheads and five barrels of beef, together with a mixed cargo of hides and wheat. In the following month, three merchants, Thomas Matire, Henry Callister and Patrick Brew landed a cargo at the same port from Douglas which included five hogsheads and a quarter of beef, as well as tallow, barley, wheat, sheepfells and salted hides. P.R.O., E 190/1323/1 and E 190/1323/10, printed in K. P. Wilson (ed.), *Chester Customs Accounts, 1301–1566*, R.S.L.C., vol. cxi (1969), pp. 78, 79.

It does not seem to have been conducted on anything approaching a large scale, even by the standards of the island, before the 1590s. Small quantities of salted beef were sent to Chester on a fairly regular basis and occasionally to Beaumaris in Anglesey in the later sixteenth century,[91] but in general the total number of cattle shipped out of Manx ports during this period was relatively low. For example, the earliest extant book of waterbailiff's accounts, for the year ending at June 24, 1579, records the export of 117 beasts and at least forty-two beef carcases,[92] a comparatively small total number when viewed alongside the figures for the seventeenth century (Table 5.1).

Table 5.1 *Exports of Livestock from the Isle of Man (years ending at June 24)*

Year	Cattle	Sheep	Pigs
1594	749	515	263
1600	405	383	42
1605	454	152	66
1610	714	8	124
1618	895	50	48
1630	589	24	30
1647	890	—	9
1667	18	20	—
1685	4	12	5
1696	582	8	—

Sources: M.M.L., I.O., 1570–99, Customs book, 1594; Waterbailiff's accounts, 1594; M.M.L., I.O., 1600–9, Ingates and outgates (Port Customs), 1600; Ingates and outgates, 1605; M.M.L., I.O., 1610–19, Ingates and outgates, 1610; Waterbailiff's accounts, 1618; M.M.L., I.O. 1630–45, Waterbailiff's accounts, 1630; M.M.L., I.O., 1646–59, Waterbailiff's accounts, 1647; M.M.L., I.O. 1660–71, Customs book, 1667; M.M.L., I.O. 1680–9, Customs book, 1685; M.M.L., I.O. 1696–1704, Customs book, 1696.

[91] Woodward, *Elizabethan Chester*, p. 35; E. A. Lewis (ed.), *The Welsh Port Books, 1550–1603*, Cymmrodorion Record Series, no. xii (1927), pp. 244, 256, 258.
[92] M.M.L., I.O. 1570–99, 'Poort Customes and other comodities receyved By Wyllm Ratclyffe wa[ter] Bailefe of [the] Isle of Man', 1579; Cubbon, 'Maritime Commerce', pp. 618–19. Cubbon incorrectly states that this book covers the year 1580–1. *ibid*, p. 618.

This level of exports was not, however, the result of a lack of demand for meat in foreign markets, particularly in England, where the consumption of beef and mutton grew steadily in the late Tudor and early Stuart periods.[93] Nor was it due to the quality of the cattle exported from the island, despite the uncomplimentary comments made about Manx beasts by contemporaries, such as William Blundell,[94] for Irish cattle, about which similarly disparaging remarks were often made, found a ready market in England in the seventeenth century.[95] The principal reason for the limited number of cattle exported from the island before 1600 was the customary obligation of the Manx farmers to pay half their rent in kind, the provisions being used to maintain the garrisons.[96]

This system of payments in kind, which supplied approximately 500 cattle to the garrisons each year in the late 1590s,[97] and a series of bad harvests during the decade[98] had the effect of curbing exports of both live animals and carcases towards the end of the sixteenth century. In 1593–4, a period during which there appears to have been no shortage of grain in the island, and no official hindrance to the transportation of beef, a total of 749 cattle were exported (Table 5.1). This relatively high level of cattle exports may well have been connected with the temporary commutation of payments in kind to payments in coin, based on market values, in 1593, which at least

[93] C. Wilson, *England's Apprenticeship, 1603–1763* (2nd edn, 1984), p. 26; C. G. A. Clay, *Economic Expansion and Social Change: England, 1500–1700* (2 vols, Cambridge, 1984), vol. i, p. 68.

[94] For Blundell's remarks, see chapter 2, p. 90. Cf. Chaloner, *Treatise*, pp. 6–7.

[95] For comments on the poor quality of Irish cattle, see F. Moryson, *An Itinerary . . . The Description of Ireland* (1617), printed in C. Litton Falkiner (ed.), *Illustrations of Irish History and Topography* (1904), p. 222; G. Boate, *Ireland's Naturall History* (1652), cited in O'Brien, *Economic History of Ireland*, p. 40. On the development of the Irish cattle trade with England, see D. M. Woodward, 'The Anglo-Irish Cattle Trade of the Seventeenth Century', *I.H.S.*, vol. xviii (1972–3), pp. 489–523.

[96] Customary payments are also discussed in chapter 3, p. 157, n. 92.

[97] This figure is based on data from M.M.L., I.O. 1570–99, Book of charge, Castle Rushen, 1597; book of charge, Peel Castle, 1597; M. M. L, Ellesmere Papers 243/C/1, Books of charge, Castle Rushen, 1599, 1600, 1601; M.M.L., Ellesmere Papers 244/C/2, Books of charge, Peel Castle, 1599, 1600, 1601.

[98] For details of harvests in the Isle of Man in the 1590s, see chapter 2, pp. 92–105.

allowed the farmer a chance to sell his animals or salted beef at a profit in a foreign market, although the officers doubtless took care to see that the castles were adequately supplied before sanctioning any shipments. The revival of the former system of customary payments in kind in 1595, and the effects of bad harvests in 1596 and probably in 1597, led to a fall in cattle exports as demand in the island rose, but some beef, whether 'quick' or in the form of carcases, continued to be exported. In early 1597, 'divers of the Cuntry' petitioned the governor, Peter Legh, for permission to 'transport [the] carcasses of dead beeves.' After consulting the receivers of both castles and the deemsters, it was decided that 'in respect the beeves be deade,' 'the poore people' could be allowed to ship their beef.[99] A restriction seems nevertheless to have remained on the transportation of live animals.

More galling to the farmer than any temporary prohibition of cattle exports were the customary payments. For each beast delivered to the garrison, the farmer was allowed only 4s., less than a third of the market value of the animal, against his rent. As prices continued to rise, the value of this allowance diminished and the amount which the farmer lost on each beast 'paid' in this manner increased. In such circumstances, discontent was inevitable and was undoubtedly growing in the late sixteenth century. In 1582, it was considered necessary for the deemsters to set out in some detail the penalties for those who disobeyed the parish moar,[100] the coroner of the sheading[101] or a garrison soldier by refusing to hand over their livestock, corn or rent in coin.[102] The grievances of the farmers were voiced on more than one occasion in the 1590s by Thomas Moore of Conchan, who fell foul of the island authorities for repeatedly refusing to render his payments in kind.[103] Greater opportunity for the farmers to export their cattle and corn, once the domestic market had been served, would very likely have eased their resentment of this system to some extent, but shipments remained at a significantly lower level in 1599-1600, when 405 cattle were transported, than five years earlier (Table 5.1). The desire to export greater numbers of cattle was perhaps stimulated in September 1600 by the request of the English

[99] Lib. Scacc. 1597, 14.
[100] The office of parish moar is discussed in chapter 1, pp. 51–2.
[101] For details of the office of coroner, see chapter 1, pp. 46–9.
[102] Lib. Scacc. 1582, 21.
[103] Lib. Scacc. 1592, 15–17; Lib. Scacc. 1599, 19; Lib. Scacc. 1601, inter 8–9.

Privy Council, addressed to the governor, Sir Thomas Gerard, for the island to supply 'somme good store and quantitie of diverse sortes of victualles,' including beef and corn, for the English army in Ulster,[104] but while the system of customary payments in kind remained in operation, the export trade of the island as a whole was always limited beyond the needs of the domestic market.

In 1601, this situation was changed. After 'the great death of Cattle and horses happening universally over the whole Isle' during the summer of that year, the farmers and other tenants in the island were 'not able as before to pay their usual customs of corne, victuals and fire unto the Garrisons.'[105] Consequently, an agreement was reached between the deputy, Robert Molyneux, the Council, the Keys and four representatives from each parish by which the customary payments were to be commuted to 'a double rent in money' from Michaelmas 1601 and the farmers were to be permitted to 'have free liberty of transportation for corne or cattle growing and increasing upon their severall farmes for the best advantage, provided allwayes that sufficient be reserved for the necessary use and relieffe of all the whole Inhabitants' of the island.[106] The implications of this agreement for the export trade in cattle were considerable. Henceforth, farmers could ship as many animals or barrels of beef produced on their own holdings as they wished, so long as the domestic market was adequately supplied as well.

The ability of the island to produce cattle for the export market was somewhat limited, but, nevertheless, there was a general rise in the number of cattle and beef carcases shipped from Manx ports in

[104] *A.P.C.E., 1599–1600*, pp. 675–6.
[105] M.M.L., MD/401/1716/4; Moore, *Manx Note Book*, vol. i (1885), pp. 61–4. Both versions of this document are copies of the original, which does not appear to be extant. The former contains a number of obvious errors made by the copyist. The cause of this 'great death' is by no means clear, but it seems most likely that it was an outbreak of a virulent disease affecting cattle and horses, though not apparently sheep and pigs, since there is no reference to the loss of such animals.
[106] Moore, *Manx Note Book*, vol. i, p. 63. Moore is incorrect in suggesting that this agreement only lasted until 1608. Moore, *History*, vol. ii, p. 878. In fact, it remained in force permanently. See, for example, M.M.L., I.O. 1600–9, Book of charge, Castle Rushen, 1607; book of charge, Peel Castle, 1607; M.M.L., I.O. 1610–19, Book of charge, Castle Rushen, 1614; book of charge, Peel Castle, 1614.

the first half of the seventeenth century. (Table 5.1). Most of this trade involved the shipment of live animals. In 1604–5, only 211 quick beasts were exported, as opposed to 243 carcases;[107] by 1609–10, however, the position was reversed, with 479 cattle and 235 carcases being transported from Manx ports,[108] and live animals appear to have remained the more important component of the export trade for the rest of the century.

Although the destination of these shipments is not normally recorded in the waterbailiff's accounts until the 1690s, it seems likely that a large proportion of the cattle exported from the Isle of Man in the seventeenth century was sent to England. The port books of Chester and Liverpool, the two most important English ports in the rapidly developing trade in live cattle from Ireland,[109] and both ports with which the island had close links, do not, however, provide conclusive evidence that this was so. The survival of a relatively small number of port books for these places during the early Stuart period makes it dangerous to generalise from the figures for isolated years, but the level of cattle imports from the Isle of Man at Chester seems to have remained low. In 1592–3, for example, only twelve live animals were imported, while in 1619–20, a total of twenty-two cows were unloaded at the port.[110] The figures for Liverpool seem to have been similarly low, at least in some years, such as 1603–4, when only twenty-one Manx cattle were imported there.[111] It may well be that in other years the totals were considerably higher, but, in the absence of a good series of port books and of contemporary estimates of this

---

[107] M.M.L., I.O. 1600–9, Ingates and outgates, 1605. Most of the entries referring to beef rather than live animals list 'carcases'; a few state the number of barrels of beef. In the case of the latter, a barrel has been taken to contain two carcases. M.M.L., I.O. 1600–9, Outgates and ingates, 1600: Derbyhaven outgates, January 24, 1600. This may, however, be an underestimate as a barrel containing three salt beefs was used by John Kellowe (Callow), a Manx merchant who traded with Beaumaris in 1577. Lewis, *Welsh Port Books*, p. 244.

[108] M.M.L., I.O. 1610–19, Ingates and outgates, 1610.

[109] D. M. Woodward, 'The Overseas Trade of Chester, 1600–1650', *T.H.S.L.C*, vol. cxxii (1971), pp. 35–40; Woodward, 'Anglo-Irish Livestock Trade', appendix A, p. 515. Ilfracombe and Minehead only became important ports in this trade in the early 1660s. *ibid*, pp. 516, 517.

[110] P.R.O., E 190/1326/6; P.R.O., E 190/1332/1.

[111] P.R.O., E 190/1328/11.

branch of England's import trade, this can not be readily established. Some cattle were probably landed at ports on the Cumberland coast, such as Whitehaven, but since no port books survive for these ports in the early seventeenth century, this, too, must remain uncertain.

Imports of cattle from the Isle of Man were associated with the vastly larger Irish cattle trade in the minds of some, for it was believed that Irish animals were re-exported from the island to England. Although this may have happened, no evidence has so far come to light to show that it took place on any scale. Nevertheless, when the English House of Commons came to debate a ban on the importation of Irish cattle in April 1621 as part of the effort to lift the current economic depression, Richard Kippax, M.P. for Newton, suggested an addition to the bill 'to provide against the Importation [of Irish cattle] out of the Isle of Man.'[112] The bill came to nothing,[113] but, inevitably, when fears about the impact of Irish cattle imports re-emerged in the early 1660s, the position of the island was carefully considered. The first Irish Cattle Act, which came into force on July 1, 1664, and which prohibited the import of cattle from Ireland into England between July 1 and December 20 and the import of sheep between August 1 and December 20, excluded cattle from the Isle of Man from its strictures.[114] Its failure to reduce the level of the Irish cattle trade significantly ensured the introduction of another bill to halt the import of all foreign cattle into England and further scrutiny of the island's contribution to the number of beasts landed in English ports. Accordingly, a provision was inserted in the bill limiting the level of cattle exports from the island to England 'so as the Number of the said Cattle do not exceed six hundred Head yearly,' the cattle to be 'not of any other Breed than of the Breed of the Isle of Man' and only landed at Chester.[115]

---

[112] *C.J.*, vol. i, p. 615. Cf. C. A. Edie, 'The Irish Cattle Bills: A Study in Restoration Politics', *Transactions of the American Philosophical Society*, vol. lx, pt. ii (1970), p. 8.

[113] Edie, 'Irish Cattle Bills', pp. 7–9.

[114] 15 Chas. II, c. 7. For the background to this Act, see Edie, 'Irish Cattle Bills', pp. 11–13. The impact of the Act on imports into England is discussed in Woodward, 'Anglo-Irish Livestock Trade', pp. 499–500 and appendix A.

[115] 18 Chas. II, c. 2. For further details of the passage of this Act, see Edie, 'Irish Cattle Bills', pp. 17–35. The effects of the second Cattle Act on Ireland are examined by Cullen, *Anglo-Irish Trade*, ch. 2 and Woodward, 'Anglo-Irish Livestock Trade', pp. 500–2.

The second Irish Cattle Act came into effect on February 2, 1667 and seems to have had an immediate impact on cattle exports from the island. Certainly in 1666–7, exports of cattle from the Isle of Man fell dramatically; only ten beasts were shipped from Manx ports, together with five barrels of beef, a total of eighteen cattle.[116] The reasons for this slump are far from clear. It would undoubtedly be going too far to suggest that it was caused by the Cattle Act, in spite of the fact that all the shipments during the year were made before it came into operation. The Act only gradually reduced the level of the Irish trade with England and this was only achieved after further measures had been taken to enforce it.[117] It seems much more likely that the export of cattle was restrained by order from Charles, eighth earl of Derby or his officers in the island, an assumption which appears to be borne out by the absence of any Manx names among those transporting cattle from the island in that year.[118]

Such orders were issued to prevent the depletion of cattle stocks and to guarantee a sufficient supply for the Lord's garrisons.[119] Since the farmers relied to a certain extent on the sale of at least some of their cattle and corn outside the island to enable them to pay their rents, a restriction on exports, if of long duration, could have serious consequences, both for the Lord and his tenants. This was particularly so when the restriction was the product of a bad harvest, as may have been the case in early 1673, when Dowager Countess Dorothea Helena apparently directed that there should be 'a restraint for transport of cattle out of the Isle.'[120] In June, the Keys complained

---

[116] M.M.L., I.O. 1660–71, Customs book, 1667.

[117] Woodward, 'Anglo-Irish Livestock Trade', pp. 500–1.

[118] Only three men exported beef in one form or another in 1666–7, all of whom had probably been exempted from any prohibition by special licence from Earl Charles: James Tayler, Nicholas Amory [Emery?] and Henry Nowell, the deputy governor. M.M.L., I.O. 1660–71, Customs book, 1667. If an order prohibiting cattle exports was given, it has not been found, despite a search through the records of the Exchequer Court.

[119] Beef cattle were more important to Manx farmers as marketable assets than as a source of food. According to Blundell, the inhabitants of the island had a diet of 'only salt butter, herrings, and oat cakes'. Blundell, *History*, vol. i, p. 57. Chaloner noted that the Manx had a 'simple Diet', 'their Drink, water; their Meat, Fish'. Chaloner, *Treatise*, pp. 10–11.

[120] Lib. Scacc. 1673, 51. For details of Manx harvests in the seventeenth century, see chapter 2, pp. 94–105.

to Deputy Governor Henry Nowell of 'the distressed condicon' of the Lord's tenants, some of which were 'comitted into Prisson for non payment of their Quarterly rents,' being unable to 'obtaine Lycence for transportacon of their cattle, which, with their Corne, is the chieffe support for the discharge of their said Rents and other dues.'[121] Nowell and the other officers granted the tenants permission to export 'Cattle of this Countreyes growth,' as well as 'other comodeties as occasion shall require,' and wrote to the dowager countess and the young William, ninth earl of Derby, to explain their actions and 'to obtaine pardon for [their] presumpcon.'[122] Earl William sanctioned 'the Transportacon of soe many Manks Beasts as are allowed,' but warned the officers to be careful that 'noe occasion of complaint be given in any particuler.'[123]

Cattle exports continued after such interruptions, although the trade with England suffered to some extent by the provision in the Cattle Act of 1667 which stipulated that animals from the Isle of Man could only be landed 'at the Port of Chester, or some of the Members thereof.'[124] Much of the island's export trade in live cattle was probably already conducted through the head port of Chester and its 'creeks,'[125] but after the second Cattle Act came into force, Manx cattle which were landed elsewhere, such as at the ports of Cumberland, were liable to be seized by English customs officers. Some Manx merchants, who were either ignorant of the new regulation – a somewhat unlikely eventuality – or who wilfully refused to abide by it, nevertheless attempted to transport cattle to havens other than those specified by the Act. Nowell and the officers reported to Earl

[121] ibid.

[122] ibid, 51, 53.

[123] ibid, 55.

[124] 18 Chas. II, c. 2.

[125] The division of the English and Welsh coastlines into 'head ports' and 'creeks' was reorganised in 1671. Before that date, the head port of Chester included the 'creeks' of Lancaster, Liverpool, Conway, Beaumaris and Caernarfon. After 1671, these havens, together with Poulton, became 'members' of the head port, the landing places of minor importance adjacent to each 'member' being designated 'creeks'. Williams, Descriptive List, p. 523; R. C. Jarvis, 'The Head Port of Chester; and Liverpool, its Creek and Member', T.H.S.L.C., vol. cii (1951), pp. 82–3; C. Armour, 'The Trade of Chester and the State of the Dee Navigation, 1600–1800' (University of London Ph.D. thesis 1956), pp. 156–7.

William that at least some of these men 'have sustained losse by landing there, their Cattle being ceized uppon and taken from them.' The deputy governor and his colleagues urged the earl to intercede with the king or parliament on the island's behalf 'for obtaininge libertie for the transport of cattle, corne and other comodeties onlie of this Islands growth into any Poart of England.' They argued that although 'some may resolve to make their markett at such Poarts as are nott prohibitted, yet by storme or contrarie wind [they] might bee constrained to other places,' their vessels 'beinge but of small burden' and, in any event, 'the loadinges not of considerable value.'[126] No such order was forthcoming from the English government, despite a further request from the deputy governor and officers to the duke of Ormonde, the young earl's guardian, at the end of 1674, and, after a brief hiatus between 1679 and 1681, the provisions of the second Cattle Act were made permanent by a third Act in the latter year.[127]

While Manx merchants who failed to comply with the regulations concerning cattle exports from the island were penalised, even those who kept within the law were sometimes troubled by overzealous customs officers or local people. In July 1675, William Christian, perhaps of Bride, landed twenty-four Manx cattle at Piel Fowdrey in Lancashire, whereupon the king's officers and others 'seised upon [them] as imported forfitted Cattle.' Christian swore on oath that they were in fact 'of the breed and growth' of the Isle of Man and part of the 'number of the six hundred allowed by law to bee imported,' and the cattle were restored to him. Shortly afterwards, he sold the beasts to John Postlethwaite of Dalton, who drove them to Hornby Fair. There the cattle were again seized and detained, despite the fact that Postlethwaite protested that they were Manx cattle and produced a certificate to that effect from the customs officers at Piel Fowdrey.[128] In 1677, customs officers at Liverpool seized about £100 sterling from three merchants, John Broughton of the Isle of Man, John Wattleworth of Ramsey and Thomas Callister,

[126] Lib. Scacc. 1673, 53.
[127] B. L. Add. MS 33,589, f. 230r. The Cattle Act of 1667 was not intended to be a permanent measure and it expired in March 1679. A new bill to prohibit the import of Irish livestock was passed in parliament in late 1680 and came into effect on February 2, 1681. See Edie, 'Irish Cattle Bills', p. 50; Woodward, 'Anglo-Irish Livestock Trade', pp. 501–2; 32 Chas. II, c. 2.
[128] L.R.O., QSP/446/6.

who were on their way back to the island after selling some Manx
cattle in England. The money was not returned to the men before
they had petitioned the Lord Treasurer, stressing the fact that the
cattle were 'of the breed' of the island.[129]

Although irksome to the merchants involved, incidents such as
these probably did little to discourage them from engaging in the
cattle trade. Nevertheless, the number of cattle shipped by both
native and foreign merchants declined during the last two decades of
the seventeenth century. For example, in 1684–5, a particularly bad
year, according to the waterbailiff's accounts, only two quick beasts
and two carcases were transported from Manx ports; a decade later,
in 1695–6, the figure was considerably higher: 580 live animals and
two carcases were exported, a total of 582 cattle. (Table 5.1). The
total for the latter year would, at first sight, seem to indicate a return
to the level of cattle exports in the early seventeenth century, but
closer examination of the accounts for 1695–6 reveals that in fact
only 226 quick beasts and two carcases were exported by merchants
in their own interest, the rest being shipped for the earl of Derby.[130]

Before about 1690, the cattle purchased in the island and shipped
for the earl of Derby are not listed in the waterbailiff's accounts,
chiefly because they were exported customs free. This makes it
difficult to assess the accuracy of the figures derived from this source.
Before 1601, when the inhabitants paid half their rents in kind, most
of the cattle 'bought' by the Lord were taken as provisions for the
officers and garrisons in the castles and only a relatively small
number of animals were exported to England for the use of the earl's
household. In 1586, for example, ten cattle were shipped from the
island by Robert Hill for Earl Henry, whose household then numbered about 118 individuals.[131] After the rents in kind were con-
verted to a double rent in money in 1601, the Lord's prerogative right
of purveyance was exercised to obtain cattle for the garrisons at the
special 'Lord's price;' the number of beasts exported to England for

---

[129] C.T.B. 1676–9, pp. 709, 743.
[130] M.M.L., I.O. 1680–9, Customs book, 1685; M.M.L., I.O. 1696–1704,
Customs book, 1696.
[131] M.M.L., I.O. 1570–99, Book of allowance, Peel Castle, 1586: carriages
and freights; F. R. Raines (ed.), *The Stanley Papers, pt. ii . The Derby
Household Books* (Chet. Soc., O.S., vol. xxxi, 1853), pp. 23–7. Cf. K. Mertes,
The English Noble Household, 1250–1600 (Oxford 1988), appendix A, p.
211.

the use of the Stanley household, however, remained low. In 1613, Lawrence Warton was paid 40s. for the freight of ten oxen for Countess Elizabeth and sixteen years later, in 1629, Ferdinando Fox transported thirty-three cattle to Lathom for James, Lord Strange.[132] In 1633, Strange, who acted as Lord of Man for his father, William, sixth earl of Derby, directed that 'there be provided forty Oxen for the use of my house,' and this seems to have been the general level of exports of cattle for such purposes in the years before 1640.[133]

After the restoration of the Stanleys in the Isle of Man in 1660, Charles, eighth earl of Derby found it necessary to obtain a certificate from the Commissioners of the Customs, discharging him from the payment of customs duties on provisions, including cattle, imported into England from the island for the use of his household in Lancashire.[134] This liberty to enter such goods without paying customs duty, which, it was claimed, had also been enjoyed by his father, Earl James, set limits on the amount of provisions which could be imported, the number of cattle being 200 head.[135] Whether or not Earl Charles observed these regulations is not certain, but it is clear that his son and successor, Earl William, did not. The ninth earl, who obtained renewals of the certificate in 1679, 1686 and 1691,[136] seems often to have ignored the limit placed on cattle imported into England from the island. An account of the goods imported for him at Liverpool between May and September 1685 reveals that a total of 238 cattle were landed from the Isle of Man during the period, 100 head of those being shipped in the Manx customs year 1684–5.[137] (Table 5.1). The demand for meat in England and a series of harvest and herring fishery failures in the island in the

---

[132] M.M.L., I.O. 1610–19, Book of allowance, Castle Rushen, 1613: freights and carriages; M.M.L., I.O. 1620–9, Book of allowance, Castle Rushen, 1629: freights and carriages.

[133] Lib. Scacc. 1633, 35. Detailed evidence of cattle exports for the Lord's household use in the later 1630s is wanting, but the indications from the levels in the preceding years suggest that this is probably an accurate assessment.

[134] M.M.L., MD/401/1717/1. The certificate was renewed in 1663 and 1667. M.M.L., MD/401/1717/4, MD/1717/15.

[135] M.M.L., MD/401/1717/54.

[136] M.M.L., MD/401/1717/52, MD/401/1717/53, MD/401/1717/54; M.M.L., MD/401/1718/47; M.M.L., MD/401/1719/1.

[137] M.M.L., MD/401/1718/38.

1690s encouraged Earl William to 'buy' cattle from the inhabitants in lieu of their money rents and to export the animals to sell on the English market. This accounts for the small number of individuals involved in the trade in 1695–6; only twelve merchants exported cattle in that year, compared to a total of fifty-two in 1629–30.[138] It also explains the fact that 354 cattle were shipped from the island on behalf of Earl William in 1695–6, almost all being certainly destined for Liverpool.[139] At the end of the seventeenth century, therefore, the export trade in cattle was being dominated, at least temporarily, by the earl of Derby. His role in the trade between 1660 and about 1690 is difficult to determine at present, and it may be that the slump in exports during these years is more apparent than real, but, if not, his activities helped to revive it during the 1690s.

b) Other Livestock Exports

The export of sheep and pigs was much less important than the shipment of cattle in the island's overseas trade. Before 1600, large numbers of sheep were exported. In 1579–80, for example, 422 sheep and ninety-five lambs, a total of 517 animals, were transported from the Isle of Man[140] and this level of trade was maintained into the 1590s. In 1593–4, 515 sheep and lambs were shipped through Manx ports to foreign markets, but the export trade seems then to have gone into irreversible decline. By 1604–5, the number of sheep exported had fallen to 152, and thereafter the island's export trade in sheep became negligible. (Table 5.1).

The island's export trade in pigs fell into decline even more rapidly. Exports of swine seem to have been relatively high in the late sixteenth century, with 365 pigs passing through Manx ports in 1579–80.[141] By the beginning of the seventeenth century, however, the number of pigs shipped had fallen to less than fifty and by 1640 the trade had all but ceased. (Table 5.1).

A modest trade in horses exported from the island continued throughout the late sixteenth and seventeenth centuries. Since the type of horse being shipped is not recorded in the waterbailiff's

---

[138] M.M.L., I.O. 1696–1704, Customs book, 1696; I. O. 1630–45, Water-bailiff's accounts, 1630.
[139] M.M.L., I.O. 1696–1704, Customs book, 1696.
[140] Cubbon, 'Maritime Commerce', p. 618.
[141] *ibid.*

accounts, however, it is impossible to determine whether these exports represent shipments of native Manx horses, re-exports of animals previously imported or a mixture of both.[142] The problem of assessing the importance of the trade in the Manx economy is rendered even more difficult by the fact that in some years the number of horses imported exceeded that of those exported (Tables 5.1 and 5.11). In 1579-80, for example, forty-nine horses were exported, while seventy were entered at the island's ports.[143] In other years, such as 1609-10, the total number of horses shipped from the island was much greater than the level of imports (Tables 5.1 and 5.11). The measures taken by the island's government in an effort to maintain and improve the quality of Manx horses, which have already been described,[144] were doubtless intended to reduce the dependence of the island on imported animals, but may also have had a beneficial effect on the export market, albeit on a limited scale. During the 1690s, at least some of the native Manx breed of horses were shipped both to England and Ireland; of the six horses exported in 1695–6, all but one were of the native breed, four being sent to Ireland and a single animal being transported to England.[145]

c) Animal Products: Hides, Skins and Wool

The skins and hides of animals reared in the island formed an important group of commodities in the Manx export trade. Large quantities of sheepskins and fells, lambskins and raw or untanned hides were shipped from the island's ports in the late sixteenth century. Like many other trades, the export of skins and hides expanded considerably towards the end of the century. In 1579-80, 2,628 sheepskins and fells were sent to foreign markets from the island, but this rose to 8,080 exported to Chester alone in the year ending at Michaelmas 1593 and 5,292 exported in general in 1593–4.[146] Lambskin exports showed a similar increase, from 1,062 in 1579–80 to 3,356 in 1593–4. The shipments of untanned hides,

---

[142] For details of the native breed of Manx horses, see chapter 2, pp. 88–9.
[143] Cubbon, 'Maritime Commerce', p. 618.
[144] See chapter 2, p. 88.
[145] M.M.L., I.O. 1696–1704, Customs book, 1696.
[146] Cubbon, Maritime Commerce, p. 620; P.R.O., E 190/1326/6, cited in D. M. Woodward, 'The Chester Leather Industry, 1558–1625', *T.H.S.L.C.*, vol. cxix (1967), p. 71.

however, remained almost at the same level of about 160 dicker.[147]
(Table 5.2).

Table 5.2 *Exports of Skins and Hides from the Isle of Man
(Years ending at June 24)*

Year	Sheep-skins[1]	Lamb-skins	Calf-skins	Rabbit-skins	Goat-skins	Kid-skins	Mixed skins	Hides (dickers)[2]	
								raw	tanned
1594	5292	3356	—	360	126	384	2580	157.8	—
1600	2308	4434	—	240	—	—	2040	77.7	24.0
1605	2400	5076	24	660	—	—	1353	48.2	—
1610	1348	3120	343	540	—	—	2086	64.8	—
1618	1886	5112	126	360	—	—	2100	66.5	—
1630	528	1536	60	240	—	—	2100	54.6	76.0
1647	2106	3124	—	600	1	—	1118	2.0	26.0
1667	900	720	—	480	24	—	900	16.0	2.0
1685	—	1080	139	708	170	—	750	29.8	25.7
1696	144	3012	234	1698	570	—	998	76.8	8.4

Sources: See Table 5.1

Notes.
1. Sheepskins and sheepfells.
2. The number of hides to the dicker varied. There were eight ox hides to
the dicker, but ten cow hides. Since a distinction is not always drawn,
hides of an unspecified nature have been taken to be cow hides.

The determination of the earl and his officers to make the most of
the island's resources is clearly demonstrated by the periodic orders
restraining the shipment of hides. As part of their regular business,
the governor and officers discussed the stocks of provisions and
other commodities to decide which items could be exported without
loss to the island and which goods had to be 'restrained.'[148] In December 1594, such a discussion took place at a session of the Chancery
Court in the Exchequer in Castle Rushen after the governor,

[147] Cubbon, 'Maritime Trade', p. 620. Compare the similar expansion, on a
much greater scale, of Chester's export trade with Ireland during the same
period. Woodward, *Elizabethan Chester*, pp. 12–22.
[148] See, for example, the meeting of the officers at Castle Rushen in October
1578. M.M.L., I.O. 1570–99, Book of licences, 1578.

Randulph Stanley, had received a request from 'divers and sundrie persons [who were] willing and desirous to have lycense for Corne and hydes.' In reply to the governor's enquiry

> whether it standeth with the better Comoditie and state of thisle to lycense the sayd Corne and hydes or to restrayne the transportacon, the demster, viz. Thomas Samsbury and others in the behalf of the Cuntrie doe answere in the behalfe of the sayd Cuntrie men That they thinke it best that hydes shall be restrayned and kept for the marchant Stranger, and that such as shall have occasion to transport their beeves in their hydes, the said hydes to be returned by the same boate upon paine of xxs. every hyde.[149]

This procedure and the order for a restraint of the trade thus guaranteed that the island would benefit from the disposal of the hides rather than merely a few merchants. Such steps, which were similar in intent to the assessments of grain in the parishes in times of shortage or dearth, were necessary if the island's economy were to remain healthy.

In the early seventeenth century, exports of hides fell to less than half the amount shipped on average in the last two decades of the sixteenth century and, while shipments of sheepskins and fells declined, the number of lambskins exported rose to 5,076 in 1604–5 and 5,112 in 1617–18. Inevitably, the exports of skins and hides fluctuated, depending to a large extent on the judgement of the Lord's Council as to the economic condition of the island, but, nevertheless, two Scottish merchants, Robert Lawson and David Murrey, considered that the trade offered sufficiently good prospects of a return to negotiate for 'the onelie libertie of transportacon of all the sheepe skins, goteskins, lambskins, kid skines and Cony skines' with the governor, John Ireland, in 1611.[150] Although 'all others [were] debarred' from shipping skins by the grant of this monopoly, it is difficult to estimate its impact since it is not clear when exactly it came into operation. Nevertheless, it was not renewed in 1612, perhaps because Lawson and Murrey had failed to make a profit; on the other hand, Countess Elizabeth, who took charge of the government of the island

---

[149] Lib. Canc. 1595, 6.
[150] M.M.L., I.O. 1610–19, Waterbailiff's accounts, 1611, 1612. Lawson and Murrey paid the sum of £5 in total for this monopoly.

on behalf of her husband, William, sixth earl of Derby, in that year, jealously guarded the prerogative rights, dues and privileges of the lordship of Man and was unlikely to accept any bargain which might leave the Lord at a disadvantage.[151]

As far as can be deduced from a small sample of waterbailiff's accounts, the export of skins continued at much the same level as that attained in the early seventeenth century, apart from the occasional fluctuation, until about 1650, when the trade began to decline somewhat in significance. During the unusual conditions of the 1640s, the island's trade seems to have been largely unaffected, and in 1646–7, native and foreign merchants were able to ship 2,106 sheepskins and fells and 3,124 lambskins through the ports. After the middle of the century, however, and despite the fact that there were sometimes years when the island's export trade was relatively buoyant, the trade in skins and fells became a much less important element in the Manx economy. Towards the end of the seventeenth century, coney skins and goat skins were apparently accounting for a growing proportion of the trade and, while lambskins were being transported in numbers roughly equivalent to those exported in 1599–1600, the traffic in sheepskins was being conducted at a much reduced level. (Table 5.2).

Shipments of untanned hides dwindled to almost nothing in the 1640s, the decade of the 'War of the Three Kingdoms', but gradually recovered thereafter. By about 1700, the export trade in such hides had returned to approximately the same level as that of a century earlier. Tanned hides, which had never been exported in any quantity, played very little part in the island's export trade and in many cases anyway probably represented re-exports of leather produced elsewhere. Some of the tanned hides exported, however, such as the dozen shipped to Scotland from Ramsey by John Young in May 1685, were doubtless processed in the island.[152] (Table 5.2).

In the late sixteenth century, the Isle of Man exported large quantities of wool in addition to the fleeces shipped with skins in the form of sheepfells. Exports of wool from the island amounted to 1,770 stones in 1579–80[153] and 1,655 stones in 1593–4, and at least

---

[151] The close supervision of the island's government by Countess Elizabeth is examined in Coward, *Stanleys*, pp. 59–61.

[152] M.M.L., I.O. 1680–9, Customs book, 1685.

[153] Cubbon, 'Maritime Commerce', pp. 620–1. This figure, and all those relating to wool exports, do not include the wool shipped in the form of sheepfells.

some of this wool was destined for the looms of the woollen textile weavers of south Lancashire. (Table 5.3).

Table 5.3 *Exports of Wool and Herring from the Isle of Man*
(Years ending at June 24)

Year	Wool		Herring		
	stones	tons	hogsheads	barrels	maze
1594	1665	1	—	—	—
1600	439	—	1	1	—
1605	435	—	8	—	—
1610	113	—	—	—	—
1618	614	54.5	—	71	3
1630	684	2	—	139	1
1647	175	—	—	60	—
1667	39	54.5	—	485	339
1685	335	—	—	388	1
1696	395	—	—	—	—

Sources: See Table 5.1

Supplies of wool within the county had proved to be insufficient to meet demand by the second half of the sixteenth century and, consequently, the raw material of the industry was being brought in from elsewhere in England and imported from Ireland and, to a certain extent, the Isle of Man via Liverpool and probably Chester.[154] Imports of Manx wool at the latter port reached a peak for the late sixteenth century of 281 stones in 1592–3, a year which also witnessed an unusually large amount of Irish wool landed at Chester.[155] Liverpool was the more important of the two ports in the wool trade, despite being merely a creek of Chester,[156] but shipments of Manx wool to the Mersey port were often very few in number and the cargoes very small. In 1603–4, for example, there was only one consignment of wool shipped to Liverpool and that comprised a bag containing 'eight

[154] Lowe, *Lancashire Textile Industry*, pp. 10–19; Woodward, *Elizabethan Chester*, pp. 7–9.
[155] Lowe, *Lancashire Textile Industry*, Table 3, p. 14; Woodward, *Elizabethan Chester*, Table 1, p. 7. The figures in these tables, based on the same source, are slightly at variance.
[156] Woodward, *Elizabethan Chester*, pp. 7–9.

stone manske woole.'[157] Equally small amounts of wool were also exported from the island to North Wales, as in August 1584, when William Christian landed four stones of wool at Beaumaris.[158]

Even before the end of the sixteenth century, however, exports of wool from the island had fallen drastically and never returned to the level of the trade before about the mid-1590s. The reasons for this are not clear. There certainly seems to have been no attempt by the English government to interfere with the import of Manx wool into England and, indeed, the clothiers called before a committee established by the Privy Council to examine the causes of the decline of the English cloth trade in 1622 wanted positively to encourage wool imports from the island.[159] Nevertheless, exports from Man remained at a relatively low level. The efforts to establish woollen cloth manufacturing in the last decade of the seventeenth century had the inevitable effect of reducing the amount of surplus wool which otherwise would have been available for export and accounts for the absence of wool from the list of commodities which, the officers informed James, tenth earl of Derby in August 1709, would have to be shipped abroad to supply the needs of the island.[160]

d) Herring

In spite of the importance of the herring in the Manx economy,[161] the fish is seldom mentioned in the waterbailiff's accounts as an export before the second half of the seventeenth century. This was partly because a large proportion of the catch was taken by Manx fishermen and consumed in the island and partly because of the reluctance of both natives and foreigners, at least in the years before 1613, to participate in the fishery because of the heavy impositions levied on each catch in kind and subsequently in coin on behalf of the Lord of Man. Herring were probably only exported after a successful fishery, as, it would seem, in 1617; all the shipments in the customs

---

[157] P.R.O., E 190/1328/11.

[158] Lewis, *Welsh Port Books*, p. 250. Christian imported a single stone of wool at the same port in the following March. *ibid*, p. 253.

[159] Bowden, *Wool Trade*, pp. 191–2.

[160] L.R.O., DDKe 80. John Rowe, Bishop Wilson *et al.* to James, tenth earl of Derby, August 4, 1709. For details of the cloth manufacturing project, see chapter 3, pp. 176–83.

[161] The herring fishery is discussed in chapter 2, pp. 110–24.

year 1617-18 were made between the end of September and the middle of the following February, that is, during the later stages of the 'Herring Fishing Time, and after the completion of fishing.'[162] The same pattern of export shipments can be traced in other years when the fishery proved successful.[163] (Table 5.3). The level of exports could, and did, therefore, vary considerably from year to year, depending on the appearance or otherwise of the herring shoals. It may also have been affected by the clause in the Navigation Act of 1660 concerning fish caught and imported into England by foreigners, which stipulated that such fish 'shall pay double aliens' customs.'[164] The figures for 1666–7, however, suggest that this provision had little practical effect.

e) Grain

In the same way that herring exports were determined to a large extent by the success or failure of the annual fishery, shipments of grain from the island varied according to the quality of the harvest. In years when the harvest was deficient or worse, the export trade in grain was restrained in order to ensure that the domestic market was served, although licences to ship grain were occasionally granted to farmers who undertook to supply the local markets with an amount of similar size to that transported.[165] After harvests which were average, good or abundant, considerable quantities of wheat, barley, oats and malt were exported from the island.

The trade in exported grain seems to have been at its height, so far as the accounts can show, during the late sixteenth and early seventeenth centuries. In 1579–80, sixty-five bolls and fifty-seven barrels of wheat, 897 bolls and 352 barrels of barley, 112 bolls and four barrels of malt and 581 bolls and twelve barrels of oats were shipped from Manx ports.[166] Exports of wheat, which does not grow well in

---

[162] M.M.L., I.O. 1610–19, Waterbailiff's accounts, 1618.
[163] See, for example, M.M.L., I.O. 1660–71, Customs book, 1667. For further details of the history of the herring fishery, see Moore, *History*, vol. ii, pp. 952–6; W. C. Smith, *A Short History of the Irish Sea Herring Shoals* (1923).
[164] 12 Chas. II, c. 18; J. Thirsk and J. P. Cooper (eds), *Seventeenth-Century Economic Documents* (Oxford, 1972), p. 521.
[165] See, for example, the case of John Stevenson of Balladoole in 1596 in chapter 2, p. 93.
[166] Cubbon, *Maritime Commerce*, pp. 618–19.

the island, and which may consequently include a proportion of re-exported grain, sometimes exceeded 200 bolls and the same number of barrels. In 1578–9, 294 bolls and 258 barrels were licensed for export, while in 1629-30, 203 bolls and 270 barrels were transported.[167] (Table 5.4).

Table 5.4 *Exports of Grain from the Isle of Man*
(Years ending at June 24)

Year	Wheat		Barley		Oats		Malt	
	bolls	barrels	bolls	barrels	bolls	barrels	bolls	barrels
1594	33	—	747	90	745	60	4	—
1600	136	134	329	140	1367	185	731	42
1605	118	220	367	253	406	—	349	68
1610	215.5	103.5	643	24	232	—	224.5	6
1618	170.5	66	473.5	26	395	—	1184	—
1630	203	270	791	292	—	—	68	8
1647	18	35	—	162	—	—	376	35
1667	16	38	—	50	—	—	—	3.
1685	3.5	9	204	90	15	61	10.5	12
1696	20	—	12	—	—	—	41	—

Sources: See Table 5.1

Barley, which was more suited to Manx conditions than wheat, was much more significant in the export trade. Although shipments rarely reached the level of 1579–80, exports of barley were always considerably higher than those of wheat. The peak of the export trade in barley in the early seventeenth century seems to have been in 1629-30, when 791 bolls and 292 barrels were shipped. Exports of oats, which was of similar importance to barley in the Manx economy, were generally higher than the level of wheat exports and more akin to the quantity of barley transported from the island. In 1599-1600, shipments of oats reached an extremely high point, with 1,367 bolls and 185 barrels passing through Manx ports. (Table 5.4). Malt exports, like all grain exports, fluctuated a great deal, the most productive year among those sampled being 1617–18, when 1,184 bolls were sent abroad. (Table 5.4).

[167] M.M.L., I.O. 1570–99, Book of licences, 1579, cited in *ibid*, p. 618.

In the later seventeenth century, the export trade in grain seems to have been much reduced, even when the island enjoyed reasonably good harvests. The series of bad harvests in the early 1670s and especially during the 1690s had a naturally depressing effect on the prospects of the trade and it never recovered the vitality of the period before 1640.

f) Cloth

Considerable quantities of raw cloth were exported from the island before the end of the sixteenth century. Most, if not all, of this cloth was 'course frize,' as the officers informed Earl James in 1709.[168] In 1579–80, 2,137 yards were shipped and, though this level of exports was not sustained until the end of the century, the island was still able to send 1,372 yards of raw cloth, 130 yards of woollen cloth and four yards of walked cloth to foreign markets in 1593–4. (Table 5.5).

Table 5.5 *Export of Cloth from the Isle of Man (in yards)*
(Years ending at June 24)

Year	Raw cloth	Woollen cloth	Walked cloth	Russet	Linen cloth	Hewerdsen cloth
1594	1372[1]	130	4	—	—	—
1600	879	—	412	—	35	—
1605	348	—	—	—	(1 footpack)	—
1610	140	4	—	—	22	—
1618	321	—	—	—	—	—
1630	10	—	—	—	—	—
1647	—	417	—	—	(3.5 pieces)	—
1667	—	—	—	—	20	—
1685	—	234	—	156	166	—
1696	35	2127	—	899.5	2602	1002

Sources: See Table 5.1

Note.
1. Plus 128 slatts of raw cloth. A slatt was a piece of cloth approximately 50 inches in length and between 20–23 inches in width. *O.E.D.*, *sub* slatt.

---

[168] L.R.O., DDKe 80. Rowe, Wilson *et al.* to Derby, August 4, 1709.

After the turn of the century, exports of unfinished woollen cloth declined significantly. Annual totals of cloth exports were frequently between 100 and 450 yards, but in some years the amount was even smaller, as in 1629–30, when a mere ten yards of raw cloth was transported. In other years, such as 1666–7, no woollen cloth was exported at all. The trade only began to revive towards the end of the seventeenth century, and particularly in the 1690s, under the stimulus of projects initiated by William Sacheverell, deputy governor in 1692 and governor from June 1693 until the summer of 1695.[169]

Sacheverell's main interests were the establishment of a trading company and the encouragement of linen manufacturing in the island with the aid of skilled workers from outside. In spite of his failure to achieve the former, however, his activities certainly seem to have had a beneficial effect on linen exports, even allowing for the fact that some of the shipments may have been re-exports. Very little linen cloth left the island during the first half of the seventeenth century, but towards 1700, particularly after the passing of the Act 'for setting up a Linnen manufacture' in 1692, exports began to increase markedly. In 1695–6, 2,602 yards of linen cloth were shipped from Manx ports, mainly to England.[170] (Table 5.5).

Although Sacheverell's energies were particularly devoted to the linen manufacture, the production and export of other types of cloth rose as a result of the general impetus provided by the implementation of his plans. By 1695–6, exports of woollen cloth had increased dramatically to 2,127 yards; thirty-five yards of raw cloth, nearly 900 yards of russet cloth and about 1,000 yards of 'hewerdsen' cloth were also transported from the island, the latter exclusively to England.[171] (Table 5.5). From this modest level, the island's cloth industry continued to develop and to diversify in the eighteenth century, exporting an average of more than 50,000 yards of linen each year between 1780 and 1800.[172]

---

[169] The projects devised by Sacheverell are outlined in chapter 3, pp. 175–88.
[170] M.M.L., I.O. 1696–1704, Customs book, 1696. The fortunes of the linen cloth industry in the late eighteenth century are briefly sketched by Moore, *History*, vol. ii, pp. 590–3.
[171] M.M.L., I.O. 1696–1704, Customs book, 1696.
[172] Moore, *History*, vol. ii, p. 592 n. 5; T. Quayle, *General View of the Agriculture of the Isle of Man* (1812), appendix D, p. 179.

g) Other Exports

Apart from the commodities already mentioned, the island exported a variety of goods which were produced by the farmers. These included ale and beer, particularly the former, although it was the latter which achieved something of a reputation. In January 1673, Richard Walmsley of Clayton-le-Moors in Lancashire wrote to Deputy Governor Henry Nowell, asking him to send some 'excellent sort of strong beer made in your island, such as my Lord of Derby drinks, some times, at Knowsley.'[173] Large quantities of honey and tallow were also exported, as were a substantial number of slates, at least during the 1690s and afterwards. The growing scale of the trade in slates is clearly indicated by the speculation of the officers in the early eighteenth century that the island might be able to produce up to 200,000 slates and 5,000 flagstones in a single year.[174]

V. THE IMPORT TRADE OF THE ISLE OF MAN

The commodities which comprised the island's import trade during the late sixteenth and seventeenth centuries can be divided into two groups : firstly, the raw materials which were either scarce or absent from the Isle of Man, such as coal, timber and iron, and, secondly, manufactured goods, including sickles, scythes, hats and cloth, and luxury items, such as wines and spices. The nature of this trade remained relatively stable throughout the period, although the scale on which it was conducted and the scope of the goods involved expanded significantly. The traffic in tobacco, for example, which did not exist before about 1630, became by 1700 perhaps the most important sector of the island's import trade.

a) Coal

There are no deposits of coal in the Isle of Man and, consequently, all supplies of the fuel in the sixteenth and seventeenth centuries had to be imported from England. This fact alone made coal comparatively expensive in the island, and ensured that its use as a domestic fuel was limited to the houses of the officers and larger farmers and

[173] *H.M.C. Kenyon*, p. 95.
[174] L.R.O., DDKe 80. Rowe, Wilson *et al.* to Derby, August 4, 1709.

to the garrisons.[175] As timber was in very short supply in the island and imported wood was invariably destined for construction work of one sort or another, coal was the principal industrial fuel. By the end of the seventeenth century, it was being used in brewing, at least for the earl of Derby, the production of lime and brickmaking[176] and there is also evidence to suggest that, despite the occasional shortages of raw materials, blacksmiths in the island worked with coal in their forges. In the late 1640s, William Blundell observed that when 'a Manksman in the country have his plowshare to be mended, or any man's horse wanteth a shoe, or but a nail being loose, and either of these do come to make use of the smith, they must both bring coals to make the fire, and iron to make the shoe or nail, for the smith is not provided with either.'[177]

Even before 1600, substantial quantities of coal were being landed in the island. In 1593–4, as much as 440 tons were imported, at least some of the coal being shipped from Parton in Cumberland.[178] (Table 5.6). This trade suffered something of a setback, albeit a temporary one, in December 1599, when the English government imposed a new tax on coal exported from all English and Welsh ports, which was levied at the rate of 5s. per Newcastle chaldron of about two tons. Coal imports into the island actually ceased for a period of about six months after the introduction of this tax, as mine-owners and merchants protested to the government. Complaints from consumers in Ireland resulted in the removal of the levy on shipments of coal to Dublin and other Irish ports, but similar petitions from the Channel Islands and the Isle of Man had little

---

[175] In some areas of England where coal was readily obtainable, it was 'still overwhelmingly a cheap fuel for the poor' during the sixteenth and seventeenth centuries. D. C. Coleman, *Industry in Tudor and Stuart England* (1975), p. 47. Turf, or peat, was the domestic fuel used by the vast majority of Manx people.

[176] For details of brickmaking, see chapter 3, pp. 182–83.

[177] Blundell, *History*, vol. i, p. 83.

[178] M.M.L., I.O. 1570–99, Customs book, 1594; waterbailiff's accounts, 1594. Coal shipments from Parton to Ireland, the major market for Cumberland coal, do not appear to have commenced until 1605, although the fact that very few port books survive for the Cumbrian ports before the late seventeenth century makes this difficult to substantiate. J. V. Beckett, *Coal and Tobacco. The Lowthers and the Economic Development of West Cumberland, 1660–1760* (Cambridge 1981), p. 39.

Table 5.6 *Imports of Coal and Iron into the Isle of Man*
(Years ending at June 24)

Year	Coal				Iron	
	tons	'loads'[1]	part loads	barrels	tons	cwt[2]
1594	—	11	—	—	9	7
1600	26	2	—	20	4	7
1605	38	5	—	—	1	4
1610	74	7	—	—	6	5
1618	46	5	—	2	6	16
1630	49	8	—	—	4	10
1647	86	19	6	—	5	12
1667	110[3]	10	5	—	7	13
1685	—	12	—	—	6	2
1696	119	—	—	5	9	5

Sources: See Table 5.1

Notes.

1. Vessels are sometimes entered in the waterbailiff's accounts as 'laden with coals'. Such a 'load' may have been a variable amount, depending on the size of the ship or, perhaps more likely, it may have referred to a 'keel load', a measure of twenty chaldrons or forty tons before 1676, when it changed to sixteen chaldrons or thirty-two tons. Zupko, *British Weights and Measures*, appendix B, p. 151. If this was the case, the imports for the period, converting whole loads into tons, would be as follows:

1594	440 tons	1630	369 tons
1600	106 tons	1647	846 tons
1605	238 tons	1647	510 tons
1610	354 tons	1685	192 tons
1618	246 tons	1696	119 tons

2. Figures to the nearest hundredweight.

3. This total includes eight chaldrons, probably the equivalent of sixteen tons, if measured by the standard used on the west coast of England and Wales throughout the seventeenth century: 1 chaldron = 2 tons. Nef, *Rise of the British Coal Industry*, vol, ii, appendix C, p. 370.

immediate effect. In 1605, however, James I agreed to exempt from the levy coal shipped to the island, the Channel Islands and Scotland,[179] but it seems that imports into the Isle of Man were already recovering, with perhaps 238 tons being unloaded at Manx ports in 1604–5. (Table 5.6). In the year ending at October 29, 1605, ninety-two tons were sent to the island from Workington alone.[180]

During the first half of the seventeenth century, the consumption of coal in the island varied considerably, but was generally between 200 and 400 tons a year. About 150 tons were imported from Workington in 1615–16,[181] and almost 250 tons, doubtless mostly from Cumberland, were unloaded in the island's ports in 1617–18. (Table 5.6).

The exemption of this traffic from the levy on coal exports was something of a problem for the Crown, since it offered the opportunity for smuggling, on the pretext that the coal was destined for the Isle of Man, and because the farmers of the impost claimed deductions from the rent which they paid to the king to the full amount of the tax levied on coal shipped to exempted ports.[182] Efforts were made to reintroduce the tax on the coal trade with Ireland, Scotland, the Channel Islands and the Isle of Man on several occasions, as in 1620, when the impost was raised from 5s. to 6s. 8d. and the syndicate negotiating for a new farm of the levy requested that consignments transported to the exempted destinations should pay the old rate. Although this provision was included in the grant issued in January 1621,[183] it was strongly and successfully attacked by the authorities in Dublin.[184] The farmers nevertheless attempted to have a quota fixed for shipments to the Channel Islands and the Isle of Man and, in respect of the latter at least, they seem to have achieved their goal by the late 1630s. In June 1638, they directed Henry Skelton, their deputy in Carlisle, 'to demand and receyve heareafter

---

[179] J. U. Nef, *The Rise of the British Coal Industry* (1932, reprinted 1966), vol. ii, pp. 220–1.

[180] B. L. Add. MS 34,318, f. 29.

[181] Appleby, *Famine in Tudor and Stuart England*, p. 87; Nef, *British Coal Industry*, vol. ii, appendix D, facing p. 380.

[182] Nef, *British Coal Industry*, vol. ii, pp. 220–1.

[183] W. Notestein, F. H. Relf and H. Simpson (eds), *Commons Debates, 1621* (New Haven, Conn., 1935), vol. vii, appendix B, pt. i, p. 431.

[184] Nef, *British Coal Industry*, vol. ii, p. 221.

but the sum of vi.d. per ton ffor 200 ton of Coales to bee transported out of your porte ffor the provicon of the Isle of Man ffrom all such Masters of ships or Barques as shalbee deputed under the hand of the Captain of the Isle or under the hande of one of the Deemsters of the same to bee transported ffor the said Island.' If exports to the island exceeded 200 tons in any one year, Skelton was ordered to extract 5s. per chaldron on every cargo above that level.[185]

The introduction of a quota system on the export of coal from England and Wales seems to have had a negligible effect on imports into the Isle of Man. Even the outbreak of war in England in 1642 seems to have had a minimal impact on the island's trade, although it is impossible to be certain about this from a limited sample of the waterbailiff's accounts. Nevertheless, in some years coal imports seem to have reached new heights. In 1646–7, for example, imports may have reached nearly 850 tons. According to William Blundell, this coal was shipped 'at very easy rates both from Whitehaven in Cumberland and Weirwater [Wyre] and Liverpool in Lancashire, or from Bagot [Bagillt], Moston and the north parts of Carnarvenshire and Flintshire in Wales.'[186]

The level of coal imports in the later seventeenth century fluctuated considerably and on several occasions there appears to have been a shortage of the fuel. In some years, such as 1666–7, imports were well above the pre-1640 average annual range of shipments, but in others they were low and supply was unable to meet demand. In May 1692, Deputy Governor William Sacheverell informed Earl William that 'your peeple want cole extremly, not only for your brick[making], which will require great quantitys, but even your necessary bruing could not be perfected had I not accidentally loden some Cole in my vessell; besides your garrisons must be supplyd before winter.'[187] Imports of coal in 1695–6 came to only 119 tons, a figure which in isolation may indicate nothing more than one of several years when shipments of coal to the island were relatively few, but which nevertheless also suggests that Professor Nef's

---

[185] Lib. Scacc. 1638, 61. Ralph Freeman, Sir Thomas Bludder and Sir John Trevor to Henry Skelton, 'Deputie to the Coale Fermors at the port of Carlile', June 19, 1638.

[186] Blundell, *History*, vol. i, p. 48.

[187] M.M.L., MD/401/1719/23. Sacheverell to Derby, n.d. (May 10–23, 1692, based on internal evidence).

estimate of annual coal consumption in the Isle of Man in this period as not exceeding between 1,000 and 2,000 tons is wildly inaccurate.[188] (Table 5.6).

b) Timber

The limited amount of woodland in the island and the efforts of the authorities to conserve it[189] meant that all the timber required for construction work and other purposes had to be imported. This timber came in many forms and in substantial quantities every year, mainly from Ireland.[190] Joists, poles and boards of various types – deal, ash, oak – were imported for use in building in the towns and the castles and oars, boat stems, poles and spars were brought in for the construction of small boats and the repair of such boats and larger vessels. In 1593–4, for example, more than 3,000 boards and 1,000 carpoles were landed in Manx ports, together with over 200 oars.[191] Barrel staves were also imported in sizeable amounts for making the casks in which to store and ship salted herring and other commodities. In 1604–5, more than 450 staves were unloaded in the island and in 1617–18, imports reached over 6,000 in total.[192] Even in years when the herring catch was reputedly poor, as in

---

[188] Nef, *British Coal Industry*, vol. i, p. 91 n. 1. Professor Nef's figures for the production of English coalfields between 1550 and 1700 have also been widely criticised for exaggerating the development of the industry during this period. Coleman, *Industry in Tudor and Stuart England*, pp. 46–7; J. L. Langton, 'Coal Output in South-West Lancashire, 1590–1799', *Ec.H.R.*, 2nd series, vol. xxv (1972), pp. 28–54; *idem, Geographical Change and Industrial Revolution: Coal Mining in South West Lancashire, 1590–1799* (Cambridge 1979).

[189] See chapter 2, p. 80, n. 16.

[190] The origin of the shipments is not stated in the waterbailiff's accounts, but, since timber formed one of the chief exports of Ulster and Munster, especially in the early seventeenth century, and many of the merchants transporting the boards, staves and other timber can be identified as Irish or Manx, there can be little doubt that these items were anything other than Irish exports. E. M. McCracken, *The Irish Woods Since Tudor Times: Distribution and Exploitation* (Newton Abbot, 1971), ch. 4.

[191] M.M.L., I.O. 1570–99, Customs book, 1594; waterbailiff's accounts, 1594.

[192] M.M.L., I.O. 1600–9, Ingates and outgates, 1605; M.M.L., I.O. 1610–19, Waterbailiff's accounts, 1618.

1695, the number of barrel staves entered could reach an equally high level.[193]

c) Iron and Lead

Small quantities of iron were imported into the island on a regular basis to supply the needs of the garrisons and the smiths in the towns and parishes. The amounts were typically between about four and ten tons and were shipped from Ireland and Spain. (Table 5.6). On at least one occasion in the late seventeenth century, iron was brought in from Cumberland. In 1671, the Quaker William Callow of Ballafayle, Maughold, purchased some iron from Force Forge, to the south of Hawkshead, in the county, but this was the only such transaction with this smelting works.[194]

Lead was also imported, but in very small quantities. In some years, less than one hundredweight entered the island, but at other times, as in 1666–7 and 1684–5, imports rose to 100 hundredweight.[195] Some of the demand for lead in the island was undoubtedly met by the limited production of the small Manx mines.[196]

d) Salt

The importance of fish, and especially herring, in the Manx diet and to some extent as an element in the island's export trade made salt a vital commodity. A 'Certayne Portion' of salt was produced in the island by brine-evaporation,[197] but, nevertheless, the inhabitants

---

[193] M.M.L., I.O. 1696–1704, Customs book, 1696. Firewood was imported on a very few occasions. In June 1599, for example, John Norres landed 'firewood [and] other tymber not ratable' at Douglas and in February 1630, William Quay unloaded 1,000 'fagotts' at Peel. M.M.L., I.O. 1600–9, Ingates and outgates, 1600; M.M.L., I.O. 1630–45, Waterbailiff's accounts, 1630.

[194] B. G. Awty, 'Force Forge in the Seventeenth Century', *T.C.W.A.A.S.*, vol. lxxvii (1977), p. 106; C. B. Phillips, 'The Cumbrian Iron Industry in the Seventeenth Century', in W. Chaloner and B. M. Ratcliffe (eds), *Trade and Transport. Essays in Economic History in Honour of T. S. Willan* (Manchester, 1977), p. 7.

[195] M.M.L., I.O. 1660–71, Customs book, 1667; M.M.L., I.O. 1680–9, Customs book, 1685.

[196] For details of Manx mining, see chapter 3, pp. 183–88.

[197] P.R.O., SP16/539/120.

were largely dependent upon imports from abroad – from France, particularly Brittany, and to a lesser degree, Spain and Portugal. In May 1594, William Abbey arrived at Derbyhaven with a cargo of nine barrels of 'portingall' [Portuguese] salt and twelve barrels of 'bretish' [Breton] salt.[198] Only a relatively small number of entries in the waterbailiff's accounts, however, record the origins of the salt in this way. Much of the salt imported which is not identified is likely to have been of continental origin, since nearly all of the coarser grades derived from seawater, which were used for preserving foodstuffs, were produced in France in quantity for export, the principal production area being the Bay of Bourgneuf.[199] Some of the salt which reached the island was clearly re-exported from English or Welsh ports rather than being shipped directly from continental Europe. In July 1587, for instance, John Corrin exported eighty barrels of 'bay salt' from Beaumaris to Man.[200] Other consignments were probably sent directly to the island, such as the eighteen tons of French salt landed by 'Peter John' of 'Croswicke' [Le Croisic] at Douglas in April 1630.[201] Some English salt was imported into the island, but was, it appears, re-exported. David Murrey, the head of one branch of the Scottish merchant family settled in Douglas since the early seventeenth century, shipped thirty tons of such salt to Scotland in October 1695.[202]

Salt imports varied considerably from year to year, perhaps according to the expectation of the success or failure of the herring fishery. (Table 5.7). In some years there certainly appears to have been a concentration of the trade in the months between June and December. In the customs year 1629–30, for instance, ten out of twelve shipments of salt landed in the island were entered between July and December 1629 accounting for approximately 75 per cent of the total amount of salt imported. Even in years when the seasonality of the imports is less pronounced, such as 1617–18, when

---

[198] M.M.L., I.O. 1570–99, Waterbailiff's accounts, 1594.

[199] A. Bridbury, *England and the Salt Trade in the Later Middle Ages* (Oxford 1955), pp. 56–75, 114. The salt produced in the 'wich' towns of Cheshire and in Worcestershire was of much higher quality and more expensive than French salt. In 1599, the price of such salt was about twice that of French salt. P.R.O., SP 63/203/105.

[200] Lewis, *Welsh Port Books*, p. 260.

[201] M.M.L., I.O. 1630–45, Waterbailiff's accounts, 1630.

[202] M.M.L., I.O. 1696–1704, Customs book, 1696.

Table 5.7 *Imports of Salt, Soap, Hops, Tobacco and Wine into the Isle of Man (Years ending at June 24)*

Year	Salt[1]		Soap firkins[2]	Tobacco		Hops	Wine
	tons	barrels	firkins[2]	cwt.	lbs	lbs	tuns
1594	27	155	10	4	—	1240	19
1600	5	171	31	—	—	874	29
1605	25	22	11	—	—	304	25
1610	1	368	41	1	—	838	21
1618	15	629	32	4	—	1086	18
1630	67	204	46	—	104	1646	21
1647	12	145	59	⌐1	2242	2102	18
1667	10	94	13	—	1046	2296	2
1685	59	6	3	18	4597	2980	25
1969	108	14	—	11	22638	2584	—

Sources: See Table 5.1.

Notes.

1. The relationship between the 'barrel' and the 'ton' of salt is not clear. If the ratio of barrels to the ton was the same as that calculated by Dr A. R. Bridbury for England in the late medieval period, with ten barrels equivalent to one ton, the figures for imports would be as follows (to the nearest ton):

1594	42 tons	1630	87 tons
1600	22 tons	1647	26 tons
1605	27 tons	1667	19 tons
1610	38 tons	1685	60 tons
1618	78 tons	1696	110 tons

See A. R. Bridbury, *England and the Salt Trade in the Later Middle Ages* (Oxford, 1955), appendix B, p. 160.

2. One firkin of soap = eight gallons. *O.E.D.*, *sub* firkin.

four out of eight shipments fell within the period from June to December, the larger cargoes tended to be brought in just before, during or immediately after the fishery.[203]

---

[203] M.M.L., I.O. 1610–19, Waterbailiff's accounts, 1618; M.M.L., I.O. 1630–45, waterbailiff's accounts, 1630.

e) Hops

Hops, which were apparently introduced into south-east England from continental Europe in the early sixteenth century,[204] were imported for use in the brewing of beer, both in the garrisons and in the towns and countryside. William Blundell claimed in the late 1640s that the Manx did not generally drink beer or ale 'till they meet at markets, where they will as familiarly, and with as much facility, drive it down their throats.'[205] An examination of the court records and the efforts of the authorities to regulate the brewing and con-sumption of ale and beer indicates that this is a far from accurate picture.[206] Certainly the notable general increase in the import of hops during the seventeenth century, after a decline during the period when the island was in the hands of the English Crown (1595–1612), suggests that the production, if not the consumption, of beer in the island was rising. Small quantities of Manx beer were exported before the later years of the century – in most years amounting to less than ten barrels – but even in the two decades before 1700, when in exceptional years, such as 1684–5, nearly 200 barrels were sent off the island,[207] the expansion in shipments dis-patched to foreign markets can not wholly account for the increase in the import of hops. (Table 5.7).

f) Tobacco

There are no recorded imports of tobacco into the island before the 1620s, but thereafter, as the output of England's American colonies soared and prices fell,[208] the import trade developed steadily until about the middle of the seventeenth century. From only 104 pounds in 1629–30, the level of tobacco imports climbed to more than 2,000 lbs. in 1646–7, although it is very likely that the latter figure was

[204] J. Thirsk, 'Farming Techniques', in *idem* (ed.), *Agricultural Change: Policy and Practice, 1500–1750* (Cambridge, 1990), p. 30. Cf. P. Clark, *The English Alehouse. A Social History, 1200–1830* (1983), pp. 31–2, 101.

[205] Blundell, *History*, vol. i, p. 57.

[206] For details of the regulations relating to brewing, see chapter 3, pp. 132–39.

[207] M.M.L., I.O. 1680–9, Customs book, 1685.

[208] Clay, *Economic Expansion and Social Change*, vol. ii, p. 138; R. Davis, 'English Foreign Trade, 1660–1700', *Ec.H.R.*, 2nd series, vol. vii (1954), reprinted in E. M. Carus-Wilson (ed.), *Essays in Economic History*, vol. ii (1962), p. 259.

boosted by the presence in the island of royalist refugees fleeing from civil war in England and a larger number of soldiers than usual. (Table 5.7).

In the second half of the seventeenth century, the growth of the import trade in tobacco was nothing short of spectacular; however, this had much more to do with the effects of English commercial policy and the consequent development of a contraband trade between the Isle of Man and the countries bordering on the Irish Sea than with rising demand in the island.[209] Without an exhaustive examination of the waterbailiff's accounts for the later seventeenth century, it is impossible to trace the remarkable increase in imports in detail, but it is evident from the data in Table 5.7 that, by the 1690s, very large quantities of tobacco were being landed at Manx ports, far greater amounts than could be consumed by the inhabitants of the island. In the early eighteenth century, it was estimated that seventy hogsheads of tobacco were sufficient for the needs of the population, but that more than seven times that amount was being imported and then re-shipped secretly from the island.[210]

g) Manufactured Goods and Other Imports

In addition to the commodities which have already been discussed, the Isle of Man imported a wide range of other goods, particularly metalware and items of clothing. Much of the 'ironmongery' which was unloaded in Manx ports was in the form of agricultural tools, especially sickles, scythes and spades. (Table 5.8). The dependence of the island on imported metal products is also indicated by the regular shipment of knives, such as the half gross of 'peny' knives which Thomas Corrin entered at Douglas on behalf of John Scarf in April 1594.[211] Other metal articles imported included iron and brass pots, griddles, cressets, hatchets and screws. In 1629-30 at least, a considerable number of 'ffisshing hookes' were also brought into the island; William Christian alone landed about 400 hooks at Ramsey in October 1629.[212] Towards the end of the century, the range of ironmongery became more diverse. In February 1696, for example,

---

[209] The measures taken by the English government and the nature of the smuggling activity in the island are considered *infra*, pp. 331–41.
[210] B. L. Add. MS 38,462, ff. 97–8.
[211] M.M.L., I.O. 1570–99, Waterbailiff's accounts, 1594.
[212] M.M.L., I.O. 1630–45, Waterbailiff's accounts, 1630.

Table 5.8 *Imports of Scythes, Sickles and Shoes
into the Isle of Man (Years ending at June 24)*

Year	Scythes doz.	Sickles doz.	Shoes pairs
1594	2	17	398
1600	2	16	104
1605	4	18	432
1610	2	19	518
1618	7	68	564
1630	6	67	95
1647	54.5	141	3
1667	4	50	213
1685	2	47	107
1696	6	145	94

Sources: See Table 5.1.

Henry Sandwitch imported window hinges, razors, scissors, 'smoth-ing Irons,' stirrup irons, tailor's shears and shoe buckles among an extremely varied cargo of metal goods and haberdashery.[213]

Most of the clothing required by the inhabitants was made up at home or by local craftsmen, but some items, particularly hats and shoes, were nevertheless imported. Shoes were by far the most important article in this trade and at least some of them were shipped from Chester, such as the three dozen entered in the *Forehound* of Douglas by John Walker of that city in November 1593.[214] Some seem to have been imported from Ireland, as in January 1696, when Thomas Kennedy entered forty-two pairs of 'Broages' from the *Bonyventure*, a Dublin wherry.[215] (Table 5.8). Hats were generally shipped in small quantities and seem to have been mainly of poorer quality; 'coorse hatts' are mentioned on several occasions in the waterbailiff's accounts, as in April 1630, when William Sumpter entered three dozen such hats at Ramsey.[216] The two 'quilted Capps'

[213] M.M.L., I.O. 1696–1704, Customs book, 1696.
[214] M.M.L., I.O. 1570–99, Customs book, 1594; M.M.L. R.D. 1579–98, 'Custome Book,' 1594 (Captain's book of licences and entries, 1594–5).
[215] M.M.L., I.O. 1696–1704, Customs book, 1696.
[216] M.M.L., I.O. 1630–45, Waterbailiff's accounts, 1630.

imported by Major Richard Stevenson of Balladoole in August 1596 doubtless represented the other end of the market.[217] Other items of clothing which were also imported included mantles, hoods, gloves and stockings, as well as lace, buttons and a variety of haberdashery.

Different types of cloth and commodities associated with the production of cloth were also regularly landed at Manx ports. There is, however, a difficulty in attempting to assess the level of trade in some of these commodities, arising from the vagueness and lack of precision in the entries in the waterbailiff's accounts. Linen, for example, comprised the bulk of the cloth imports, but it is probably also concealed behind some of the shipments described as Scottish or Irish cloth. There is certainly evidence from the late seventeenth century to show that linen was shipped from Scotland to the Isle of Man. In 1695, for instance, John Quayle entered fifty yards of 'scotch linnen' in a small boat at Ramsey.[218] Woollen cloth in general was of minor importance as an import, probably because it was the main type of cloth produced in the island and output was usually sufficient to answer most of the needs of the inhabitants. Kerseys and fustians also attracted little attention on the Manx market, being imported only infrequently – as far as can be deduced from the terminology of the accounts – and in small quantities. (Table 5.9). Alum, which was used as a dye-fixing agent in cloth-making, was brought into the island in most years, as were dye-stuffs of one sort or another, such as indigo, copperas, galls and saffron, but only in limited amounts. At the end of the seventeenth century, imports of alum were generally no more than about six hundredweight a year, a level which was not significantly higher, in terms of quantity, than that in about 1600, while, with the exception of copperas and to a certain extent galls, inward shipments of dye-stuffs could be measured in pounds weight rather than hundredweight. Woollen cards were imported in most years, an indication of the importance of woollen cloth production in the island.

Throughout the seventeenth century, native and foreign merchants entered a variety of household items among a miscellany of manufactured goods which were probably mainly produced in England or re-exported from English ports. Large consignments of treen ware – wooden vessels and dishes – were shipped to the island, as

---

[217] M.M.L., I.O. 1696–1704, Customs book, 1696.
[218] *ibid.*

Table 5.9 *Imports of Cloth into the Isle of Man (in yards)*
(Years ending at June 24)

Year	Linen cloth	Broad cloth	Scottish cloth	Irish cloth	Woollen cloth	Kerseys	Fustians
1594	1000[1]	12	—	60	—	—	8
1600	1480[2]	48	550[3]	—	10	28	—
1605	598[4]	—	—	100	12	—	—[5]
1610	40[6]	—	—[7]	—	—[8]	8	—
1618	195	—	—	—	—	—	31
1630	569[9]	74[10]	60	—	—	44[11]	10
1647	667[12]	—	140[13]	55	—	—	—
1667	—	—	—	—	—	—	—
1685	152	—	—	—	—	—	—
1696	139	—	50	—	2.5	—	23[14]

Sources: See Table 5.1.

Notes.

1. Plus two footpacks of linen.

2. Plus one horsepack and one footpack containing linen.

3. Plus 80 ells of cloth. The ell was a Scottish cloth measure, equivalent to 37 English inches. Zupko, 'Weights and Measures of Scotland', p. 128.

4. Plus one footpack containing linen.

5. Half a footpack of linen was imported.

6. Plus three horsepacks, two 'foot fardels', a footpack and an unspecified, though probably small, amount of linen cloth.

7. One 'foot fardel' of Scottish cloth was imported.

8. One piece of narrow cloth was imported.

9. Plus three pieces.

10. Plus one remnant.

11. Plus two pieces and one remnant.

12. Plus 18 slatts of linen. A slatt of linen cloth was approximately 50 inches in length and between 20 and 23 inches in width. *O.E.D.*, *sub* slatt.

13. Plus six pieces.

14. One half piece of fustian was imported.

well as varying amounts of earthenware, such as the two cart loads of mugs and the single 'Creedles [*sic*] of Cupes' imported by John Ottiwell at Castletown in May 1667.[219] Some furniture, probably destined for the castles or the houses of the officers or wealthier farmers, was also landed in Manx ports. This was mostly in the form of chairs, but on at least a few occasions cupboards and tables were imported. In November 1646, for example, John Crellin imported a 'drawinge table' and a 'Cubbord' at Peel.[220] Soap was regularly imported from at least the late sixteenth century, some of it in vessels from Chester and Formby.[221] (Table 5.7). The type of soap shipped is rarely mentioned in the accounts, although it seems unlikely that much of it would have been high quality soap, such as the Spanish Castile variety, which has been described as the Lux of its age.[222] On one occasion, in May 1594, some white soap was imported at Douglas by William Shapley of Barnstaple and, while this may have been Castile soap, it is equally likely that it was the hard, white English equivalent.[223] Most of the soap imported was probably of lower quality, such as the 'blacke soape' entered at Douglas by Danold Callister in June 1599,[224] and sold to those who could not afford the more expensive varieties.

Glass was transported to the island in small amounts in the 1590s and throughout the seventeenth century. There is no apparent indication of the source of this glass, but some was definitely shipped from Ireland and from Chester in 1593.[225] While most of these imports were drinking glasses for the tables of the governor, officers and more affluent inhabitants of the island, there were a few shipments of sheet glass which was used for windows in the castles, the governor's house and perhaps elsewhere.[226]

---

[219] M.M.L., I.O. 1660–71, Customs book, 1667.

[220] M.M.L., I.O. 1646–59, Waterbailiff's accounts, 1647.

[221] See, for example, I. O. 1570–99, Ingates and outgates,1583; Woodward, *Elizabethan Chester*, p. 36 n. 1.

[222] Thirsk, *Economic Policy and Projects*, p. 54.

[223] *ibid*, pp. 53–4; M.M.L., I.O. 1570–99, Waterbailiff's accounts, 1594; M.M.L. R.D. 1579–98, 'Custome book', 1594 (Captain's book of licences and entries, 1594–5).

[224] M.M.L., I.O. 1600–9, Ingates and outgates, 1600.

[225] M.M.L., I.O. 1570–99, Customs book, 1594.

[226] Glazing work was carried out on a number of occasions in the castles and at the governor's house in the Castletown. See, for example, M.M.L.,

Other manufactured goods arrived in the island from time to time and in limited quantities. Among these were arms, ammunition and gunpowder, which were particularly important for the defence of the island in times of crisis, bellows, wooden combs, lanterns, plough beams, starch and, from the 1640s onwards, tobacco pipes.

Wine and other luxury items enjoyed a strictly limited market and were consequently imported in very small amounts. Wine imports showed a remarkable stability during most of the seventeenth century, generally ranging from about twenty to about twenty-five tuns a year, until the war between England and France, the principal supplier of the island's imports, in the 1690s brought the trade to a temporary halt. (Table 5.7). Nearly all of the imported wine originated in the Bordeaux region of France, although, in the late sixteenth and early seventeenth centuries, shipments of Spanish sack also entered the island's ports.[227] The consumption of wine was inevitably restricted to those with a little money to spend, although the occasional bottle might not be outside the reach of those of moderate means. In about 1680, Thomas Denton of Warnell Hall in Cumberland found on his visit to the island that 'you may have a good Spanish wine for 10d. a quart, and ffrench wine for a groat [4d.] a quart.'[228] Not all of the wine imported was consumed by the wealthier sort, however, for some was re-exported. In June 1584, for example, John Callow transported two tuns of French wine in the *Elizabeth* of Ramsey to Beaumaris in Anglesey, and two months later William Christian shipped a hogshead of 'Gascony' wine to the same port.[229] Some small quantities of French wine were also re-shipped to Chester.[230]

The level of spice imports into the island fluctuated but remained low during the seventeenth century. In many years, there were no imports of spices at all. Shipments of cinnamon, nutmeg and ginger were, however, landed on a fairly regular basis and entries of the latter were on the increase in the 1680s and 1690s. Indeed, ginger

Ellesmere Papers 243/C, 86: Book of allowance, Castle Rushen, 1601: Reparations and works.

[227] France was also the most important source of Irish wine imports in the early seventeenth century. H. F. Kearney, 'The Irish Wine Trade, 1614–15', *I.H.S.*, vol. ix (1955), p. 405.

[228] Denton, 'Description', p. 439.

[229] Lewis, *Welsh Port Books*, p. 251.

[230] Woodward, *Elizabethan Chester*, p. 35.

appears to have been the most frequently imported spice, though usually in small parcels until the late seventeenth century. In 1684–5, more than sixty pounds of ginger were imported and a decade later, in 1695–6, imports stood at seventy-six pounds.[231] By contrast, the island's consumption of pepper, another commodity classifiable as a luxury in 1600, grew significantly during the course of the century. Imports of pepper varied considerably, but towards the end of the seventeenth century, the amount landed in the island seems to have risen from about forty pounds or less to between about eighty and 100 pounds a year.[232] The same growth in demand can be seen in the case of sugar, which was being shipped into the Isle of Man from time to time during the 1590s. Some of the individual shipments could be large, as in May 1594, when Richard Ferris of Barnstaple landed 200 pounds of sugar from the *Mary* of Fremington at Douglas, but it was not a regular import until after 1650. The level of imports in the second half of the seventeenth century seems to have been above 200 pounds a year. In 1695–6, for instance, more than 250 pounds of sugar was imported.[233] It is likely, though it is not easily demonstrated, that the development of this import trade in spices, pepper and sugar was connected with the growth of the contraband traffic in the Irish Sea, but its expansion may have been partly the result of an increase in demand in the island.

Varying amounts of paper and small numbers of books were imported into the island during the seventeenth century, but the trade in these items was very limited. Paper was required by the island's administration for court books, the waterbailiff's and other accounts, cockets and various certificates and there was also probably a small market among the native and naturalised merchants and larger farmers in the island. Some paper may have gone unrecorded in the waterbailiff's accounts if purchased for the use of the island's government in England, but the level of imports in some years suggests that there may have been a periodic restocking of supplies;

[231] M.M.L., I.O. 1680–9, Customs book, 1685; M.M.L., I.O. 1696–1704, Customs book, 1696.

[232] See, for example, M.M.L., I.O. 1610–19, Ingates and outgates, 1610; M.M.L., I.O. 1680–9, Customs book, 1685; M.M.L., I.O. 1696–1704, Customs book, 1696.

[233] M.M.L., I.O. 1570–99, Waterbailiff's accounts, 1594; M.M.L. R.D. 1579–98, 'Custome book', 1594 (Captain's book of licences and entries, 1594–5); M.M.L., I.O. 1696–1704, Customs book, 1696.

in 1609–10, for example, twenty-six reams of 'white paper' were imported in a single shipment.[234]

Most of the books which came into the island appear to have been primers and horn books[235] for the petty schools in the towns and parishes.[236] There is a good deal of evidence, however, to indicate that a much broader range of books was imported. These included bibles, such as the three copies entered by John Casement at Ramsey in October 1695, and Common Prayer Books, seventeen of which – one for each parish in the island – were dispatched 'for the better performance of the Church service' by Bishop Isaac Barrow in 1664.[237] Sir Charles Coole, vicar of Lezayre, who died in 1658, owned a library of at least twenty theological works, while his colleague, Sir John Crellin, vicar of Arbory, amassed a collection of some seventy-one volumes during his lifetime, sixty-eight of which were of a devotional nature.[238] Books of a more secular nature were also imported. When Mary Whetstone of Malew died in August 1662, she possessed ten books, including a copy of Stow's *Survey of London* and an 'old Turkish history.'[239] George Harrison, the schoolmaster at Castletown, left a total of sixty-five books at his death in 1661, among which were seventeen 'Latine Worke Bookes' and sixteen 'English Bookes.'[240] Almanacs, which offered practical

[234] M.M.L., I.O. 1610–19, Ingates and outgates, 1610.

[235] A horn book was a leaf of paper containing the alphabet, perhaps the numerals from one to ten, some rudimentary spelling guidance and the Lord's Prayer, protected by a plate of translucent horn and mounted on a wooden tablet. *O.E.D.*, *sub* horn book. On the use of the horn book in seventeenth-century England, see D. Cressy, *Literacy and the Social Order. Reading and Writing in Tudor and Stuart England* (Cambridge, 1980), pp. 20–1.

[236] In the late 1640s, William Blundell found a 'free school' in each town in the island. Elementary schools were established in the parishes by Bishop Barrow after 1663. Blundell, *History*, vol. i, p. 67; Moore, *History*, vol. i, p. 471; P. G. Clamp, 'English Schooling in the Isle of Man, 1660–1700: The Barrovian Design', *Journal of Educational Administration and History*, vol. xx (1988), pp. 10–21.

[237] M.M.L., I.O. 1696–1704, Customs book, 1696; M.M.L., MF/EW/17. Bishop Barrow to the officers of the island, March 17, 1664.

[238] Unpublished Document no. 96, *J.M.M.*, vol. ii (1930–4), p. 220; Craine, *Manannan's Isle*, p. 121.

[239] M.M.L., MF/EW/16, Malew, 1662.

[240] M.M.L., MF/EW/17, Malew, 1663.

advice on everyday matters, were brought into the island in limited numbers. In November 1695, for example, Thomas Kennedy imported a dozen almanacs in a small boat at Ramsey, possibly from Scotland.[241] Since most of the books which found their way into the island probably originated in London, however, it seems likely that they were normally shipped mainly from Chester, the port which also handled a large part of the trade in books between the English capital and Ireland.[242]

Comestibles formed another branch of the import trade. Most such commodities were shipped in small consignments on an irregular basis and included butter – in one instance 'Flemishe butter' – currants, raisins, cabbages, beans, peas, turnips and prunes. Fruit of various types was also imported, some of it, such as figs and oranges, clearly the produce of continental European countries and probably re-exported through English ports. Other varieties, especially apples, which were shipped to the island in most years, were doubtless chiefly of English origin. Not all of this fruit reached its destination in a state of merchantable quality. When John Quirk unloaded his cargo of eighteen barrels of apples at Douglas in October 1616, the customer or perhaps the searcher found that 'many of thees apples were Rotten.'[243] Limited amounts of grain entered the island. Even in years when there seem to have been considerable shipments inwards, these were generally matched by the exports of grain. (Tables 5.4 and 5.10). Some items which could be regarded as consumables, but which were in demand because of their medicinal uses, such as aniseed and liquorice, were also imported in small quantities.[244]

---

[241] M.M.L., I.O. 1696–1704, Customs book, 1696. The origin of Kennedy's shipment is not clear, but the rest of the cargo was Scottish cloth.

[242] R. J. Hunter, 'Chester and the Irish Book Trade, 1681', *I.E.S.H.*, vol. xv (1988), p. 89. In view of the limited output of Irish and Scottish presses, it is very unlikely that books were imported from either Ireland or Scotland. R. Gillespie, 'Irish Printing in the Early Seventeenth Century', *ibid*, p. 81; R. A. Houston, *Scottish Literacy and the Scottish Identity. Illiteracy and Society in Scotland and Northern England, 1600–1800* (Cambridge, 1985), pp. 164–5.

[243] M.M.L., I.O. 1610–19, Waterbailiff's accounts, 1617.

[244] Aniseed was imported occasionally throughout the seventeenth century, usually, it appears, in quantities of less than twenty pounds a year. Liquorice did not apparently become popular until towards 1700, when it was shipped

Table 5.10 *Imports of Grain into the Isle of Man*
(Years ending at June 24)

Year	Wheat		Barley		Oats		Malt	
	bolls[1]	barrels	bolls	barrels	bolls	barrels	bolls	barrels
1594	45	53	186	290	46	42	133	40
1600	—	—	—	—	50	146	—	—
1605	—	—	—	12	—	—	20	—
1610	—	1	23	11	23	16	—	—
1618	—	—	—	—	—	—	—	—
1630	—	—	0.5	—	—	—	—	—
1647	30	88	—	14	40	36	3	4
1667	—	—	—	—	—	—	—	—
1685	—	—	—	6	—	—	—	—
1696	1	—	—	—	—	—	12	—

Sources: See Table 5.1.

Note.
1. The relationship between the boll and the barrel is not clear, but it
very likely that after 1628 at least, they were identical measures. *Statutes*,
pp. 81, 102.

While the Isle of Man was principally an exporter of livestock, some
animals were brought into the island. Much of the beef which was
shipped into Manx ports was in the form of carcases, but some live
beasts were landed, perhaps to be used as breeding stock. (Table 5.11).
In June 1684, Thomas Thompson arrived at Peel with a yearling
bullock and twelve months later he entered a further eight bullocks at
Ramsey. Also in June 1685, John Cunningham imported eight yearling bullocks and nine two-year olds at Peel. These cattle, like the ten
'Ireish beast' landed at Peel by Captain Charles Christian in August
1684, unquestionably came from Ireland.[245] Horses were transported
both to and from the island, as previously noted,[246] and in some years

in similar amounts, though not in every year. M.M.L., I.O. 1600–9, Ingates
and outgates, 1605; M.M.L., I.O. 1610–19, Waterbailiff's accounts, 1618;
M.M.L., I.O. 1680–9, Customs book, 1685; M.M.L., I.O. 1696–1704, Customs book, 1696.
[245] M.M.L., I.O. 1680–9, Customs book, 1685.
[246] See *infra*, p. 259–60.

Table 5.11 *Imports of Livestock into the Isle of Man*
(Years ending at June 24)

Year	Cattle	Sheep	Pigs	Horses
1594	13[1]	40	—	13
1600	21	—	—	159
1605	15	—	—	7
1610	14	—	120	14
1618	14	—	2	112
1630	9	—	—	39
1647	71	—	—	58
1667	2	2	—	39
1685	59	15	—	14
1696	32	—	—	2

Sources: See Table 5.1.

Note.
1. Plus two boat loads of quick beef (live animals). These animals may not have been landed since the merchants only paid anchorage dues.

the number of animals entered exceeded that of those exported. Although it was technically illegal to export horses from England until January 1657,[247] there can be little doubt that some of the animals which were imported into the island originated on the English side of the Irish Sea. Permits could be obtained for shipment abroad from England, or, failing that, customs officers could be bribed or the horses could be smuggled out of the country.[248] In the unusual circumstances of the 1640s, William Kaye, a servant of Governor John Greenhalgh, was dispatched to the horse fair at Malton in Yorkshire 'to buy horses for my Lord for the Island' and seems to have encountered few problems in taking the four animals which he purchased there to Liverpool for shipment to Man.[249] Scotland, which had

[247] P. R. Edwards, *The Horse Trade of Tudor and Stuart England* (Cambridge, 1988), pp. 48, 50.
[248] *ibid*, pp. 48–9.
[249] F. R. Raines (ed.), *The Stanley Papers, pt. iii, vol. i*, Chet. Soc., O.S., vol. lxvi (1867), pp. cxxxiii–iv n. 58. There seems to be little evidence of the presence of buyers or sellers of horses from the island at the specialist horse

benefited from the illicit trade in horseflesh across the border with England, was another source of the island's imports. In June 1593, John Clucas entered two horses from Scotland at Douglas and, in the following May, two Scottish 'nagges' were landed at the same port by Ellis Rymer.[250] It is unlikely that Ireland supplied any animals since the shortage of horses there was a frequent cause of complaint in the sixteenth and seventeenth centuries.[251]

VI. THE DIRECTION OF THE ISLAND'S TRADE

It is difficult to provide more than a rough outline of the direction of the island's overseas trade in the late sixteenth and seventeenth centuries because of the general lack of details concerning the origins of shipments and the destination of exports in the waterbailiff's accounts. This problem is compounded by the uneven survival of the relevant English, Welsh and Scottish port books and the almost complete absence of such records for Ireland during the period from about 1590 to 1700.[252] The position is somewhat better, so far as the

fairs in England. Dr Edwards has noted only one purchase by a Manxman at the Chester horse fairs in the second half of the seventeenth century. P. R. Edwards, 'The Horse Trade of Chester in the Sixteenth and Seventeenth Centuries', *Journal of the Chester Archaeological Society*, vol. lxii (1980), p. 105.

[250] M.M.L., I.O. 1570–99, Customs book, 1594; waterbailiff's accounts, 1594.

[251] Gillespie, *Colonial Ulster*, pp. 72–3; O'Brien, *Economic History of Ireland*, pp. 63–4.

[252] There are many gaps in the series of port books for Chester and its dependent creeks and members in North Wales and Lancashire in the late sixteenth and seventeenth centuries and less than a dozen books for Carlisle and the ports of Cumberland before 1700. Williams, *Descriptive List*, pp. 523–560, 561. The Scottish Import and Export Books for the ports of south-western Scotland are equally imperfect and in any event generally only provide information about inward shipments. The accounts of the collector of bullion dues, which were levied on certain imports in Scottish ports, rarely contain details of the origin of shipments. *The Custome Buik of Dumfreis, 1578*, printed in R. C. Reid (ed.), An Introduction to the History of Dumfries, by Robert Edgar, *Records of the Western Marches*, vol. i (1915), appendix B, pp. 261–8; T. C. Smout, *Scottish Trade on the Eve of Union, 1660–1707* (1963), p. 37; A. Murray, 'The Customs Accounts of Dumfries and Kirkcudbright, 1560–1660', *T.D.G.N.H.A.S.*, 3rd series, vol.

Manx customs accounts are concerned, in the later seventeenth century, when, after about 1680, the customer or waterbailiff began to record the name of the vessel in which an incoming cargo was shipped, together with its home port, and to note down the country, though not the port, to which outgoing shipments were consigned.[253]

There is no suggestion in the waterbailiff's accounts or elsewhere that the pattern of Manx overseas trade changed significantly in the course of the seventeenth century and the available evidence, especially that from the decades after 1680, indicates that the island's commercial links with northern England were of prime importance. (Tables 5.12, 5.13 and 5.14). The nature of the Manx economy, and in particular the demand for raw materials, such as coal, and for manufactured goods, made this inevitable, for coal mining was developing in west Cumberland and south Lancashire and the ports of the region, especially Chester, which lay on the most direct route between London and Ireland, and Liverpool, could draw on extensive areas beyond their immediate hinterlands to supply finished goods for the export trade. (Map 5).

The trade between the ports of west Cumberland and the island was dominated by the export of coal from Parton, Workington and Whitehaven. Before about 1600, Parton, where the harbour could apparently accommodate up to sixteen vessels at one time, seems to have been an important port, although Workington was apparently handling a substantial part of the traffic by the early seventeenth century.[254] The destruction of the pier at Parton by a gale in the early 1630s and the failure to rebuild it until sixty years later brought the coal trade from that port finally to an end.[255] Workington subsequently lost its pre-eminence as a coal exporting port to Whitehaven, which was developed by Sir Christopher Lowther and his

note 252 *continued*
xlii (1965), pp. 114–132; Smout, 'Foreign Trade of Dumfries and Kirkcudbright', pp. 36–7. Port books exist for only four Irish ports – Coleraine, Strangford, Carrickfergus and Derry – for part or the whole of the period from Michaelmas 1612 to Michaelmas 1615. Leeds City Library, Temple Newsam MSS PO/7/1–4.

[253] See *infra*, pp. 234–35.
[254] See *infra*, pp. 271–74.
[255] Beckett, *Coal and Tobacco*, p. 39.

Map 5. Overseas trade: the Irish Sea.

Table 5.12 *Vessels trading with the Isle of Man,
by country of port of provenance
(Years ending at June 24. 1595: year ending at April 27)*

i) *Vessels entering Manx ports*

Country of Origin	Year			
	1595	*1618*	*1696*	*1701*
Isle of Man	10	18	40	30
England	18	11	12	30
Ireland	11	15	19	13
Scotland	10	10	4	9
Wales	—	1	1	2
Jersey	—	—	—	1
France	—	4	—	1
Uncertain	48	72	15	4
Total	97	131	91	90

ii) *Vessels leaving Manx ports*

Country of Origin	Year			
	1595	*1618*	*1696*	*1701*[1]
Isle of Man	—	—	46	2
England	—	—	12	2
Ireland	—	—	8	1
Scotland	—	—	4	—
Wales	—	—	—	—
France	—	—	—	1
Uncertain	—	—	9	2
Total	—	—	79	8

Sources: M.M.L., R.D. 1579–98, 'Custome Book', 1594 (Captain's book of licences and entries, 1594–5); M.M.L., I.O. 1610–19, Book of licences and entries, 1618; M.M.L., I.O. 1696–1704, Customs book, 1696; ingates and outgates, 1701.

Note.
1. The low total for 1701 is due to the omission in most entries of details of the vessels.

Table 5.13 *Vessels trading with the Isle of Man,*
by port of provenance
(Years ending at June 24. 1595: year ending at April 27)

i) *Vessels entering Manx ports*

Port of Provenance	Year			
	1595	*1618*	*1696*	*1701*
Isle of Man				
Douglas	2	2	15	5
Castletown	1	—	3	10
Ramsey	3	12	19	9
Peel	—	3	3	5
Michael	1	1	—	—
Laxey	3	—	—	—
Bride	—	—	—	1
England				
Chester	7	2	—	3
Hilbre	1	—	—	—
Liverpool	—	1	5	8
Formby	1	—	—	—
Alt	4	1	—	—
Ribble	—	—	—	1
Poulton	—	—	3	3
Wyre	2	—	—	—
Lancaster	—	—	1	2
Grange	—	—	—	3
Ravenglass	1	—	—	—
Whitehaven	—	—	3	8
Parton	—	4	—	—
Workington	—	2	—	—
Carlisle	—	—	—	1
Bristol	—	—	—	1
Fremington	1	—	—	—
Barnstaple	1	1	—	—
Ireland				
Dublin	—	1	4	4

Port of Provenance	Year			
	1595	1618	1696	1701
Coleraine	—	—	1	—
Carrickfergus	2	1	—	—
Donaghadee	—	—	4	—
Portaferry	—	—	—	1
Strangford	1	3	6	2
Downpatrick	—	—	2	—
Ardglass	—	5	—	—
Killough	—	—	1	—
Newry	—	—	—	1
Carlingford	—	—	—	1
Clonard	—	—	—	1
Wicklow	—	—	1	3
Wexford	2	5	—	—
Unspecified	6	—	—	—
Scotland				
Glasgow	—	2	—	1
Renfrew	—	1	—	—
Greenock	—	—	—	2
Wemyss	—	—	—	1
Largs	—	2	—	—
Saltcoats	—	3	—	—
Irvine	—	—	—	1
Ayr	1	1	—	—
Campbeltown	—	—	2	—
Portpatrick	—	—	—	1
Kirkcudbright	1	—	2	2
Dumbries	1	—	—	—
Preston	1	—	—	—
Kintyre	—	—	—	1
Unspecified	6	1	—	—
Wales				
Mostyn	—	1	—	—
Caernarfon	—	—	—	1

Port of Provenance	Year			
	1595	1618	1696	1701
Clwyd	—	—	1	1
Jersey	—	—	—	1
France				
Plousganou	—	1	—	—
Le Croisic	—	1	—	—
La Rochelle	—	1	—	—
Bordeaux	—	—	—	1
Granville	—	1	—	—
Uncertain	48	72	15	4
Total	97	131	91	90

ii) *Vessels leaving Manx ports*

Port of Provenance	Year			
	1595	1618	1696	1701
Isle of Man				
Douglas	—	—	20	—
Castletown	—	—	2	1
Ramsey	—	—	21	1
Peel	—	—	3	—
England				
Liverpool	—	—	6	1
Poulton	—	—	3	—
Lancaster	—	—	1	—
Whitehaven	—	—	2	1
Ireland				
Belfast	—	—	1	—
Portaferry	—	—	1	—
Strangford	—	—	4	—
Killough	—	—	1	—
Carlingford	—	—	1	—
Wicklow	—	—	—	1
Scotland				
Kirkcudbright	—	—	3	—
Dumfries	—	—	1	—

Port of Provenance	Year			
	1595	1618	1696	1701
France				
Bordeaux	—	—	—	1
Uncertain	—	—	9	2
Total	—	—	79	8

Sources: See Table 5.12.

Note. These tables record the number of entries and departures by vessels from a particular port and not the number of individual vessels involved in the trade.

Table 5.14 *Destinations of shipments licensed for export from the Isle of Man (Years ending at June 24)*

Destination	Year		
	1685	1696	1701
England	59	88	60
Ireland	11	13	32
Scotland	3	15	9
Wales	—	—	—
Jersey	3	—	3
France	2	—	2
Uncertain	13	—	3
Total	91	116	109

Sources: M.M.L., I.O. 1680–9, Customs book, 1685; M.M.L., I.O. 1696–1704, Customs book, 1696; Ingates and outgates, 1701.

son, Sir John, from the 1630s onwards.[256] By the end of the seventeenth century, Whitehaven was supplying about half, and very probably more, of the island's coal, a fact which was reflected by both the high output of the mines in the area surrounding the town and its importance in the export trade.[257] Tobacco was also shipped to the island from Whitehaven in the late seventeenth century and in return small quantities of wool and cargoes of slates were dispatched.[258]

Of the Lancashire ports, Liverpool was the most important to the Isle of Man . Together with Chester, Liverpool supplied most of the island's needs for manufactured goods, as well as shipping small quantities of salt and coal from the south Lancashire coalfield.[259] Liverpool was also the port nearest to the principal residences of the earl of Derby, at Lathom and Knowsley, and consequently it was the main port through which the officers of the island passed when required to appear before the Lord of Man and through which the annual revenues of the island were sent under guard.[260] On the rare occasions when the earl of Derby himself crossed to the Isle of Man, Liverpool was the most convenient embarkation point. In April 1577, Earl Henry celebrated the feast of St George in the town while waiting for a favourable wind for the island.[261] Liverpool was also the port through which many of the provisions which the earl

---

[256] *ibid*, pp. 39, 43–6; P. Ford, 'Tobacco and Coal: A Note on the Economic History of Whitehaven', *Economica*, vol. ix (1929), pp. 192–3; Nef, *British Coal Industry*, vol. i, pp. 71–3.

[257] In 1695–6, at least forty-seven tons of coal were imported from Whitehaven, slightly less than half of the total amount of coal imported (Table 5.6). M.M.L., I.O. 1696–1704, Customs book, 1696. For details of the output of the collieries in the Whitehaven area and the level of export sales in the late seventeenth century, see Beckett, *Coal and Tobacco*, Table 2.3, p. 47 and appendix 4, pp. 229, 231.

[258] P.R.O., E 190/1448/8, cited in Appleby, *Famine in Tudor and Stuart England*, p. 177; M.M.L., I.O. 1696–1704, Customs book, 1696.

[259] J. E. Hollinshead, 'The People of South West Lancashire during the second half of the Sixteenth Century' (University of Liverpool Ph.D. thesis, 1987), vol. i, p. 360; M.M.L., I.O. 1696–1704, Customs book, 1696.

[260] In 1594, for example, John Blundell of Formby was paid 47s. for 'Carrying the officers from the Audyt'. Although the place of embarkation is not recorded, it seems most likely that it was Liverpool. M.M.L., I.O. 1570–99, Book of allowance, Castle Rushen, 1594.

[261] Bagley, *Earls of Derby*, p. 63.

obtained from the island were imported, including cattle, fish, puffins, samphire and beer.[262] Manx exports which were otherwise shipped to Liverpool were similar to those transported to other ports and consisted mainly of cattle, wool, sheepfells, tallow and herring.[263] Trade between the island and other Lancashire ports, such as Lancaster, Poulton and Wyre, was generally conducted on a small scale and was based on exports of Manx cattle. Some of the beasts imported at Wyre were destined for Lathom, like the ten animals landed there by Ferdinando Fox in 1630.[264] The outward shipments from these ports, particularly Poulton and Wyre, largely consisted of salt and a certain amount of coal.[265]

At the end of the sixteenth century, Chester was a more important port than Liverpool for the shipment of manufactured goods to the Isle of Man. Despite this fact, Chester's position in this trade can not be readily demonstrated by reference to the books of licences and entries, since so many of the vessels entering Manx harbours can not be identified. In 1594–5, for example, the port of provenance of about half of all the ships arriving in the island is not recorded; of the English vessels whose home port is known, however, the greatest number belonged to Chester. (Table 5.13). A clearer indication of the importance of the Chester trade can be found in the waterbailiff's accounts, which reveal that ships sailed between the island and the Dee on a fairly regular basis in the late Tudor period. In 1582–3, at least seven vessels from Chester arrived in Douglas Bay, carrying shoes, caps, soap, wool cards, treen ware and scythes, as well as some hops, salt and iron.[266] In 1594–5, the same number of Chester vessels are recorded in the island's ports, together with a single vessel of Hilbre, an islet which served as an anchorage at the mouth of the Dee. The cargoes landed included the items previously mentioned and in addition drinking glasses, spades, brass and beer.[267] The

---

[262] M.M.L., MD/401/1718/38, MD/401/1718/47.

[263] P.R.O., E 190/1328/11.

[264] M.M.L. R.D. 1627–50, Book of allowance, Castle Rushen, 1630: Rewards.

[265] M.M.L. R.D. 1579–98, 'Custome book', 1594 (Captain's book of licences and entries, 1594–5).

[266] M.M.L., I.O. 1570–99, Ingates and outgates, 1583.

[267] M.M.L. R.D. 1579–98, 'Custome book', 1594 (Captain's book of licences and entries, 1594–5). Since the merchants who shipped goods in these vessels were Manx, or of Manx origin, with close connections with Chester, it seems most likely that the ships sailed from the Dee.

Chester port books of the late sixteenth and early seventeenth centuries provide further evidence of the extent of this trade. Although in 1565-6 only two vessels are recorded as entering the port from the Isle of Man and none are listed as sailing for it, in the remaining years of the sixteenth century for which there are extant port books for Chester, the number of ships arriving in the Dee was always between two and four and the total of vessels clearing for the island was in the range from four to nine. In 1602-3, nine ships departed from Manx ports bound for Chester, while four sailed from the Dee to the island.[268] By contrast, six vessels landed cargoes from Man at Liverpool in 1603-4, but no shipments were made in the other direction.[269]

By the late seventeenth century, it seems that Chester was losing its position of importance as a source of manufactured goods, as the Dee continued to silt up and Liverpool and Whitehaven developed, but the evidence from the Manx customs accounts, which rarely record the port of origin of a shipment at this time, is far from conclusive in the matter. It is certainly true, however, that Chester vessels played a smaller part in trade with the island in 1700 than a century before, though in itself this is not a sign that the traffic with the port was in decline. (Table 5.13). The Chester port books appear to confirm the reduction in the number of shipments to Manx ports. In the quarter year ending at Michaelmas 1680, for example, only one vessel sailed from Chester to the Isle of Man, and in the corresponding period in 1700, there were no shipments at all.[270]

The goods shipped to Chester from the island were much the same as the commodities sent to other English ports. These chiefly comprised cattle, including, in the early seventeenth century, some for the household of William, sixth earl of Derby, at Bidston in Wirral,[271] skins and sheepfells for the tanners and glovers in Chester, wool, herring, tallow and smaller quantities of honey, malt, re-exported wine and salt.

---

[268] Woodward, *Elizabethan Chester*, appendix i (B), p. 131; K. P. Wilson (ed.), *Chester Customs Accounts, 1301-1566*, R.S.L.C., vol. cxi (1969), pp. 74-99, especially pp. 78, 79. The figures quoted refer to arrivals and departures and not to individual vessels.

[269] P.R.O., E 190/1328/11.

[270] P.R.O., E 190/1342/1; P.R.O., E 190/1361/8, cited in Armour, thesis, pp. 325, 338-40.

[271] M.M.L. R.D. 1627-50, Book of allowance, Castle Rushen, 1630: Rewards.

Ships from more distant English ports also traded with the island from time to time. Barques from Barnstaple in Devon landed cargoes at Manx ports on several occasions, such as in July 1582, when John Wilson, the factor of a certain Mr Norris of that place, entered in the *Peter* of Barnstaple a wide range of commodities, including salt, calico, ginger, pepper and sugar.[272] Another Barnstaple vessel arrived at Douglas in July 1617 in which Richard Stradling imported Gascon wine, sack, iron and a variety of other wares.[273] Bristol vessels were also involved in trade with the island. In October 1700, John Murrey, a member of the Douglas merchant family, entered a cargo of horseshoe nails and spikes in the *Crown* of Bristol.[274] Ships from ports further afield sometimes put in to the island to ride out storms or to take on provisions. In 1600, for example, the *Primrose* of Dover anchored in the bay at Peel; in 1604, a Dartmouth ship paid anchorage dues at Douglas; and, in 1609, a Weymouth barque took shelter in the same port.[275]

There was also a limited amount of contact between the Isle of Man and the Channel Islands, chiefly Jersey. Two shipments of corn, together with some hides, yarn, butter and cheese were exported from Ramsey by William Button in 1685 and in 1700 the *Mary* of Jersey arrived with a cargo including brandy and paper.[276]

Trade between the Isle of Man and the ports of Wales seems to have been fairly limited throughout the period under consideration. In the late sixteenth century, the only Welsh port with which the island apparently had commercial links was Beaumaris in Anglesey. The main feature of this trade was the shipment of grain from Manx ports and indeed it seems that the island was an important source of wheat, barley, malt and oats for Anglesey. In addition, quantities of salted beef, herring, wool, salt and French wine were

---

[272] M.M.L., I.O. 1570–99, Ingates and outgates, 1583.

[273] M.M.L., I.O. 1610–19, Waterbailiff's accounts, 1618; book of licences and entries, 1618.

[274] M.M.L., I.O. 1696–1704, Ingates and Outgates, 1701.

[275] M.M.L., I.O. 1600–9, Ingates and outgates, 1600; ingates and outgates, 1605; M.M.L., I.O. 1610–19, Ingates and outgates, 1610.

[276] M.M.L., I.O. 1680–9, Customs book, 1685; M.M.L., I.O. 1696–1704, Ingates and outgates, 1701. For a discussion of the trading network of Jersey in the sixteenth and seventeenth centuries, see J. C. Appleby, 'Neutrality, Trade and Privateering, 1500–1689', in A. G. Jamieson (ed.), *A People of the Sea. The Maritime History of the Channel Islands* (1986), pp. 74–96.

shipped from the island, and, in return, millstones, lime and salt were periodically sent from Beaumaris.[277] There appears to have been no trade between the island and the other Welsh ports, either during the late Tudor period or in the early seventeenth century, although vessels from north Welsh ports, such as Mostyn and Caernarfon occasionally called at the island. (Tables 5.12, 5.13 and 5.14).[278] After the leasing of the copper mines in the island in 1700, however, several shipments of ore were made from Castletown and Port St Mary to Bagillt on the Flintshire side of the Dee, although this trade came to an abrupt end when the project apparently collapsed some years later.[279]

A fairly regular trade existed between the ports of eastern Ireland and the ports of the island, especially Peel, which was well placed to benefit from this traffic. The commodities imported into the island from all the Irish ports were much the same and were typical of that country's exports in general, consisting principally of timber, together with smaller shipments of linen yarn, cloth, caddows,[280] shoes, herring, grain, cattle and butter.[281] No single item predominated in the Manx export trade to Ireland, which, in terms of outward shipments, was second only in importance to that with England, though by a considerable margin. (Table 5.14). Consignments of re-exported train oil, cloth, Manx wool and, particularly before the later seventeenth century, ale and beer were transported in most years. Tobacco became an important re-export commodity in the trade to Ireland in the 1690s. Although the limitations of the surviving evidence and the loss of almost all the Irish port books render it difficult to construct an exact picture of Manx trade with

[277] Lewis, *Welsh Port Books*, pp. 244–6, 248–51, 253, 256–61, 268.
[278] *ibid*; W. Rees (ed.), *The Port Books of Cardiff and its member ports, Swansea and Neath, for the years 1606–1610*, South Wales and Monmouth Record Society, vol. viii (1954).
[279] M.M.L., I.O. 1696–1704, Ingates and outgates, 1701. Some copper ore was also shipped to England. In January 1702, for example, Nicholas Harley of Castletown exported twenty tons from Port St Mary in the *Sarah* of Wicklow, bound for England. M.M.L., I.O. 1696–1704, Ingates and outgates, 1702. For details of the copper mining project, see chapter 3, p. 188.
[280] Caddows were coarse woollen blankets. *O.E.D.*, *sub* caddow.
[281] A. Clarke, 'The Irish Economy, 1600–1660', in Moody, Martin and Byrne, *New History of Ireland*, vol. iii, pp. 177–182; L. M. Cullen, *Anglo-Irish Trade*, ch. 2.

Ireland, it seems clear that the Irish ports with which the island traded stretched from Derry in the north to Waterford in the south. In 1582–3, for example, two vessels arrived at Douglas from Ardglass, one from each of the ports of Carlingford, Dublin and Wexford and four other ships from unspecified ports in Ireland.[282] The Carrickfergus port book of 1614–15 reveals that the *Gift of God* of the Isle of Man entered that port on two occasions in 1614.[283] Suits brought for debt in the island's chancery court by merchants from Derry, Carrickfergus, Belfast, Dublin and Waterford clearly indicate commercial connections with these towns.[284]

The island also traded with the ports of south-west Scotland as far north as Glasgow. Manx exports to Scotland included skins, dried fish, honey, oil, beer and slates, as well as re-exported items such as tobacco, brandy and wine.[285] Vessels arriving in the island from the ports of the north coast of the Solway and the Firth of Clyde brought various types of cloth, but mainly Scottish linen cloth, shoes, iron, 'Scotts Daggers,' salt, soap and cheese.[286] Small amounts of coal also appear to have been shipped from Kirkcudbright, the coal probably originating in the mining operations on the Ayrshire coast.[287] The trade between the island and ports such as Dumfries, Kirkcudbright, Ayr and Irvine was normally conducted on a small scale throughout the seventeenth century, although it undoubtedly expanded during the 1690s as a result of the growth of unofficial trafficking in commodities such as tobacco.[288]

Direct commercial links between the Isle of Man and continental Europe were few and, with the exceptions of the trade in salt and

---

[282] M.M.L., I.O. 1570–99, Ingates and outgates, 1583.

[283] Leeds City Library, Temple Newsam MS PO/7/3, summarised in R. Sweetnam, 'Early Seventeenth Century Ships' Masters and Merchants', *Carrickfergus and District Historical Journal*, vol. ii (1987), pp. 11, 12.

[284] Lib. Canc. 1605, 7; Lib. Canc. 1613, 9; Lib. Canc. 1618, 15, 18; Lib. Canc. 1622, 16–17, 20, 22; Lib. Canc. 1624, 15; Lib. Canc. 1630, 8.

[285] Smout, 'Foreign Trade of Dumfries and Kirkcudbright', pp. 41–2; M.M.L., I.O. 1696–1704, Customs book, 1696; ingates and outgates, 1702.

[286] M.M.L. R.D. 1579–98, 'Custome book', 1594 (Captain's book of licences and entries, 1594–5); M.M.L., I.O. 1696–1704, Customs book, 1696.

[287] M.M.L., I.O. 1696–1704, Customs book, 1696; S. G. E. Lythe, *The Economy of Scotland in its European Setting, 1550–1625* (1960), p. 48; Smout, *Scottish Trade*, p. 225.

[288] For details of the smuggling trade, see *infra*, pp. 331–41.

wine, of minor importance. The very small market in the island for continental products, apart from salt, inevitably directed the attention of merchants to the much larger markets of England and, to a lesser extent, Ireland, Scotland and Wales, and consequently much of the salt and wine brought into the Isle of Man was re-shipped from ports in those countries.[289]

Nevertheless, there were occasionally direct shipments of salt, wine, brandy, vinegar and some iron from France during the late sixteenth and seventeenth centuries. In 1582–3, 'Francis Rychart' entered thirty-two tuns of French wine from the *Mary* of 'Oulderone' [Ile d'Oléron] at Douglas.[290] Vessels from Le Croisic, La Rochelle and Granville arrived at the same port in 1617–18, each carrying some salt as well as quantities of wine, vinegar, iron and pitch.[291] In the years around 1630, 'Peter John' of Le Croisic made several journeys between France and the island, bringing the same sort of commodities and returning with wool, hides and tanned leather.[292] War between England and France after 1689 and the English embargo on trade between the two countries disrupted this trade, but shipments from France to Man continued, some of the wine imported doubtless finding its way secretly into England, Ireland or Scotland. David Murrey of Douglas sent cargoes to France, chiefly to Bordeaux, on an irregular basis during the 1680s and 1690s. In 1700-1, he dispatched at least two shipments of hides, tallow and lead to Bordeaux from Douglas, one aboard the *François Sct. George* of the former town.[293] Some wine was also imported into the island from Portugal, although such cargoes appear only infrequently in the customs records. The *Loyalty* of Chester, for instance, anchored in Douglas Bay in July 1701 with red and white wines from Oporto on board.[294] There was apparently no significant direct trade with

---

[289] See *infra*, pp. 276–78, 285. Cubbon states that the waterbailiff's accounts do not record the source of wine imports, but that it was thought that the shipments came from France, Spain, Portugal and the Netherlands. Cubbon, 'Maritime Trade', pp. 623–4. Some of the accounts do, however, record the place of origin. See, for example, M.M.L., I.O. 1570–99, Ingates and outgates, 1583.
[290] M.M.L., I.O. 1570–99, Ingates and outgates, 1583.
[291] M.M.L., I.O. 1610–19, Book of licences and entries, 1618.
[292] See, for example, M.M.L., I.O. 1630–45, Waterbailiff's accounts, 1630.
[293] M.M.L., I.O. 1696–1704, Ingates and outgates, 1701.
[294] *ibid.*

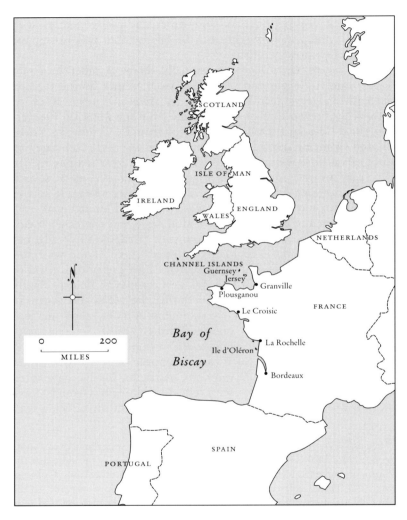

Map 6. Overseas trade: Europe.

the Netherlands, though Dutch vessels called at the island from time
to time. In April 1604, a ship from Flushing arrived at Douglas, but
landed no merchandise and paid only anchorage dues.[295] The *Golden
Fortune* of Middelburg was en route from St Martin in the Ile de Ré
to Kirkcudbright via Cork in March 1647 when it was forced to put
in at Douglas because it was leaking badly.[296] Dutch merchants, such
as Maximilian Vanderleere, occasionally traded with the island in the
early 1600s, but he at least was probably by that time settled in
Ireland.[297] Such limited direct trade as existed between the island and
the continent, therefore, remained focused on France throughout the
seventeenth century. (Map 6).

Of the island's ports, Douglas was by far the most important in
overseas trade, whether it was conducted with the continent or, as
was most often the case, the other countries of the British Isles. This
relative prominence as a commercial centre, which is quite clear from
even a cursory examination of the waterbailiff's accounts and from
the lists of recorded anchorages (Table 5.15), was due to the quality
of the town's harbour.

Table 5.15 *Recorded Anchorages in the Isle of Man,*
by Port. (Years ending at June 24)
(* An asterisk denotes defective figures)

Year	Douglas	Castletown	Ramsey	Peel	Total
1594	27	7	9	6	49
1595	33	17	12	16	78
1596	61	17	11	19	108
1597	40	24	16	33	113
1598	3	13	3*	4*	23*
1599	15	5	5	3	28
1600	20	15	12	11	58
1601	27	18	5	14	64

[295] M.M.L. R.D. 1600–26, Deputy's book of ingates and outgates (licences
and entries), 1604.
[296] Lib. Canc. 1647, 25–9, 33, 35, inter 82–5.
[297] M.M.L. R.D. 1600–26, Deputy's book of ingates and outgates (licences
and entries), 1604; R. Loeber, 'English and Irish Sources for Dutch Economic Activity in Ireland, 1600–1689', *I.E.S.H.*, vol. viii (1981), p. 82.
Vanderleere (Vanderleur) had settled in Co. Fermanagh by 1609.

Year	Douglas	Castletown	Ramsey	Peel	Total
1602	17	10	6	3	36
1603	38	13	9	9	69
1604	32	22	1	7	62
1605	39	16	3	11	69
1606	67	16	9	21	113
1607	60	8	5	13	86
1608	27	21	2	5	55
1609	32	9	2	12	55
1610	31	12	2	3	48
1611	46	26	8	11	91
1612	37	17	1	13	68
1613	26	7*	–	–	33*
1614	34	8	3	9	54
1615	78	15	—	13	106*
1616	—	—	—	—	—
1617	95	19	5	23	142
1618	121	23	6	30	180
1619	146	21	12	24	203
1620	125	9	—	24	158*
1621	98	8	2	20	128
1622	—	—	—	—	—
1623	101	1	7	14	123
1624	103	4	9	13	129
1625	126	14	23*	6	169*
1626	45	19	9*	25	98*
1627	94	3	3	18	118
1628	83	4	1	1	89
1629	96	3	1	16	116
1630	70	—	—	17	87*
1631	63	—	—	17	80*
1632	74	—	—	10	84*
1633	—	—	—	—	—
1634	—	10	—	—	10*
1635	—	—	—	—	—

Year	Douglas	Castletown	Ramsey	Peel	Total
1636	—	12	—	13	25*
1637	83	6	—	8	97*
1638	—	14	4	4	22*
1639	—	17	—	9	26*
1640	29	10	—	6	45*
1641	82	10	—	5	97*
1642	—	—	—	—	—
1643	—	—	—	—	—
1644	—	—	—	—	—
1645	—	—	—	—	—
1646	—	—	—	19	19*
1647	51	—	—	17	68*
1648	29	—	—	19	48*

Sources: M.M.L., I.O. 1600–19; I.O. 1629–9; I.O. 1630–45; I.O. 1646–59; R.D. 1579–98; R.D. 1627–50, Waterbailiff's accounts, 1594–1648.

Although, as William Blundell observed, 'Castletown be the principal town, yet Douglas is acknowledged to have the best, fairest, and securest haven of any other in all the Island,' a view subsequently echoed by James Chaloner.[298] In Blundell's opinion, the port was 'most inviting [to] foreigners' commerce, and therefore [was] the most frequented'. The haven was capable of accommodating ships of 'great burthen', which could

> cast anchor within the road under the shelter of two high rocks, mountains on each side, but if any do rashly presume to approach near unto the town without a Manks guide to conduct him, the ship is in an inevitable danger to miscarry by reason of latent rocks, on every side of the fort, lying undiscoverable either at the high or low water.[299]

There were also dangers for vessels anchoring in the island's other ports. Derbyhaven, or Ronaldsway, acted as the main harbour for Castletown, where large vessels were able to anchor in safety, except

[298] Blundell, *History*, vol. i, p. 89; Chaloner, *Treatise*, p. 6.
[299] Blundell, *History*, vol. i, p. 89.

during a storm, 'for either a south-east or a south wind drives them upon rocks, shelves which are not visible during the tides, and many have miscarried.'[300] By contrast, Ramsey offered 'a safe bay and road for ships to ride at anchor.'[301] The bay had 'a very large reception for ships,' Blundell reported, 'as so all of any burthen and many at once shall find easy entrance;' Ramsey did not, however, provide 'that shelter from winds nor that safe riding which is found at Douglas.'[302] Peel was not able to accommodate large vessels, but

> only small barks, because the channel betwixt this town and the island called Pile is very narrow, and therefore the sea is too boisterous at this haven, and therefore is seldom frequented, but upon necessity, except only by reason of proximity.[303]

Consequently, Irish merchants frequented Peel more than other foreign traders. The haven at Laxey, which was not noticed by Blundell or Denton, was, according to Chaloner, 'the meanest' of all the island's anchorages.[304]

VII. MERCHANTS, SHIPPING AND THE CONDUCT OF TRADE

The most striking feature of Manx overseas trade at the end of the sixteenth century is the comparatively large number of individuals who were engaged in it. A century later, this number had fallen by more than half, and commercial activity was increasingly concentrated in the hands of a relatively small group of merchants. In 1593–4, for example, approximately 208 persons made shipments to or from the island; by 1629–30, the total had dropped to about 168; in 1684–5, the number of those shipping merchandise of one sort or another through Manx ports was only eighty-three, and in 1695–6, it stood at eighty-seven.[305] A majority of the individuals

---

[300] *ibid*, p. 90.
[301] Denton, 'Description', p. 441.
[302] Blundell, *History*, vol. i, p. 91.
[303] *ibid*, p. 92.
[304] Chaloner, *Treatise*, p. 6.
[305] These figures are based on the names appearing in the waterbailiff's accounts, on the assumption that no two individuals shared the same name, except where this is clearly the case. This may be a dangerous assumption,

concerned – more than 50 per cent in each of the years mentioned – made only one small shipment of goods in the course of a year, according to the entries in the waterbailiff's accounts, while a limited number of merchants, always, it seems, composed of less than twenty, handled the trade on a more regular basis, shipping five or more cargoes a year.

Problems of identification and definition make it extremely difficult to determine statistically the share of the island's trade in the hands of native and foreign merchants respectively. A great deal of additional research would be required before such an analysis could be made, and then it might only serve to confirm the impression derived from the waterbailiff's accounts that Manx overseas trade was mainly conducted by Manxmen, whether resident, immigrant or emigrant, and that, while individual foreign merchants often played a significant part, English, Irish and Scottish merchants were of secondary importance.

This impression of the dominance of Manxmen in the island's trade appears to be borne out by an examination of the leading merchants at various times during the late sixteenth and seventeenth centuries. In 1593–4 there were eighteen merchants who came into this category, ten of whom were natives of the island. Of these men, Danold Christian and John Callow, the customer at Ramsey, were marginally the most active, making ten and nine inward and outward shipments respectively.[306] Two others, Danold Callister and Thomas Corrin, were based in Chester, although they are also sometimes described as of Douglas.[307] Callister, who had been apprenticed to Hugh Cally, a Chester sherman, was entered as a freeman of the city in October 1593, and traded between Chester and Douglas until about 1620.[308] Corrin, who owned the barque *The Gift of God* of Chester, regularly carried goods on behalf of other merchants or traded in his own right between the Dee and Douglas during the

particularly in relation to Manx names, but, even if it were possible to identify individuals more exactly, it is unlikely that these totals would be significantly lower.

[306] M.M.L., I.O. 1570–99, Customs book, 1594; waterbailiff's accounts, 1594.
[307] M.M.L. R.D. 1579–98, 'Custome book' 1594 (Captain's book of licences and entries, 1594–5).
[308] J. H. E. Bennett (ed.), *The Rolls of the Freemen of the City of Chester*, pt. i: *1392–1700*, R.S.L.C., vol. li (1906), p.71; M.M.L., I.O. 1610–19, Waterbailiff's accounts, 1618.

1590s and early 1600s.[309] The remaining eight merchants comprised three Englishmen – two from Chester and one from Neston in Wirral – two Scotsmen and three men of uncertain origin.[310]

The position of Manxmen in the island's trade was similar in 1629–30, although naturalised Manxmen, as opposed to natives, were beginning to play an important part. Nine of the twelve leading merchants in this year could be described as Manx, but only five were natives of the island.[311] The naturalised merchants[312] included Herbert Anderson and David and George Murrey, all doubtless of Scottish origin. The Murrey family appear to have settled in the island in the early seventeenth century and quickly became established in Douglas, from where David and George Murrey traded until their deaths in 1635.[313] The other merchant in this group was Henry Finch, a member of another family which was later to be important in the development of Douglas and which was presumably of English origin. Finch, like the Murreys, traded almost exclusively through Douglas.[314] Among the leading native Manx merchants were Robert Quayle of Douglas and Arthur Caesar of Ballahick, Malew. The other three principal merchants were English and included George Squire, the waterbailiff.

By the late seventeenth century, a large portion of the island's trade was being controlled by a handful of Manx merchants. Although substantial quantities of merchandise could be shipped by those merchants who made only one shipment to or from the Isle of

[309] M.M.L. R.D. 1579–98, 'Custome book' 1594 (Captain's book of licences and entries, 1594–5); M.M.L., I.O. 1610–19, Ingates and Outgates, 1610.
[310] M.M.L., I.O. 1570–99, Customs book, 1594; waterbailiff's accounts, 1594.
[311] M.M.L., I.O. 1630–45, Waterbailiff's accounts, 1630.
[312] Including the descendants of foreigners who had recently settled in the island. Foreigners could obtain the rights of a 'free denizen' of the island by swearing an oath of fealty to the Lord and paying a fine. See, for example, the payments made by John Cawsten and John Shittlington, both Scotsmen, in 1597 and 1622 respectively. Englishmen were theoretically not regarded as foreigners. Lib. Scacc. 1597, 31; Lib. Scacc. 1622, 24; M.M.L., MD/15,040, Parr, *Abridgement*, p. 8; Moore, *History*, vol. i, pp. 297–8.
[313] M.M.L., MF/EW/19. Testamentary Court File (Episcopal), 1635: will of David Murrey, October 30, 1635; inventory of George Murrey, November 7, 1635.
[314] Finch (Vinch) was trading from Douglas in 1618 and was perhaps still active in the late 1640s. M.M.L., I.O. 1610–18, Waterbailiff's accounts, 1618; M.M.L., I.O. 1646–59, Waterbailiff's accounts, 1647.

Man, such operations could not match the sustained enterprises of David Murrey senior and junior of Douglas or John Casement of Ramsey, who dominated Manx commerce in the 1680s and 1690s. In 1684–5, only one English merchant, William Button, was among the ten individuals who shipped most frequently through Manx ports.[315] The five native Manx merchants, including Phillip Moore of Douglas and John Wattleworth of Ramsey, who fell into the same category were overshadowed by the frequent shipments made by immigrant merchants such as Nicholas Harley, late of Wexford, then of Castletown,[316] Thomas Ottiwell of Castletown and the Murreys, though the latter were probably coming to be regarded as natives by this date. Harley supervised ten shipments during the year, the Murreys handled a total of fourteen, while Ottiwell was the most energetic, with eighteen cargoes either sent or received. A decade later, in 1695–6, the Murreys had increased their share of the trade still further, making thirty-eight shipments between them. Their nearest rivals were John Casement, who had expanded his dealings since the 1680s and in that year handled thirteen cargoes, and John Wattleworth, who managed a total of ten shipments in the same period.

Although it is scarcely possible to obtain a full picture of any merchant's operations from the fragmentary evidence available, it is clear that naturalised Manxmen were among the most successful merchants involved in the island's trade during the seventeenth century. The probate inventories of such merchants, which, despite their significant limitations, may be used as a crude indication of an individual's standing, show that some of these men accumulated a considerable amount of wealth by the standards of the island. Jeffrey Galloway, who settled in Castletown in about 1590, was an active merchant, trading between the island and England, on several occasions arriving at Liverpool in the first decade of the seventeenth century.[317] In spite of a tendency to speak his mind too often to criticise the behaviour of the deputy governor and officers, which led to his indictment for treason and punishment by fines,[318]

---

[315] M.M.L., I.O. 1680–9, Customs book, 1685.
[316] L.R.O., DDKe 80. Statement of Nicholas Harley, June 23, 1691.
[317] Lib. Plit. 1592, 2; P.R.O., E 190/1328/11; M.M.L., I.O. 1600–9, Water-bailiff's accounts, 1605.
[318] See, for example, Lib. Scacc. 1598, 2; inter 2–3; Lib. Scacc. 1601, 11–12; Lib. Plit. 1601, 29; Lib. Scacc. 1603, 8, inter 8–9; Lib. Scacc. 1606, 10.

Galloway seems to have been relatively prosperous. After his death in 1610, his estate was valued at £160 15s. 7½d. at least.[319] His household possessions were fairly basic, apart from four silver spoons, and amounted to only about £25 8s. 10d. of that total. Shop wares and trade goods, which included considerable quantities of cloth – fustians, medleys, kerseys, silk and velvet lace – as well as hats, gloves, stockings, spurs, arrowheads and bowstrings, paper and spices, accounted for £56 6s. 9½d.; the remainder of Galloway's estate was in the form of £70 in gold and silver and an 'ould barke,' which was sold for £9.

The inventory of John Black, another Scottish merchant who became a naturalised Manxman, reveals a similar degree of affluence. Black appears to have settled in Ramsey some time in or before 1651.[320] He traded as a merchant stranger until 1654, when, after being 'for severall yeares past a shopkeeper and inhabitor in Ramsey towne,' he paid 13s. 4d. to become a 'free denizon' of the island.[321] When he died ten years later, in 1664, Black left a personal estate amounting to £198 16s. 3d., although he does not appear to have lived in especial comfort. There was no silver amongst his household goods, all the plates and utensils being of wood, earthenware, pewter or horn. The merchandise in his shop came to at least £28 and consisted of a wide range of items, including haberdashery wares, such as buttons, pins, hooks and eyes, various types of cloth, clothing, knives, hatchets and other hardware, some paper, spices, books, looking glasses and 'apothecary stuffe.'[322]

Merchants such as Galloway and Black may have been comparatively wealthy by Manx standards, but the general level of prosperity which their probate inventories suggest was dwarfed by the success of David Murrey of Douglas, who died in 1702. The son of another David, with whom he can easily be confused,[323] he was

[319] M.M.L., MF/EW/6. Inventory of Jeffrey Galloway, June 6, 1610. Several entries in the inventory are slightly damaged and therefore the actual total was probably a little higher.
[320] Radcliffe, *Ramsey, 1600–1800*, p. 16.
[321] Lib. Scacc. 1654, 41.
[322] Radcliffe, *Ramsey, 1600–1800*, p. 111; M.M.L., MF/RB/517. Inventory of John Black, April 20, 1665.
[323] David Murrey (d. 1702) was probably the great grandson of the merchant of the same name who died in 1635. See *infra*, pp. 312–13. His father (d. 1701) and grandfather (date of death uncertain) both shared the same

a member of perhaps the third or fourth generation of this branch of the Murrey family based in Douglas. Together with his father and on his own account, he expanded the family's trading enterprises so that, by the mid 1690s, the Murreys were the most important merchants in the island in terms of the number of shipments made and the volume of goods transported. In the previous decade, the Murreys concentrated mainly on exporting skins and quantities of wool, tallow, butter, cheese and beer, principally to England, and importing iron, brandy, wine and tobacco, as well as occasional large cargoes of miscellaneous goods.[324] During the 1690s, the range of commodities in which the Murreys dealt regularly became broader. Spices, dyes, haberdashery wares and especially tobacco were all imported, the latter apparently being the foundation of the family's prosperity. A thriving re-export trade in tobacco rapidly developed, ostensibly between the island and Scotland and Ireland, although some was doubtless sent secretly to England as well.[325] In 1695–6, the Murreys were, with one exception, the only merchants handling the tobacco trade, entering 21,627 pounds of Virginia leaf and re-exporting 8,787 pounds to Irvine in Scotland and to Ireland, according to the Manx customs accounts.[326] The wealth generated by this traffic in particular is clearly reflected in the value of David Murrey's personal estate, which amounted to £3,657 at the time of his death.[327]

Merchants such as David Murrey probably supervised most of their commercial enterprises in person, although in some cases they were represented by factors or agents.[328] It has been suggested by D. M. Woodward that the absence of factors was a noticeable

name. M.M.L., MF/PR/5, Braddan Parish Registers: Burials; Lib. Canc. 1650, 71; W. Cubbon (ed.), 'Unpublished Document no. 227,' *J.M.M.*, vol. iv (1938–40), p. 154 n. 3.

[324] M.M.L., I.O. 1680–9, Customs book, 1685.

[325] For a discussion of the smuggling from the island, see *infra*, pp. 331–41.

[326] M.M.L., I.O. 1696–1704, Customs book, 1696.

[327] M.M.L., MF/EW/27. Inventory of David Murrey, junior, June 21, 1704. The inventory of David Murrey survives only in the form of an abstract. Cf. Cubbon, 'Unpublished Document no. 227', p. 154. The total of Murrey's estate is inexplicably given here as £3,396.

[328] The role of the factor in overseas trade has generally been neglected, but see Willan, *Studies in Elizabethan Foreign Trade*, pp. 1–33; Lythe, *Economy of Scotland*, pp. 128–9; Smout, *Scottish Trade*, pp. 8off., 96ff.

feature of the trade between Chester and the Isle of Man in the late sixteenth century and that consequently merchants engaged in this trade probably made the voyage to or from the island to oversee the shipment of their goods.[329] Some merchants certainly did so. In October 1586, Roger Darwell, a Chester glover who frequently traded with the island between about 1580 and 1610, was unable to appear before the portmote court in the city as he was bound, because he was 'then in the Isle of Man, the wind not servinge to Retorne.'[330] Darwell does not seem to have owned a ship, either in his own right or in partnership, but many of the merchants involved in this and in other branches of the island's trade were shipowners and, indeed, were masters of their vessels. Phillip Kewley, a Chester merchant of Manx origin, made several journeys between the city and Douglas during the 1590s, probably all of them in his own barque; John Martin, a Scotsman who took up residence in Ramsey, regularly ventured with his boat to the ports of south-west Scotland in the years between about 1590 and 1620; and Patrick Audley of Strangford was a periodically frequent visitor to Peel over the same span of time.[331]

Some of these merchant shipowners appear to have also acted as factors, transporting goods for other traders,[332] although the

[329] Woodward, *Elizabethan Chester*, p. 36.

[330] C.C.R.O., Assembly Minute Books, AB/1, f. 206r.

[331] See in general M.M.L., I.O. 1570–99, Customs book, 1594; waterbailiff's accounts, 1594; M.M.L. R.D. 1579–98, 'Custome book', 1594 (Captain's book of licences and entries, 1594–5); M.M.L., I.O. 1600–9, Waterbailiff's accounts, 1600; waterbailiff's accounts, 1605; M.M.L. R.D. 1600–26, Deputy's book of ingates and outgates (licences and entries), 1600 (1600–1). These sources do not provide details of the ports with which John Martin traded, but his association with William Clugston of Whithorn in 1599–1600 and the fact that he paid £3 to the burgh treasurer of Ayr for a licence to sell his beef and hides there in 1607–8 clearly indicates the direction of Martin's main trading activities. G. S. Pryde (ed.), 'Ayr Burgh Accounts, 1534–1624', *Scottish History Society*, 3rd series, vol. xxviii (1937), p. 234.

[332] It was by no means unknown for English, Irish and Scottish merchants to commission other merchants to supervise the shipment of goods on their behalf. See, for example, M. H. B. Sanderson, 'The Edinburgh Merchants in Society, 1570–1603; the Evidence of their Testaments', in I. B. Cowan and D. Shaw (eds), *The Renaissance and Reformation in Scotland* (Edinburgh 1983), p. 191; J. J. Brown, 'Merchant Princes and Mercantile Investment in Early Seventeenth Century Scotland', in M. Lynch (ed.), *The Early*

evidence of this practice is limited to occasional references in the waterbailiff's accounts, mainly before 1600, and may rather indicate a partnership or at least a temporary association between merchants. In May 1594, for example, Phillip Kewley entered a shipment of earthenware and soap at Douglas for Patrick Kelly, who may have commissioned Kewley as his factor for the voyage or who may have been his partner; similarly, in the same month and at the same port, Thomas Corrin landed cargoes of corn, woollen cards, soap and spades for four individuals who may have retained him as their agent or who may have been engaged with him as fellow merchants.[333] In one case at least, after November 1633, a prominent Manx merchant, Robert Quayle of Douglas, served as a resident factor for an English merchant, Christopher Lowther of White-haven. Quayle was responsible for receiving, storing and selling any wines which might be unloaded from one of Lowther's ships and for selling any other goods which were landed; in return for his factorage, Quayle received two per cent 'upon all sayles and imploy-ments' with 'all your extraordinaries in my busines.'[334] This rate may have been slightly lower than the contemporary standard, but Lowther allowed the same rate to his other agents in Irish Sea ports.[335]

Partnerships, whether lasting only for the duration of a single voyage or for a longer term, were not unusual among the merchants who traded in the island on a regular basis, although associations of the former type were apparently more common than those of the latter. When merchants continued to ship goods together over a period of years, it was most often because they were joint owners of

---

Modern Town in Scotland (1987), p. 135; Willan, *Studies in Elizabethan Foreign Trade*, pp. 14–15; Woodward, *Elizabethan Chester*, p. 34.

[333] M.M.L., I.O. 1570–99, Waterbailiff's accounts, 1594.

[334] Hainsworth, *Commercial Papers of Sir Christopher Lowther*, p. 137. Robert Quayle of Ballaquayle, Conchan, was a member of the Keys from 1608 until 1636, when he became a deemster. He died in March 1644. Lib. Scacc., *passim*; M.M.L., MF/EW/5. Braddan Parish Registers: Burials.

[335] Hainsworth, *Commercial Papers of Sir Christopher Lowther*, p. 137. Lowther had factors at Dublin, Belfast, Carrickfergus, Bristol, Liverpool, Lancaster, Milnethorpe, Ravenglass and Whitehaven, as well as at Douglas. D. R. Hainsworth, 'Christopher Lowther's Canary Adventure: A Merchant Venturer in Dublin, 1632–3', *I.E.S.H.*, vol. ii (1975), p. 22, n. 4.

a barque or wherry.[336] In the last decade of the sixteenth century, John Cure and John Quayle, both of Douglas, owned a boat of unspecified type and made several shipments through that port.[337] At least one of the cargoes entered by William Watterson at Douglas in 1629 was unloaded from the vessel which he owned with William Billinge, and Danold Christian and John Black of Douglas landed a consignment of coal from their barque in the same year at the same place.[338] In 1688, David Murrey and another Douglas merchant, William Kelly, made the joint purchase of a ship which was named the *Rose* and which became the chief Manx-based carrier of the Murreys' merchandise during the 1690s.[339]

Most of the leading figures in the Manx mercantile community seem to have owned a vessel of some description, but the nature of the entries in the waterbailiff's accounts, which in general before the late seventeenth century merely record ownership of an unnamed vessel, makes it difficult to establish whether any merchants owned more than a single ship, in full or in part. Nevertheless, it seems that a merchant generally transported his goods in his own vessel, unless it was already engaged in another trading enterprise. In such circumstances, he had to charter a vessel to carry his cargo, either in his own right or in combination with one or more fellow merchants.

The chartering of vessels by individual merchants or by a temporary or longer term partnership was a part of normal business practice in the island's trade, but the precise nature of such arrangements is not clear. Agreements between shipowners and merchants for the hiring of a vessel for a particular overseas trading venture were usually formalised in a charter party, which recorded the names of the owners and master of the vessel, or at least the latter, the name of the merchant or merchants and of the vessel itself and the purpose

---

[336] A wherry was 'a little light boat with two masts', with fore and aft rig. Megaw and Megaw, 'Manx Fishing Craft', pp. 14, 16. It is possible, however, that apparent joint ownership may conceal specific arrangements for the use of the vessel on a series of voyages.

[337] M.M.L., I.O. 1570–99, Customs book, 1594; waterbailiff's accounts, 1594; M.M.L., I.O. 1600–9, Ingates and outgates, 1600.

[338] M.M.L., I.O. 1630–45, Waterbailiff's accounts, 1630.

[339] M.M.L., MD/401/1718/75; M.M.L., I.O. 1696–1704, Customs book, 1696.

of the voyage in detail.[340] In the opinion of Gerard de Malynes, writing in the early seventeenth century, 'no Ship should be fraighted without a Charterpartie,' which was 'a Charter of Covenant betweene the two parties.'[341] It has been suggested, however, that, although charter parties were in general use by the seventeenth century, such commercial instruments may not have been widely employed in trade across the Irish Sea and were perhaps only drawn up on occasions when several merchants planned to load a ship to capacity.[342] This may well have been the case in trade with the Isle of Man, although the fact that no charter parties involving Manx shipowners or merchants seem to have survived does not necessarily prove that these documents were never used. From references to trading arrangements in disputes between merchants and shipmasters, it appears that some form of written agreement was made between the parties involved, probably similar to that entered into by shipowners who hired out their vessels for coastal shipments in England. This type of agreement embodied an undertaking by the owner or the master, who were often one and the same, to deliver the goods specified by the merchant to a particular port at a certain date.[343] As in a charter party, the merchant promised to pay the freight charges and dues and both parties bound themselves in a sum of money to observe the terms of the arrangement.[344] A merchant who had good reason to believe that the shipmaster had broken his contract could also seek restitution through the courts. In December

[340] For examples of charter parties, see D. M. Woodward, 'Sixteenth-Century Shipping: The Charter Party of the *Grace* of Neston, 1572', *I.E.S.H.*, vol. v (1978), pp. 67–8; Williams, *Maritime Trade*, pp. 293–5; Lib. Canc. 1636, inter 58–9 (1); Lib. Canc. 1647, inter 82–5; Smout, *Scottish Trade*, p. 293. Charter parties are discussed in Williams, *Maritime Trade*, pp. 208–10; R. Davis, *The English Shipping Industry in the Seventeenth and Eighteenth Centuries* (2nd edn, Newton Abbot, 1972), pp. 166–7; Lythe, *Economy of Scotland*, pp. 128–9.

[341] G. de Malynes, *Consuetudo, vel Lex Mercatoria, or the Ancient Law Merchant* (1622), p. 134.

[342] Woodward, 'Sixteenth-Century Shipping', p. 64.

[343] Williams, *Maritime Trade*, p. 212 and n. 28. For references to covenants of this kind, see, for instance, the suits brought by Thomas Tubman of Peel against Edward and James Taylor of 'Milep' (Millom?) in Cumberland and by Deemster Ewan Christian against William McNuskey. Lib. Canc. 1600, 18; Lib. Canc. 1630, 12, inter 12–13.

[344] Williams, *Maritime Trade*, pp. 209–10.

1687, Henry Cottier of Castletown brought a suit against William Corrin of Douglas for damages which he had incurred through the mariner's negligence. Cottier had chartered Corrin's vessel to carry his goods from Wicklow to the island, but when Corrin arrived off the coast, he 'neglected to secure the said vessell and bring her into safe harbour whereby the complainant hath lost his said goods.' The Admiralty Court[345] ordered Corrin to pay Cottier the sum of £5 10s., 'together with all the charge,' and 50s. in damages at a later date.[346]

The small size of the merchant community in the island meant that commercial transactions were conducted by a mixture of cash payments, credit and a sort of 'book-keeping barter.' It is difficult to assess the importance of cash as a means of exchange for, though it was probably more plentiful throughout the seventeenth century than previously thought, the quantity in circulation was still relatively small.[347] Nevertheless, cash was used for minor transactions, such as the purchase from Mary Corkan of four pots of honey at a cost of £1 19s. by Christopher Lowther, who was en route from Dublin to Whitehaven in November 1635.[348] Some Manx merchants doubtless exchanged specie for goods but, in line with the widely held contemporary view that such an outflow of sound coin was a recipe for economic disaster, it was a practice which was not encouraged.[349] The limited resources of most of the island's mercantile community essentially restricted the use of credit mechanisms, such as bills of exchange, to the relatively wealthy merchants who traded with ports where these facilities were readily available. The bill of exchange was a negotiable credit instrument which was basically an order to pay and it became increasingly common during the seventeenth century.[350] The extent to which it was used by the principal merchants in the island is not certain, but the debts which they

[345] The jurisdiction of the Admiralty Court is discussed in chapter 1, pp.73–4.
[346] Lib. Canc. 1687, 63.
[347] For further details about the coinage in the island, see chapter 3, pp. 160–66.
[348] Hainsworth, *Commercial Papers of Sir Christopher Lowther*, p. 165.
[349] Despite repeated legislation prohibiting the export of coinage, merchants often sent or took specie abroad on their trading ventures. Sutherland, *English Coinage*, pp. 69, 83, 92; O'Brien, *Economic History of Ireland*, p. 65; Lythe, *Economy of Scotland*, pp. 140–1.
[350] E. Kerridge, *Trade and Banking in Early Modern England* (Manchester 1988), pp. 45–6 and *passim*.

accumulated may indicate the employment of such methods of obtaining credit. At the time of his death in 1664, John Black of Ramsey, for example, owed one Richard Townsend the sum of £42 and a further £14 to two other, unnamed English merchants.[351] For the vast majority, who had very little in the way of capital, the usual commercial practice was to exchange their goods for foreign items of equivalent value, a process embodied in the common bargain with the merchant stranger.[352] More prosperous merchants were also sometimes ready to adopt this means of exchange if ready cash were in short supply. In 1624, John Veasey, a Belfast merchant, was quite prepared to accept, in lieu of specie, 'soe much good and merchantable wares as would extend to the full woorth and valewe' of the debt of £64 6s. 1od. owed to him by Danold Christian and Patrick Finch.[353]

Most of the vessels owned or freighted by merchants engaged in trade with the island were small craft, even by contemporary standards. Although no relevant information is recorded in the waterbailiff's accounts, details of the burthen of Manx and foreign vessels trading between the island and England and Wales in the late sixteenth and early seventeenth centuries are contained in the port books of Chester, Liverpool, Beaumaris and other ports of the Irish Sea littoral. Such data were increasingly omitted during the seventeenth century, but it is clear from the evidence available that the great majority of Manx vessels involved in this trade were of less than twenty tons burthen.[354] In the first Chester port book, for 1565–6, the *Anne* of Castletown of eight tons and the *Katherine* of Douglas of four tons are recorded as entering the port.[355] The four Manx

---

[351] M.M.L., MF/RB/517. Inventory of John Black of Ramsey, 1665.

[352] See *infra*, pp. 240–42.

[353] Lib. Canc. 1624, 21.

[354] Woodward, 'Port Books', p. 154. The burthen represented the potential cargo capacity of a vessel, but it is not clear how this was measured. Variations in the tonnage quoted for the same vessel in the port books suggest that it was probably merely an approximation. R. W. Unger, *The Ship in the Medieval Economy, 600–1600* (1980), p. 29; Hinton, 'Port Books of Boston', pp. xxi–xxii; Williams, *Maritime Trade*, pp. 223–4. For examples of such variations relating to Manx vessels, see the entries for the *Elizabeth* of Ramsey and the *Margaret* of Douglas in the Beaumaris port books for 1583–4, 1585 and 1587. Lewis, *Welsh Port Books*, pp. 250, 256 and 259.

[355] Wilson, *Chester Customs Accounts*, pp. 78, 79.

vessels which arrived at Liverpool in 1570 ranged in size from the *Katherine* of four tons – perhaps the same craft which traded with Chester several years previously – to the *Sunday* of sixteen tons.[356] As many as six vessels entered Beaumaris from the Isle of Man in 1577, the smallest of which was the *Margaret* of Peel of six tons, while the largest was the *Michael* of Ramsey of eleven tons.[357] Two of the three Manx ships which entered the Mersey in 1603–4 had a burthen of ten tons or less – the *Grace of God* of nine tons and the *Grace* of Douglas of ten tons; the third vessel, the *Gift of God*, was substantially larger, having a burthen of fifty tons.[358] The single Manx barque which traded at Carrickfergus in 1614–15 was the *Gift of God* of fourteen tons.[359]

Small though these Manx vessels generally were, they were not significantly smaller than the craft engaged in some other branches of Irish Sea trade. In the later sixteenth century, for instance, Irish vessels, chiefly from Wexford, trading with Milford in south Wales had an average burthen of less than eight tons.[360] Vessels involved in other Irish Sea trades tended to be somewhat larger. The average cargo capacity of ships clearing from Chester for Ireland during the reign of Elizabeth varied between about sixteen and about thirty tons.[361] The barque with a burthen of about fifteen tons which carried Sir William Brereton from Portpatrick in Scotland to Ireland

---

[356] P.R.O., E 190/1323/12, cited in Hollinshead, thesis, vol. i, pp. 360–1.

[357] Lewis, *Welsh Port Books*, pp. 244–6.

[358] P.R.O., E 190/1328/11. It seems likely that the *Gift of God*, which was described merely as of the Isle of Man, was the barque of Thomas Corrin of Douglas and Chester. The burthen of Corrin's vessel was stated as thirty tons in the Beaumaris port book for 1599–1600, but, as previously noted, variations in the tonnage recorded were by no means uncommon. Lewis, *Welsh Port Books*, p. 290. Cf. note 354.

[359] Sweetnam, 'Early Seventeenth Century Shipmasters and Merchants', p. 12. In the second half of the sixteenth century, there were apparently a few larger Manx vessels, such as the *Nicholas* of Douglas and the *Anne* of Douglas, both of fifty tons, but these ships traded with Spain and France and cleared from foreign ports, principally, if not exclusively, Chester. Wilson, *Chester Customs Accounts*, pp. 75, 81, 84.

[360] D. M. Woodward, 'Irish Sea Trades and Shipping from the Later Middle Ages to c. 1660', in M. McCaughan and J. C. Appleby (eds), *The Irish Sea. Aspects of Maritime History* (Belfast, 1989), p. 42.

[361] Woodward, *Elizabethan Chester*, appendix I, p. 131.

in 1635 was probably typical of the most common size of vessel traversing the Irish Sea for commercial purposes.[362]

The largest contingents of foreign shipping which traded with the Isle of Man, in terms of entries and departures, originated in England and Ireland, and most of these vessels were probably little larger than their Manx counterparts. The smallest English vessels in the trade appear to have been of about six tons burthen, such as the *Jonas* of Formby, which was one of four Lancashire craft, ranging in size from six to ten tons, which sailed from the island for Beaumaris in March 1587.[363] Many of the English vessels transporting goods to and from the island had a carrying capacity of between ten and twenty tons. In 1583, John Meyrick, bishop of Sodor and Man, was conveyed to his home in Anglesey aboard the *Michael* of Liverpool of fifteen tons.[364] In 1603–4, shipments from Douglas arrived at Liverpool in the *Unicorn* of Frodsham of ten tons, the *Margaret* of Alt of twelve tons and the *James* of Liverpool of fourteen tons.[365] Some English vessels of greater burthen also entered Manx harbours. In the last three decades of the sixteenth century, four Liverpool ships of between twenty and thirty-six tons arrived in the island on one occasion or more, the largest of these vessels being the twenty-six ton *Lantern* and the thirty-six ton *Elizabeth*.[366] All four ships were considerably larger in size than the average English vessel in the Manx trade, which, when sailing from the Dee at the beginning of the seventeenth century, had a mean cargo capacity of sixteen tons.[367] Little information is available about the size of Irish ships trading with the island, but such data as can be derived from the customs accounts indicate that some Irish vessels were of about six tons burthen, such as the *Sunday* of Wexford which entered Douglas Bay in 1594.[368]

---

[362] *W. Brereton's Travels in Holland and the United Provinces, England, Scotland and Ireland*, (ed.), E. Hawkins (Chet. Soc, O.S., vol. i, 1844), pp. 123–6; Woodward, 'Irish Sea Trades', p. 42.

[363] Lewis, *Welsh Port Books*, p. 258.

[364] *ibid*, p. 248.

[365] P.R.O., E 190/1328/11.

[366] Hollinshead, thesis, vol. ii, appendix xxv, pp. 845–6.

[367] Woodward, *Elizabethan Chester*, appendix i (B), p. 131.

[368] M.M.L. R.D. 1579–98, 'Custome book', 1594 (Captain's book of licences and entries, 1594–5). Cf. P.R.O., E 190/1328/11.

The pace at which commercial enterprises proceeded, once the merchant had loaded his goods aboard his vessel or a charter ship and paid the customs duties and other dues, was determined mainly by the weather. Crossings of the Irish Sea could be relatively swift in favourable conditions, particularly from Irish ports to the Isle of Man or from the island to England and Scotland, taking advantage of the prevailing south-westerly winds. A Dublin merchant, Bartholomew Rossynell, informed William of Worcester in 1479 that a voyage from Dublin to the Isle of Man was 'four kennings'[369] – a day and a night's sailing – and, with a fair wind and a light sea, this seems to have been the normal duration of such journeys. Christopher Lowther's crossing from Dublin to Douglas in 1635, for example, appears to have lasted about twenty-four hours, approximately the same length of time as the second leg of his journey from Douglas to Whitehaven.[370] The duration of journeys between Chester and the island was probably similar,[371] although crossings between the more northerly parts of England and the Manx ports, particularly those on the east coast of Man, could be considerably shorter. In 1687, William Stout of Lancaster sailed from that port in a vessel bound for Dublin 'and in twelve hours came over against Douglas.'[372]

Bad weather frequently caused delays for shipping, whether the vessels were in port or at sea. The lack of a favourable wind could

[369] *Statute Rolls of the Parliament of Ireland, Henry VI*, ed. H. Berry (Dublin 1910), p. 483ff., cited in T. O'Neill, *Merchants and Mariners in Medieval Ireland* (Dublin 1987), p. 118. A kenning was a maritime measure equivalent to twenty or twenty-one miles. *O.E.D.*, *sub* kenning.

[370] Hainsworth, *Commercial Papers of Sir Christopher Lowther*, p. 165. The entries in Lowther's accounts concerning the first part of the journey are, however, somewhat ambiguous – the time of departure and of arrival being merely referred to as '10 of the clocke' – but, unless his ship was becalmed or encountered a storm, it seems unlikely that the voyage would have lasted for thirty-six hours. In view of the distance between Dublin and Douglas, it is equally unlikely that the journey was of only twelve hours duration.

[371] The distance between Chester and the Isle of Man and between Chester and Dublin is practically the same and a voyage between the two cities took about a day or so. D. M. Woodward, 'Ships, Masters and Shipowners of the Wirral, 1550–1650', *Maritime History*, vol. v (1977), p. 9.

[372] J. D. Marshall (ed.), *The Autobiography of William Stout of Lancaster, 1665–1752* (Chet. Soc., 3rd series, vol. xiv, 1967), p. 86.

prevent departure for some little time and, after the ship finally put to sea, further delays could arise from storms, which were not uncommon in the Irish Sea. In 1622, the *Mayflower* of Derry, bound for London from her home port with a cargo of beef, tallow and hides, ran into such a storm, during which the vessel lost her rudder. After three days, the crew managed to bring the *Mayflower* into Douglas, where repairs were made, but when the ship set sail ten days later, more foul weather drove her into Holyhead.[373] The *Sarah* of Castletown, owned by Nicholas Harley, was carrying a cargo of cattle for the earl of Derby from the island to Liverpool in 1692 when, 'within four leagues of Highlake' [Hoylake], she was forced back by 'very tempestious wether,' 'with great difficulty escapeing, being once in hazard of oversetting.' Two cattle died and four others were 'much bruised' as a result of the high seas, but the ship eventually reached port.[374] Other vessels were less fortunate, even though they were sheltering in the comparative safety of one of the island's havens. En route from Belfast to England in 1687-8, the *Supply* of Lancaster was blown into Castletown 'by contrary winds,' and, while she lay at anchor, 'was bulged by a stone' and a large part of her cargo of Irish yarn, hides and linen cloth was spoiled.[375] Severe storms sometimes caused ships to be wrecked off the island's coast, as in 1650, when a Workington barque 'was broken uppon the rockes att the stack of Scarlett,' to the west of Castletown.[376] No fewer than three Manx vessels were lost in the 'very tempestious weather' of December 1687.[377]

---

[373] J. C. Appleby, 'Merchants and Mariners, Pirates and Privateers: An Introductory Survey of the Records of the High Court of Admiralty as a Source for Regional Maritime History', in McCaughan and Appleby, *Irish Sea*, p. 52.

[374] M.M.L., MD/401/1719/16. John Rowe, comptroller, to William, ninth earl of Derby, September 8, 1692.

[375] M.M.L., MD/401/1718/63. Rowe to Robert Roper, secretary of the earl of Derby, January 4, 1688.

[376] M.M.L., MF/PR/19. Malew Parish Registers: Burials.

[377] M.M.L., MD/401/1718/63. Rowe to Roper, January 4, 1688.

VIII. PIRACY IN THE IRISH SEA

Apart from the hazards of the weather, the merchants' other major source of uncertainty sprang from the activities of pirates in the Irish Sea. Until the second half of the seventeenth century, the waters between England and Ireland were infested by vessels of various nations whose crews were eager to prey on merchant shipping. British pirates operated from remote areas, such as south-west Ireland, where the local population made a part of their living by entertaining them.[378] While it does not seem to have been extensively used as a base, the Isle of Man, which had no laws against fraternising with pirates, was often a port of call for vessels stocked with booty. In 1588, the *Pelican* of Bremen was seized by Anthony Weekes and taken to the island, where parts of its cargo, valued at more than £1,400, were sold.[379] Ten years later, the Privy Council believed that some of the plunder taken from a Waterford barque by Thomas Venables and his crew had been disposed of in Chester and the Isle of Man.[380] Some merchants suspected the officers of the island of complicity in such matters, but, while the latter may have often turned a blind eye to the dealings between pirates and the inhabitants, they did not always do so. In 1603, Daniel Tucker and his crew landed forty tuns of plundered Gascon wine in the island, but were arrested by Deputy Governor Robert Molyneux and sent to London in the charge of the constable of Castle Rushen.[381] In an effort to stamp out the practice of receiving pirates in the island, Elizabeth, countess of Derby, who was effectively Lord of Man between 1612 and her death in 1627, commissioned Bishop John Phillips, Edward Rigby of Burgh and Henry Radcliffe, the waterbailiff, in 1614 to examine 'all and everye offendors or persons suspected in or with the offence of Pyracye, aswell the Pyrators themselves, as all Ayders, Receyvors, or Relievers of them within the said island' and to imprison the guilty parties.[382] The

---

[378] C. M. Senior, *A Nation of Pirates. English Piracy in its Heyday* (Newton Abbot, 1976), pp. 53–7, 138–9; M. MacCarthy-Morrogh, *The Munster Plantation. English Migration to Southern Ireland, 1583–1641* (Oxford, 1986), pp. 215–222.
[379] *A.P.C.E., 1588*, pp. 367–9.
[380] *A.P.C.E., 1597–8*, pp. 281–3.
[381] B. L. Add. MS 5,664, ff. 331r., 333r.; M.M.L., Ellesmere Papers, 244/C/2, 172; 246/D/2, 158.
[382] Lib. Scacc. 1614, 41.

results of this commission are not certain, but its effects appear to
have been very limited. In 1615, two pirate vessels anchored at Ramsey and traded for victuals with some of the inhabitants, including Sir
William Norris, vicar general and vicar of Lonan, and John Curghey
of Ballakillingan, Lezayre. John Halsall, the attorney general, claimed
that these individuals were guilty of treason by virtue of the statute
of 1423 which stated that 'whosoever relieves or receipts Rebells,
knowing the Rebellion, he is a Traytor;' the deemsters and Keys,
however, informed him that this only applied to 'cases of government
within the Island, namely in insurrections made against the Lieutenant or the Lords Royalties.'[383] No orders prohibiting dealings with
pirates or laws against piracy were made in the island and consequently Manx harbours continued to be at least a temporary refuge
for those who lived from the looting of merchant vessels.

In the early 1630s, Thomas, Viscount Wentworth, Lord Deputy
of Ireland, found his determined efforts to reduce the pirate threat
to Irish Sea commerce partially undermined by the actions of Edward Christian, governor of the Isle of Man from 1627 until 1634.
In April 1631, Christian detained John Downes, a notorious pirate
who had long eluded the vessels sent out by the English government,
but subsequently released him, claiming that 'no Body came to
prosecute against [Downes], although he had sent divers Times into
England and into Ireland.'[384] Two years later, Christian received
John Gayner, an English pirate with a Spanish commission 'for the
takeing of Hollanders,' who had recently seized the *St Jacob* of
Rotterdam in Dublin Bay. Protesting that 'Means [he] had not any
to take the Prize from them by Force,' Christian informed
Wentworth that he had purchased as much of the cargo as possible
so that it could be returned to the owner on petition to the Lord of
Man.[385] Wentworth's representative, Captain Thomas James of the
Ninth Lion's Whelp, was not convinced, warning that

This Island, if it be not governed by an honest and faithful Man,
may be a most dangerous lurking Place for Pirates, for a Ship

[383] Lib. Plit. 1649, inter 100–1; *Statutes*, p. 10.
[384] Lib. Plit. 1631, October 18, 1631; Senior, *Nation of Pirates*, p. 144; W.
Knowler (ed.), *The Earl of Strafforde's Letters and Dispatches* (2 vols, 1739),
vol. i, p. 127.
[385] Knowler, *Strafforde's Letters*, vol. i, pp. 118, 126–7; *C.S.P.D., 1633–4*, p.
506.

may ride round about it for all Winds, and from it you may see England, Wales, Scotland and Ireland, and endanger all the Shipping that pass any Ways in those Seas, as being not twenty Leagues from Dublin, Beaumaris, and the Streight of Carickfergus.[386]

Wentworth pressed for action against Christian, who was summoned to appear before the Lords Commissioners of the Admiralty. Doubtless to the Lord Deputy's dismay, Christian's explanations seem to have been accepted in London, but, nevertheless, James, Lord Strange, who was acting as Lord of Man for his father, William, sixth earl of Derby, tactfully decided to dismiss the governor from office.[387]

The dangers facing merchant shipping crossing the Irish Sea during the 1640s were probably significantly greater than in the previous decade. In the 1630s, two or three English naval vessels guarded the seas from the North Channel between Ulster and the Mull of Galloway in the north to the Scilly Isles and Cape Clear, County Cork, in the south – a practically impossible task, for the area to be patrolled encompassed 'above 400 leagues of water.'[388] The wars of the 1640s brought an increased naval presence in the Irish Sea to combat Royalist privateers, who were little better than pirates and who operated from a number of bases including Wexford[389] and the Isle of Man. Merchant vessels could, however, be stopped by either side, and sometimes by both, the crews of the navy ships being quite as likely to take cargo as the licensed privateers. In 1649, James Cotterell, a privateer who frequented the island, captured the *Speedwell* of Dublin, bound for Strangford, off the Ulster coast and brought her in to Peel. According to John Blythe, one of the merchants aboard, this was not the first time that the vessel's passage had

[386] Knowler, *Strafforde's Letters*, vol. i, p. 127.

[387] *ibid*, vol. i, p. 136; *C.S.P.D.*, *1634–5*, pp. 74, 139. Christian was replaced temporarily by Deemster Ewan Christian and subsequently by Sir Charles Gerard of Halsall. Lib. Scacc. 1634, inter 32–3; Lib. Canc. 1634, 29.

[388] *C.S.P.D.*, *1634–5*, p. 202.

[389] Many of the Wexford privateers were Dunkirkers who had sometimes entered the Irish Sea in the previous decade. See J. H. Ohlmeyer, 'The Dunkirk of Ireland: Wexford Privateers during the 1640s', *Journal of the Wexford Historical Society*, vol. xii (1988), pp. 23–49; *idem*, 'Irish Privateers during the Civil War, 1642–1650', *Mariner's Mirror*, vol. lxxvi (1990), pp. 119–133.

been interrupted, for some of the cargo of sack which he was shipping 'was wasted and druncke by the Company of two parliament Frigots who before tooke them and kept them three or four dayes.'[390]

Other privateers, including George Bradshaw and John Bartlett, also used the island as a base from which to harry merchant vessels. In June 1650, Bradshaw seized the *Mary* of Liverpool off the Irish coast near Carrickfergus 'with a longe boate from the Iland of Man, manned with Sixteene Oares,' and armed with 'two guns, one murderer, and several musketts.' The prize was taken to the island, where George Sayer, the factor of Robert Massey of Warrington, petitioned James, seventh earl of Derby, for the restitution of his master's goods which formed part of the cargo. He received no satisfaction and had to be content with Derby's uncompromising answer that 'a fifteenth parte he did take for the Kinge, a tenth parte for himself, and the Remainder for the taker.'[391] Bartlett, who often cleared from Manx harbours, was particularly active during the summer of 1650, capturing the fishing boat *Hopewell* of Yarmouth near the Faroe Islands and, having returned to home waters, the *Michael* of Liverpool en route for that port from Drogheda.[392]

Significantly, none of the privateers operating out of Manx waters seem to have spoiled merchant vessels trading with the island, although such ships were as vulnerable as any shipping to the depredations of licensed privateers based elsewhere. In 1647, a Wexford frigate under the command of Cornelius Dann seized the barque of John Crellin of Peel, which was returning to Man with a consignment of corn. After transferring the cargo to his vessel, Dann held Crellin to ransom for his son and three other members of his company detained in the island, sending a message to Earl James to inform him 'how that [Crellin] was taken at sea' and to request the release of the prisoners; Crellin was carried to Wexford, where he endured twelve weeks in prison before an undertaking was received that Dann's men would be freed.[393]

In the second half of the seventeenth century, a new danger arose to jeopardise merchant enterprises in the Irish Sea in the form of

---

[390] Lib. Scacc. 1650, 45.
[391] J. H. Stanning (ed.), *The Royalist Composition Papers, vol. ii*, R.S.L.C., vol. xxvi (1892), p. 131.
[392] Lib. Scacc. 1650, 83.
[393] *ibid*, inter 79–80.

foreign privateers. French and Spanish privateers made occasional appearances in British waters in the 1620s and 1630s,[394] but, after 1650, the three wars between England and the United Provinces and subsequently, from 1689, the war between England and France meant that Dutch and French privateers became a major threat to vessels crossing the Irish Sea. During the Second Dutch War (1665–67), there were unsubstantiated reports that some Manxmen had entertained 'severall Pikeroons and Dutch men of Warr.' Charles, eighth earl of Derby, dismissed such rumours, but warned Deputy Governor Henry Nowell and the other officers that no inhabitant was 'to hold any Correspondence with any persons whatsoever that are enemies to the King.' He considered that it was 'very probable' that the Dutch and their French allies might 'attempt an invasion of the Isle of Mann the better to carry on their designe against the king's subjects, and also [to] hinder traffic and Commerce betweene England, Scotland and Ireland.'[395] However unlikely it is that the Dutch ever contemplated such a plan, there is evidence that foreign privateers did cause some disruption to Irish Sea trade, despite the presence of naval vessels and the fact that merchantmen increasingly sailed in convoys.[396] In the mid-1690s, for example, three French ships were cruising in the North Channel and the Irish Sea between Ireland and the Isle of Man.[397] In June 1695, two Manx vessels fell victim to a French privateer 'to the west part of the Island' and, two years later, William, ninth earl of Derby, cancelled his planned visit to Man 'because of the danger of the sea, and the many privateers who are now in St George's Channell, waiteing for the ships that will come to Highlake [Hoylake] for Chester fair.'[398]

The potential risk to merchant shipping in the Irish Sea should not, however, be exaggerated. Vessels were more likely to encounter storms than pirates or privateers in the course of their passage and the overwhelming majority of merchantmen arrived safely at their destination, even during periods such as the 1640s and 1690s, when the dangers were probably greater than usual.

---

[394] Senior, *Nation of Pirates*, p. 144; *C.S.P.D.*, *passim*; *C.S.P.Ire.*, *passim*.
[395] Lib. Scacc. 1666, 9.
[396] *C.S.P.D.*, *1665–6*, p. 415; Woodward, 'Anglo-Irish Livestock Trade', p. 513.
[397] *C.S.P.D.*, *1696*, p. 206.
[398] M.M.L., MD/401/1719/38. William Sacheverell to William, ninth earl of Derby, June 25, 1695; *H.M.C. Kenyon*, p. 419. Cf. Marshall, *William Stout*, pp. 99, 115.

IX. SMUGGLING

The location and peculiar constitutional position of the Isle of Man,[399] together with its comparatively low customs duties,[400] made it a natural centre from which to smuggle goods into the adjacent countries. The scale of this activity at any time can never be established with any degree of precision, since successful smugglers leave few traces, but it seems likely, in view of the infrequent complaints made by the English government to the island's authorities, that the contraband trade was of minor significance, as far as England was concerned, before the mid-seventeenth century. By 1671, however, when the English government resumed direct administration of the customs revenue, the smuggling problem was clearly beginning to assume considerable proportions, in no small part due to the restrictive legislation passed by the English parliament in the form of the Navigation Act of 1660. The 'running trade' from the Isle of Man received further impetus from the Navigation Act of 1671 and the increase in English tariffs after 1689, so that, by 1700, it was causing the government in London much concern, as well as costing a great deal in lost customs revenue.

Smuggling in the island, which was almost exclusively export smuggling, as elsewhere, was not a new phenomenon in the late sixteenth and seventeenth centuries, but the low number of cases on record in this period suggests that it was very limited. There were clearly occasions when it was suspected that certain commodities were being exported without licence. During 1596, Henry Billinge spent nearly twenty weeks 'lying in Ramsey' at the direction of Deputy Governor Cuthbert Gerrard, attempting to 'search and see what Corne or other wares were transported from thence without lycense.'[401] This step may have been taken at the queen's behest, for Elizabeth, who had assumed control of the island in the previous year pending the outcome of the dispute over the various Stanley family estates,[402] was anxious to prevent supplies from Man reaching

---

[399] For details of the relationship between the island and the English Crown, see chapter 1.

[400] See *infra*, pp. 235–38.

[401] M.M.L. R.D. 1579–98, Book of allowance, Peel Castle, 1596: Expenses Abroad.

[402] For information about the disputed succession to the Stanley estates following the death of Ferdinando, fifth earl of Derby in 1594, see R. A.

the rebels in Ulster. The results of Billinge's endeavours do not appear to have survived, though it seems that some trade in corn continued, causing the Privy Council to require the governor, Sir Thomas Gerard, 'to take espetiall care and order that from hence forthe no manner of grane be transported out of that Isle under your charge into the realme of Irelande but to suche places and the people as ar knowne to be in due obedience to her Majesty.'[403]

Some of the unlicensed cargoes which were reported by the searchers, customs or other officers and placed on record in the early seventeenth century were of unspecified size, although the valuation of the goods seized and the severity of the punishment imposed on the offender may provide an indication of the quantity of merchandise involved. In 1606, William Bankes of Douglas was fined 20s. and sentenced to fourteen days in prison 'to be inflicted upon him at the Discretion of Mr Deputie,' Robert Molyneux, for transporting 'certen wooll without license.'[404] The hides and corn unlawfully 'imbarqued' and consequently forfeited by Thomas Stevens, merchant stranger, in 1614 were sold for 20s., and four carcases similarly loaded for transportation from Ramsey without permission raised a further £2 9s. 0d. for the Lord's exchequer in the same year.[405] In other cases, the amount of unlicensed goods confiscated or shipped was recorded and, though generally quite small, the quantity could sometimes be relatively large. At Douglas in 1628, for example, the officers seized four stone of wool which John Dickson 'was to bring away more then he was licensed,' but also noted that Richard Stradling had transported without licence 154 pounds of hops, valued at £15 8s. 0d.[406]

In an attempt to prevent the unlicensed shipment of goods, an order was issued by the island's government in the early seventeenth century which laid down regulations about the loading and unloading of cargoes. In October 1609, Christopher Young, the

note 402 continued
Curphey, 'The Background to the Disputed Derby Succession, 1594–1612', M.N.H.A.S., vol. vii (1964–72), pp. 602–17; Coward, Stanleys, ch 4.
[403] A.P.C.E., 1597–8, p. 590.
[404] Lib. Scacc. 1607, 7.
[405] M.M.L., I.O. 1610–19, Waterbailiff's accounts, 1614.
[406] M.M.L., I.O. 1620–9, Waterbailiff's accounts, 1629.

waterbailiff's deputy,[407] informed Governor John Ireland and the Council that

> much goodes and merchandize are conveyed foorth of this Isle without any custome for them, to the Losse of the Lord, and that many licenses are concealed and kept backe from the Customers of everye severall port and cheeflie at the Peele, to the great losse of the waterbalif, the onlie Reason and Cause whereof is that ordinarilie the owners of barques take aboord goodes in the night season and at such unconvenient tymes as the Customers and searchers of everye port cannot attend the same.[408]

As a result, it was ordered for the future that no shipowner or master was to allow any cargo to be loaded after sunset and that no merchant was to attempt to 'lade goodes aboord' after the setting of the sun on penalty of forfeiture of the vessel and the merchandise.[409] Few such forfeitures are, however, recorded, either in the water-bailiff's accounts or the books of revenue charge,[410] but this does not necessarily mean that the order was punctiliously observed and that no smuggling took place or that it was easily circumvented and smugglers were able to ship unlicensed goods without difficulty. For it to be effective, it was essential that merchants or masters flouting the regulations should be reported immediately, before the vessel carrying the goods had a chance to leave harbour; if the illegal shipment was discovered only subsequently, the officers would have no alternative but to exact a fine from the merchant, since, by that time, the cargo would almost certainly have been sold off. Action could still be taken against the owner or master of the vessel who shipped the merchandise – often the same person – but, in practice, this seems rarely to have happened. In December 1647, John Woods

---

[407] M.M.L., I.O. 1600–9, Waterbailiff's accounts, 1609. Young was a clerk, but the waterbailiff's deputy was generally another member of the Lord's Council.

[408] Lib. Scacc. 1610, 7.

[409] *ibid.*

[410] There are two series of books of charge, one for Peel Castle, which records the revenue collected from the Northside parishes, and the other for Castle Rushen, which contains the details of the revenue from the Southside parishes. After 1661, the books were amalgamated. See M.M.L., I.O. and R.D.

stated that Hugh Shimmin of German had shipped some salt and wool before midsummer and, although he did not know if Shimmin had an export licence, it was clearly significant that the latter's boat had departed from Peel 'about the middle of the night.' Shimmin confessed that he had transported two barrels and two firlots of salt and thirty-six pounds of wool to Ireland, where he sold the goods to buy oats, wheat and beans, 'and all this without lycense.' Instead of seizing his boat, however, the court imposed a fine of 40s.[411]

The low level of smuggling activity in the island which the water-bailiff's accounts, books of revenue charge and court records apparently reveal in the first half of the seventeenth century was greatly increased after 1650 as a result of measures taken by the English government. The initial stimulus to a contraband trade between the island and the other countries of the British Isles was provided by the Navigation Acts of 1651[412] and 1660,[413] which extended previous restrictive orders concerning the conduct of trade between England and the eastern Mediterranean and the Baltic.[414] Both Acts provided that henceforth English colonial products, including tobacco and sugar, were to be carried only in English, Irish, Welsh or colonial vessels and the 1660 Act, in a deliberate move to develop a re-export trade, further stipulated that such cargoes were only to be landed in England, Ireland or Wales, whatever the ultimate destination of the cargo. The Navigation Act of 1671[415] concentrated the colonial trade on England to an even greater extent by prohibiting direct trade between the colonies and Ireland, and thus gave additional encouragement to the illicit trade in goods which, by the later seventeenth century, were rapidly becoming staple requirements.

The Isle of Man was ideally placed to become an entrepôt in such a trade because of its geographical location and the fact that it lay outside the jurisdiction of the English customs system. Situated almost in the centre of the northern part of the Irish Sea, about twenty miles from the Mull of Galloway in Scotland and about thirty-five miles from both the Irish and English coasts, the island

---

[411] Lib. Scacc. 1647, inter 83–4.
[412] Thirsk and Cooper, *Seventeenth-Century Economic Documents*, pp. 502–5.
[413] 12 Chas II, c. 18.
[414] Davis, *Rise of the English Shipping Industry*, pp. 302–3; R. W. K. Hinton, *The Eastland Trade and the Common Weal* (Cambridge 1959), pp. 9–11. Cf. L. A. Harper, *The English Navigation Laws* (New York 1939), ch. 4.
[415] 22 & 23 Chas II, c. 26.

was in a convenient position for the 'running trade.' Vessels carrying cargoes such as tobacco could enter Manx harbours and unload their merchandise quite legitimately, as long as the import duty and anchorage dues were paid. The bulk cargo could then be broken down into small parcels and re-shipped in wherries and other small craft without having to pay any further duty. Little of the tobacco, the principal contraband commodity, which passed through Manx ports in this way arrived directly from the colonies; most of it was duty-paid tobacco which was re-exported from England to obtain drawbacks, or rebates of customs duty.[416] Once the tobacco had been landed in the island, it could then be run into England or smuggled into Ireland or Scotland. Technically, as far as the island's authorities were concerned, this was all quite legal since the Navigation Acts did not apply to the Isle of Man and no Manx laws were broken in the process. The English government, however, took a different view.

During the 1670s, after direct collection of the customs revenue had been resumed,[417] the English government became increasingly aware of the growing contraband trade based on the island and began to consider ways to curb it. In 1673, the Lord Treasurer, Thomas, Lord Clifford, believed that it was 'very necessary' to send an itinerant officer to the Isle of Man as well as to Ireland 'to prevent abuses in the Plantation trade.'[418] It was subsequently suggested that a customs officer should be established in the island to look to the Crown's interests, but none was appointed until 1682, when Christopher Eyans was nominated as surveyor, waiter and searcher.[419]

[416] S. Walpole, *The Land of Home Rule. An Essay on the History and Constitution of the Isle of Man* (1893), p. 208; Harper, *English Navigation Laws*, p. 155.

[417] With the exception of the years during the wars of the 1640s and the Interregnum, the collection of English customs revenue had been in the hands of farmers since 1604. A. P. Newton, 'The Establishment of the Great Farm of the English Customs', *T.R.H.S.*, 4th series, vol. i (1918), pp. 129–155; F. C. Dietz, *English Public Finance, 1558–1641* (New York, 1932), ch. 14–16; C. D. Chandaman, *The English Public Revenue, 1660–1688* (Oxford, 1975), ch. 1.

[418] *C.T.B.*, *1672–5*, p. 144.

[419] *C.T.B.*, *1681–5*, pp. 449, 452. Eyans is often referred to as J'Ans in these books.

It did not take long for Eyans to encounter opposition to his presence, and this intensified when, in May 1683, he accused Ferdinando Calcott, the waterbailiff, of 'inderect Practises very Injurious to his Majestie in his Customes.' Eyans specifically charged Calcott with allowing a ship from the West Indies to discharge its cargo of tobacco at Ramsey without an entry being made in the customs book, the contraband being stored in the Lord's warehouse under the watchful eye of the customer, Edward Curghey, whom the king's officer found to be 'siding with the smucklers.'[420] Governor Robert Heywood called the parties to Castle Rushen for the case to be heard, but Eyans, 'disowning the jurisdiction of this Court, utterly refused to have any trial here,' stated that he would 'make his application to the Lords of his Majesty's Treasury, and would proceed according to such measures as he should receive from them.' Heywood reported to William, ninth earl of Derby, that it would damage the Lord's prerogative rights in the island if the officers were to be called to 'any Court of England for trial of misdemeanours committed here;' far worse in the short term at least was 'the great hindrance of commerce and trade here, by having such an officer placed amongst us, to the utter destruction and ruin of the natives and inhabitants as also the great prejudice to your Honor in your customs.'[421] This incident set the tone for the future relationship between the earl's officers and the king's customs officers, two of whom were normally resident in the island during the remainder of the seventeenth century.[422]

In addition to the appointment of customs officers for the island, the English government attempted to negotiate a lease of the Manx customs from the earl of Derby. The suggestion that the king should farm the island's customs seems to have been first made in early 1683 by the Irish Revenue Commissioners. They advocated this course of action to prevent the fraudulent practices of some merchants, who took advantage of the Isle of Man 'to break bulk and run their wine, tobacco and fine goods thence in small boats to the creeks of the

---

[420] *ibid*, p. 568; M.M.L., MD/401/1718/24. Christopher Eyans to Governor Robert Heywood, May 16 and 19, 1683.

[421] *H.M.C. Ormonde*, pp. 44–5.

[422] In July 1683, Francis Michelbourne was appointed as surveyor, waiter and searcher to inspect Peel and Ramsey, while Eyans was to be responsible for Douglas and Castletown. *C.T.B., 1681–5*, p. 876. There was a fairly regular turnover in these offices between 1683 and 1700. *C.T.B., passim*.

three kingdoms.'[423] A lease of the island's customs by the Crown
would secure control of commercial activity in Manx harbours and,
it was hoped, bring an end to the contraband traffic, something
which the presence of English customs officers had been unable to
achieve.[424] The English Customs Commissioners were accordingly
entrusted with the task of approaching Earl William to obtain detailed information about the island's customs and to come to terms.
The earl, however, was as reluctant to comply with these proposals
as he was with the suggestion that bonds should be imposed on
merchants exporting goods from the island to ensure that the merchandise was landed at the port stated in the cocket. He claimed that
any farm of the customs would cause him considerable loss 'because
it is evident that heerby the trade of the Island will suddenly decay,
and thereby the Earle's tenants will be disabled to improve his lands
and pay the rents they are now let for.' The earl would only counten-
ance a lease if he received the sum of £500 for the customs and
damages, an amount which the English government was apparently
not prepared to pay.[425] The scheme was revived in 1687, but on this
occasion, Earl William countered by informing the English Treasury
Commissioners that his counsel told him that, since the island was
strictly entailed on his family by private Act of Parliament, he was
'restrayned' from making any lease of the customs. He did, however,
consent to the imposition of bonds on merchants shipping goods
from the island, as requested by the Privy Council. Negotiations
concerning the customs continued, with the earl only supplying a
copy of the island's Book of Rates after repeated requests, but finally
broke down in 1688.[426]

The failure of the English government to obtain a lease of the
island's customs allowed the contraband trade to continue, while the

---

[423] *C.T.B., 1681–5*, pp. 716, 734; Jarvis, 'Illicit Trade', p. 250.
[424] The Irish Revenue Commissioners believed that Eyans was 'a fraudulent
or at least a useless officer' in the island on account of the 'notoriety of the
Plantation and other prohibited trade that to this day is slipt through that place
contrary to two Acts of Parliament in force there [*sic*]'. *C.T.B., 1681–5*, p. 895.
[425] *C.T.B., 1681–5*, p. 742; M.M.L., MD/401/1718/32, MD/401/1718/33,
MD/ 401/1718/34, MD/401/1718/35, MD/401/1718/49.
[426] *C.T.B., 1685–9*, pp. 1505, 1507, 1562, 1563, 1604, 1615, 1669, 1786, 1869;
M.M.L., MD/401/1718/49, MD/401/1718/50, MD/401/1718/51, MD/401/
1718/ 52, MD/401/1718/53, MD/401/1718/54, MD/401/1718/59, MD/401/
1718/61, MD/401/1718/72, MD/401/1718/79.

outbreak of war between England and France in 1689 caused it to expand significantly. After a temporary embargo on French imports, very high duties were imposed on such items in an attempt to discourage trade with the 'enemy.' The necessity for additional revenue to pay for England's war effort led to a substantial increase in the level of duties on imported goods in general in the 1690s; the standard 5 per cent *ad valorem* rate levied on most commodities was raised to 10 per cent in 1697 and even heavier duties were placed on certain goods.[427] Both these measures provided greater temptation to merchants to engage in smuggling to some extent, and there can be little doubt that the illicit trade between the island and the adjacent countries, though impossible to quantify, grew considerably during the last decade of the seventeenth century.

There was certainly a dramatic increase in the recorded amount of tobacco, the most important contraband cargo, which was landed annually in the Isle of Man between 1680 and 1700.[428] In 1684–5, for example, 4,597 pounds were unloaded from vessels entering Manx harbours; about a decade later, in 1695–6, imports had soared to 22,638 pounds (Table 5.7); five years later, the figure stood at 23,485 pounds.[429] This rise in tobacco imports was by no means steady, the quantity landed varying from year to year, but imports were nevertheless maintained at a high level throughout the 1690s and beyond. The number of inward shipments was low and individual cargoes were therefore generally very large. In August 1691, Thomas Hodson entered 54,091 pounds of tobacco in three consignments at Douglas, of which 8,450 pounds was 'sold and consumed in this Isle,' the remaining 45,641 pounds being re-shipped.[430] In 1695–6, there were only half a dozen shipments officially landed in Manx ports, the smallest comprising 1,011 pounds of Virginia leaf tobacco.[431] In

---

[427] R. Davis, 'The Rise of Protection in England, 1669–1786', *Ec.H.R.*, 2nd series, vol. xix (1966), pp. 306–10; Clay, *Economic Expansion and Social Change*, vol. ii, p. 213.

[428] Some shipments of tobacco clearly went unrecorded. See, for example, *infra*, p. 336.

[429] M.M.L., I.O. 1696–1704, Ingates and outgates, 1701. This book covers the eighteen month period from June 24, 1700, but this total applies only to the year commencing at that date.

[430] M.M.L., I.O. 1680–9, Customs book, 1690.

[431] M.M.L., I.O. 1696–1704, Customs book, 1696.

1700-1, eight shipments accounted for the entire amount of imported tobacco, ranging in size from 240 pounds to 10,629 pounds.[432]

While any assessment of the scale of undeclared imports is scarcely possible, it seems likely that the waterbailiff's accounts record a substantial part of the island's trade in commodities such as tobacco. Duties were comparatively low and, although the handful of merchants in whose hands the tobacco trade was apparently concentrated – men such as David Murrey (d.1702), David Murrey the younger (d.1709), John Murrey and Phillip Moore – were unquestionably engaged in smuggling shipments into England, Ireland and Scotland to some extent, and doubtless evaded customs duties on occasion, there was little incentive for them to attempt to defraud the island's customs on a regular basis, except in the case of consignments arriving in vessels directly from the colonies, which the English customs officers would attempt to seize.

Although merchants required a licence for its transportation, re-shipped tobacco bore no duty[433] and consequently it is likely that the waterbailiff's accounts similarly provide a reasonably accurate picture of the quantity, though not the direction, of the island's re-export trade. In common with the import trade, the level of outward tobacco shipments rose sharply in the last two decades of the seventeenth century. From practically nothing before 1680, re-exports rose to 9,470 pounds in 1695–6 and 11,842 pounds in 1700–1.[434] This trade was similar in form to the import traffic, with a small number of shipments of considerable size. In 1695–6, for example, David Murrey, who, with his son of the same name, dominated the tobacco trade in this year, shipped the largest single cargo, comprising 3,867 pounds of leaf tobacco.[435]

According to the customs records, most of the tobacco shipped from Manx ports was dispatched to Ireland or Scotland,[436] which were both legitimate destinations in the view of the English government, provided that the cargo had first been landed in England and had paid duty there. Whether or not the tobacco actually reached the country or port stated in the merchant's cocket and in the

[432] M.M.L., I.O. 1696–1704, Ingates and outgates, 1701.
[433] M.M.L., MD/401/1715/20. Book of Rates, 1692. Cf. M.M.L., I.O. 1696–1704, Customs book, 1696.
[434] M.M.L., I.O. 1696–1704, Customs book, 1696; ingates and outgates, 1701.
[435] M.M.L., I.O. 1696–1704, Customs book, 1696.
[436] M.M.L., I.O. 1690–5, I. O. 1696–1704, Customs books, *passim*.

waterbailiff's accounts remains to be seen. It was an easy matter for a vessel to set sail for Ireland or Scotland and then alter course once at sea and make for one of the many unguarded creeks on the English coast. In the unlikely event of an encounter with an English naval vessel, the master could explain his position by claiming that his ship or wherry had been blown off its planned course by stormy weather or contrary winds.[437] It was this facility which caused the English customs officers in the island to be extremely wary of the movements of cargoes of tobacco and which ultimately led to the clashes between them and the merchants and the Manx authorities. In January 1694, for instance, the *Ann* of Wemyss, which departed from Dumfries bound for Greenock with a cargo of tobacco, was driven 'by distress of weather' into Douglas Bay, where the vessel anchored. Several days later, Jonathan Antrobus, one of the English customs officers in the island, boarded the ship and impounded twenty-three rolls of tobacco. Despite undertakings by the master, John Hunter, that he would give 'good security to the double value of the tobaccoe' to obtain a certificate that duty had been paid on the goods in England and an invitation to Antrobus to accompany him to Greenock 'to see the king was not defrauded,' the customs officer was not satisfied. The matter was only resolved when the merchant who had shipped the tobacco, John Browne of Dumfries, obtained a duplicate cocket 'amply informing that waiter or who itt may conscern that it was truly entred in Whythaven and came here by cockett.'[438]

To avoid confiscation by the English customs officers and payment of Manx duties, some merchants smuggled tobacco and other commodities into and out of the island. In December 1698, Governor Nicholas Sankey received

> private intimacon that considerable quantitys of tobaccoe and other goods were of late secretly and in the dead time of the night put on shipboard in the Port of Douglas as also that

---

[437] B. L. Add. MS 38,462, ff. 22–4; Harper, *English Navigation Laws*, p. 154. The development of the fore and aft rig before the late seventeenth century clearly made the smugglers' task a great deal easier, since it meant that vessels rigged in this manner could, when properly handled, land contraband and sail away with the wind in almost any quarter. Jarvis, 'Illicit Trade', pp. 247–8.

[438] M.M.L., MD/401/1719/34, MD/401/1719/41.

certaine parcells were landed in the port afforesaid after the same unseasonable and clandestine manner, perticularly by one John White sometime in the month of October last or thereabouts.[439]

Consequently he issued a commission to the comptroller, John Rowe, Deemster Daniel McYlrea and Silvester Huddleston to investigate 'all secrett and illegall importacons and exportacons' in the preceding year, to examine 'all such boatmen, Porters and Sailors as are comonly imployed by the merchants of Duglas in shiping and unshiping goods' and to demand the cockets of two 'Tobaccoe ships' then in Douglas Bay.[440] The sole result of this exercise seems to have been the discovery that the younger David Murrey and Thomas Joyner of Douglas had shipped some tobacco from Douglas at night, ostensibly to Port Erin; near the Calf of Man at dawn, the cargo was transferred to another boat and conveyed to Ballywalter, County Down. Murrey and Joyner, the 'principall contrivers in this peece of fraude,' were each fined the sum of 10s. for loading the goods secretly and their boat, as well as the other vessel involved, belonging to Daniel Callister and William Kelly of Rushen, was confiscated 'for goeing of the Island without the Governors Lycence as the Law requires.'[441] Earl William took the opportunity of his visit to the island in 1700 to issue an order requiring the officers to implement all previous directives concerning such frauds and to prevent the 'running of severall goods and merchandizes with [the] design of defrauding the king of his just rights.'[442] In spite of such gestures, well intentioned though they might be, the contraband traffic based on the island continued to flourish and indeed grew very considerably in the early eighteenth century. By the 1720s, it had become a major problem for the British government and, although the Revestment of the island in the Crown in 1765 may have significantly reduced the importance of the Isle of Man as a centre of the illicit trade, smuggling nevertheless continued.[443]

[439] Lib. Scacc. 1699, inter 63–4.
[440] ibid.
[441] ibid, 66–75.
[442] Lib. Scacc. 1700, 12–13.
[443] On the growth and decline of smuggling based in the Isle of Man in the eighteenth century, see Moore, *History*, vol. i, pp. 428–38 and vol. ii, pp. 597–601; Jarvis, 'Illicit Trade', pp. 251–67; L. M. Cullen, 'The Smuggling

Overseas trade, whether legitimate or illicit, was always an integral part of the Manx economy. Animals, skins and a limited range of primary products were exported from the island, allowing the inhabitants to sell their goods in a foreign market and to obtain money to pay their rents to the Lord. In return, manufactured goods and raw materials in which the island was deficient were brought in to supply the requirements of the Manx. Interruptions to this trade could, therefore, cause some hardship, if protracted, since any restraint on the transportation of merchandise would inevitably affect the ability of the inhabitants to pay their rents; however, this seems to have been generally avoided. The development of the smuggling trade in the late seventeenth century and afterwards meant that commercial activity took on a greater importance in the island's economy than previously, as many profited from it. The Lord benefited from the increased level of trade by the higher yield from the customs revenue; some merchants, such as David Murrey senior, acquired a considerable degree of wealth through legal ventures and those which, in the eyes of the English government, were illicit; and even many of the inhabitants at large gained a little from it by the employment offered to mariners and to those who serviced maritime needs, such as the coopers who made the barrels for storing and shipping goods. While agriculture and, to a lesser extent, domestic manufactures were more immediately important to the inhabitants of the Isle of Man, overseas trade was nevertheless a more significant element in the Manx economy in 1700 than it had been a century earlier.

note 443 *continued*
Trade in Ireland in the Eighteenth Century', *Proceedings of the Royal Irish Academy*, vol. lxvii, section C (1969), pp. 149–75; *idem*, 'Economic Development, 1750–1800', in T. W. Moody and W. E. Vaughan (eds), *A New History of Ireland, vol. iv: Eighteenth-Century Ireland, 1691–1800* (Oxford, 1986), p. 190; *idem*, 'Smugglers in the Irish Sea in the Eighteenth Century', in McCaughan and Appleby, *Irish Sea*, pp. 85–99. For a comparison with the smuggling trade of Guernsey, which, like the Isle of Man, also lay beyond the jurisdiction of the English Customs Commissioners, see A. G. Jamieson, 'The Channel Islands and Smuggling, 1680–1850', in *idem, People of the Sea*, pp. 195–210.

Conclusion

The Isle of Man was only one of the possessions which the Stanleys acquired through service to successive kings in the fifteenth century, but it differed significantly from the other estates in England and Wales which they obtained by grant or purchase in the nature of the powers which the lordship conferred on the holder. The Lord of Man exercised authority which was broadly similar to that of his feudal superior, the English king, and jealously guarded his prerogative rights. The title and authority of Lord of Man probably did not enhance the status of the Stanleys at court, where the lordship of such a small island in the Irish Sea might count for little, but together with the offices of lord lieutenant of Lancashire and Cheshire, which the earl generally held from the inception of the lieutenancy in the early sixteenth century onwards,[1] it helped to consolidate the influence of the Stanleys in the north west.

The fact that the Stanley Lords of Man seldom visited the island should not be taken as an indication that they were uninterested or unconcerned about their Irish Sea possession. Indeed, as Dr Coward has shown, the Stanleys were nothing if not astute, level-headed landlords who would be unlikely to neglect any of their estates.[2] In the same way that the earl of Derby supervised the running of his estates elsewhere, the Lord of Man was determined to receive all his rents and perquisites and was ready to take action against inefficient or possibly corrupt servants. The Lord kept in contact with his officers in the island, who were regularly pestered with queries from Lathom, Knowsley or one of the other Stanley residences. Wherever the earl of Derby might be, matters concerning the island, and any of his other estates, received speedy attention. Periodically the earl deemed it necessary to dispatch commissioners to report on the state of the

---

[1] B. Coward, The Lieutenancy of Lancashire and Cheshire in the Sixteenth and Early Seventeenth Centuries, *T.H.S.L.C.* vol. cxix (1967), p. 40; Coward, *Stanleys*, pp. 151–7, 180–2; J. J. Bagley, *The Earls of Derby, 1485–1985* (1985), pp. 111, 116.

[2] Coward, *Stanleys*, pp. 58–64.

island's administration, to negotiate leases or deal with other specific business.[3] When, for whatever reason, the earl considered it necessary to be present in the island in person he made the voyage across the Irish Sea from Liverpool although, with the exception of the residence of the seventh earl between 1643 and 1651, such visits tended to be somewhat brief. The fact that the earl had more pressing domestic and political responsibilities in Lancashire meant that the Lord of Man only appeared in person on a handful of occasions during this period.[4]

While it can not be denied that possession of the Isle of Man did provide the Stanleys with an additional source of patronage it is also true that there were few posts in the island's establishment of sufficient importance and prestige to satisfy the ambitious. The Stanleys could only reward a handful of their servants with high positions in the island's government, although a larger number of men of humble status could be accommodated by a place in one of the garrisons. Of those who did obtain a post in the Lord's Council or serve as coroner or Captain of the Parish, most were natives, either Manx or from English families resident in the island for long enough for them to be regarded as indigenous. Few such men seem to have had ambitions to pursue careers off the island on a permanent basis, though doubtless some aspired to do so. In reality, those men who served in one of the principal posts in the Stanley administration in the island rarely, if ever, went on to higher, more lucrative office. Even most of the Englishmen who held the post of governor in the seventeenth century either left the island and returned to their homes and, it seems, obscurity, or died in office. One or two of these Englishmen, however, probably viewed the governorship as a comparatively minor reward, having already established a career in public office. One such individual was Sir Philip Musgrave of Hartley in Westmorland, who

---

[3] Commissions seem to have been appointed on an irregular basis. As far as can be deduced from the extant records, commissions were sent to the island in 1417–18, 1490, 1505–6, 1511(?), 1522, 1532, 1541, 1550–1, 1561, 1562–3(?), 1614, 1630, 1651–2, 1660, 1691. *Statutes*, pp. 1–3, 29, 31; Cl.R.O., Nantlys D/NA/905, 1; 'Unpublished documents in the Manx Museum no. 6', *J.M.M.*, vol. ii, p. 21; Lib. Scacc. 1644, post 37; J. Gell, (ed.), *An Abstract of the Laws, Customs and Ordinances of the Isle of Man, compiled by John Parr, vol. i [Notes]*, Manx Society, vol. xii (1867), pp. 89–90; Lib. Scacc. 1691, 13–14

[4] For details of the visits to the island made by the Stanley Lords of Man, see chapter 1, pp. 23–5.

had been returned twice as M.P. for his county in 1640 and was the commander of the Royalist forces in Cumberland and Westmorland in the first civil war. Retiring to the Isle of Man in the summer of 1650, Musgrave was governor when the island was surrendered to Parliament's forces little more than a year later. After the Restoration, he again served as M.P. for Westmorland.[5] James Chaloner had also achieved a degree of prominence, being returned as Member of Parliament for Aldborough in Yorkshire in 1645, before he was appointed governor in 1657.[6] Roger Kenyon of Peel in Lancashire, who had longtime connections with the earl of Derby, served as clerk of the peace for the county (1671–98), receiver general of the duchy of Lancaster (1680–3) and was elected M.P. for Clitheroe in 1690 before taking up the post of governor in the following year.[7]

It was a similar story in the Manx Church, which offered few positions for clergy seeking advancement from the Stanleys. The bishopric was poor and many of those appointed to the see by the earl of Derby held the diocese *in commendam* and scarcely visited the island, leaving the everyday running of the diocese to the archdeacon and the vicars general. Henry Bridgman was dean of Chester and rector of Bangor in Flintshire as well as bishop between 1671 and 1682 but apparently only visited his diocese on two occasions.[8] Other bishops during the period were rather more diligent and a few were able to secure 'promotion,' even if the benefits in material terms might not always be immediately evident. The industrious John Phillips was appointed archdeacon in 1587 and continued to hold that office after he was made bishop in 1604.[9] Bishop Isaac Barrow, who also acted as governor (1664–8), was translated to the see of St Asaph in North Wales – hardly a rich diocese – in 1669 and continued to hold the see of Sodor and Man *in commendam* until 1671.[10] John Lake, who resigned his prebend at York to become bishop of the diocese in 1682, visited the island only once before being translated first to Bristol in 1684 and then Chichester in 1685.[11] The

[5] *D.N.B.*, vol. xiii (1917), pp. 1318–19.
[6] *D.N.B.*, vol. iii (1917), p. 1365.
[7] R. Somerville, *Office-Holders in the Duchy and County Palatine of Lancaster from 1603* (Chichester 1972), pp. 107–8; *H.M.C. Kenyon*, pp. 236, 238.
[8] Moore, *History*, vol. i, p. 483.
[9] A. W. Moore, *Sodor and Man* (1893), p. 182.
[10] Moore, *History*, vol. i, p. 483.
[11] Moore, *Sodor and Man*, pp. 182–3.

other posts in the church were less prestigious, although the two offices of vicar general offered the opportunity of promotion to able native-born clerics. The parish livings in the island were very poor and were inevitably reserved for native Manx clergy.

One of the more remarkable features of the island in this period is the evident complexity of the administrative structure in both church and state. Considering the size of the island and the probable size of its population in the later seventeenth century, a perhaps surprisingly large number of officers were entrusted with specific duties. The compulsory nature of service for all parishioners, except for those in high office, in posts such as members of the day and night watch[12] compelled the inhabitants to become part of the administrative machine. All major landholders in the parish served in rotation as the moar for a year and were personally liable for the collection of the Lord's rent for that period.[13] Only when the last penny had been paid into the exchequer was the moar's tally broken to signify receipt of the rent in full. Failure to carry out any of the duties of theses offices was invariably punished. To ensure that none of the inhabitants could escape from their responsibilities, it was ordered that no native could depart from the island without a licence from the governor. In view of the ease with which any Manxman could get access to a boat and slip across to England, Scotland or Ireland it is perhaps doubtful whether this law had as great an effect as the Stanley administration would have liked.[14]

It was clearly in the interests of the Stanleys to employ the more influential men of island society in positions of authority. Members of families such as the Christians of Milntown, Lezayre, the Stevensons of Balladoole, Arbory, the Qualtroughs of Kentraugh, Rushen and the Quayles of Ballaquayle, Conchan, regularly occupied posts in the Lord's Council and the Keys as well as serving as Captain of the Parish and coroner of the sheading. This not only helped to gain the co-operation of this group but also permitted these men to exercise a degree of power which they might otherwise have been

---

[12] W. Cubbon, 'Watch and Ward in A. D. 1627', *M.N.H.A.S.*, vol. iii (1932–42), pp. 258–65.
[13] The office of moar is discussed at greater length in chapter 1, pp. 51–2.
[14] This order was first recorded in c. 1418 and was reissued in 1422 and 1687. *Statutes*, pp. 5, 21 and 143. It is perhaps surprising that it was not reissued more often. Similar orders specifically concerning servants were made in 1655 and 1665. *ibid*, pp. 107, 117.

denied. The position of governor was generally restricted to members of the English gentry, chiefly from Lancashire, whom the earl believed he could trust and, perhaps as a matter of policy to avoid internal tensions, he therefore appointed few leading Manxmen to the office. The difficulties which could arise in such circumstances were clearly indicated by the case of Captain Edward Christian of Maughold, who attempted to stir up rebellion against the Stanleys in 1643.[15] The other principal offices of the island's administration and lesser posts, such as that of coroner, were normally filled by members of prominent native families or families of English, mainly Lancastrian, origin.[16]

It has been suggested that in the later seventeenth century the Stanleys may have found possession of the Isle of Man increasingly burdensome as discontent arising from the earl's attempts to replace the island's customary copyhold 'tenure by the straw' with leasehold tenure resurfaced.[17] Fears about the ability of the Lord to dispossess tenants at will and the level of entry fines led to moves to secure an agreement with the earl of Derby. Negotiations between members of the Keys, representing the influential landowners in the island, and the earl ultimately produced the Act of Settlement in 1704, which established the level of entry fines payable by the Lord's tenants and the procedure by which such fines were to be paid in future.[18] The importance of this Act went far beyond securing the inheritance rights of the Lord's tenants. It marked a significant step forward in the development of the Keys as a political force in the island. Even the format of the text of the Act suggests that there may have been a shift in political power; like the legislation passed in 1691, the Act has much more the appearance of parliamentary legislation than of a declaration made by the Lord or the governor and officers.[19] The dispute over land tenure in itself, however, was not enough to make

---

[15] For a brief account of Edward Christian's 'rebellion,' see J. R. Dickinson, 'The Earl of Derby and the Isle of Man, 1643–1651', *T.H.S.L.C.*, vol. 141 (1992), pp. 42–8. The origins of the governors and deputies are considered in chapter 1, pp. 34–43.

[16] The names of the principal office-holders in the island are listed in appendices ii–vii.

[17] Coward, *Stanleys*, p. 106.

[18] *Statutes*, pp. 161–76.

[19] *ibid*, pp. 144–54.

the Stanleys wish to rid themselves of the island, especially as the island still held some economic value for them.

The economy of the Isle of Man was mainly geared to providing the essentials of daily life for the inhabitants, with primary products, surplus foodstuffs and goods being exported in return for raw materials and limited quantities of manufactured items. The island therefore shared many of the characteristics of the economies of the upland areas of the rest of the British Isles. The similarities between the island and the countries of the Irish Sea littoral were perhaps most evident in agricultural activity. The island's agrarian economy was essentially pastoral, based on cattle and sheep rearing, but considerable quantities of cereals, mainly barley and oats, which were better suited to the damp climate, were also grown.[20] As such, farming activity in the island was little different from that in some adjacent parts of northern England and southern Scotland.[21] Certainly the inhabitants of the island were as dependent on the success or failure of the harvest as their counterparts on either side of the Irish Sea.

Unlike most of the people who fished the waters of the Irish Sea, the Manx relied to an equally large extent on the herring fishery. The evidence for the fluctuations of the fishery during the period is somewhat limited, but it seems that, in the second half of the seventeenth century, there may have been a fall in the size of the total catch.[22] Whether this was related to an apparent reduction in the number of fishing boats at the fishery or the result of fishermen landing their catch elsewhere is not clear.

Manufacturing in the Isle of Man in the early modern period mainly served the basic requirements of the inhabitants for food and clothing. More specialist craftsmen, such as slaters and glasiers, were employed in the garrisons, where they often served as soldiers, and worked on the houses of the officers and the more affluent members of island society. Many craftsmen, particularly in the towns, had more than one occupation, which is an indication of the undeveloped nature of the Manx economy and the small scale of demand in the island. Close supervision of craftsmen's wages was, nevertheless, maintained by the officers, who were also careful to ensure that

[20] See chapter 2, pp. 87–92.
[21] I. D. Whyte, *Agriculture and Society in Seventeenth-Century Scotland* (Edinburgh 1979), p. 20.
[22] See chapter 2, pp. 119–22.

standards of workmanship were kept at an acceptable level by punishing those who attempted to pursue a trade without having been apprenticed for the customary period of about seven years.[23]

The manufacturing projects which were planned in the last decade of the seventeenth century were an attempt to reduce the dependence of the island on imported goods which originated in more industrially advanced areas, such as south Lancashire. Attempts were made to induce foreign craftsmen and prospectors to settle in Man and set up ventures and, although many of these plans came to nothing, the cloth manufacture which was established continued into the eighteenth century and became an important industrial concern.[24]

In the Isle of Man, as elsewhere, internal trading activity was probably more significant than overseas trade, but this is practically impossible to demonstrate because of the lack of evidence. The town markets were of major importance in the economy of the island, since they were the basic mechanism of exchange and also the means by which the supply of corn was regulated during times of shortage or dearth. The officers consequently took special pains to ensure that the markets were properly served with corn on these occasions and that none were guilty of engrossing or forestalling.[25] Steps were also taken to see that only weights and measures carrying the Lord's seal were used in transactions.[26] These moves were vital after a harvest failure to prevent starvation in the island and, so far as can be deduced from the records of the island's government, seem to have been generally successful.[27]

Although the internal market was probably many times more important to the Manx economy than overseas trade, the fact remains that the island relied on imports of raw materials which were absent or in short supply in the island, such as timber, salt, coal and iron, and on imports of basic manufactured goods, such as metalware.[28] The export trade also performed a crucial role by allowing Manx farmers to transport their produce, particularly cattle, to England and elsewhere to sell, the money which resulted being used to pay the Lord's rents. The export trade in cattle was adversely affected by

[23] See chapter 3, pp. 145–47.
[24] ibid, pp. 175–88.
[25] See chapter 2, pp. 92–105.
[26] See chapter 4, pp. 208–19.
[27] See chapter 2, pp. 92–105.
[28] See chapter 5, pp. 280–84.

the Cattle Acts of the 1660s, which limited the number of Manx animals which could be imported into England, and only continued at a reduced level thereafter.[29]

The development of the 'running' trade in the later seventeenth century replaced the cattle trade as the island's most important commercial activity. The geographical and constitutional position of the island made it an ideal entrepôt for smuggling and the increased duties placed on tobacco in the 1690s and the embargo on French goods imposed by the English government inevitably stimulated the trade. The inhabitants of the island benefited not only from employment as sailors in smuggling vessels, but also from the work generated by the trade, such as the construction of casks and the repair of boats. Merchants and shipmasters who engaged in the running trade could make substantially greater profits.[30] By the early eighteenth century, smuggling in the Irish Sea was assuming major proportions and the British government was endeavouring to stamp it out or at the very least reduce its impact on revenue from the customs.

In common with other men of his rank, the earl of Derby jealously guarded his rights and prerogatives and was reluctant to surrender any of those semi-regal powers which he enjoyed in the Isle of Man, as was clearly demonstrated by the response of the earl and his officers to the activities of English customs officers in the island and the proposals made by the Crown to lease the Manx customs in the late seventeenth century. The Isle of Man did not make the earl rich financially, but it did provide him with a source of provisions, particularly beef, for his household in England and with an additional source of patronage from which to reward some of his servants. In the later seventeenth century, as the contraband trade expanded, he benefited from a small, though general rise in the level of Manx customs revenue arising from that development and his position as Lord of Man did give him a certain potential for political leverage with the Crown. Possession of the Isle of Man after c.1670 may have brought with it more trouble than the ownership of his other estates, but it also meant that the earl of Derby had a material interest in the flourishing maritime trade of the Irish Sea. The lordship of Man might not in itself have endowed the Stanleys with

[29] *ibid*, pp. 247–59.
[30] *ibid*, pp. 314–15, 338–39.

greater political influence on the national stage but it did help to consolidate the growing strength of the family in the north west in the fifteenth century and remained as a symbol of their status in the region throughout the period.

Appendix I

Appendix II

GOVERNORS AND DEPUTY GOVERNORS
OF THE ISLE OF MAN, c. 1590–c. 1700

(The figure in brackets denotes successive appearances in the list)

Dates in Office	Name	Title of Office	Origin
1578–1591	Richard Shireburne	Captain	Lancs. (Stonyhurst?)
1584	Sir Richard Shireburne	Lieutenant	Lancs. (Stonyhurst)
1592?	Cuthbert Gerrard (1)	Captain	Lancs.?
1592	Thomas Mortimer	Deputy Captain	?
1592–4	William Stanley[1]	Captain	Lancs. (Knowsley)
1594	Thomas Burscough	Deputy	Lancs.?
1594	Edward Ellis (1)	Deputy Captain	?
1594–5	Randulph Stanley	Captain	Ches. (Alderley)
1595–1608	Sir Thomas Gerard[2]	Captain, Governor	Staffs.
1596–1608	Robert Molyneux (1)	Deputy	Lancs.?
1596	Cuthbert Gerrard (2)	Deputy	Lancs.?
1596–7	Peter Legh	Captain	Ches. (Lyme)
1597	William Lucas	Deputy	Man
1599	Edward Ellis (2)	Deputy	?
1601	Edward Moore	Deputy	Lancs. (Bank Hall)
1601	Charles Young	Deputy	?
1604	Thomas Molyneux	Deputy	Lancs.?
1605	Cuthbert Gerrard (3)	Deputy	Lancs.?
1609–12	John Ireland	Governor, Lieutenant and Captain	Lancs. (Hutt).
1612	Thomas Ireland	Deputy	Lancs.? (Hutt)

1612–21	Robert Molyneux (2)	Captain	Lancs.?
1621–2	Edward Fletcher (1)	Governor	Man (Braddan)
1622–4	Sir Ferdinando Legh	Captain	Yorks. (Middleton?)
1624–5	Edward Fletcher (2)	Governor, Deputy	Man (Braddan)
1625–7?	Edward Holmewood	Captain	?
1626–7	Edward Fletcher (3)	Deputy	Man (Braddan)
1627–34	Edward Christian (1)	Lieutenant and Captain	Man (Maughold)
1630–1	Ewan Christian (1)	Deputy Lieutenant, Deputy Governor	Man (Lezayre)
1632	Edward Fletcher (4)	Deputy	Man (Braddan)
1634	Ewan Christian (2)	Lieutenant and Governor	Man (Lezayre)
1634–8	Sir Charles Gerard	Lieutenant, Captain and Governor	Lancs.
1636–9	John Sharples (1)	Deputy Lieutenant	Lancs.?
1636	Edward Christian (2)	Lieutenant	Man (Maughold)
1639	Radclif Gerard	Deputy	Lancs.
1639–40	Ewan Christian (3)	Deputy Lieutenant	Man (Lezayre)
1640–51	John Greenhalgh	Governor and Lieutenant General	Lancs. (Brandlesholme)
1641–2	John Sharples (2)	Deputy Lieutenant	Lancs.?
1651	Sir Philip Musgrave	Governor	Westm.
1651–2	Col. Robert Duckenfield	Governor	Ches. (Duckenfield)
1652	Samuel Smith	Deputy Governor	?
1652–3	Major Philip Eyton	Lieutenant Governor	?
1652	John Sharples (3)	Deputy Lieutenant	Lancs.?

1653	Capt. Francis Duckenfield	Deputy Governor	Ches. (Stockport)
1653	Major John Wade [?]	Governor	?
1654–6	Capt. Matthew Cadwell	Governor	?
1656–8	William Christian	Governor	Man (Malew)
1658–60	James Chaloner	Governor	Yorks.
1660–2	Roger Nowell	Governor	Lancs. (Rede)
1660–2	Richard Stevenson (1)	Deputy Lieutenant, Deputy Governor	Man (Arbory)
1661–3	Henry Nowell (1)	Deputy Governor	Lancs. (Rede)
1662	Richard Stevenson (2)	Deputy Lieutenant	Man (Arbory)
1663–4	Henry Nowell (2)	Governor	Lancs. (Rede)
1664–8	Bishop Isaac Barrow	Governor	Camb.
1664–74	Henry Nowell (3)	Deputy Governor	Lancs. (Rede)
1674–7	Henry Nowell (4)	Governor, Lieutenant	Lancs. (Rede)
1677–8	Richard Stevenson (3)	Deputy Governor	Man (Arbory)
1677–8	Henry Stanley	Governor, Lieutenant	Lancs.?
1678–91	Robert Heywood	Governor	Lancs. (Heywood)
1681–2	Richard Stevenson (4)	Deputy Governor	Man (Arbory)
1691–3?	Roger Kenyon	Governor	Lancs. (Peel)
1691–2	Richard Stevenson (1)	Deputy Governor	Man (Arbory)
1691–2	John Rowe (1)	Deputy Governor	?
1691–2	William Sacheverell (1)	Deputy Governor	Oxon.
1693	Richard Stevenson (2)	Deputy Governor	Man (Arbory)
1693	John Rowe (2)	Deputy Governor	?
1693–5	William Sacheverell (2)	Governor	Oxon.
1695–1701?	Nicholas Sankey	Governor	Lancs.?
1697	Peter Heywood	Deputy Governor	Lancs. (Heywood)
1697	John Rowe (3)	Deputy Governor	?
1697	John Parr (1)	Deputy Governor	Man (Arbory)

1701	Thomas Huddleston	Deputy Governor	Man (Malew)
1701–2	James Cranstoun	Governor	?
1702–4?	Charles Stanley	Governor	Lancs.
1703	John Parr (2)	Deputy Governor	Man (Arbory)
1703	Robert Mawdesley (1)	Deputy Governor	Lancs.?
1704–13	Robert Mawdesley (2)	Governor	Lancs.?

Sources: See Table 1.1

Notes.

1. Subsequently, in 1594, sixth earl of Derby.

2. From 1603, Lord Gerard of Gerrards Bromley.

Appendix III

COMPTROLLERS, *c.* 1590–*c.* 1700

Term of Office	Name	Place of Origin
1591–3?	Francis Holt	?
1594?–9	Humphrey Scarisbrick	Lancs.
1599–1607?	Edward Moore	Lancs. (Bank Hall)
1611?–30	John Halsall	Lancs.
1630?–52	John Sharples	Lancs.?
1652–73?	Richard Tyldesley	Man (Arbory)
1676?–86	Thomas Norris	Man (Malew?)
1687-post 1720	John Rowe	?

Sources: Lib. Scacc., *passim*; Lib. Canc., *passim*.

Appendix IV

RECEIVERS OF THE ISLE OF MAN, c. 1590–c. 1700

Term of Office	Name	Place of Origin
c. 1578–93	Thomas Burscough [PC][1]	Lancs.
1591–4	Thomas Mortimer [CR][1]	?
1594–1613?	William Radcliffe [PC]	Man?
1594–1613?	William Lucas [CR]	Man
1614–16	John Halsall	Lancs.?
1616–36?	Edward Fletcher	Man (Braddan)
1636–43	Edward Christian	Man (Maughold)
1643–8	William Smyth	?
1649–59	William Christian	Man (Malew)
1659–60	Arthur Squibb	?
1661–82	Richard Stevenson	Man (Arbory)
1683–1701	Revenue commissioners [members of Lord's Council]	
1701-post 1709	Christopher Parker	?

Sources: See appendix iii.

Note.
1. Until 1614, there was a receiver at both Castle Rushen [CR] and at Peel Castle [PC].

Appendix V

PROVISIONAL LIST OF DEEMSTERS, c. 1590–c. 1700

Term of Office	Name	Property
c. 1570–1595	John Lucas	
1585–1626	Thomas Samsbury	Ronaldsway, Malew
1595–1605	John Curghey	Ballakillingan, Lezayre
1605–55	Ewan Christian	Milntown, Lezayre
1627–31	Henry Ratcliffe	Gordon, Patrick
1631–5	George Stanley	Ballakeighan, Arbory
1627–55	John Christian [assistant to Ewan Christian]	
1636–44	Robert Quayle	Ballaquayle, Conchan
1644–52	John Cannell	
1655–67?	John Christian	Milntown, Lezayre
1652–63	William Qualtrough	Kentraugh, Rushen
1660–75	Thomas Norris	
1661–9?	Edward Christian [assistant to John Christian?]	Milntown, Lezayre
1663	Thomas Fletcher	Ballafletcher, Braddan
1664–9	Hugh Cannell	
1669–80	Edward Christian	Milntown, Lezayre
1678	Charles Christian [deputy for Edward Christian]	
1675–93	Thomas Norris	
1680–93	Edward Christian	Milntown, Lezayre
1693–1724?	John Parr	Arbory
1696–1734?	Daniel McYlrea	

Sources: Lib. Scacc., *passim*; Lib. Canc., *passim*; R. B. Moore, 'The Deemsters and the Manx Courts of Law', *J.M.M.*, vol. vi (1957–65), p. 160.

Appendix VI

WATERBAILIFFS OF THE ISLE OF MAN,
c. 1590–c. 1700

Term of Office	Name	Place of Origin
c. 1593–4	Henry Radcliffe	?
1594–1602	John Quayle	Man
1602–7	James Hey	?
1607–9?	Bell Edwardes	?
1608	Thomas Leech [deputy]	?
1608	Christopher Young	?
1612–23	Henry Radcliffe	Man (Gordon, Patrick)
1622	John Halsall [deputy]	Man?
1624?	Fermor Coote	?
1624–31	George Squire	?
1630–7?	Fermor Coote	?
1638	Sir Charles Gerard	Lancs.
	John Halsall [acting]	Man?
1638–41	Humphrey Barrowes	?
1641–3	John Cannell	Man
1643	Fermor Coote	?
1643–4	John Sharples [deputy]	Lancs.?
1644–9	William Christian	Man (Malew)
1649–50	Robert Barrey	?
1651–2	William Huddleston	Man (Malew)
1652–60	Hugh Moore	Man
1660–6?	Richard Calcott	Man
1668–70	Hugh Cannell	Man
1670–3	Richard Baxter	?
	Thomas Fletcher	Man (Braddan)
	Thomas Huddleston	Man (Malew)

1670–3	Thomas Norris the younger	Man (Malew?)
1673–7	Robert Roper	Lancs.?
1677	Ferdinando Calcott	Man (Malew)
1677–80	John Thompson	?
1680–91	Ferdinando Calcott	Man (Malew)
1692–7?	Richard Stevenson	Man (Arbory)
1697–1701	Thomas Huddleston	Man (Malew)
1701–2	Silvester Huddleston	Man (Malew)
1702-post 1704	William Ross	?

Sources: See appendix iii.

Appendix VII

LORD'S ATTORNEYS, c. 1590–c. 1700

Term of Office	Name	Place of Origin
c. 1579–1600	Henry Halsall	Man?
1600–1629?	John Halsall	Man?
1605	Christopher Young [deputy]	?
1629–36	John Sharples	Lancs.?
1636–51?	Robert Calcott	Man (Braddan)
1652–60	John Caesar	Man (Malew)
1661–2	Hugh Cannell	Man
1662–5	William Quayle	Man
1666–82?	William Qualtrough	Man (Rushen)
1682–6	Thomas Norris [deputy]	Man
1687–94?	Peter Heywood	Lancs.
1692	Charles Christian [deputy]	Man
1694	Vacant	—
1696–1701	Thomas Huddleston	Man (Malew)
1698	Silvester Huddleston	Man (Malew)
1701-post 1704	John Bridson	Man (Malew)

Sources: See appendix iii.

Appendix VIII

LIST OF MILLS IN THE
ISLE OF MAN 1500–1700

Patrick	Peel Castle
	Peel (Holmtoun)
	Glen Maye (1703: Mullin Glonna?)
	Ballahig (1703: Mullin e Chlugg)
	Abbey Mill [Monastic]
	Colvill's Mill (1703)
	Knockaloe (?) (1703)
German	Mullen e Kew (1643)
	Mullen Renash (Rhenass Mill)
	Greeba
	Mollen e Cowle (1643)
	Mollen Beg
Michael	Mullen e Kelley (1643)
	Mullin Harry (1643: Harry's Mill)
	Mullengaw (1703: Mill of the Smiths)
	Borodaill (1627)
	Ballagawne Mill (1703)
	Glen Wyllin [1703: 'now lying wast']
Ballaugh	Scrandall (1703)
Jurby	Killane (1643: Kerlane)
Andreas	Lhen Mooar (1669: Lane More)
	Mwyllin ny geayee (?)
	Mwyllin ny liargee (Ballacamain)
Lezayre	Altadale (Glen Auldyn)
	Alia Altadale
	Breryk (1703: Brerick)
	Sulby [corn mill and walk mill]
	Middle Mill (1703)

	Cloddaugh Mill (1703)
	Mullen a Jammag (1703) [Abbey mill]
	Carretts Mill (1703)
Bride	Gill's Mills (1660)
Rushen	Kentraugh
	Rhenwyllan
Arbory	Colby
Malew	Castle Rushen
	Meadow Mill [two grain mills near the Castle]
	Abbey Mill [Ballasalla. Monastic]
	Scarlett [two corn mills]
	Mullenaragher (1703) (Faragher's Mill)
	Creg [Silverdale Glen. Monastic]
	Grenaby
Santan	Glen Grenaugh (1643: Glanagreenagh)
	Mwyllin y Quinney (Quinney's Mill)
	[fulling mill on Santan Burn]
	[flax mill near Quinney's Mill]
Marown	Ballayemany (Eyreton)
	Ballanicholas (1703: Mullin Balniclas)
	Sandbrick (1703)
	Droghed hollan [replaced by Mullenglongaroo]
	Mullenglongaroo (Glonne Krow. 1644)
	Mullen e Caine (1703)
Braddan	Baldal (1643. Baldwin) [two mills]
	Mullen Oates (Doway)
	Middle Mill [Kewaigue?]
	Nunnery Mill
	Fletcher's Mill
	Mullin Aspick (Ballaughton Mill)
	Mullen e Corran (1703) [Abbey]
Conchan	Tromode
	Haralett (1643)

	Groudle
	'Burnt Mill,' near Howstrake
	Ballacreetch (1703)
	Corran's Mill (1643)
Lonan	Laxey (1637: Quayle's Mill)
	Mwyllin Beg (1703)
	Glion Wyllin (1703)
	Garwick
Maughold	Cornaa [two corn mills; flax mill?]
	Ballure
	Port e vullen (Purt y wyllin)

Sources: J. J. Kneen, *The Place Names of the Isle of Man* (Douglas, 1925–8, reprinted Ilkley, 1970); T. Talbot (ed.), *The Manorial Roll of the Isle of Man, 1511–1515* (1924); M.M.L., MF/RC/1. Lord's Composition Book, 1703; M.M.L., MS 510C, J. Quayle, *A Book of Precedents* (n.d., c. 1725), p. 121; Lib. Scacc. 1585, 21; Lib. Scacc. 1630, inter 53–4 (1); Lib. Scacc. 1644, inter 4–5 (2); Lib. Scacc. 1660, 76; Lib. Scacc. 1662, inter 88–9; T. A. Bawden et al., *The Industrial Archaeology of the Isle of Man* (Newton Abbot, 1972); W. Radcliffe and C. Radcliffe, *A History of Kirk Maughold* (Douglas, 1979), p. 172.

Appendix IX

CUSTOMS REVENUE OF THE ISLE OF MAN,
C. 1590–c. 1700

(Years ending at 24 June. 1701–4: years ending at Sept. 29)

(Gross totals to nearest penny)

Year	Ingates			Outgates			Total		
	£	s.	d.	£	s.	d.	£	s.	d.
1590	—	—	—	—	—	—	—	—	—
1591	—	—	—	—	—	—	—	—	—
1592	9	9	3	26	19	4	36	8	7
1593	—	—	—	—	—	—	—	—	—
1594	14	13	5	49	3	2	63	16	7
1595	12	10	3	40	8	8	52	18	11
1596	18	17	10	28	17	4	47	15	2
1597	17	1	9	20	7	10	37	9	7
1598	11	4	0	29	13	4	40	17	4
1599	8	2	10	33	7	0	41	9	10
1600	16	4	9	32	17	11	49	2	8
1601	19	17	6	20	4	7	40	2	1
1602	15	6	8	14	0	10	29	7	6
1603	14	16	4	32	9	3	47	5	7
1604	19	14	10	36	13	5	56	8	3
1605	14	17	4	29	0	5	43	17	9
1606	13	19	4	35	1	2	49	0	6
1607	13	9	0	31	15	4	45	4	4
1608	14	3	5	35	16	4	49	19	9
1609	11	9	8	34	12	1	46	1	9
1610	12	12	4	37	7	6	49	19	10
1611	26	19	6	71	12	10	98	12	4
1612	21	9	1	52	5	2	73	14	3
1613	17	7	0	35	0	1	52	7	1

Year	Ingates			Outgates			Total		
	£	s.	d.	£	s.	d.	£	s.	d.
1614	14	19	4	37	19	3	52	18	7
1615	11	11	5	57	19	9	69	11	2
1616	—	—	—	—	—	—	—	—	—
1617	17	18	0	62	18	11	80	16	11
1618	17	10	6	64	4	8	81	15	2
1619	24	4	2	67	6	4	91	10	6
1620	16	9	7	47	9	1	63	18	8
1621	16	9	9	35	2	1	51	11	10
1622	—	—	—	—	—	—	—	—	—
1623	17	7	10	43	7	3	60	15	1
1624	24	9	9	86	1	1	110	10	10
1625	16	5	0	75	10	8	91	15	8
1626	15	16	11	88	18	3	104	15	2
1627	11	17	8	41	4	10	53	2	6
1628	11	8	10	50	18	11	62	7	9
1629	14	4	10	44	10	0	58	14	10
1630	16	9	0	46	14	0	63	3	0
1631	10	12	4	46	13	5	57	5	9
1632	8	6	1	52	0	11	60	7	0
1633	—	—	—	—	—	—	—	—	—
1634	10	8	10	61	4	9	71	13	7
1635	—	—	—	—	—	—	—	—	—
1636	11	19	9	30	7	9	42	7	6
1637	14	0	10	84	11	1	98	11	11
1638	20	4	10	61	7	10	81	12	8
1639	15	11	10	67	4	2	82	16	0
1640	9	15	6	40	14	3	50	9	9
1641	10	7	0	43	18	6	54	5	6
1642	16	16	6	41	18	11	58	15	5
1643	14	19	1	19	15	9	34	14	10
1644	12	14	8	13	4	2	25	18	10
1645	14	5	4	81	5	1	95	10	5
1646	17	12	1	79	9	10	97	1	11

Year	Ingates			Outgates			Total		
	£	s.	d.	£	s.	d.	£	s.	d.
1647	28	9	6	83	8	0	111	17	6
1648	22	4	2	49	2	11	71	7	1
1649	28	17	7	26	12	4	55	9	11
1650	23	8	7	36	11	2	59	19	9
1651	8	15	10	20	9	1	29	4	11
1652	9	13	3	29	2	2	38	15	5
1653	12	7	4	12	13	6	25	0	10
1654	17	9	7	16	12	7	34	2	2
1655	15	15	10	14	12	9	30	8	7
1656	19	15	9	33	8	7	53	4	4
1657	17	13	8	32	7	1	50	0	9
1658	14	13	0	21	12	1	36	5	1
1659	17	8	7	64	2	7	81	11	2
1660	15	19	8	32	4	10	48	4	6
1661	16	7	6	54	10	5	70	17	11
1662	—	—	—	—	—	—	—	—	—
1663	15	1	11	30	2	3	45	4	2
1664	14	8	7	18	10	9	32	19	4
1665	23	17	9	36	16	0	60	13	9
1666	15	18	8	22	11	1	38	9	9
1667	16	1	2	13	2	3	29	3	5
1668	30	16	2	41	6	0	72	2	2
1669	31	4	1	75	6	11	106	11	0
1670	36	7	2	38	10	10	74	18	0
1671	29	18	10	45	12	6	75	11	4
1672	37	19	4	72	13	5	110	12	9
1673	38	17	9	29	9	1	68	6	10
1674	37	15	8	52	18	11	90	14	7
1675	25	0	6	63	17	1	88	17	7
1676	40	3	5	128	19	8	169	3	1
1677	31	0	10	35	1	0	66	1	10
1678	30	5	4	76	10	2	106	15	6
1679	39	1	0	46	3	5	85	4	5

Year	Ingates			Outgates			Total		
	£	s.	d.	£	s.	d.	£	s.	d.
1680	26	4	1	14	5	7	40	9	8
1681	21	0	5	13	5	9	34	6	2
1682	21	0	5	22	6	6	69	7	8
1683	38	15	3	42	6	0	81	1	3
1684	21	6	1	30	1	0	51	7	1
1685	34	0	5	22	18	5	56	18	10
1686	31	6	11	22	11	3	53	18	2
1687	88	17	2	16	14	2	105	11	4
1688	62	16	6	18	13	11	81	10	5
1689	79	17	6	20	17	0	100	14	6
1690	40	2	4	28	7	2	68	9	6
1691	94	18	7	20	10	6	115	9	1
1692	48	18	4	51	18	3	100	16	7
1693	59	3	6	43	5	1	102	8	7
1694	73	2	9	30	4	6	103	7	3
1695	70	13	8	32	0	0	102	13	8
1696	79	12	4	37	6	5	116	18	9
1697	76	2	0	31	0	10	107	2	10
1698	54	15	9	31	8	1	86	3	10
1699	43	14	8	53	0	8	96	15	4
1700	98	19	2	19	13	8	118	12	10
1701	118	17	0	56	11	7	175	8	7
1702	109	14	4	22	17	1	132	11	5
1703	87	19	5	29	4	9	117	4	2
1704	74	10	8	24	19	9	99	10	5

Sources: M.M.L., I.O.1570–99, 1600–9, 1610–19, 1620–9, 1630–45, 1646–59, 1660–71, 1672–9, 1680–9, 1690–5, 1696–1704, Waterbailiff's accounts; M.M.L., R.D. 1579—98, 1627–50, 1651–70, 1700–4, Waterbailiff's accounts.

Bibliography

I. UNPUBLISHED PRIMARY SOURCES

Manx Museum Library, Douglas

a) Court records

Lib. Scacc.	Libri Scaccarii (Exchequer books), 1580–1704
Lib. Canc.	Libri Cancellarii (Chancery books), 1578–1704
Lib. Plit.	Libri Placitorum (Books of pleas), 1496–1704

b) Ingates and Outgates

Bundles. 1570 [1576]-1704

c) Receipts and Disbursements

Bundles. 1579–1704

d) Manuscript Collection

510C	J. Quayle, *A Book of Precedents* (n.d., *c.* 1725)
MD401	Derby Papers
MD15,040	J. Parr, *An Abridgement or Short Tract of the most usefull Lawes Actes and Ordinances conteyned in the Statute Book of this Isle of Mann* (1679)

e) Microfilms

EW	Episcopal Wills
PR	Parish Registers
RB	Archidiaconal Wills

Lancashire Record Office, Preston

DDK	Stanley of Knowsley papers
DDKe	Kenyon of Peel papers
DDLx	Trappes Lomax of Clayton-le-Moors papers
DDSt	Weld (Shireburne) of Stonyhurst papers
QSP	Quarter Sessions Petitions

Chester City Record Office

A/B	Assembly Minute Books
M/MP	Mayors' Military Papers

Liverpool City Record Office

NOR	Norris of Speke papers

Clwyd Record Office, Hawarden

Nantlys MS.
D/NA/905. Anon., An account of the Isle of Man, *c.* 1665

Public Record Office, London

E 190	Queen's Remembrancer, Port Books
SP 14	State Papers, Domestic, James I
SP 16	State Papers, Domestic, Charles I
SP 29	State Papers, Domestic, Charles II

British Library, London

a) Additional MSS

5,664	Letter from Sir John Trevor to the Lord Admiral, the Earl of Nottingham, October 19, 1603.
33,589	Letters concerning the government of the Isle of Man, 1673–5
34,318	Exchequer accompts and other official papers, 1516–1656
38,462	Letter from the Commissioners of Customs to William, Earl of Derby, February 19, 1692.

b) Lansdowne MSS

82	Letter from William, sixth Earl of Derby to Lord Burghley, July 10, 1596

Public Record Office of Northern Ireland, Belfast

D695	Waring MSS

Knowsley Hall, Prescot

H/41	Laws of Man (n.d., *c.* 1705)
H/44a	Papers relating to the Isle of Man

II. PUBLISHED PRIMARY SOURCES

Armytage, G. (ed.), *Pedigrees made at the Visitation of Cheshire, 1613*, by Richard St George, R.S.L.C., vol. lviii (1909)

Bennett, J. H. E. (ed.), *The Rolls of the Freemen of the City of Chester, pt. i: 1392–1700*, R.S.L.C., vol. li (1906)

Bennett, J. H. E. (ed.), 'Chester Apprentices, 1557–1646', *Cheshire Sheaf*, 3rd series, vol. vii (1909)

Bennett, J. H. E. (ed.), 'Chester Apprenticeship Indentures, 1603–1684', *Cheshire Sheaf*, 3rd series, vol. viii (1910)

Blundell, W., *A History of the Isle of Man, (1648–56)*, ed. W. Harrison, 2 vols., Manx Society, vols. xxv, xxvii (1876, 1877)

Brereton, W., Travels in Holland and the United Provinces, England, Scotland and Ireland, ed. E. Hawkins, (Chet. Soc., O.S., vol. i, 1844)

Broderick, G. (ed.), *Chronicle of the Kings of Mann and the Isles* (Edinburgh 1973)

Brownbill, J. (ed.), *A Calendar of that part of the Collection of Deeds and Papers of the Moore Family of Bankhall, Co. Lanc., now in the Liverpool Public Library*, R.S.L.C., vol. lxvii (1913)

Calendar of Carew Manuscripts

Calendar of Close Rolls

Calendar of Patent Rolls

Calendar of State Papers, Domestic

Calendar of State Papers, Ireland

Calendar of Treasury Books

Camden, W., *Britannia* (1586)

Camden, W., *Britannia*, ed. E. Gibson (1695)

Camden, W., *Britannia*, ed. E. Gibson (1722)

Caulfield, R. (ed.), *The Council Book of the Corporation of Youghal* (Guildford 1878)

Chaloner, J., *A Treatise of the Isle of Man*, (1656), ed. J. G. Cumming, Manx Society, vol. x (1854)

Coke, E., *The First Part of the Institutes of the Laws of England* (2nd edn., 1629)

Coke, E., *The Fourth Part of the Institutes of the Laws of England* (2nd edn., 1648)

Cregeen, A., *A Dictionary of the Manks Language* (Douglas 1835 [1838], reprinted Ilkley 1984)

Cubbon, W. (ed.), 'An Important Balladoole Document', *J.M.M.*, vol. ii (1930–4)

Cubbon, W. (ed.), 'Description of Ballaugh Parish in the year 1774', *J.M.M.*, vol. iv (1938–, 40)

Cubbon, W. and Megaw, B. R. S. (eds.), 'Our Oldest Legal Records. Extracts from the Sheading Court Rolls of A.D. 1417–18', *J.M.M.*, vol. v (1941–6)

Denton, T., 'Description of the Isle of Man and its Customs' (*c.* 1681), ed. G. W. Wood, *Y.L.M.*, vol. iii (1895–1901)

Dietz, B. (ed.), 'The Port and Trade of Early Elizabethan London', *London Record Society*, vol. viii (1972)

Earwaker, J. P. (ed.), *A List of the Freeholders in Lancashire in the year 1600, Miscellanies relating to Lancashire and Cheshire, vol. i*, R.S.L.C., vol. xii (1885),

Elton, G. R. (ed.), *The Tudor Constitution* (2nd edn, Cambridge 1982)

Foster, J. (ed.), *The Visitation of Yorkshire made in the year 1584/5 by Robert Glover . . . to which is added the subsequent visitation made in 1612 by Richard St George* (1875)

Foster, J. (ed.), *Alumni Oxoniensis* (4 vols., 1891)

Foster, W. (ed.), *The Voyage of Thomas Best to the East Indies, 1612–1614*, Hakluyt Society, 2nd series, vol. xv (1934)

Gill, J. F. (ed.), *The Statutes of the Isle of Man, vol. i, 1417–1824* (1883)

Graunt, J., *Natural and Political Observations on the Bills of Mortality* (3rd edn., 1665)

Hainsworth, D. R. , *The Commercial Papers of Sir Christopher Lowther, 1611–1644*, (ed.) Surtees Society, vol. clxix (1977)

Hainsworth, D. R. (ed.), *The Correspondence of Sir John Lowther of Whitehaven, 1693–1698. A Provincial Community in Wartime*, Records of Social and Economic History, new series, vii (1983)

Harrison, W. (ed.), *The Old Historians of the Isle of Man*, Manx Society, vol. xviii (1871)

Hinton, R. W. K. (ed.), *The Port Books of Boston, 1601–1640*, Lincoln Record Society, vol. l (1956)

Hollis, D. (ed.), *Calendar of the Bristol Apprentice Book, 1532–1565, pt. i: 1532–1542*, Bristol Record Society, vol. xiv (1949).

Hull, C. H., *The Economic Writings of Sir William Petty*, (2 vols., Cambridge 1899)

Irvine, W. Fergusson et al. (eds.), 'Annals of Chester', *Cheshire Sheaf*, 3rd series, vol. ix (1913)

Knowler, W. (ed.), *The Earl of Strafforde's Letters and Dispatches* (2 vols., 1739)

Langton, W. (ed.), *The Visitation of Lancashire and a part of Cheshire, 1533*, Chet. Soc., O. S., vol. xcviii (1876)

Lansdowne, Marquess of (ed.), *The Petty Papers* (2 vols., 1927)

Lewis, E. A. (ed.), *The Welsh Port Books, 1550–1603*, Cymmrodorion Record Series, no. xii (1927)

Macfarlane, A. (ed.), *The Diary of Ralph Josselin, 1616–1683*, Records of Social and Economic History, new series, vol. iii (1976)

Mackenzie, W. (ed.), *Legislation by Three of the Thirteen Stanleys, Kings of Man*, Manx Society, vol. iii (1860)

Malynes, G. de, *Consuetudo, vel Lex Mercatoria, or the Ancient Law Merchant* (1622)

Marshall, J. D., *The Autobiography of William Stout of Lancaster, 1665–1752*, Chet. Soc., 3rd series, vol. xiv (1967)

Munch, P. A. and Goss, Dr (eds.), *Chronica Regum Manniae et Insularum*, 2 vols., Manx Society, vols. xxii and xxiii (1874)

Notestein, W., Relf, F. H. and Simpson, H. (eds.) *Commons Debates*, 1621 (7 vols., New Haven, Conn. 1935)

Parker, F. (ed.), *Chetwynd's History of Pirehill Hundred, 1679, Collections for a History of Staffordshire, pt. ii*, William Salt Archaeological Society (1914)

Pryde, G. S. (ed.), *Ayr Burgh Accounts, 1534–1624*, Scottish History Society, 3rd series, vol. xxviii (1937)

Quayle, B., *General View of the Agriculture of the Isle of Man* (1794)

Quayle, T., *General View of the Agriculture of the Isle of Man* (1812)

Raines, F. R. (ed.), *The Stanley Papers, pt. ii: The Derby Household Books*, Chet. Soc., O. S., vol. xxxi (1853)

Raines, F. R. (ed.), *The Stanley Papers, pt. iii: Private Devotions and Miscellanies of James, Seventh Earl of Derby*, Chet. Soc., O. S., vols. lxvi, lxvii and lxx (1867)

Raines, F. R. (ed.), *The Visitation of the County Palatine of Lancaster made in the year 1567 by William Flower*, Chet. Soc., O. S., vol. lxxxi (1870)

Raines, F. R. (ed.), *The Visitation of the County Palatine of Lancaster made in the year 1613 by Richard St George*, Chet. Soc., O. S., vol. lxxxii (1871)

Raines, F. R. (ed.), *The Visitation of the County Palatine of Lancaster made in the year 1664–5 by Sir Wm. Dugdale*, Chet. Soc., O. S., vols. lxxxiv, lxxxv, lxxxviii (1872, 1873)

Reid, R. C. (ed.), *An Introduction to the History of Dumfries, by Robert Edgar*, Records of the Western Marches, vol. i (1915)

Rylands, J. P. (ed.), *Lancashire Inquisitions Post Mortem returned into the Chancery of the Duchy of Lancaster, Stuart Period, pt. i*, R.S.L.C., vol. iii (1880)

Rylands, J. P. (ed.), *The Visitation of Cheshire in the year 1580, made by Robert Glover*, Harleian Society, vol. xviii (1882)

Sherwood, R. (ed.), *The Constitution of the Isle of Man, consisting of part the third of the Report of the Commissioners of Enquiry for the Isle of Man, made in the Year 1792*, Manx Society, vol. xxxi (1882)

Skeat, W. W. and Britten, J. (eds.), *Reprinted Glossaries and Old Farming Words*, English Dialect Society, vol. iii (1879–80)

Smith, T., *De Republica Anglorum*, ed. M. Dewar (Cambridge 1982)

Stanning, J. H. (ed.), *The Royalist Composition Papers, vol. ii*, R.S.L.C., vol. vi (1892)

Talbot, T. (ed.), *The Manorial Roll of the Isle of Man, 1511–1515* (1924)

Twemlow, J. A. (ed.), *Liverpool Town Books. Proceedings of Assemblies, Common Councils, Portmoot Courts, etc., 1550–1862, vol. i: 1550–71* and *vol. ii: 1571–1603* (1918, 1935)

Waldron, G., *A Description of the Isle of Man*, ed. W. Harrison, Manx Society, vol. xi (1864)

Willan, T. S. (ed.), *A Tudor Book of Rates* (Manchester 1962)

Index

In memory of T. S. Willan
and Owen Ashmore

THOMAS STUART WILLAN, 1910–1994

T. S. Willan, who died in Manchester 4 June 1994, aged eighty-four, was a member of the council of the Chetham Society from 1969 to May 1994. Tall and quiet, characteristically smoking a pipe, Willan was possessed of a dry but gentle wit. He was professor of Economic History in the History Department at Manchester University from 1961 until 1973 (emeritus), and had begun his teaching at the university in 1935. When I joined the staff there in 1969 Willan was immediately an interesting and encouraging senior colleague and, as the years passed, a wise friend as well. He was regularly to be found in the Manchester Common Room long after his retirement.

Manchester University provided many of the leading members of council. Although he is barely mentioned in Alan Crosby's recent history of the society, Willan will be remembered with his friends Prof. J. S. Roskell, and the late Prof. W. H. Chaloner, the two who seemed predominant in the society in the 1970s. One member of the time has recorded that Willan's independent contributions in council meetings were always perspicacious and relevant.

Willan is the only author to have written two volumes in the society's third series, both on topics at the core of his historical interest. *The Weaver Navigation* (vol. iii, 1951) was part of his initial interest in England's economic infrastructure, particularly water transport. It stands alongside his first book, the more general *River navigation in England 1600–1750* (1936; reprinted 1964), and parallels his specialist books on part of the Great Ouse (1946), and the Don (1965), and papers on other rivers. *Elizabethan Manchester* (vol. xxvii, 1980), his last book, emerged from his concentration on later sixteenth-century England, his second field of enquiry on which he had begun to publish books in the 1950s. These two volumes were by no means the sum of his involvement in the Society's third series however. His help and advice was acknowledged by Stella Davies in vol. x, while Norman Lowe's vol. xx had begun as his M.A. thesis under Prof. Willan's supervision.

Though he also chaired the committee of the Lancashire Bibliography for nearly two decades from 1954, published with his native county's Yorkshire Archaeological Society, and used the papers of an ancestor for his *An eighteenth-century shopkeeper: Abraham Dent of Kirby Stephen* (1970), T. S. Willan did not think of himself as a local or regional historian. The main thrust of his work was on English trade, and England's transport network.

The English coasting trade 1600–1750 (1938) like *River navigation* has been reprinted (1967), while his specialist studies of trade with Russia and with Morocco took him into the organisation of international commerce. His penultimate book, *The inland trade* (1976) saw him back to old water-borne haunts, but mainly illumined the routine workings of credit and internal trade. Bill Chaloner was something of a numismatist, and here Willan took particular pleasure in developing his colleague's suggestion that trade tokens had stories to tell of early shopkeepers.

His innovative work on water-borne trade remains the starting point for modern studies, and the quality of his scholarship was acknowledged with his election as a Fellow of the British Academy in 1991. Former colleagues and students presented him with a collection of essays in 1977, entitled *Trade and transport. Essays in economic history in honour of T.S. Willan.*

C. B. Phillips
Manchester University

OWEN ASHMORE, 1920–1995

Owen Ashmore, a long-standing member of this society and its Honorary Treasurer from 1972 to 1983, died in July 1995.

Owen was a Cheshire man by birth and, his education at Cambridge and wartime service in the Royal Artillery apart, he spent his life in the three counties of Cheshire, Derbyshire and Lancashire. He began his career in the late 1940s as a history teacher in Derbyshire but in 1950 joined Manchester Extra-Mural Department as a resident tutor. From this highly traditional role he was drawn into the administration of the department to become its director and professor from 1976 to 1982. In 1982 he took early retirement but a sad decline in health then restricted his activities and shadowed the rest of his life. In his retirement he had the comfort and consolation of a close family, his wife Sheila and the children Geoffrey, Anne, Matthew and David, and the support of St George's church at Stockport to which he had given devoted service.

Owen was first a schoolmaster and, throughout his career, his teaching was clear and serious, well illustrated with slides, xerox maps or documents and the precise blackboard recording of facts, always in cursive hand because it was relatively silent. During the 1960s he was an early exponent of 'hands on' local history, setting up study groups working both on documentary sources and in the field. His field trips in the north-west and in north Wales at the annual Bangor summer schools were popular and highly purposeful though some extra-mural students were taken aback by his assumption that no-one would engage in a field trip without map and field note-book and preferably compass and tape measure. What animated both classroom and field trip was Owen's ability to bring students to see everyday landscapes, sites or buildings in their historical context, to understand the chains of events that produced them and the consequences that then followed.

As his administrative career advanced Owen could undertake less and less teaching but he could maintain his research. This had grown out of his teaching. In Derbyshire he wrote about the early cotton mills in the Derwent valley, in Lancashire he researched and wrote the guidebook to Whalley Abbey which is still used today and, a little later, illuminated the history of the Low Moor mill and community, the first of many similar studies. He had already begun to explore the use of probate records, enclosure maps and surveys, tithe awards and enumerators' returns from the Parliamentary census of 1851, only fragments of which work found their way into print. It would be interesting to know how many local historians first saw the potential of probate records from his modest articles in the *Amateur Historian* in 1959 or his substantial work on the household inventories of the Lancashire gentry in 1958. However, the progressive erosion of the industrial landscape drew him away from local history into the study of industrial archaeology. Here he combined the close study of his comprehensive collection of maps with documentary and field research to record industrial sites in the region. This meticulous approach bore fruit in the two industrial archaeology volumes for Lancashire in 1969 and the north-west in 1982 but these are really only summaries of the vast knowledge he had accumulated. It is all the more impressive that this work was done principally in the evenings and at weekends when he was free from administrative work at the university. His family have the keenest recollections of holding tape measures in dusty, derelict mills or standing on windy banks as he photographed canals and railways.

Research in industrial archaeology brought other commitments from the 1960s. As one of the pioneers in the region Owen was an early member of the Industrial Archaeology Society and organised their memorable conference at Owens Park in 1977. He then became a founder member of the Manchester Region Industrial Archaeology Society, played a part in the establishment of the Helmshore Mill Museum Trust, was involved in discussions about the future of Liverpool Road Station and was an expert witness in the public enquiry into the Chapel en le Frith by-pass in relation to the Bugsworth canal basin. A very private man, he shunned the limelight, and the full record of his initiatives and involvements in regional conservation is now lost. In effect he acted as a consultant to a great range of individuals and groups concerned about understanding or conserving artifacts from the past whether mills like Helmshore, or the machinery of Plant's hat block works in Manchester, or a cache of archives like that of the Stockport hatters, the Christys. No one approached him in person without receiving a prompt and courteous response without stint of his time.

Industrial archaeology did not absorb all Owen's energy. His activities in the Chetham Society have already been mentioned and the Lancashire and Cheshire Antiquarian Society found him a good servant as a council member from 1961, secretary from 1964 to 1969 and a vice-president from 1969. More locally he was very active as a member and later President of the Stockport Historical Society where, typically, he organised an industrial archaeology group which conducted and published a valuable survey of the town's industrial past. His F.S.A. in 1975 recognised his work in the field to which he had given so much.

It is easier to record what Owen did than it is to portray the man. He was, above all, a scholar, perceptive in identifying a gap in our knowledge and how to fill it, meticulous in research and clear in exposition. He was also punctilious in acknowledging the contributions of others, whether published or private. Nor were these qualities confined to his research: as an administrator he considered every decision and prepared for every meeting with the same close attention to detail. An abiding memory is that of Owen at his desk patiently listening to some interruption but still with fountain pen poised in his hand. His colleagues, friends and students found him a modest man of principle and integrity, kind and considerate, reserved but not distant and quite lacking in self-importance or the trappings of personal status. His tolerance did not extend to low standards of work or behaviour: the rebukes they attracted were as effective for their rarity as their sharpness. Though a serious man he was not solemn but had an appreciation of the rich variety of life and the humour that flows from it and himself had a dry wit that could startle the unwary. As tutor and scholar, colleague and friend, Owne was the epitome of the liberal adult educator. He deepened our perception of our own history, helped to conserve exemplary sites and resources and encouraged a great many people to develop their own interests and abilities. Now we can meet him only through his books and they must speak for him.

J. H. Smith
Manchester University